THE BLACK SHOALS

THE BLACK SHOALS

OFFSHORE FORMATIONS *of* BLACK *and* NATIVE STUDIES

TIFFANY LETHABO KING

DUKE UNIVERSITY PRESS DURHAM AND LONDON 2019

© 2019 Duke University Press
All rights reserved
Printed in the United States of America on acid-free paper ∞
Text designed by Amy Ruth Buchanan
Cover designed by Aimee Harrison
Typeset in Arno and Avenir by Tseng Information Systems, Inc.

Cataloging-in-Publication Data is available from the Library of Congress.
ISBN 9781478005056 (hardcover : alk. paper)
ISBN 9781478006367 (pbk. : alk. paper)
ISBN 9781478005681 (ebook)

Cover art: Charmaine Lurch, *Sycorax Gesture*. Courtesy of the artist.

To those who dance, share drum skins,
chase smoke rings, and brush tongues
to know each other's languages.

CONTENTS

Something about listening to this Anishinaabe woman's story, with its un-familiar contours, brought into sharp relief the grooves, dips, depressions, and crevices that I had never paid attention to all of the times I had run my fingertips over the familiar skin of my own narrative of slavery. I thought I knew all of its dry patches, oil slicks, depressions, raised surfaces, grooved fault lines, and loosening jowls. I know the texture of that face. However, when I listened intently to her talk about how she and her people, the Anishinaabeg, and the other Indigenous peoples in this hemisphere have been stalked by the death shadow of genocide daily, then I began to know something new. As she spoke, I paid attention to the depth of the grooves, took the time to pursue the strange feeling of each rough cut that had been etched over time. A particular line between my eyebrows took on a new curve and depth. Running my finger over it, I found that I could poke clear through its threshold into new regions of "my slavery." On the face of my Blackness, I could feel a new clammy and terrorizing cavern whose depths swallowed the length of my finger.

When I felt around and realized the new and unfamiliar about the slavery with which I had become so comfortable, it changed me — and I do not mean changed in a neat, orderly, or containable way. It unmoored and disassembled me in ways that I and others did not expect. I could no longer be accountable only to myself, my ancestors, and my story of experienc-ing Blackness and its slavery that had been passed down over my lifetime. When I say unmoored, I mean that I could not continue life as I knew it. In the fall of 2007, I decided to take a leave of absence from the doctoral program I had just begun at the Ontario Institute for Studies in Education (OISE). I told my department at the time that I was having "health issues."

I needed to sort out what had happened. "Health issues" provided a cover for the undoing that I had experienced. This was more than a mental health crisis. I do not believe that we have any language available for what I experienced so intensely in 2007 and what I experience less acutely now.

There was something about the way this Anishinaabe woman spoke of genocide. I knew that it had everything to do with now, with tomorrow, with yesterday. With then. And more so, it had everything to do with slavery. Someone else's "story bearing" informed me that there was more to the experience of slavery.[1] My ancestors knew something more; they knew, tasted, smelled, and felt the edges of multiple deaths. They knew more than just their own death.

To share the hemisphere with Indigenous people also experiencing the day-to-day terror of conquest molds the form of your own experience with conquest as slavery. What my unnamed ancestors knew of slavery was life- and world-altering. They knew of a terror that exceeded the memory and understanding of what we think we know of slavery. I do not believe that genocide and slavery can be contained. Neither has edges, yet each is distinct. Each form of violence has its own way of contaminating, haunting, touching, caressing, and whispering to the other. Their force is particular yet like liquid, as they can spill and seep into the spaces that we carve out as bound off and untouched by the other.

Slavery and genocide linger in places we do not expect and cannot yet see or define. Their touch can arrive in an illness, a "not feeling right," or not wanting to rest your feet on the ground. Their presence can feel like not being able to fully expand your lungs. In a more profound sense, it and they are a haunt. In the words of Eve Tuck and Christine Ree, "The United States is permanently haunted by the slavery, genocide and violence entwined in its first, present and future days. Haunting does not hope to change people's perceptions, nor does it hope for reconciliation. Haunting lies precisely in its refusal to stop. Alien (to settlers) and generative for (ghosts), this refusal to stop is its own form of resolving. For ghosts, the haunting is the resolving, it is not what needs to be resolved."[2]

Genocide and slavery do not have an edge. While the force of their haunt has distinct feelings at the stress points and instantiations of Black fungibility and Native genocide, the violence moves as one. To perceive this distinct yet edgeless violence and its haunting requires a way of sensing that allows moving in and out of blurred and sharpened vision, acute and dulled senses of smell. It requires the taste buds at the back of the throat and the pinch of the acidic in the nerves of the jawline. Edgeless distinction is a haptic moment, shared, and a ceremonial Black and Indigenous ritual.[3] This project is an act and ritual that spans ten years.

When Marika, Christine, Abi, Larissa, and I sat together (to listen and watch smoke rise, shift, and disappear) as Black and Native women,[4] we developed a capacity to know something more—something my ancestors had known but had been rendered unimaginable within the rehearsals and protocols of remembering slavery. Slavery and genocide do not have edges. My ancestors who were enslaved knew more than slavery; they knew the terror of conquest. An Anishinaabe woman helped me understand that. The terror I felt was specifically and unmistakably Black. It was not the terror of a long-lost Native ancestor. It was not a transference of her ancestral terror and blood memory that I picked up on. It was a different kind of vision of yourself that you experience in a truly ethical encounter, a kind of co-witnessing that enables people not only to mirror back pain but also to also implicate one another in our survival. However, also in the witnessing to understand with one another, one realizes that "innocence" does not exist within the lifeways of this hemisphere or the modern world. The endeavor of surviving under conditions of conquest is never clean.

Under relations of conquest, Black and Indigenous people made difficult and agonizing choices when it came to negotiating and fighting for their existence. Often when Black and Indigenous people encountered one another their meetings were mediated by the violence of an evolving humanism organized through their captivity and death.[5] The terms of survival—or, said another way, the circumstances under which you as a Black or Indigenous person lived—were often tethered to the death of the Other. Claims to innocence on the part of Black or Indigenous people are disingenuous and deprive Black and Indigenous life of the agonizing texture and horrific choices that often had to be (and have to be) made to survive under relations of conquest. What is true for Black people is that they also fear for their lives and make shrewd and difficult decisions that at times fall outside their own, as well as larger and shared, ethical frames. Black people can be backed against the wall, make choices out of the need for brute self-preservation. The buffalo soldier can be called into the "war for America."[6] After all, the Five Civilized Tribes made a choice to enslave Black people to prove the measure of their own humanness.[7] This was, but does not have to be, life and death in this hemisphere.

The conquistador and settler, who perhaps need to be renamed the "conquistador-settler," established the violent terms of contemporary social relations.[8] Further, the conquistador-settler also mediates Black and

Indigenous relations through the nation-state, press, academic discourse, and even leftist politics. To become or "ascend" to Whiteness is to enact a self—or self-actualize—in a way that requires the death of others. The position of the conquistador is tethered to the process of "ascending to whiteness," or becoming human under the terms required by multiple versions of the human that keeps the category an exclusive and privileged site of unfettered self-actualization. This historical process of what Rey Chow and Jasbir Puar call the "ascendancy to whiteness" is an open and changing space.[9] Even if people of color (or non-Black and non-Indigenous) can over time occupy the structural position of the "settler," then critical social theory needs another name for the position previously held by the white settler. If postcolonial subjects, former "Natives" and racialized others, can become the settler, then the white settler has continued to occupy the structural and ontological position of the conquistador, and should be named as such.

The stains and occasional hard, crusty residue of gore that line the crease and gutter where the sidewalk meets the street in Ferguson, Missouri; Baltimore; Seattle; Morton County in Sioux Territory; Vancouver; and Toronto tell the ongoing story of conquest. The brutal violence required to distinguish the human conquistador from the Black and Indian continues into the current moment. The tributaries of blood that M. Jacqui Alexander, Leslie Marmon Silko, Toni Morrison, Joy Harjo, Stormy Ogden, and Junot Díaz describe so vividly and evocatively paint a hue that refuses to coagulate. It is a river with a pulse in the contemporary moment with the capacity to drive its witnesses beyond a place of wellness.

I write this because I still need to heal. And my own healing, Black healing, is connected to Indigenous healing. I also write this as homage to the Black radical politics that have nursed and nurtured me. The Black radical struggle that I know intimately has always contained a mode of self-critique that frequently requires adjustment and revision. Black people constantly "on a move" and remaking the world maintain on ongoing intramural discussion that allows Black politics, movement, and thought to think about itself in relation to an expanding notion of itself connected to others.[10] This open conversation taking place among a dynamic and fluid Black "we" also takes place among Indigenous people. The Black radical tradition that informs this project is the one that I am also writing back to in gratitude. I write back to a porous and forever transforming practice that is an ethical project concerned with encounter.

I write this because I trust Black people. I trust the radical and always shifting ground of Black freedom dreams.[11] I also trust Black freedom dreams when they consider Native freedom. This project confronts the various ways that Black politics and Black studies continue to deal with and incorporate the struggle against Native genocide into its ethical frame. This book is a multivoiced conversation. First, it is a Black intramural conversation. Second, it is a conversation with Native studies and Native peoples who face genocide and a dispossession so profound that even "land" cannot adequately speak to the loss. Third, it is a "talking at" and back to conquistador-settler knowledge formations. Specifically, this conversation is a confrontation with the ways that conquistador forms of discourse, like colonial and settler colonial studies, attempt to mediate discussions between Black and Native peoples, Black studies, and Native studies. White colonial and settler colonial discourse structure the ways that people think about and simultaneously forget the ways that Black and Native death are intimately connected in the Western Hemisphere.

Finally, and most important, like most scholars, artists, and people, I write to live with myself. Beyond keeping one up at night, a haunting can grant an inheritance. My inheritance is that, as a Black person living under relations of conquest, I care about Native people's survival. And I do not care because I have a Native grandmother or ancestor. I care because the Black radical politics that I have inherited cares about Native people.[12] It does not do it in response to political cajoling or guilt. It does not do it in the hope of coalition. It does not do it out of self-hatred. This ethics that eschews and actively resists genocide as an order of modernity and making of the human subject proper is an ethics of Black radical struggle, period. It is a Black radical politics that proceeds and moves toward Black and Indigenous futures.

PROCEEDING TOWARD THE RIDGE

I write from atop a ridge, which is a part of the Appalachian foothills. The Muskogee Creek and the Cherokee were the first to caress the curve of the slope that started at the lips of the Chattahoochee River's banks and stretched into an immense mountain range. Pines once sprouted at whim at the very top of the peak. A special pine served as a meeting place between the two nations; a place of encounter, shared breath, speaking a rhythm, flow, and exchange between two peoples at the base of the tree. The place of Creek and Cherokee encounter would be cleared of its meaning, name, and vibration to serve as an artery of commerce. Commerce—

rice, cotton, bodies, chattel — would flow into this artery from a railroad terminus. The rail line that ran through the new city would connect the port at Savannah across the mountains and to the Midwest.

The rise and fall of the city's topography forces drivers to modulate their speed as they move through Atlanta. Over the five years I lived in the city, I had become so used to the hilly terrain that I barely took the time to notice how I moved. My movements became more guided by proprioception, force, and the steering wheel and the gears than any conscious and measured movement. Only in the last stages of writing this book did I consciously begin to search out the best geographic metaphors for this project and start to pay attention to the naming and renaming of the space I traversed daily.

For instance, if I am not in a rush to get home in the evening, I will drive through the city. I will take Auburn Avenue through the "Old Fourth Ward," where Martin Luther King Jr. grew up, and make a right on Boulevard, which takes me south to Memorial Drive. Memorial Drive takes me east to Moreland Drive. As I bear right and south on Moreland, I cross Interstate 20, named after Ralph David Abernathy, and shortly reach a road on my left (to my east) called Flat Shoals.[13] Once I get to Flat Shoals, I can take it across Glenwood Avenue all the way to where Flat Shoals runs into Bouldercrest.

When I take Flat Shoals I always have to watch carefully and reduce my speed to be ready for young folks racing across the street and to linger long enough to identify the range of music blaring from local establishments. It could be hip hop, bluegrass, New Orleans brass bands, or punk that cuts the panes of my car windows and seeps into the space of my car on any given afternoon. Even the smell of a "wanna be" New York City pizza joint on a particular day will make me trust my bad faith that what comes out of Grant Pizza East in Atlanta will approximate what I can find at home in the Northeast and Mid-Atlantic region of the country. A number of the activities on Flat Shoals make you slow down or shoal your movement on the road. Until I lived here, close to the Flat Shoals interchange, I was unfamiliar with the geologic and oceanomic term "shoal." It was only as the last chapters of this book ran their fingers along the Black contours of this landscape of conquest in the Western Hemisphere that I felt compelled to look for a better organizing metaphor and thread that readers could use to guide their way through the book that I got the notion to look up the term. And like other authors in the final phases of their work, I found what I was looking for very close by. In some sense, I found it under my feet, in the very geography that my Blackness was now living on, creating on, and contending with.

I soon found shoals everywhere. The crease on my forehead between my eyes that felt different after receiving the wisdom and witness of an Anishinaabe friend became a shoal. It slowed or shoaled my movement. It gave me pause. After finding it again for the first time, it made me slow down whenever I ran my fingers over my face and my own history and experience of being a descendent of the enslaved. Any dry patch under my nose or oily patch on my forehead became a new and concerning place to study and care about.

Throughout this book, I meditate on this place — the spot in the road, on the route home, and on the way to the familiar places that force you to slow down; the space that forces you to move from the automaton to a more alert driver and navigator. In this project, I both map and trace this geological, geographic, and oceanic place called the shoal. By titling this book *The Black Shoals*, I posit that Black thought, Black study, Black aesthetics, and Black expression function as a shoal that interrupts the course and momentum of the flow of critical theories about genocide, slavery, and humanity in the Western Hemisphere. More specifically, the book intervenes in contemporary discourses and theories of colonialism and settler colonialism in North America that dictate how the academy and "the left" talk about (or do not talk about) Indigenous genocide, Indigenous peoples, settlers, arrivants, and Black people. *The Black Shoals* approaches the territory and social relations of Indigenous genocide, slavery, settlement, place making, and contemporary extension of the bloody project of conquest. *The Black Shoals* also offers up the possibility that specifc forms of Black abolition and Native decolonization interrupt normative processes of white human self-actualization. In fact, Black abolition and Native decolonization as projects that frustrate liberal (and other) modes of humanism offer new forms of sociality and futurity.

ACKNOWLEDGMENTS

As the shoals emerge as a process of accretion over time, this project has also come into form due to the individual and collective contributions of so many people and divine creative forces. I have so many people to thank. I want to acknowledge the vibrant community of activists, artists, and scholars who made Toronto home for me for two years. This is where this project began. Marika Schwandt, Abi Salole, and Larissa Carincross ensured that I had Black diasporic community to welcome me. The work that we attempted with Toronto INCITE! has changed me. The work of IN-CITE! in the city also brought Christine Luza's path to mine. I will always be grateful for the deep building of intimacy I was called to do while in her presence. Christine welcomed me into a community of dynamic and fierce Anishinaabe, Cherokee, and other Indigenous people in Toronto. I also give many thanks to Zainab Amadahy, who has been my muse for thinking about the creative capacity of Black (African American) and Cherokee life as one. Amai Kuda and Charmaine Lurch are Black Toronto-based artists who helped me imagine this project anew every time I was lucky enough to encounter them. My colleagues at the Ontario Institute for Studies in Education (OISE) at the University of Toronto — Cassandra Lord, Donna Outerbridge, Ricky Varghese, and Paloma and Fransicso Villeagas — were always true and dear during my time at OISE. My formal academic engagement with Black studies began in Toronto, and I am grateful for the work and pedagogy of Jacqui Alexander, Alissa Trotz, and Njoki Wane. Thank you, Katherine McKittrick and Rinaldo Walcott, for introducing me to Sylvia Wynter's work. McKittrick's work has been an important light: her encouragement to write toward Black "livingness" — even through violence — changed the very terrain of this book. The presence and work of these scholars at the beginning of my journey was invaluable and has been a well of sustenance. I must also thank Kari Dehli, Sherene Razack, and the late Roger Simon for their generosity and time. I thank Shaista Patel and the ungovernable Nadine Chambers.

After I left Toronto, my intellectual family at the University of Maryland, College Park, welcomed me and cared and nurtured my intellectual project. My deepest gratitude to my dissertation adviser, Psyche Williams Forson, and my committee members, Elsa Barkley Brown, Sheri Parks, Michelle V. Rowley, Mary Sies, and Andrea Smith. The Department of American Studies houses the finest humanities scholars on campus. I am so grateful to Nancy Struna; Christina B. Hanhardt; and my cohort members, Aaron Allen, Gina Callahan, Portia Dene Hopkins, Douglas Ishi, Gabriel Peoples, and Maria Vargas. I am still so full of the tremendous and gut-busting fun I shared with Jennie Chaplin, Kenyatta Dorsey Graves, Robb Hernandez, Bettina Judd, Angel Miles, Izetta Mobley, Ana Perez, and Shanna Smith while at College Park. We created so many memories. Our time together made the journey to the doctorate sweet.

My other deep well of sustenance and pleasure has come from the scholars in Black and Indigenous studies whose work continues to sustain and push a conversation about abolition and decolonization. I am grateful for the work of Jacqui Alexander, Julie Dash, Saidiya Hartman, Tiya Miles, Jennifer Nash, Jared Sexton, Hortense Spillers, LaMonda Stallings, Greg Thomas, Alex Weheliye, Frank Wilderson, and Sylvia Wynter. Christina Sharpe's wake work in particular came at the perfect — right — time and created a moment that awakened me to other registers of attending to black life and death. The task of Black study is ever evolving and changing. Its capaciousness enabled an ethical space and frame from which to approach Native studies. I thank my guides in Native and Native feminist studies: Maile Arvin, Jodi Byrd, Chris Finley, Jenell Navaro, Audra Simpson, Eve Tuck, and Melanie Yazzie. Thank you for engaging me and my work. I would not have been able to think about Blackness, Indigeneity, and New World geographies without you. I am changed by my encounters with both Native and Black studies accounts of what it means to forge life on landscapes meant to kill you.

My colleagues at the Institute for Women's, Gender, and Sexuality Studies at Georgia State University supported me during the final leg of the journey, when I struggled to imagine how writing another manuscript after the dissertation was possible. Amira Jarmakani, Julie Kubala, Andrew Reisinger, Megan Sinnott, and Susan Talburt have been more than supportive. I am so grateful to be a member of such an exceptional department that has the fortune of working with some of the brightest and most creative graduate students, who have been an immense help to this book project. I especially thank Sumita Dutta, Kristin Johnson, Taryn Jordan, Kara Lawrence, Megha Patel, and Shawquita (Quita) Tinsley for their diligence as graduate assistants. Your work was so important to making this book what it has become. I thank Lia Bascomb and Julia Gaffield for their interdisciplinary friendship and insisting on forming a writing group on our first day as assistant professors at Georgia State. I thank you for keeping me inspired and diligent. I thank my colleagues and family in African American studies, especially Sarita Davis, Jonathan Gayles, and Akinyele Umoja. Shout out to my Atlanta fam! I love you. Shannon Miller, thank you for the summer 2017 writing sessions where I was blessed to be able to "grind" with Black women scholars in Altanta. Thank you to my creative muses Brandi Pettijohn, Monica Simpson, and Camille Williams, who fed my creative and curatorial ambitions. To my good friend Susana Morris, it has been such a gift to have met you at this time in my life. Thank you for working with me as an editor, as well. Jillian Ford, thank you for the trip to Montgomery, Alabama, and the Legacy Museum. Thank you, SisterSong, Southerners on New Ground, Women on the Rise, and the Racial Justice Action Center for keeping the pulse of activist Atlanta inspiring. I thank Nigel Jones and Red, Bike, and Green for the Black and Indigenous people's histories bike tours. I promise to buy a bike before I leave Atlanta.

For folks both near and far who have given me love and support as we have collaborated on projects big and small, I thank you. The entire Working Board of Critical Ethnic Studies from 2015 through the present have been wonderful friends and colleagues. Thank you Shana Griffin, Jin Hiritaworn, Leeann Wang, K. Wayne Yang, and Syrus Ware for inviting me aboard. Tiffany Willoughby Herard, thank you for always being in the space when I need to see you. Billy-Ray Belcourt, Sara Caplan, Jay Kameron Carter, Sarah Cervenak, Ashon Crawley, Mishuana Goeman, Alyosha Goldstein, Ruth Goldstein, Bethany Hughes, Chad Infante, Mark Jerng, Isabel Altamirano-Jimenez, Vanessa Agard Jones, Justin LeRoy, Kyle Mays, Leilani Nishime, Sherene Razack, Anna Thomas, Alex Weheliye, and Kim Hester Williams, thank you for inviting me to share my work with your scholarly communities.

Finally, to the folks who held this book close and invested in its possibilities, I thank you for your endurance. Elizabeth Ault, you are such a wonderful and generous thinker and editor. Thank you again, Melanie, Sarah, Michelle and Andy, Shona Jackson, and Melanie Newton for reading chapter draft after chapter draft of this manuscript. Your supple and loving eyes and hearts are much appreciated. I thank Sharon Byrd at the Special Collections Division at Davidson College, who gave me access to the William Gerard de Brahm map. Roberto Sirvent and Vincent Lloyd of the Political Theology Network provided me with generous funding during the 2017–18 academic year. Michele Balamani reminded me of, and stood as witness to, the workings of the creative in my life and the healing it brings. And to my parents, Joyce and Robert King, thank you for your ever unfolding and widening love.

An earlier version of chapter 1 appeared in "New World Grammars: The 'Unthought' Black Discourses of Conquest," *Theory and Event* 19, no. 4 (2016). Parts of chapter 3 have been revised from "The Labor of (Re)reading Plantation Landscapes Fungible(ly)," *Antipode* 48, no. 4) (2016): 1022–39, and "Racial Ecologies: Black Landscapes in Flux," in *Racial Ecologies*, ed. Kim Hester Williams and Leilani Nishime (Seattle: University of Washington Press, 2018), 65–75.

The Black Shoals

shoal, n. and adj.

n.
A place where the water is of little depth; a shallow, a sand-bank or bar.

adj.
of water, etc.: not deep; shallow
ex. The boat could not come to land the water was so shoale.

The year 1441 is a palindrome. The date's symmetry, doubling and mir-
roring, slows the eye's movement over it. Fourteen forty-one is also a
temporal-spatial marker within Black diaspora studies that scholars use to
chart the navigational routes of the Portuguese around the deadly reef-
filled waters and rocky shoals of Cape Bojador to the shores of Guinea
(Senegal).[1] Gomes Eannes de Azurara, who drafted "The Chronicle of the
Discovery and Conquest of Guinea," reported that in 1441 sailors — perhaps
including Antham Gonçalvez — brought back the first Negroes and "gold
dust" to Portugal.[2] The date slows the easy and swift movement of colonial
studies, settler colonial studies, postcolonial studies, and some tendencies
within Native studies toward 1492 and the shores of the "Americas" as the
accepted inaugural time-space of the modern mode and era of conquest.
For a number of Black studies scholars, the 1440s mark the commence-
ment of the Portuguese slave trade, as well as European voyages poised
for the conquest of territory on the coast of West Africa.[3] These errant
and out-of-sync time and space coordinates of Black thought and study
produce a shoaling effect — a disruption in the movement and flow — of

time and space reflected in and narrated by Western disciplinary formations and their seminal texts. Throughout *The Black Shoals*, Black thought, movement, aesthetics, resistance, and lived experience will be interpreted as a form of chafing and rubbing up against the normative flows of Western thought. Specifically, *The Black Shoals* will interrupt and slow the momentum of long-standing and contemporary modes and itineraries for theorizing New World violence, social relations, Indigeneity, and Blackness in the Western Hemisphere.[4]

Through the mid-nineteenth century, ship captains' nautical journals, logs, and maps revealed the deep anxiety that unexpectedly running into a shoal caused ships' crews. As a geological and oceanic formation, shoals force one to pause before proceeding. Prior to the 1860s, mariners and sailors lacked a scientific or systematic methodology for measuring depth to the ocean floor.[5] Before the invention of bathymetry, the calculation of probability curves that estimated the latitude and longitude of shoals — rock formations, coral beds, and sandbars — were very difficult to map and, therefore, avoid.[6] For captains, sailors, and others on board a ship, the perils of the sea included crashing into a shoal and the sinking of their vessel. The unexpected appearance of rocks or a change in sea level could force the ship to reroute, turn around, cancel its voyage, or even kill all of the passengers (and cargo).

The word "shoal" has a number of meanings. Geological sources define it as the area in which the sea or a body of water becomes shallow. As a process, it is the movement of the ocean from greater to shallower depths. It is not the shore; it is a formation before the shore or offshore. As a location and geological formation it is often described as a sandbar or a coral reef. It is an accumulation of granular materials (sand, rock, and other) that through sedimentation create a bar or barrier that is difficult to pass and, in fact, a "danger to navigation."[7] As a geological unit, it is a physical place, a shallower place in the ocean before one arrives at the shore.

When the ocean is at low tide, one might be able to wade from the shore beyond a break in the waves and into deeper water or a trough to then come upon very shallow water (or a place where the ocean floor surfaces), where one can finally stand on sand again. Many who fish find the shoal to be an ideal spot. A school, or gathering of fish, also sometimes described as a shoal, often gathers at the sandbar's edges to feed on vegetation. Thus, a shoal is a good spot for catching fish. While also used to describe nongeological matter such as a school of fish, the term is rarely used in humanistic terms, however. Declining in use after the eighteenth century, the word "shoal" is generally used in the form of a verb to describe how a ship or vessel slows down to navigate a rocky or rough seabed that has risen toward the surface of the ocean. As the waters became shallow, a ship would shoal to avoid running aground.

Because these sedimentations of sand, rock, or coral were often imperceptible until they sank a vessel, the mysterious and shoal-filled ocean floor posed a problem for navigating the sea. As a sandbar, and a particularly shifty formation, a shoal can erode over time, drift, and eventually accumulate in another location. Its unpredictability exceeds full knowability/mappability and in some senses it is what Sylvia Wynter and Katherine McKittrick would call a "demonic" space.[8] Because the shoal's shape, expanse, and density change over time, the shoal is as much a dynamic and moving set of processes and ecological relations as it is a longitudinal and latitudinal coordinate that cartographers attempt to fix in time and space. It is a mobile, always changing and shifting state of flux. As an ecological space, it represents an errant and ecotonal location made of both water and not water. Ecotones are classified within environmental science as a combination or meeting of at least two distinct ecological zones.[9] The shoal is liminal, indeterminate, and hard to map.

As elements of the ocean that not are stable or readily mappable and therefore knowable, shoals slow the movement of a vessel. They cause the ship's velocity and momentum to change direction, to adjust, and on occasion they force the voyage to stop. The shoal is an impediment and a danger to navigation. Materially, it is a site where movement as usual cannot proceed. Within cultural studies, and more specifically performance studies, Michael LeVan invoked the nautical and geological term to elaborate on the productive tension created within the discipline due to the use of digital technologies.[10] LeVan describes shoals as places, metaphors for contact and encounter, as well as emergent formations. Rising and falling with the tide, the shoal is an interstitial and emerging space of becoming:

> Rather, than forming a boundary between land and water, shoals are spaces of contact, friction, and interaction among land and water (framed above, of course by another space of contact: air or atmosphere). The phenomenon of "shoaling" is a sign of this contact: when the surface waves approach a shoal, they slow down, their height increases, the distance between them decreases, and sometimes they are diffracted. Though not an absolute obstacle, a shoal transforms the qualities of the movement of water. Simultaneously, beneath the surface

the movement of water constantly remakes the topography of the shoal. With each give and take of the waves, the zone of contact and encounter is reformed. The encounter transforms each, and each is constituted in part by its transformations.[11]

Like LeVan's interpretation, the Black shoal is certainly a moment of friction and the production of a new topography. *The Black Shoals*, as an analytical and a methodological location, constitutes a moment of convergence, gathering, reassembling, and coming together (or apart). The shoal, like Black thought, is a place where momentum and velocity as normal vectors are impeded. It is the place where an adjustment needs to be made. As an in-between, ecotonal, unexpected, and shifting space, the shoal requires new footing, different chords of embodied rhythms, and new conceptual tools to navigate its terrain. The shoal enables this book to shift its conceptual lens to a liminal space between the sea and the land.

At its surface, the shoal functions as a space of liminality, indeterminacy, and location of suture between two hermeneutical frames that have conventionally been understood as sealed off from each other. I offer the space of the shoal as simultaneously land and sea to fracture this notion that Black diaspora studies is overdetermined by rootlessness and only metaphorized by water and to disrupt the idea that Indigenous studies is solely rooted and fixed in imaginaries of land as territory.[12] Scholars in Black diaspora studies, giving specific attention to late twentieth-century scholars, have mobilized oceanic and water metaphors to theorize Black life, aesthetics, and decolonial politics as breaks with continental European discourse. Similarly positioning itself as a challenge to Western and colonial epistemes, Native studies has centered land at the fulcrum of its analytical, theoretical, and metaphorical maneuvers that challenge coloniality. The shoal creates a rupture and at the same time opens up analytical possibilities for thinking about Blackness as exceeding the metaphors and analytics of water and for thinking of Indigeneity as exceeding the symbol and analytic of land.

The genesis of the shoal in this project emerges from the larger project of Black diaspora studies. More specifically, the shoal gains its force from the traditions of Caribbean poetics and studies. Black diaspora studies as a project concerned with landscapes of domination and struggle has attended to and meditated on the sea and oceanic relations for some time. The Atlantic emerges as a central geographical body of the field, as well of as this project. During the late twentieth century and into the early twenty-first century, the enduring metaphor and actual space of the ocean has pulsed through Black diasporic literature, criticism, art, and theory. The Middle Passage and "crossings" of African-descended people in particular has animated and served as an arterial through line in Anglo–African American, Anglo-Caribbean, and Black Canadian, as well as Hispanophone and Lusophone, traditions. Hard to escape, the ocean and its legacy has crested again and again in Hortense Spillers's notion of the "oceanic," Édouard Glissant's "archipelagic thought," Paul Gilroy's "Black Atlantic," Kamau Brathwaite's "tidalectics," Antonio Benítez-Rojo's "rhythm," and Omise'eke Natasha Tinsley's "Black Atlantic, queer Atlantic."[13] While often evoking a space of connection, transit, passage, and flow, the ocean has also functioned as a complex seascape and ecology within Black diaspora studies that ruptures normative thought and European discourse.

Glissant's archipelagic thought in *Caribbean Discourse* that moves away from and out of sync with continental thought figures the ocean as a space that striates or interrupts the smooth flow of continental thought. More recently, Christina Sharpe's *In the Wake* and its wake work has reanimated Black studies' capacity to ripple and disturb the surface of the ocean. While these diasporic currents all offer modes of intervention, what I intend to think more carefully with is Brathwaite's conceptualization of tidalectics. I tarry with tidalectics because of the way that Brathwaite brings it into consciousness as a ritual enacted by Caribbean people with the sea and sand (and land). It is also important to note the ways that Brathwaite's tidalectics function as a form of what McKittrick calls Glissant's "poetics of landscape" that make space for Black geographical expressions of saying, feeling, writing, and imagining space.[14] In 1995, Brathwaite and Nathaniel Mackey had a conversation about poetry and Brathwaite's body of work. In the book *ConVERSations with Nathaniel Mackey*, which records moments from the poets' dialogue with each other, Brathwaite reconjures an image that helped him explain the arc of his poetic mediations on the question "What is Caribbean/the Caribbean?"[15] Looking from a house on a sandy cliff, Brathwaite takes in the following image:

> This is an ole yard, okay? and this old woman is
> sweeping, sweeping the sand of her yard away
> from her house. Traditional early morning old
> woman of Caribbean history.[16]

The old woman is described as temporally belonging to the "early morning" and spatiotemporally as a "woman of Caribbean history." She is engaged in a peculiar dawn ritual that Brathwaite cannot fully understand the first time he views it. While Brathwaite can feel how the ritual is urged on by a compulsion to hold off impending collapse — specifically, the chaos that poverty can bring — he does not understand the "why" or the usefulness of the act of separating sand from sand. Why would the woman enact a ritual to sweep sand away from sand and a residue that will return before the next break of dawn? Brathwaite ponders:

> She's going on
> like this every morning, sweeping this sand — of
> all things! — away from . . . sand from sand
> seen? . . . And I say Now what's she doing?[17]

After another gander, Brathwaite realizes that "she is in fact performing a very important ritual which [he] cannot fully understand but which [he is] tirelessly trying to."[18] Initially, the woman's movements and ritual were perplexing and opaque. He recalls waiting for another dawn to catch the woman's silhouette moving against the "sparkling light." When Brathwaite looks again, he says that it "seems" as if the woman's

> feet,
> which all along I thought were
> walking on the sand . . . were
> really . . . walking on the wa-
> ter . . . and she was tra
> velling across that middlepass
> age constantly coming from wh
> ere she had come from — in her
> case Africa — to this spot in
> North Coast Jamaica where she
> now lives.[19]

The movement of the woman — who "was always on this journey" — forward and then back again mimics the movement of the sea. There is more than a "sandy situation" at hand.[20] The woman is not just walking across the sand. The woman is also walking on water. Although Brathwaite uses "really" as a clarifying adverb, I do not interpret the "really" as a displacement of the sand. I see an interplay between the sand and the ocean. The ocean does not simply burst through and overwhelm the entire scene. The sand that will (always) return remains entangled with the ocean.[21] I hold on to Brathwaite's image of the sand — and ocean — to move with it to his discussion of how his way of doing Caribbean poetics disrupts the time, meter, and rhythm of the colonial imposition of the pentameter on poetry and prose. Much like Brathwaite's poetics, the shoal also disrupts colonial geographies, scales, and measures that separate the sand and the sea.

To be able to attend to and write about this old Caribbean woman of history and her humble morning ritual, Brathwaite needed to write in a different meter. More specifically, for Brathwaite to see (and for me to see) "the sand between her toes" as she crosses the ocean, he will have to write toward a knowledge and understanding of the Caribbean through his poetry in another rhythm.[22] "'They' (these imposed meters) could not allow me to write the sunlight under her feet—she walk on water and in the light, the sand between her toes, the ritual discourse of her morning broom."[23] Brathwaite's image of a morning ritual of survival, gratitude, and perpetual crossing of the "middlepass age" keeps the ebb and flow of the tides touching the shores of the continent of Africa and the coasts of the Caribbean.[24]

Brathwaite writes of this ebb and flow as another errant movement that puts Caribbean life and history outside Western traditions such as Hegelian dialectics. Of the Caribbean people and their tidalectic movement against Western linearity and progress, Brathwaite writes: "Why is our psychology not dialectical—successfully dialectical—in how Western philosophy has assumed people's lives should be, but tidalectic, like our grandmother's—our nanna's—action, like the movement of the ocean she's walking on, coming from one continent/continuum, touching another, and then receding (reading) from the island(s) into the perhaps creative chaos of the(ir) future."[25]

Brathwaite's tidalectics resonate with the kinds of connections and disruptions that *The Black Shoals* attempts to achieve. First, tidalectics confound the binary and dialectical thinking that would separate ocean from land and render Black people and Indigenous people as an antagonism. Second, Brathwaite's meditation on the confounding movement and ritual of the old woman gestures toward a kind of life that is beyond transparency, a Black life that does not willingly show or give itself away to any observer and a penetrating gaze. Brathwaite's initial state of confusion summons Glissant's notion—or, rather, his "demand"—for "the right to opacity."[26] Glissant described his notion of opacity as an "irreducible singularity," writing, "The opaque is not the obscure, though it is possible for it to be so and be accepted as such. It is that which cannot be reduced, which is the most perennial guarantee of participation and confluence."[27] Elucidating on Glissant's poetics of landscape as a challenge to traditional geographical formulations and their "familiar tools of maps, charts, official records, and figures," McKittrick draws attention to the ways that Glissant's language — and in this case, Brathwaite's Caribbean and diasporic "poetic politics" — can conceptualize a kind of "uncharted" surroundings that are continually made, remade, or unmade by Black fugitives working with furtive Indigenous communities.[28] The Black shoals are a part of the "uncharted" and at times invisible geographies of everyday Black life and ritual.

The woman's movement as something that could not be reduced to a daily ritual of moving/cleaning sand held deeper (and unknown) meanings for Brathwaite. This nonreducibility is an element of Black thought, Black life, and Black aesthetics that *The Black Shoals* desperately honors and protects. As a metaphor, the shoal cannot be reduced to the ocean, the shore, or an island. It always has the potential to be something else that cannot be known in advance. In addition, the shoal exceeds easy liquid metaphors. The shoal as a metaphor and an analytic can slow the reflex and compulsion to always anticipate that Blackness (people, aesthetics, symbols) will show up as liquidity, fluidity, and flow.[29] Liquidity as a totalizing metaphor for Blackness is not just an ethical problem for depictions of Black life and the Black radical (and political) imagination — it also effaces the generative conceptual problem of Blackness.[30] For instance, what happens — or needs to happen conceptually — when Black diasporic people, aesthetics, and politics land and encounter Native peoples' cosmologies and resistance to conquest? In an attempt to register this shift, the shoal disrupts the nautical and oceanic coherence of Blackness as only liquid and enables other modes of thinking about Blackness that opens up other kinds of potentialities, materialities, and forms. Anna Reckin reads Brathwaite's tidalectic as a "creative process" that brings various texts (struggles and experiences) together and creates new ones.[31] Reckin writes of Brathwaite's tidalectic as process, as gathering space and "Legba's crossing."[32]

The shoal is an alternative space always in formation (expanding or eroding) and not already overwritten or captured by the conceptual constraints of the sea or the land. If we conceptualize the shoal as a geological, oceanic, and geographical place, we can also imagine it as an actual and metaphorical place of juncture or a crossroads. Shoals are often found a few hundred feet offshore. Sometimes as sandbars or, at times, limestone formations, shoals often prevented vessels from coming all the way to the shore to anchor. When a vessel anchored offshore, small boats would travel up to the side of a ship to retrieve passengers and cargo to take to shore.[33] If a vessel could anchor near a sandbar—a shoal—offshore, crew, cargo, and captive slaves from the hold could stand, sit, and wait on the sandbar for a boat or could wade to shore themselves. For the members of the community/shoal that emerge from the ship's hold, it is perhaps the last shallow place to rest your feet before the last canoe ride or swim to shore. It is another in-between space other than the hold to temporarily squat and reassemble the self on new terms.

In the fifteenth century, for those who did not enter (or leave from) the arched threshold of the Door of No Return, sandbanks and shoals were the last spots of sand that an African embarking the slave vessel stepped on before being carried into the hold. The shoal was also a place just off the coast of the archipelagos of the Caribbean and the ports of the British Carolinas where the enslaved Africans arrived in the New World and took their first wobbly steps on a small bar of sand, where they stumbled forward, slipped, or crashed and were made to stand before wading into a shorter stretch of water that would finally bring them to the shore—a place where an adult could hoist a child higher on a hip to get a better grasp before wading to shore; a place that caused unsteady sea legs to slip beneath themselves into a tumble and tangle of coffles and iron banging together. At the beginning or end of other planned voyages, the sandbars could also present another opportunity to kill the ship's crew, seize the vessel, and head back to the sea in the other direction. Or, as in Paule Marshall's retelling of the story of Ibo Landing, the shoal could have been the place that Ibo decided they would turn around and walk past the boat back home.[34] The shoal is a small uncovered spot of sand, coral, or rock where one must quickly gather, lose oneself, or proceed in a manner and fashion not yet known. In a temporal sense, the shoal is also the location that offers a moment to reassemble the self as an amphibious and terrestrial subjectivity. Not just water (fluid, malleable, and fungible) but also a body landed. A place and time of liminality where one becomes an ecotone, a space of transition between distinct ecological systems and states. A place to come to terms with a changing terrain that demands that you both walk and swim to shore—and whatever the shore may bring.

In addition to rethinking Black epistemologies and conceptual ecologies, I also use the shoal as a way of moving Black diaspora studies to reconceptualizing Indigenous people as also connected to water and the oceanic. Vincente Diaz, a scholar of Pacific Island communities that constitute Oceania, works within seafaring epistemologies (ocean travel, chant, moving islands) to honor the ways that "land, sea and humans are mutually constitutive of one another."[35] Taking into consideration the "very long history of geo and oceanographic dispersal" and travel, Diaz's work, as well as other Pacific Islander Indigenous scholars, challenge notions of Indigenous "rootedness" in static time and space.[36] Thinking with Indigenous mobilities, migrations, and relationships to the sea, I hope to engage an important proposition that Seneca scholar Mishuana Goeman poses. More specifically, Goeman asks, what might "forms of analysis or action" that center "indigenous conceptions of land as connected, rather than land as disaggregate parcels at various European-conceived scales" of accumulation look like?[37] Colonial European scales disaggregate space into reservations, nation-states, continents, hemispheres, and water. Goeman offers that we "position land and water as always connected."[38] Goeman asks, "what if we think of waterways in the way my Pacific Islander colleagues, particularly Vincente Diaz and Alice Te Punga Somerville, have positioned waters as connected with the currents rather than water as that which divides continents, islands, and land?"[39] For Goeman, Somerville, and Diaz, "the binding of land and water to the political, cultural and social life of indigenous peoples requires an ethics of care and responsibility."[40] *The Black Shoals* is a site where Black studies connects land and water. The shoals also represent an analytical and geographical site where Black studies attempts to engage Native studies on ethical terms that unfold in new spaces.

This project tracks where and how Blackness interrupted the linear and smooth flow of modern and postmodern thought on the questions of slavery and genocide. Ultimately, this book asks, What changes does the Black shoal require of normative routes and knowledge systems that consider the ways that Black presence in the Americas casts a shadow on and informs the projects of genocide, settlement, and the remaking of "the human" under ongoing relations of conquest? As an accumulation of Black thought, aesthetics, and politics, the shoals of this project halt the all too smooth logics of White settler colonial studies. More specifically, *The Black Shoals* arrests settler colonialism's tendency to resuscitate older liberal humanist modes of thought to create new poststructural and postmodern forms of violent humanisms that feed off Indigenous genocide and Black social death. The shoals as the analytical, theoretical, and methodological sandbars in this book place White settler colonial studies, as well as certain tendencies within Indigenous/Native studies (and Black studies) that align with White humanist thought, under stress. *The Black Shoals* forces a tarrying within hemispheric Black studies' discourse of conquest and its traditions of interrogating the terms on which the human comes into formation through Black and Indigenous death in the Western hemisphere.

At this contemporary juncture, many Black and Indigenous people in this hemisphere experience the current political moment as one marked by mass carnage. Everyday life is marked by grotesque interludes with Black and Indigenous death in the streets or in the plains. Even as Black and Indigenous people and the world bear live witness — on the street, Twitter, Instagram, and Facebook — to the real-time murder of their kin and relations, liberal political commentary, the academy, and the White left continue to use a form of speech that refuses to name the quotidian spectacle of death as conquest.

THEORETICAL SHOALS

The way that shoals slow the movement and momentum of vessels acts as the organizing metaphor that structures the theoretical frame of the book. The Black shoal functions as a critique of normative discourses within colonial, settler colonial, and postcolonial studies that narrowly posit land and labor as the primary frames from which to theorize coloniality, anti-Indigenism, and anti-Black racism. *The Black Shoals* introduces an alternative reading practice and an analytical suture or thoroughfare that reveals the ways that Blackness mediates the relations of conquest in the Western Hemisphere. *The Black Shoals* works to disrupt the movement of modern thought, time, and space to enable something else to form, coalesce, and emerge.

An essential analytical move that shapes the theoretical contributions of *The Black Shoals* is how the book uses a hemispheric approach that exceeds conventional Black diasporic analytics and spaces. Throughout the book, the space of the hemisphere, which includes the westernmost coast of Africa and the Americas, functions as the landscape in which the practice of enslaving Black people and making them fungible and accumulable symbols of spatial expansion happens alongside and in relationship to Indigenous genocide. Very much as Brathwaite's "tidalectics" as performed in Caribbean and Black diaspora literature moved between the experiences of dispersal and landing, the analytical approach of this book traces the relationship and dialogic traffic between Black and Indigenous thought in the hemisphere.[41] Brathwaite's tidalectics, which lap up against Glissant's archipelagic thought and poetics of landscape, produce what Mc-

Kittrick identifies as "different sets of geographic tools . . . which are anchored, primarily in nonlinearity, contradictory histories, dispossession, and an infinite variety of landscapes."[42] Tidalectics as a mediation between the sea and land tends to privilege geographies and analytical sites such as the dock, stelling, and liminal spaces that are an intermediary location between ocean and shore. It is also an analytical location that forecloses settlement and permanent landing on its always shifting and dissolving terrains. Rather than read these ruptures, dissolving and ephemeral spaces suspiciously, I encourage the reader to engage the nontraditional geographies (visible, uncharted, and invisible) that connect Indigenous and Black diasporic thought reparatively.[43]

The theoretical frame of the book gathers, much like shoals gather, disparate granules of sand, rock, and coral to make new and varied theoretical formations within Black diaspora studies. While some of the theoretical pairings may seem disparate and sound dissonant, their placement in conversation with one another produces a generative friction. More important, the scholarly voices that I have curated for this project all ask important questions about how the human — or its apex, Man — is defined in relationship to Black and Indigenous people. In the theoretical formation that is the Black shoals, readers will recognize the sand mounds and coral patterns of Wynter, Spillers, and McKittrick, as well as Saidiya Hartman, Frank Wilderson, and Denise Ferreira da Silva. Their bodies of work contribute to a lineage and legacy of scholarship that arrests the normative epistemic flow and the violence of the narrativity of humanist (or what Wynter calls "monohumanist") thought. While the book recognizes that the authors and the respective traditions from which they are a part and help form (Caribbean studies, Black and African diaspora studies, U.S. Black studies, Black Canadian studies, Afro–Latin American and Brazilian studies) address specific and unique challenges that arise at the level of the nation-state and supranational regions, the book refuses to silo or treat the intellectual traditions as bounded. Black studies in its Caribbean, Canadian, U.S, Brazilian, North American, and Latin American iterations all shift and respond to one another (albeit unequally) like living shoals that are connected to one another like an archipelago.

Rather than conflate distinct intellectual formations, traditions, and practices of study, I trace the nerves of a gathering or shoaling (however fleeting and temporary that it may be) of a Black diasporic and hemispheric conversation about middle passages, geographies, rootless relations to nation-states, and encounters with Indigenous peoples amid the violence of New World modernity. I attend to the violence of conquest in Anglo imperial regimes and nation-states that connect Black people in the Western Hemisphere. I also attend to the ways that Black people who are subject to the legacy of this violence have always been trying to communicate with Indigenous people.

Each tradition and practice of Black study has its own approach to configuring and enfleshing the spaces and cracks where Black and Indigenous life caress each other. In the Anglo North American academy, Black Canadian studies — which continues to demand institutional resources and recognition — has sustained the most explicit and intentional exchange with Indigenous people, genocide, and the discourse of settler colonialism as evidenced by their scholarly imprint. Canadian racial discourses prioritize the settler-Indigenous binary and subordinate — erase — the nation's own history of slavery and anti-Black racism through a Canadian project of multiculturalism that focuses on assimilating (Black) immigrants into its national project.[44] Because of the way that the Canadian nation-state organizes and narrates its racial conflict and reconciliation along settler and Indigenous lines, Black Canadian studies has a long and established record of theorizing racial violence and through a triadic European-Native-Black frame. Further, the influence of Black diaspora studies, particularly a practice inflected by Anglo-Caribbean Studies in Toronto, privileges an Afro-diasporic tradition with a long history of studying and critiquing coloniality. The influence of Caribbean philosopher Wynter is evident in the work of Black Canadian scholars like Rinaldo Walcott, whose essay "The Problem of the Human: Black Ontologies and 'the Coloniality of Our Being'" (2014) limns the limits of a settler colonial critique in the face of anti-Black racism. In "The Problem of the Human," Walcott draws on the Wynterian tradition of studying the violent enclosures of the human in order to elaborate the ways that the Canadian nation-state's project of multiculturalism expands to incorporate modes of Indigenous representation into its notion of the human/Man at the expense of Black subjects in Canada.[45]

In comparison, U.S. Black studies' engagement with Native studies and Indigenous sovereignty as a political and intellectual project, while longer, has been less even and consistent. U.S. racial discourse tends to be organized by a White-Black paradigmatic frame that often erases Indigenous peoples. When U.S. Black studies has engaged Indigenous thought and politics, the field has been less likely to articulate Black-Indigenous relations through a discourse of settler colonial relations until recent, twenty-first-century scholarship.[46] Tracking the history of Black popular and scholarly treatments of the subject of Native America, scholar Arika Easley-Houser has discovered an antebellum African American print culture in which Native Americans figured centrally in the nineteenth-century African American imagination.[47] These print cultures ranged from those that sought to explore alliances with Native peoples to comparative projects that tried to prove African American superiority to Native peoples, as well as those that investigated Native practices of enslavement.[48] Shortly after founding the Association for the Study of African American Life and History (ASALH) in 1915, Carter G. Woodson published his article "The Relations of Negroes and Indians in Massachusetts" in the *Journal of Negro History* in 1920. During the late 1960s and early 1970s, the first Black studies programs producing scholarship at the nexus of Black activism and the development of academic departments created fertile ground for conversations between Black and Native scholars and activists. With the establishment of Black studies departments, a noticeable uptick in scholarship by Black scholars on Black and Native American relations emerged after Powhatan-Renape scholar Jack D. Forbes's *Africans and Native Americans: The Language of Race and the Evolution of Red-Black Peoples* was published in 1993.

In the first decades of the twenty-first century, scholars began to pay particular attention to the practice of slavery among the Five Civilized Tribes. In 2006, Tiya Miles and Sharon Holland coedited the anthology *Crossing Waters, Crossing Worlds: The African Diaspora in Indian Country.* The contributors to the collection used a variety of interdisciplinary methods and rooted their work in primary sources, archival records, and Black and Native literary traditions that told stories of Black and Native relations in North America. In the wake of Miles and Holland's *Crossing Waters, Crossing Worlds,* Frank B. Wilderson authored one of the first interdisciplinary Black studies texts that introduced a theoretical frame for elaborating the complex structural and ontological—political economic and libidinal—positions of Black and Native people in the United States.

Caribbean and Latin American studies' attention to complicated processes of racialization and identity formation like creolization and mestizaje refract Blackness and Indigeneity differently from Black North American racial frameworks. Blackness and Indigeneity do not function as frequently as bounded ancestries, identities, or ontological positions. However, Anglo-Caribbean scholars such as Shona Jackson and Melanie Newton have noted that in the Anglo Caribbean, anticolonial and postcolonial national origin stories often erase Amerindian presence through a Calibanesque tradition that indigenizes African-descended people.[49]

However, Black and African diaspora scholarship that emerges from the Caribbean and from Central and South America directly engages questions of coloniality from theoretical and experiential perspectives. For example, Sylvia Wynter's body of work, which traces the "epistemic revolutions" of Western humanism, attends to the ways that Black (Niggers) and Indigenous (Indios) identities are made and remade as a perpetual limit point or outside to the boundaries of Man across various colonial formations. Wynter's critique of humanism and its systems of overrepresentation has functioned as a crucial pivot point in Black studies that has enabled the emergence of a shared critique to emerge between Black and Native Studies. A Black studies reading practice that attends to African diaspora studies as they unfold in the Caribbean and South America has the conceptual space to acknowledge philosophical, literary, and historical traditions that can attend to histories of both enslavement and colonialism. Despite these different and, at times, divergent tendencies in each respective Black tradition of study, factions within each tradition have sustained unique and meaningful conversations with Indigenous peoples and Indigenous/Native studies on their own terms.

As a way of eroding (while attending to specificities of) nation-bound approaches for tracking Black and Indigenous dialogue, I turn to Black diasporic methods. More specifically, I rely on Gilroy's analytic of the Black Atlantic as a way to track mobile and shifting diasporic thought, activism, and aesthetics that engage Indigenous people.[50] At times, the diasporic movement will travel with and identify Black and Indigenous dialogue at the level of the nation, the region, the hemisphere, or imagined spaces that exceed all of these geographical scales. Diasporic itineraries and thought act as methods and practices of study that present other frames for attending to Black diaspora people's engagement with Indigenous people.

BLACK NOTES ON WESTERN HUMANISM

Humanism is generally defined as a philosophy or worldview that puts the human at the center of the world. This point of view displaces God (and the clergy) as the center and puts the rational (man with reason) there, emerging during the Renaissance of the fourteenth and fifteenth centuries into what we know as the Enlightenment of the seventeenth and eighteenth centuries. A more recent form of humanism that stretches into the contemporary moment is liberal humanism, which privileges the bourgeois individual as a self-contained and competitive economic subject within the capitalist system. The Caribbean philosopher Sylvia Wynter is far more surgical in her schematic of humanism, particularly in the ways she maps its shifts and epistemic ruptures and the areas in which there is overlap between, or residue (a transmutation) that carries over into, different forms of humanism. For example, during the period of Renaissance humanism, there was shift from a religious or God-centered paradigm to a more secular and reason-oriented paradigm. As this shift occurred, due to a particular population (the laity) overturning a hegemonic cognitive or system of knowledge, some elements of Christianity persisted. In a conversation with David Scott, Wynter explains that Columbus was a millennial Christian, which was an "underground form" of the Christian humanism of the time.[51] While he was not as radical as the lay/secular humanists who challenged the "orthodox theocentric conception of the Christian God," he did want to be free of the constraints of a theocentric absolutism that held on to the social structures that benefited what Wynter calls the "hegemonic medieval-aristocratic order."[52] Overthrowing certain aspects of the social hierarchies within Christian humanism allowed for a "lowly born mapmaker-*cum*-merchant" to rise through the ranks and build the Spanish state, as well as his own personal wealth, through imperial conquest. Columbus's humanism is a hybrid form in which the residual ideologies of the religious order that place the Christian over the heathen (evil, unbaptized) still linger and influence the newly emerging form of secular humanism. During this shift, the former heathens (pagans, enemies of Christ, idolaters) were being transformed into secular forms of human otherness (irrational, lack, symbolic death). From the end of the fifteenth century into the sixteenth century when Christian explorers traveled, Africans and Amerindian peoples were turned into the human others called Negroes and Indians. Rational "Man," or the ideal version of the human, was being invented through the construction of the sensuous and irrational Negro and Indian as "a category of otherness or of symbolic death."[53] Western European men wrote and represented themselves (through cultural production such as Shakespeare's *The Tempest*) as conquerors in this era. This form of conquistador humanism and its view of the Native and Black Other — as a space of death — produced and sustained a genocidal violence and brutal system of enslavement that relegated Niggers and Indios to the bottom ranks of the human order. This ranking system, though revised, still positions Indigenous and Black people at its bottom rungs. I argue in this book that this form of conquistador humanism, which requires Black and Indigenous dehumanization (as death bound), continues to this day.

In the human's overrepresentation of itself as Man (Wynter), the ideal and proper human remains an exclusive category.

Wynter argues that even when the boundaries of the category have expanded and changed over time, how the human is culturally depicted (for Wynter, overrepresented) always produces other humans or less than fully human figures. Wynter and other Black decolonial scholars such as Frantz Fanon and Aimé Césaire have argued that there are multiple, competing, and non-European forms of humanism that seek to overturn this conception of Man and its hierarchies. For instance, Marxist and feminist versions of humanism have emerged to expand who can be considered a subject worthy of dignity, rights, and a place within the universal narrative of the struggle for human progress.[54] However, finding them insufficient, Fanon and decolonial scholars have called for more just or new humanisms. A part of anticolonial and decolonial projects has been the reinvention of the human and humanism on more just terms. Wynter has cautioned the anticolonial male subject and the Native Caribbean and Black American womanist subject that their versions of humanism should also be subjected to scrutiny. The Caribbean scholar Tonya Hayes has argued that Wynter was "critical of the attempts of Black nationalists" to create the African or Antillean Man as the norm.[55] Wynter urges a disruption of the very order that creates a norm and, inevitably, an "Other." In "Whose Time Is It," Michelle V. Rowley has argued that Fanon's new humanism largely reconfigures the human in ways that expand to include the Black man but not to incorporate Black women unless they can fit under the sign of the maternal, heterosexual, Black, subaltern women committed to the Black man and nation in the Caribbean. While this stretching of the category of the human in the Caribbean includes some women, its reorganization around the concept, or "code," of gender leaves other subjects and bodies out.[56] Alongside Wynter, Rowley argues that new and evolving humanisms "coincide with the empirical reality" in which we live.[57] Wynter argues that we continue to revise what it means to be human and keep the human an open question that can never be resolved in advance.

One of the places that one might feel some theoretical tension, I argue, is where Wynter and Frank Wilderson meet. While Wynter argues that Black and Indigenous people occupy a degraded position on the bottom rung of the human chain—the missing link between human and animal—Black people are nonetheless a part of the human-biological species. Black and Indigenous people represent other kinds of humans. Wilderson, by contrast, argues at a more extreme—or less orthodox—end of Fanon's notion of the zone of nonbeing that the Black is nonhuman. In fact, the Black must be rendered nonhuman for White subjects to know their own humanity. Although Wynter can argue for a continual reworking of the human, and Wilderson argues for a destruction of the human as an epistemic system, both scholars argue that the current conception of humanity is anti-Black and, to a large degree, anti-Indigenous. Further, they proffer a triad (Indian-European-Negro or Red-White-Black) model to explain the modern ruptures and antagonisms that order the world. They subvert the prosaic colonial dyad of settler and Native that structures most colonial discourses, including settler colonial studies.

A crucial theoretical intervention that Wynter, Spillers, and Wilderson introduce are discourses of Black conquest that rupture and break with the humanist tradition and hegemonic hold of White settler colonial studies. Like an unexpected rock formation, Wynter's and Spillers's reorganization of the traditional spatial and temporal frames used to talk about conquest function as a shoal for White settler colonial studies and some tendencies within Indigenous and Native studies. By starting on the shores of what is today's Senegal and extending the inaugural moments of conquest back half a century to 1441, Wynter and Spillers push back the curtains and position Blackness, which was previously positioned just offstage, directly under the spotlight of the epic drama of conquest. According to Wynter, the invention of Blackness — as heathen under the fifteenth-century Christian humanism of Bartolomé de las Casas and Juan Ginés de Sepúlveda — and Black lands as terra nullius (or torrid and inhabitable) are required to establish the terms of conquest. Further, the epistemological revolution of Enlightenment's Man requires the presence of the Negro as an irrational and sensual human Other. Because Wynter insists on a "triadic model" (White-Native-Black) rather than a dyadic model (White-Native) to understand the sets of relations and conflict that would bring forth the notion of the modern human and inform conquest, her work is essential to the Black errancy of *The Black Shoals*.[58] Particularly important in guiding the theoretical interventions of the book are four of Wynter's theoretical contributions: her "European-Negro-Indian" triad; the notion of Man as a concept under constant revision; her adaptation of C. L. R. James's *pieza* consciousness as a critique of political-economic reason/criticism; and her notion of ceremony.

Equally essential to this intervention, Spillers reorganizes the geo-temporal dimensions of conquest in ways that expand their spatial and temporal frames beyond the conventional time-space coordinates of 1492 and the New World by locating conquest on the shores of Guinea. When Spillers turns to the archive in the essay "Mama's Baby, Papa's Maybe," she finds Gomes Eannes de Azurara's *The Chronicle of the Discovery and Conquest of Guinea, 1441–1448* and says that "we learn that the Portuguese probably gain the dubious distinction of having introduced Black Africans to the European market of servitude."[59] For both Wynter and Spillers, conquest begins before Columbus with the landing of the Portuguese on the shores of western Africa.[60] In this hemispherical treatment of the relations of conquest, the coasts of western Africa—the reefs, rocks, and fog of Cape Bojador—function as shoals to Western and normative theorizations of the geography and temporality of New World conquest. Wynter's and Spiller's theoretical disfigurement of time-space represents a tradition of Black studies' ability to shoal the linear and normative treatment of conquest in the Americas.

The coast of West Africa works not so much to displace the horrors and legacies of Indigenous genocide in the Americas as to insert the invention of Blackness as a crucial line of demarcation for the thinking and writing of the human as Man. I also use the shoal as a peripheral point or location off the shore—or offshore—of the Americas to bring home the full force of this intellectual and political intervention. Rather than place Black studies at the "center" of the discourse of settler colonial studies, *The Black Shoals* pulls settler colonial studies offshore—and away from its position as a discursive center—to make it contend with Black thought. *The Black Shoals* puts Black studies into a productive friction with settler colonial studies. The discourse of conquest within Black studies is something that "settler colonial studies" must bump into and adjust for before it comes ashore and lands. *The Black Shoals* tests the navigational skills of settler colonial studies, as well as other humanist critical theories, as they attempt to cross the terrain of Black life, thought, pain, pleasure, and modes of resistance and expression in the hemisphere. Settler colonial studies breaks open when crashing into the rock, coral, and sandbank of the shoal and must contend with the ways that its own discourse of settler and settlement disavows the violent ways that settler human self-actualization depends on the most violent forms of Black and Indigenous death.

Scholars of the British Empire and colonial studies marked a shift in the discursive paradigms used to invoke and describe Indigenous genocide, racial (Black) slavery, imperial expansion, and colonial rule in the eighteenth century. Carole Pateman and Anuradha Gobin have argued that, in an attempt to create distance from the violence of Spanish conquest and

disavow Britain's own brutal practices of genocide and slavery, British par-
lance, visual art, maps, and other discursive performances of power shifted
from using the term "conquest" to employing terms such as "settlement"
and "plantation."[61] These words were the preferred terms and syntax for the
active and brutal process of British and Anglo forms of imperial domination in the eighteenth century. For example, the British, French, and Dutch
began to distinguish their brand of colonialism from the "Black Legend,"[62]
or the barbarism and gratuitous violence of the Spanish Empire, which was
temporally marked as a sixteenth-century phenomenon and relegated to
the practices of the Spanish and Portuguese. In the eighteenth century,
British and, soon after, Anglo American modes of colonialism began to describe and name their form of colonialism as settler colonialism or a form
"that implied alteration of the land only through planting."[63]

In "Red, White and Black," Wilderson also tracks this grammatical
shift in the language of White civil society to hide the violence that White
human life requires as its condition of possibility. Wilderson helps us think
about the kind of discursive and material violence that occurs within what
he calls the "Settler/Master/Human's grammatical structure."[64] Within
this grammatical structure, he argues, there is a disavowal of the violence
of genocide in how the settler narrates the formation of the United States.
On one level, the disavowal occurs through the settler's preferred part of
speech. For example, "clearing" is spoken of only as a noun in the Settler/
Master/Human's grammatical structure and never used as a verb. Wilderson draws our attention to its use: "*Clearing*, in the Settler/'Savage' relation, has two grammatical structures, one [as] a noun and the other as a
verb. . . . But prior to the clearing's fragile infancy, that is before its cinematic legacy as a newborn place name, it labored not *across* the land as a
noun but as a verb *on* the body of the 'Savage.'"[65]

The Black Shoals halts the ways that invocations of settlement, land,
clearing, and territory efface the violence of conquest. The eighteenth-
century and contemporary discourse of "settler colonialism," particularly
as deployed by White settler colonial studies, continental theory, and
some strands of ethnic studies, continues to disavow the gratuitous violence that is ongoing and, in fact, necessary for the "human" to continue
to self-actualize without sufficient scrutiny as a category of Whiteness.
More specifically, the "human" as an exclusive category demands an outside and requires the death of Indigenous and Black people. For the human
to continue to evolve as an unfettered form of self-actualizing (and expanding) form of Whiteness, Black and Indigenous people must die or be

transformed into lesser forms of humanity—and, in some cases, become nonhuman altogether. *The Black Shoals* traces the ways that Black studies, as well as Black thought, expressive culture, social movements, and alternative modes of life, illumine the ways that White humanity and its self-actualization require Black and Native death as its condition of possibility.

In chapter 1, Wynter's, Spillers's and Wilderson's theorizations of conquest interface with Native and Indigenous studies' theorizations of conquest and imperialism. I put Leslie Marmon Silko's *The Almanac of the Dead*, Huanani-Kay Trask's *Notes from a Native Daughter*, Joanne Barker's theorization of imperialism, and Andrea Smith's *Conquest* in conversation with Wynter, Spillers, Wilderson, and other Black literary artists to trace the contours of a shared speech. Silko, Trask, Barker, and Smith establish intellectual and political traditions within Native and Native feminist studies that provide unflinching accounts of the ways that Indigenous genocide and the violence of colonization make White and human world-making possible. Silko, Trask, Barker, and Smith use a particular grammar of violence that exposes the ways that White settler colonial discourse avoids explicit discussions of how Native death ensures White settler life and self-actualization. I name conquest as a lingua franca or shared dialogic space to articulate genocide and slavery as forms of violence that are essential to the emergence of conquistador humanism or what Wynter names "Man1." In this way, *The Black Shoals* posits a new kind of speech. Conquest as a grammar represents a form of Black and Native speech that contests the ways that White settler colonial studies attempts to constrain Black and Native thought and speech. Further, conquest as a dialect resists the ways that White settler colonial studies currently mediates dialogues between Black and Indigenous people. Discursively, Black and Native grammars of conquest attempt to speak into existence a dialogic space less mediated by White settler colonial studies and other liberal humanist communicative acts.

THE SHOALS OF FUNGIBILITY

Perhaps the most important theoretical intervention of *The Black Shoals* is how it searches for utterance and grammar outside of what Black studies calls the narrativity of the liberal subject or human. While not situating itself as an Afro-pessimistic text, *The Black Shoals* does take Wilderson's claims seriously when he argues that the "grammar of suffering," or theory of violence articulated by liberal humanists, Marxists, feminists, and queer and trans subjects, does not have the capacity to speak for how Black people experience violence in the world.[66] While at times positioned as an optimist vis-à-vis Wilderson's work, Fred Moten on a number of occasions cites Wilderson's contention that Black thought and what Moten would call Black sociality does in fact emerge from "the hold of the ship."[67] Black life and expression is an utterance or moan that emerges from the hold of the ship and continues on the plantation, like Aunt Hester's scream.[68] Black thought and theory break with normative modes of narrativity and intelligibility. *The Black Shoals* therefore stages an extended rumination on the theoretical, methodological, creative, and ethical potential of Black fungibility as a way of articulating a world-altering mode of existence.

Hartman's theorization of fungibility represents a Black mode of expression, screaming, or utterance that exceeds the narrow humanist and settler grammars of labor (and land as property). Jared Sexton has argued that the theoretical intervention of settler colonial studies—and its critique of colonial studies—while changing the terms of engagement to settlers, settlement, invasion, and occupation, still relies on humanist epistemes and units of analysis of "the body in relation to land, labor, language, lineage" to ask its "most pertinent" questions about settler decolonization.[69] Hartman's theorization of fungibility, as well as Afro-pessimist critiques of Marxism, challenge the notion that White revolutions (reforms) often fail Black subjects and fall short of abolition's aspirations. While not thoroughly rejecting Marx's theoretical contributions, Hartman does challenge the overriding logic of labor in his formulations of value and questions its applicability for the Black enslaved person. Thinking with (and against) Marx's notion of primitive accumulation, Hartman theorizes racialization, accumulation, and domination rather than labor as the primary mode of Black subjectification.[70] In the first chapter of *Scenes of Subjection*, Hartman establishes the role of enjoyment in the economy of chattel slavery and identifies the overriding value of the slave as the "figurative capacities of blackness."[71] She goes on to elaborate the figurative capacities of Blackness as fungibility. Hartman states her intentions this way: "I contend that the value of blackness resided in its metaphorical aptitude, whether literally understood as the fungibility of the commodity or understood as the imaginative surface upon which the master and the nation came to understand themselves."[72] I situate Hartman's theorization of Black fungibility within the genealogy of Spillers's explication of Black enslaved flesh in the essay "Mama's Baby, Papa's Maybe" as unanchored, malleable, and open signs.

Spillers's notion of Black flesh is an important touchstone because of how it helps this book elaborate that Black fungible flesh is a "[territory] of cultural and political maneuver" that can be arranged and rearranged infinitely under relations of conquest in the Americas.[73] As a Black fleshy analytic, I argue, Black fungibility can denote and connote pure flux, process, and potential. To be rendered Black and fungible under conquest is to be rendered porous, undulating, fluttering, sensuous, and in a space and state at-the-edge and outside of normative configurations of sex, gender, sexuality, space, and time to stabilize and fix the human category. Black fungibility is an expression of the gratuitous violence of conquest and slavery whose repertoire has no limits or bounds. It operates both materially on the body and produces Blackness (as idea and symbol) as a discursive space of open possibility.

Similar to Hartman, I argue that Black fungibility—rather than labor—defines and organizes Black value within relations of conquest. Black fungible bodies index the imagined (surfaces) and actual sites of colonial spatial expansion and, in turn, the space of Indigenous genocide. While Hartman's and Wilderson's critiques of labor are not achieved in conversation with Native studies, this project identifies critiques of labor within both fields as a possible shoal and shared terrain that interrupts Lockean and Marxian valorizations of labor.

Since the emergence of Native studies, a number of scholars, from Vine Deloria to more contemporary scholars, such as Mishuana Goeman, have critiqued the Lockean ethos of labor. More recently, Goeman has argued that "property, as has been argued by Indigenous scholars and their allies, is distinctly a European notion that locks together (pun intended) labor, land, and conquest. Without labor to tame the land, it is closely assigned the designation 'nature' or 'wilderness.'"[74] Within this Lockean formulation, Indigenous subjects who do not labor across the land fail to turn the land into property and thus fail to turn themselves into proper human subjects. In *Red Skins, White Masks*, Glen Coulthard, in a fashion similar to Hartman, interrogates the usefulness of Marx's liberal humanist tendencies that reify the laborer as the paradigmatic subject of suffering and agency. Coulthard also stretches the potential of Marx's notion of primitive accumulation rather than labor to rethink Indigenous people's relationship to settler states. Plumbing the usefulness of primitive accumulation, he argues that "the history and experience of dispossession, not proletarianization, has been the dominant structure shaping the historical relationship between Indigenous peoples and the Canadian [and U.S.] state."[75] On the way toward a larger project of articulating and affirming Indigenous politics of resurgence that do not capitulate to statist modes of recognition, Coulthard finds it necessary to jettison the deterministic and recognizable rubric and nomenclature of labor.

This challenge to the overriding frame of labor that appears in Hartman's and Coulthard's work is also explored by Shona Jackson as a potential onto-epistemic rupture that both Black creole subjects and Indigenous subjects in the Caribbean can embrace. In *Creole Indigeneity: Between Myth and Nation in the Caribbean*, Jackson argues that "the modern teleology of labor" simultaneously locks the Black creole subject and Indigenous subjects into European notions of progress and modernity that at once enslave and turn the Black subject into a civilized subject while negating Indigenous subjects and marking them for death. Jackson asks that certain modes of Caribbean philosophy and political thought that tend to overvalorize labor reconsider the consequences. She makes a distinction between jettisoning labor and rethinking a particular attachment to it when she argues, "I am not suggesting that to be truly postmodern the Caribbean must move beyond labor, but rather to truly exit modernity it must reject the metaphysics of labor deployed in the opposition of the 'Creole' self to the 'native' other."[76] Further, Wynter's reclamation of C. L. R. James's "pieza framework" challenges labor's determinism to expose the multiple and intersecting modes of oppression that shape the violence of coloniality and, subsequently, the lives of Black diasporic people.[77]

In this project, Black fungibility — rather than Black labor — represents the unfettered use of Black bodies for the self-actualization of the human and for the attendant humanist project of the production and expansion of space. As a project of human and geographical possibility, the invention of Blackness (material and symbolic bodies) in the New World has certainly enabled the human to self-actualize as an expression of unfettered spatial expansion and human potential. The invention of Blackness as the conceptual fodder for the rhizomatic imagination of the conquistador figures the Black body as an open space of possibility.

Just as Black fungibility is a form of gratuitous violence that is unending and unpredictable, Black struggle's resistance to and maneuvering within fungibility is as unpredictable and uncontainable. As a Black mode of critique, it elaborates and gives texture to various forms of violence while also revealing unexpected and ever emerging modes of freedom — or a "loophole of retreat."[78] Following C. Riley Snorton's argument in *Black on Both Sides* that under enslavement "fungibility and fugitivity figured two sides of a Janus-faced coin, in which the same logic that figured blackness as immanently interchangeable would also engender its flow," this book argues that Black fungibility resists conventional understandings and deployments of fungibility as solely a space of Black death, accumulation, dereliction, and limits.[79] In *The Black Shoals*, Black fungibility also represents a space of alterity and possibility, or what Snorton calls "fungible fugitivity."[80]

While fungibility is a key concept in the book, it is not the animating analytic, theory, or metaphor. The shoal is an expansive analytic of disruption and becoming that includes and puts fungibility into play as one of several ways to elaborate how Black studies disrupts Western humanist thought. For example, fungibility as theorized by Hartman and Wilderson critiques the hegemonic and totalizing regime of labor within political economic theory. Fungibility is but one intervention that constitutes the disruptive force of the shoal. As a capacious metaphor of slowing, becoming, merging, formation, and indeterminacy, the shoal animates and shapes how fungibility is construed and elaborated as unknowability and unpredictability. Much like the Wynterian and McKittrickian notion of the "demonic," fungibility evades capture.[81]

Further, fungibility elaborated through the space of the shoal turns into a confounding, liminal, and shifting space that cannot be reduced to water. As the shoal is a space in the ocean that is both water and other (rock, sand, etc.), fungibility is a concept that exceeds the metaphor of liquidity, as well as neat categorization. Fungibility is a formation that emerges in response to power, its particular form (rupture, destabilization, materiality) cannot be predicted in advance. It is more elusive than liquid and its mapped states (vapor, solid, liquid). This indeterminacy distinguishes it from water and liquid metaphors.

While fungibility as theorized by Hartman and Wilderson emerges from a place of unfettered domination and marks "Blackness" as an open space of figurative and material exchange, I argue that fungibility is, in fact, a product of White anxiety and representation, an attempt to "get in front of" or anticipate Black fugitive movement. In chapter 2, I argue that the ever present threat in the eighteenth century of Black rebellion required the production and projection of errant, unpredictable, and uncontainable movement onto Black enslaved bodies. In chapter 2, I read the cartographic depiction of Black bodies as fungible — open, exchangeable, shifting, and ever in flux — as a failed attempt by British settlers to control Black movement through representation. Subverting the logic of fungibility as an unfettered form of the one-directional flow of White domination, I rewrite fungibility and fugitivity as the product of a dialectical relationship. In very much the same ways that Black fugitivity morphs and changes according to the vicissitudes of power, fungibility and its modes of manipulating Blackness respond to Black fugitivity. Reclaiming fungibility as a resource for Black enslaved people rather than an impediment to Black practices of — or, as Snorton argues "for" — freedom stretches Blackness's terrain. Black "fungible fugitivity" as an expansive and unwieldy concept also interfaces with Indigeneity in resourceful and unpredictable ways.[82]

The final theoretical intervention that the book stages is a reimagination of Black and Indigenous ethics. Through a discussion of Black and Indigenous erotics in chapter 4, the project argues that a shared Black and Indigenous erotics that is oriented toward Black and Indigenous futures introduces an ethical frame that addresses some of the shortcomings of "coalition." My working understanding of ethics emerges primarily from Black feminist notions of the term. More specifically, my notion of ethics is inspired by what I heard Black queer women and femmes who are members of the Black Lives Matter Atlanta chapter express as an ethics of "we leave no one behind." This coincides with other Black feminist and womanist conceptions of ethics. For example, the womanist theologian Katie Cannon has argued that oppression and the "real-lived texture of black life requires a moral agency that may run contrary to the ethical boundaries of Protestantism."[83] Normative notions of ethics that align with Protestantism value and conflate ethical action with activities related to "economic success, self-reliance, frugality and industry."[84] Cannon also argues that normative notions of ethics assume that a subject is free and unconstrained and experiences reality as offering a "wide range of choices." Anti-Black racism creates conditions of oppression and constraint that force Black people to "create and cultivate values and virtues on their own terms."[85] As there is no one Black community, and no one experience with anti-Black racism, I limit my discussion of ethics to a frame for thinking about how Black people in the Americas can work toward Black and Indigenous peoples' futurity. The ethical orbits around a notion of mutual care. Ethical acts in this project also complement Audre Lorde's notion and elaboration of the erotic in *Uses of the Erotic: The Erotic as Power* (1978) and later in her essay "The Master's Tools Will Never Dismantle the Master's House" (1983).[86] The Lordean notions of the erotic that this project extends draw inspiration from Lorde's positing of the erotic in 1978 as a "power that rises from our deepest and non rational knowledge"; "a provocative force of revelation"; and a "measure between the beginnings of our sense of ourselves and the chaos of our strongest feeling."[87] In chapter 4, I draw on these notions of the erotic to read moments in which Black and Indigenous subjects in two novels "share deeply" with each other and give each other access to an erotic form of knowledge that acts as a "bridge which connects them."[88]

I honor and expand Lorde's notion of the erotic to reimagine it as a state of ecstasy—or a coming undone and moving outside of oneself— that moves an individual into the liminal space of the "measure between the beginnings" of the self and a kind of chaos that opens them up to their own and another's deepest feelings, wants, and desires. The Cree poet and scholar Billy-Ray Belcourt similarly writes about sex, and what I also interpret as the erotic, as having the capacity to unmoor individuals. For Belcourt, "Sex talk makes us talk about states of fragility" in ways that transcend the capacity and ethics of "political speak."[89] According to Belcourt, unlike sovereignty, sex "engenders a discourse about the future that hinges on the tenuousness of being beholden to others in determining one's sense of a livable life."[90] Belcourt's meditation on sex and the "erotic," which draws from queer Native studies and politics, shares deep resonances with Lorde's notions of the erotic. Within queer Native studies, the erotic is a form of Two Spirit and a queer source of knowledge, one that challenges the biopolitical and colonial discourse of "sexuality."[91] Rather than subject Native bodies to the violence of biopolitical knowledge production around sexuality, this notion of the erotic invokes a relationship to "bodies and pleasures" that can displace the power of sexuality.[92] The erotic becomes a source of power and information that is crucial for decolonial resistance. This feminist, Two Spirit, queer, and errant form of critique also compels decolonizing movements to move outside of dominant logics and narratives of "nation."[93] I situate and discuss the erotic as a site of Black and Indigenous gathering (shoaling) or coming together. These instances of coming together gesture toward an otherwise mode of being human that holds space for one another's well-being, joy, and future.

METHODOLOGICAL SHOALS

This book's methodological approach is a practice in listening for, feeling for, and noticing where things have come into formation together, or where they are one. The methodological capaciousness of the shoal has helped me avoid reproducing what I have called elsewhere "discovery narratives."[94] What I mean by this is that, in the important work that Black and Native studies has developed to better understand how the lives of Black and Native peoples in the Americas intersect, there is often an attempt to uncover and or prove the existence of histories of Black and Native contact, coexistence, intermarriage, alliance and collision, or conflict.[95] This archival, historical, literary, and sociological work that historicizes and theorizes the ways that Black and Native lives are intertwined in the Western Hemisphere is essential and provides the conditions of possibility for my work. However, my use of the shoal attempts to overcome the analytical constraints of looking for connection and encounter in ways that reproduce regimes of representation that make Black people and Native people appear as if they are isolated, bounded, and discrete communities and historical processes that come together only after their separate and respective emergences. The formation and methodology of the shoal works to challenge forms of what I am calling "applied intersectional frames" that attempt to discover, connect, or wrangle together experiences and power dynamics that are conceived as emerging independently of one another.[96] The conceptual tools of "discovery" assume a binary that must be overcome or discrete phenomenon that must be connected in ways that occlude their co-constitution or oneness. Part of the methodological contribution of *The Black Shoals* is its attunement to and disruption of the binaries and chasms that are overrepresented as an epistemological truth. Methodologically, the shoal functions as a site that introduces new formations, alternative grammar and vocabularies, and new analytical sites that reveal the ways that some aspects of Black and Indigenous life have always already been a site of co-constitution. The book in some cases revisits older analytical sites, such as Christopher Columbus's humanism, and in other cases it develops new analytical sites, such as composite maps of indigo processing—an overlay of eighteenth-century and twentieth-century depictions of indigo processing to illustrate where anti-Black and anti-Indigenous resistance emerged simultaneously. More important, the book attempts to show where Black and Indigenous death, resistance, and life have appeared simultaneously.

Materially and conceptually, the shoal—as simultaneously water and land—presents a site of conceptual difficulty. The shoal represents a process, formation, and space that exists beyond binary thinking. Chapters in the book attend to where Black and Indigenous speech and grammar share the same tongue; where Black and Indigenous resistance disrupt the master codes and cartographic representations of Man on an eighteenth-century map; where Black porous bodies tell histories of Black and Indigenous survival in "uninhabitable zones," where Black and Indigenous erotics force an unmooring of the self; and where decolonial aesthetic practices sculpt new epistemologies and sensibilities that shape the contours of humanness in more expansive ways. The shoal offers an analytical site where multiple things can be perceived and experienced simultaneously.

Because sites where the simultaneity of Black and Indigenous life, or anti-Black and anti-Indigenous violence, do not always come into view, this book at times must create these spaces or create the conditions of possibility for them to emerge. This act of creating analytical sites and new primary sources expresses itself most vividly in chapter 3. For example, to disrupt the iconicity of the Black laboring body as the paradigmatic violence that orders slavery and conquest, I combine two disparate and conflicting primary sources—Julie Dash's blue-handed slaves and an eighteenth-century map's cartouche depicting indigo processing—and read them through each other in a way that creates a composite speculative map. This new map creates a speculative bricolage that renders Blackness as porous representations of Black embodiment on indigo plantations to trouble—or shoal—the iconicity of the laboring Black body on plantation landscapes. Further, the usual momentum and demarcations of a book that moves neatly from one source to the next and from one chapter to the next are interrupted. For example, the book tarries with an analysis of an eighteenth-century map in chapters 2 and 3. Similarly, the work of the filmmaker and novelist Julie Dash is discussed in chapters 3 and 4. Some sites and objects of analysis are stretched, pulled, and linked to one another from chapter to chapter in ways that make the reader aware of their relationship to and palimpsestic indent on other sites.

Black women's films, historiographies, and novels are also read and treated as primary sources in a different way. For instance, I approach and treat Dash's and Tiya Miles's bodies of work that attempt to address, grapple with, or resolve a particular problem or question raised in a past work in a newer work and through a different genre as a compendium. Reading Dash's novel (and sequel to her film) *Daughters of the Dust: A Novel* and Miles's *The Cherokee Rose: A Novel of Garden and Ghosts* in the context of their attempts to work out questions and obsessions that emerged in former iterations of their work, I treat their practices of manipulating the porosity of the archive and using speculation as forms of what Hartman calls "critical fabulation."[97] Their labor to wrestle with an enduring question over time and shift form and genre when necessary become particularly apparent in both authors' attempts to confront Black and Indigenous relations. I read the love affairs and the erotic encounters between Dash's and Miles's Black and Indigenous (Cherokee, specifically) characters as longer sagas that reappear from text to text (and performance to performance) in ways that present themselves as important and enduring ethical questions that deserve attention.

Finally, throughout each chapter—and, more explicitly, in the second chapter of the book—I attempt make my eye softer and more supple to attend to what McKittrick terms a "noticing" or attention to (and for) "black Atlantic livingness."[98] Evolving within her body of work after the publication of *Demonic Grounds: Black Women and the Cartographies of Struggle* (2006), McKittrick urges Black studies scholars to move beyond simply theorizing or "analytically reprising" anti-Black violence.[99] For McKittrick, naming violence has never been the only, or the most important task, of Black studies projects. Recognizing that it is difficult to sift through an overwhelming archive and contemporary landscape shaped by anti-Black violence, McKittrick attempts in more recent essays, such as "Mathematics Black Life" (2014) and "Diachronic Loops/Deadweight Tonnage/Bad Made Measure" (2016), to create a methodology, ethics of care, and way of "noticing" the "other possibilities" in the midst of Black death and Black degradation.[100]

While there is no methodological formula for developing this awareness and capacity to notice "Black livingness," part of the effort involves reading intertextually.[101] By assembling, shoaling, and rubbing disparate texts against one another, unexpected openings emerge where different voices are brought into relationship. As new relationships among texts and voices are made, new and "transgressive ground[s] of understanding" emerge where one can begin to notice where rupture and "momentary dislodgings" reveal that the archive is not a closed system that contains only one story.[102] McKittrick argues that it is in these moments of rupture that we can—and must dare to—betray the archive of violence to look, listen, and feel for "what else happened."[103]

McKittrick argues that within the historical and contemporary records of anti-Black violence there remains a surplus or pulse of Black resistance and "Black livingness."[104] In chapter 2, I adopt this practice and desire to notice Black and Indigenous livingness as I read an eighteenth-century map that intends to mark Black people and Native people as natural and sensuous bodies and spaces marked for death. Rather than read the map as primarily a scene of horror and violence, I develop a Black geographical reading practice that mines it for where Black and Indigenous signs of life bleeds through the surface to disrupt a single narrative of Black and

Indigenous death. I use this practice of noticing and caring for Black and Indigenous life throughout the chapters and analytical sites of the book. McKittrick's method and noticing of Black life functions as a crucial intervention that shoals and disrupts the current impulse and tendency within the academy that seems to focus on and find Black death wherever it looks.

Throughout the book, the reader will notice that the shoal functions theoretically as a disruptive mechanism that interrupts and slows normative thought and violent knowledge production. The theoretical shoal is primarily one of disruption and displacement where necessary. As a methodological practice and approach, the shoal functions as a process and space where boundaries and binaries constructed between sea and land, Black and Native, aesthetics and theory, and human and nonhuman are blurred. Each chapter engages the shoal on its own, unique terms and at different theoretical and methodological registers. Ultimately, the theoretical and methodological shoals bring the reader to new and, at times, "unthought" terrain from which to reconsider the relational and ethical spaces of Black and Indigenous scholarship and the liberatory practices of abolition and decolonization.

OVERVIEW OF CHAPTERS

The shoal as a place, a site of disruption, a slowing of momentum, and a process of rearrangement takes on various forms throughout each chapter of the book. Chapter 1 focuses on the defacing of a statue of Christopher Columbus on the Boston waterfront in 2015 by allegedly "Black actors" in the name of the Black Lives Matter movement. The chapter focuses on the ways that this act of Black rebellion functions as a defilement of the aesthetic practice and ongoing monumentalization of the overrepresentation of the human in the form of the conquistador human Christopher Columbus.[105] The incidents of beheading and defacement of the Columbus statue by Black and Indigenous activists function as the conceptual shoal that disrupts the modernist and postmodernist humanist logics of White settler colonial studies that tend to read power through political economic rubrics of land, labor, and settlement.

The chapter returns to a discourse of conquest in both Black studies and Native studies to exhume and render visible contemporary modes of violent White/human self-making that settler colonial studies often invisibilizes through discourses of settlement. The discourse of conquest acts as a discursive and theoretical shoal that exposes the ways that discourses of "settler colonial relations" function as a ruse and cover up ongoing, gratuitous anti-Black and anti-Indigenous violence. Chapter 1 slows the momentum of White settler colonial studies and, for that matter, continental theory as forms of conceptual and analytical common sense. The defacements and beheadings of the statue in Boston demonstrate the ways that contemporary movements such as Black Lives Matter, along with Indigenous women's organizing under the hashtag #MMIW to highlight the issue of missing and murdered Indigenous women, are still trying to stop the often unspeakable violence required to make the human in the image of Man.

Chapter 2 introduces and reinterprets William Gerard de Brahm's eighteenth-century map of the coast of South Carolina and Georgia as an active process of cartographically writing the human through the spatial and orthographic negation of Native and Black people. The map reflects the ways that the British settlers attempted to represent Black and Indigenous embodiment as regions and spaces of what Denise da Silva calls "affectability," or overdetermined by nature and exteriority. In contrast to Black fluidity and fungibility and wild Native anaspace, British humanity writes itself on the map as a symbol of logocentric order and rationality that materializes what da Silva also calls the interior or "transparent I."[106] As a Cartesian subject, the "transparent I" (and transcendent I) both invents and masters space and exterior, affectable bodies.[107]

By conducting what I call a Black geographical reading practice that is informed by McKittrick's notion of noticing "black Atlantic livingness," chapter 2 also maps the ways that Black and Indigenous resistance to conquest frustrate British attempts to settle in the Low Country and write themselves as human through dominating Black and Indigenous people.[108] Looking closely at the map for Black and Indigenous livingness, I read de Brahm's map that was intended to facilitate projects of genocide and enslavement as an incomplete project frustrated time and time again by Black and Indigenous rebellion. What McKittrick calls the "what else happened" of Black and Indigenous life amid violence erupts onto the surface of the map and forces de Brahm and British subjects to adjust to Cherokee resistance and Black slave rebellions.[109] By reading the map alongside archives such as Eliza Lucas Pinckney's letter book and her accounts of absconding slaves and Native assaults on frontierspeople, I read the making of the map within a context of British fear and anxiety about Black fugitivity and Cherokee aggression. Reading the map this way, Black and Indigenous life rises up to shoal the momentum of British conquest and settlement in the Low Country.

In chapter 3, images of Black porous figures destabilize the iconicity of Black laboring bodies on plantations. The Black porous figure and the plantation depicted in the cartouche of de Brahm's map and in Julie Dash's film *Daughters of the Dust* reconfigure the plantation and the bodies on it as a process in motion. By conducting a visual analysis that attends to Blackness as a dynamic state of transition and flux, I reread renderings of Black slaves on indigo plantation landscapes as states of flux that exceed the regime of labor. Theoretically and conceptually, Black porosity, much like Black fungibility, slows down the tempo of the homogenizing force of humanist and Marxian regimes of labor. Black theoretics of porosity and fungibility align with Indigenous critiques of labor and function as another shoal or gathering space that unsettles normative Lockean and Marxist notions of the laborer as a modern and civilized human who masters the land and the bodies on it. By rejecting what Shona Jackson refers to as the onto-epistemology of labor and its modernizing telos that disciplines Indigenous and Black subjects, I posit porosity, fungibility, and fugitivity as other ways to discuss human relations to the land and nonhuman life forms.

More specifically, the chapter pairs Dash's more than human depictions of the formerly enslaved's indigo-stained hands with the eighteenth-century map's cartouche to establish a composite visual of Black bodies and indigo as a punctum point that transforms bodies into chemical processes (hands merging with indigo plants) and disrupts the visual regime of labor. Rather than simply overwrite Blackness as vegetation and a state of abjection, the Black bodies stained indigo that appear coterminous with nature transform the laboring body into indigo flesh that represents forms of Black alterity and pleasure. Black porosity also collapses distinctions between bodies and plants in ways that resonate with Indigenous notions of human and nonhuman relationality. Further, thinking with Spillers's notion of the "flesh," Black indigo-stained pores contest Western notions of gender differentiation and challenge queer theory's genital-anus complex as the primary site of penetrability, self-annihilation, or pleasure. The Black pore becomes a place to reimagine Black embodiment as a space of transit for conceptions and revisions of the human on more ethical terms.[110] Gathering and reading de Brahm's map and Dash's cinematic images in relation to, in friction with, and through one another (re)presents Black life as a vibrant space where porosity and open-endedness can offer generative sites of reinvention.

In chapter 4, a strange branch on the ancestral tree and lineage of a Cherokee and Black family disfigures the notion of Victorian erotics and reveals the ways that Black and Native sexualities under conquest both trouble and exceed queer theoretical impulses toward antisocial (i.e., Leo Bersani) and queer futureless (i.e., Lee Edelman) sociality.[111] Chapter 4 returns to Dash's *Daughters of the Dust* compendium (film, novel, and other cultural productions) to examine the Black and Native erotics performed by the characters Iona Peazant and St. Julien Lastchild as nonnormative sexual subjectivities that simultaneously mark spaces of death and new forms of life. The chapter also explores Miles's depiction of Ruth Coleman and Jennifer/Jinx Micco's love affair in *The Cherokee Rose* to explore how Black and Native erotics can open portals to intergenerational healing. Dash's and Miles's Black decolonial imaginaries rework Black and Native death as sites of futurity for alternative modes of Black and Indigenous life.

The chapter also expands on the work of Native feminist and queer thought, such as Qwo-Li Driskill's and Daniel Heath Justice's theorizations of Cherokee queer subjectivity to illumine the ways that decolonial notions of the erotic contain their own critiques of heteronormative kinship structures that undergird anti-Black racism and nationalist notions of sovereignty. Chapter 4 concludes with an exploration of how Cherokee-descended characters such as St. Julien Lastchild and Jinx Micco rework Native masculinities in ways that make space for Blackness within Cherokee and Creek notions of sovereignty and communities.

Chapter 5 uses "Revisiting Sycorax," a sculpture by the Black Canadian painter, sculptor, and educator Charmaine Lurch, as a point of departure. Lurch's sculptures attempt to take up Wynter's notion of the demonic through the manipulation of wire to produce a fifth (and other) dimension(s) that Lurch calls the "tesseract."[112] I argue that "Revisiting Sycorax" creates a Black errant dimension of aesthetic space. Further, Lurch's Black diasporic aesthetic, which uses the tesseract, represents a break in the spatial and narrative conventions that attempt to represent Black and Indigenous relations on Turtle Island and on its archipelagos (in the Caribbean). "Revisiting Sycorax" is a multidimensional and porous black and copper wire sculpture that produces positive and negative space as it configures the Black and Native female figure (body form) in a state of flux and change in relationship to each other.

Throughout the chapter, Sycorax operates as conceptual and aesthetic shoal that indexes a space of flux, change, and indeterminacy. On a representational level, the intertwining of Black and Indigenous "flesh" represented by the black and copper wire makes the viewer contend with the twoness and edgelessness of the sculpture. Lurch's "Revisiting Sycorax" enables those who encounter it to think about the distinct world and subject-making violence of slavery (and its afterlife) and Indigenous genocide as unique and irreducible social relations without producing hard borders and edges around them. Her craftswomanship and interpretive and curatorial practices work to slow down, and perhaps even rearrange, normative modes of looking, reading, thinking, and feeling about Blackness and Indigeneity. Furthermore, Lurch's Black diasporic "Canadian" aesthetic reassembles Black diasporic expressive culture in ways that disrupt easy movement to Black nationalisms or Black politics dictated by Black U.S. hegemonies. Echoing Dionne Brand's refrain, "I don't want no country, none of it," Lurch's sculpture "evokes a kind of Black exilic relationship to the nation and narrow notions of Black and Indigeneity."[113] Lurch's wiry sculptures and aesthetics wrinkle the smooth surface of the time space of Black diaspora studies.

Overall, *The Black Shoals* aims to create an alternative site of engagement to discuss Indigenous genocide, anti-Black racism, and the politics of Black and Native studies. Within the academy and in some activist circles, Black and Indigenous dialogue continues to be mediated by White modes of speech and liberal humanist protocols for understanding, theorizing, and addressing genocide and the afterlife of slavery. *The Black Shoals* locates a space off the shores of White academic and political discourse to continue ongoing conversations, and create new ones, among Black and Native peoples within and outside the academy.

1

ERRANT GRAMMARS

Defacing the Ceremony

And what was Columbus doing on the coasts of West Africa in 1468?
—JOHN HENRIK CLARKE, "Christopher Columbus and Genocide"

They say it came first from Africa, carried in the screams of the enslaved; that it was the death bane of the Tainos; uttered just as one world perished and another began; that it was a demon drawn into Creation through the nightmare door that was cracked open in the Antilles. *Fukú americanus*, or more colloquially fukú—generally a curse of doom of some kind, specifically the Curse and Doom of the New World. . . . No matter what its name or provenance, it is believed that the arrival of Europeans on Hispaniola unleashed the *fukú* on the world, and we've all been in the shit ever since.
—JUNOT DÍAZ, *The Brief Wondrous Life of Oscar Wao*

I want to draw a map, so to speak, of a critical geography and use that map to open space for discovery; intellectual adventure, and close exploration as did the original charting of the New World—without the mandate for conquest.
—TONI MORRISON, *Playing in the Dark: Whiteness and the Literary Imagination*

"Why here? I mean it just seems so out of place," lamented Jean Brady, a volunteer who helps the Friends of Christopher Columbus Park maintain stewardship of the park in Boston's North End.[1] Brady was responding to the red paint simulating blood that covered portions of the sailor Columbus's forehead and face, a shoulder, and portions of his folded arms. The crimson paint ran down the conquistador's back into a pool of bloody red surrounding his feet. A tag spray-painted in black letters, with each word stacked on another, read "BLACK LIVES MATTER!" For Brady, as well as other onlookers, the statue of Columbus, defaced by allegedly Black actors,

FIGURE 1.1. Back of the defaced and tagged statue of Christopher Columbus, North End waterfront, Boston, 2015. Photograph by Stephen Passacantilli.

confounded North American common sense and frustrated conventional narratives about the origins of the New World.

When local residents and visitors to the park were confronted with the bloody defacement of Columbus "the discoverer," they expressed their sense of incredulity. People could not seem to wrap their heads around why Columbus had become a target of despoilment by "allegedly" Black actors. The local ABC News affiliate in Boston interviewed two individuals who became aware of the event during their visit to the waterfront the day the story was being covered. When the ABC reporter showed them images of the defaced statue, one of the visitors responded confoundedly, "Oh look, there's blood there," as if the association of blood with Christopher Columbus was some kind of non sequitur or had some oblique kind of re-lationship to the historical figure.[2] In the White "American" imagination, if bloodletting was associated with Columbus at all, it was confined to Indigenous peoples and failed to touch the bodies and lives of Black people.

The defacing of the statue in June 2015 became a news item because of its association with the Black Lives Matter movement. Since its design and placement in the park, the statue has been defaced several times. Often around annual Columbus Day celebrations, Indigenous and Native activists deface the statue in protest of the "bloody" festivities. In 2006, in response to upcoming Columbus Day commemorations, protestors beheaded the statue. The removed head remained missing for days.[3] Accustomed to these ongoing acts of protests from the usual suspects, the Native American community, local and national news outlets covering the defacement found the event novel and newsworthy on June 25. This particular act of defacement was new because the accused perpetrators were Black. The Black actors of this form of symbolic violence created a cognitive dissonance for the mainstream U.S. news audience and their journalists.

Beyond local stories about the incident in the Boston metro area, national news sources covered the incident. Labeled an act of "vandalism," the incident was presumed to be part of the string of acts of vandalism and defacement of Confederate monuments across the southeastern part of the United States immediately following the massacre of nine African Americans in Charleston, South Carolina. This incident of "vandalism" in the northeastern city of Boston elicited a number of responses. For the North End resident Jean Brady, it did not sync within the space and time of Boston, Christopher Columbus, or the Movement for Black Lives. As a sympathizer with the movement, Brady found it hard to believe that the people who belong to or believe in Black Lives Matter's cause would participate in an act like this. In a state of disbelief, she stated, "This is not what they would do."[4] A few days later, the *Boston Herald* interviewed Daunasia Yancey, the local founder and lead organizer of Black Lives Matter Boston. While Yancey maintained that members of Black Lives Matter Boston had nothing to do with this political act of public resistance, she also stated, "We fully support it."[5]

In the comments sections that appear on a number of the online sources that reported the story, commentators left a range of responses that evinced an inability to make the connection between Black death and Black rage and Columbus. Readers' comments covered a wide range, from those that insulted the intelligence of the "vandals" to ones that characterized the act as an appropriation of Native American issues and responses that relegated Black death and White-supremacist violence to the Confederate South. One comment left on the Media Equalizers website, where the news article appeared, is particularly telling.[6] A commenter with the username "Jack Sparrow" simply weighed in with, "What a moron. Columbus had nothing to do with Africans in America."[7]

This kind of historical amnesia or willful North American ignorance of Columbus's role in the slave trade and how conquest invented and instantiated Blackness as a form of abjection in the modern world is due to North American quotidian circulations of settler colonialist common sense. For many, Columbus and the unfortunate yet inevitable genocide of Indigenous peoples are traditionally treated as unrelated to Black life and death within the public discourse of the history of the Americas. Even leftist critiques of the normalized acts of commemoration (Columbus Day) and public forms of pedagogy that naturalize conquest typically are singularly focused on Columbus the murderer, not Columbus the enslaver. More important, what remains uninterrogated about Columbus is his role in inaugurating the modern notion of the human and affixing it to a "European self." This European self knows itself and continually performs its existence through the dehumanization of Indigenous and Black people. This aspect of conquest, a violent and repetitive process of making the modern human through extinguishing Black and Indigenous life, is disavowed and willfully forgotten. One legacy of the Columbian rupture was the creation of a Christian humanism that would transmute into various forms of secular humanism, which, in turn, would maintain their parasitic relationship to Indigenous and Black life.

It is clear that various news sources disavow Columbus's role in the Atlantic Slave trade through circulating the idea that the supposedly Black vandals were misdirected in their public act of protest. The tone and framing of most of the coverage presumed that Columbus and conquest had nothing to do with Black people. One of the problems with settler colonial common sense's erasure of Black suffering from the equation is that Black critiques of the notion of the human are simultaneously disavowed. When Black performances of resistance focus on conquest, the making and remaking of the human as non-Indigenous and non-Black becomes central to Black critique. I invoke performance here and cite how Diana Taylor uses the term in her work *The Archive and the Repertoire*. Taylor argues that theatrical and embodied scenarios of conquest and discovery "haunt our present."[8] Scenarios are performed, repeatable, and flexible "meaning-making paradigms" that make "visible yet again, what is already there: the ghosts, the images, the stereotypes."[9] For example, Taylor asserts that twenty-first century shows such as *Survivor* and *Fantasy Island* are examples of scenarios of discovery and conquest. In fact, the "discoverer, conqueror, 'savage,' and native princess for example might be staple characters in many Western scenarios," as well as in these televisual productions.[10]

As scenarios are "flexible and open to change," the "scenario of conquest, restaged in numerous acts of possession as well as in plays, rituals, and mock battles throughout the Americas, can be and often has been subverted from within."[11] I argue that the "vandals," as performers and actors, restage the scenario of Columbian discovery and conquest in a way that momentarily disrupts its temporal, spatial, and narrative power to disavow and "unknow" the ongoing violence of conquest. The act of defacing or bloodying the statue of the conquistador in 2015 (and over and over again) short-circuits the idea that conquest is a past sin committed for the greater good. The presumably Black actors, or agents acting in the name of Black life, deface Columbus, as well as open up the possibility of contending with the ongoing violence of conquest. The defacement as performance simultaneously shoals conventional settler colonial logics and puts a number of events and performances into motion. The theatricality of the act makes conquest a "living present" and an occasion of the now. More important, the theatrics make the historical and ongoing resistance to conquest by Indigenous and Black peoples visible, alive, and, in effect, repeatable.[12] Conquest, as well as resistance to conquest, is a living, quotidian, and ever present moment that actors can interact with and interrupt. It is not an event, not even a structure, but a milieu or active set of relations that we can push on, move around in, and redo from moment to moment.[13]

In addition to situating conquest in the present motion of "the now," the act of defacing and tagging the itinerant sailor illumines a Black critique of the human that is at the heart of interrogating the violence of contemporary social relations. The placement of blood on the statue's face, shoulders, arms, hands, feet, and back transports us to the inaugural scenes of genocide and capture that produced the human and the other human (and less than human) Native and Black bodies. Sylvia Wynter reminds scholars that the inaugural violence of conquest and the "scene" of the making of the European human and the Black (human other) occurred on the shores of what is now Senegal in the 1440s. In this recurring scene starting in the mid-1400s, Black people become lesser humans; Indigenous peoples soon follow in the 1490s, when the bloody theatrics and overrepresentation of the human are restaged at the site of Indigenous bodies who become lesser humans on the other side of the Atlantic in what will become the Americas.

FIGURE 1.2. Front of the statue with red paint (blood) on Columbus's face, chest, arms, and feet. Photograph by Stephen Passacantilli.

However, in this 2015 scenario, it is Columbus who is trapped and subjected to violence. The scenario and ceremony of blood is disrupted. Black actors throw blood on or bloody the conquistador this time. I read the act of defacing, bloodying, or perhaps even killing the symbol of the modern human-as-European conquistador as a performance of Black critique and revolt. The power of reading this as a form of Black performance and critique is that it renders the act alive and repeatable. Further, Black performance as a critique of the violence of conquistador humanism enacts a kind of utterance, "speech," and extratextual act outside of and against the overrepresentation of the human as a violent and normative state of existence. In conversation with Fred Moten's understanding of Black performance, the bloodying of Columbus illustrates how "Black performance has always been the ongoing improvisation of a kind of lyricism of surplus — invagination, rupture, collision, augmentation."[14] Black actors and their performances can interrupt the narrative commonsense and quotidian processes of making the human. Further, the defacement of the statue in the name of Black Lives is a critique of the human from a space outside of full and proper humanity — Blackness. For Black actors, the human — and its overrepresentation as Columbus — becomes a site for the potential destabilization and reorganization of the idea of the human outside of the normative mandates of conquest and the death of Native and Black peoples.

Further, Black revolt as performance sits both within and outside the bounds of translatability.[15] Sometimes the meaning can be discerned within humanist modes of speech and gesture, and at other times, it is elusive because it speaks outside humanist systems of signification and corporeal protocols. The performed revolt and defacement of Columbus as a stand-in for the human is part of a set of intentional kinetic motions in the act of throwing the red paint and bloodying the statue. It is also an alternative form of Black writing.[16] This particular form of Black writing disfigures the notion of the normative human as it makes space for something else or otherwise.[17]

In *The Archive and the Repertoire*, Taylor attends to the ways that Indigenous peoples in Mesoamerica in the fifteenth century developed a unique relationship between embodied performance and writing that marked an epistemic rupture and illumined a precolonial (and, in 2015, perhaps *decolonial*) orientation to logos, or "the word." Taylor explains that the theatricality of the scenario "does not rely on language to transmit a set pattern of behavior or action."[18] While the Black Lives Matter action on the Boston waterfront may have involved a "tag," or a form of writing that operates through shared Anglo linguistic systems, it is hard to tell whether embodied performance, ceremony, song, utterance, or the words came first and animated the force of the performance/disruption. Taylor goes on to describe the relationship of the Indigenous peoples of the America to writing: "Although the Aztecs, Mayas, and Incas practiced writing before Conquest—either in pictogram form, hieroglyphs, or knotting systems—it never replaced the performed utterance. Writing though highly valued, was primarily a prompt to performance, a mnemonic aid. . . . Writing was far more dependent on embodied culture than the other way around."[19]

In Mesoamerica, writing was a prompt and an aid, not the totality of the performance. In other words, writing was not the goal, the achievement, or what carried authority, as it was in Europe.[20] While I speculate here, I wonder whether the bloodying and the tagging (writing on) the statue of Columbus could also be read as a combination of antihumanist and anticolonial theatricality and writing. Without needing to decide which came first—as only the taggers know—the acts of bloodying and tagging can be interpreted as interdependent. Further, as there were no witnesses, it is difficult to tell which came first: the bloodying (embodied performance or throwing of paint) or the tag (writing as an embodied performance of defacement and erasing/revision). The ordered logic and mechanics of writing are also altered or rewritten in this act of defacement.

The ceremonial defacing of Columbus exists within the Black tradition of the destruction of property as a feature of abolition and fugitivity. More important, property destruction as part of the repertoire of Black revolt is always an act that remains partial and beyond full knowability as part of its act erases or destroys evidence of its full meaning. The tag or the writing itself, "BLACK LIVES MATTER!" also does not offer full knowability as a phrase, despite how it is currently invoked by those affiliated with the Movement for Black Lives (M4BL). What I infer from this act of defacement is that it marked an active and living moment in which the inaugural scenes of violence that created the understanding of who is human were interrupted. The taggers crashed this ceremony of the violent making, remaking, and monumentalizing of the human and disrupted and changed it.

The utterances, performances, and statements of Black abolition and Native decolonization that meet at the space of Columbus's monument (in 2006, 2015, and the future) require new words, syntax, tense, visuality, and senses. They require a transformation of the person encountering them for them to be felt and, one hopes, understood. I chose the defacing of the Columbus statute and, more important, its illegibility for some "White humans" as a point of departure for exploring what the White conquistador human cannot, fails, or refuses to see. More important, this is an invitation to talk about everyday modes of parasitic self-actualization in North America in ways that are blunt and direct. The second decade of the twenty-first century and its forms of documentary technology—such as the cell phone and digital images—have saturated everyday life with scenes of carnage. While the gratuitous bloodletting of Black and Indigenous communities since 1492 has not stopped, the modes of erasing them through academic and political discourse are challenged by digital technologies and movements such as Black Lives Matter and the Standing Rock Sioux's protectors. These contemporary social movements confront the genocidal violence of the state and White supremacy in ways that require new and old forms of speech. Social movements now explicitly center the abolition of white genocidal violence in ways that have required a shift in speech and activity toward what Wynter would call "street speech."[21]

The Black performances of revolt and Black theorizations of conquest and the human in this chapter interrupt and shoal the monumentalization of the violence of becoming and staying human under the relations of conquest. Black performative and theoretical critiques also function in ways that throw European and continental critical theories such as settler colonial studies into crisis. This chapter holds as its objects of inquiry the human as a product of conquistador relations—conquistador humanism—and the field of settler colonialism as an epistemic site that reproduces the liberal human and its attachments to conquistador violence. It argues that an analytical return to conquest enables a different kind of conversation and ethical engagement among scholars in Black studies, Native studies, ethnic studies, settler colonial studies, and other critical discourses. The Black grammars, literary traditions, and engagements with Indigenous studies explored in the chapter function as a shoaling mechanism, or series of disruptions, that attempt to slow the momentum that naturalizes the field of White settler colonial studies as the commonsense response to genocide, slavery, and social relations in North America.

BLACK GRAMMARS OF CONQUEST

While North Americans' general disavowal of the violence of Christopher Columbus is certainly a form of "colonial unknowing" worthy of interrogation, a similar form of ignorance is reproduced within contemporary leftist critical theories that include (white) settler colonial studies in North America.[22] The preoccupation of North American and Oceanic White settler colonial studies with settlement, settler subjectivity, and land make it increasingly difficult to register the far-reaching and ongoing violence of conquest in everyday life. To counter this disavowal, this chapter revisits and reclaims Black "grammars" of conquest within Black studies, African diaspora studies, and Black gender and sexuality studies. Reclaiming the work of "Black grammarians" of conquest such as Toni Morrison, Junot Díaz, Sylvia Wynter, Hortense Spillers, and the graffiti artists who tagged Columbus forces urgent and enduring questions — about the concept of the human and the violence required to sustain it — to the surface of consciousness.

The bloody relations of conquest have far from abated. By choosing to tarry with the discourse of conquest within both Indigenous and Black studies, this book works against the current tide and trend that compels scholars to ride the newest theoretical waves of intellectual currency (i.e., White settler colonialism). Rather than identify where Blackness appears or fits within (White) settler colonial discourses or place Blackness at the center of settler colonialism, this book pursues different questions and concerns: How has Black studies been talking about genocide, colonization, settlement, and slavery? How has Black studies engaged and sustained a conversation with Indigenous/Native studies? And more important: Why has the Black discourse of conquest remained a space of "unthought" within contemporary discussions about Indigenous genocide, colonialism, slavery, and settlement in North America? Black studies and its discourses of conquest shoal the movement of settler colonial studies. The shoals of Black studies make setter colonial studies stop offshore and contend with 1441 and the shores of West Africa. This book prevents the easy landing of settler colonialism and its set of disavowals from planting itself in and fixing the imagination.

While slowing and intervening in the field of White settler colonial studies, the "unthought space" of the Black vernacular of conquest also serves a number of other functions. Linguistically, it speaks directly to and addresses the gratuitous violence that discourses of "settlement" often evade through euphemisms such as "elimination," "disappearance," and "removal from the land." The directness of "conquest," "genocide," and "murder" short-circuits and avoids the kinds of understatements proffered by theoretical and analytical frames parried by settler colonialism and postcolonial studies. "Conquest," "genocide," and "murder," though seemingly blunt terms, possess expansive lexicons, affects, sensations, and grammars that explicate power, violence, transformation, and shifts over time. The macro, spectacular, and bloody as well as the micro, mundane, discursive, and "ephemeral" repertoires of genocide and Black fungibility can be uttered and given language within the Black discourses of conquest. Black vernaculars of conquest more importantly situate Black fungibility and anti-Black modes of modernity in relation to Native and Indigenous genocide.

As Black vernaculars of conquest—specifically, in their mode of making Blackness fungible—direct our attention to the violent project of the making of the human, they enable a conversation with Native studies and Native "talk" on new terms.[23] Rather than speaking only in the terms or vocabulary of liberal notions of Indigenous sovereignty and Black citizenship, what Frank Wilderson terms Black and Native "grammars of suffering" have space to produce utterances.[24] The screams of Africans or the "grammar of accumulation and fungibility," as well as Native death banes or "grammar of genocide," become audible and can create new soundscapes. No longer drowned out by humanist hymns, the Black and Native chorus's harmonies and dissonances that ring outside of Western measures, keys, and notions of the human can be taken up on their own terms—flesh moaning and humming to more flesh.

These fleshly ballads of Black and Native utterances of freedom do not speak or aspire to humanist ideas of nation, sovereignty, and rights. Black and Native calls for the abolition of genocide, the desecration of life, and the orders of thought that require a pound of flesh for the birth of the human do not always happen in ways that are legible or knowable in advance. Black cultural production and its literary tradition in particular will be approached to consider the ways that Black fiction and nonfiction writers write and affect the Black vernacular of conquest.

THE UNFINISHED BUSINESS OF CONQUEST, OR BEING FUCKED

I quote Toni Morrison and Junot Díaz at the start of this chapter because I situate them as grammarians of the Black vernacular of conquest. In *Playing in the Dark*, Morrison recognizes the contemporary order as one that is mandated by the violence of conquest, and she urges people to develop new navigational skills and cartographies that can map outside the paradigmatic ordering. For Morrison, conquest is a geography and spatiality that humans are still trying to refashion and make work. In the Pulitzer

Prize-winning novel *The Brief Wondrous Life of Oscar Wao* (2007), Díaz's narrator recounts the pan-Caribbean idioms that circulate throughout the Black diaspora to explain the shape, quality, texture, smell, and taste of the *fukú*,[25] or the curse that the New World violence of the fifteenth century unleashed across the world and that was felt acutely in the Antilles and the Western Hemisphere in the Americas. For Díaz, conquest remains with his protagonist Oscar, as well as with the Dominican diaspora—and with the reader. The narrator also names this particular story—the story of Oscar and the members of the Dominican diaspora told in the novel—a fukú story. In the opening of the novel, the narrator Yunior laments that "that the arrival of Europeans on Hispaniola unleashed the *fukú* on the world, and we've all been in the shit ever since."[26]

Being "in the shit" has been a present and long-standing reality since the arrival of the conquistadors in the Caribbean. Further, Díaz narrates the centuries-old yet reverberating "screams" of Africans and the death "banes" and rattles of the Taíno (Indigenous peoples) as the first utterances and manifestations of the fukú. The soundscape or first grammars of conquest are a patois made of both Indigenous and Black noise. Díaz's novel archives through footnotes and narrates through prose the trace of conquest in the lives of his characters.

The novel's backdrop of Black and Indigenous violation and death colors the arc of each character, especially that of Yunior, whose joy, ambivalence, and pain are associated with a quest for a deferred and patriarchal (conquistador) masculinity. I once thought that the words of Díaz, the historian turned fiction writer—especially "fukú"—rang too blunt, shallow, transparent, and trite in their attempt to evoke the depth, the horizon, the feel of conquest. "Fukú," I thought, was too taut a word to describe the kind of stretching, oozing, and ever present, gratuitous violence it denotes. However, since members of the literary community alleged Díaz had lurked among them as a sexual predator, his choice of the term "fukú"—to be fucked or cursed—has acquired new meaning and significance.

In an article published in 2018, Díaz painstakingly reveals how the legacy of childhood sexual abuse has scarred his life and the lives of others with whom he has been in intimate relationships. He describes the sexual abuse that he and other African-descended people have experienced in the Americas, as a "revenant that won't stop," much like the ever present haunt of conquest (the fukú). For Díaz, it is "the ghost that's always coming for you. The nightmares, the intrusions, the hiding, the doubts, the confusion, the self-blame, the suicidal ideation—they didn't go away." In fact, the "nightmares, the intrusions, the hiding, the doubts, the confusion, the self-blame, the suicidal ideation—they followed," he says. "All through college. All through graduate school. All through my professional life. All through my intimate life. (Leaked into my writing, too, but you'd be amazed how easy it is to rewrite the truth away.)"[27]

Far from being rewritten away, rape and sexual violence as allegories and metaphors for the ever present terror of conquest occur again and again in *The Brief Wondrous Life of Oscar Wao* and Díaz's other work. Rather than center his own trauma and pain in his novels, he transfers (and projects) his experiences of rape and sexual violation onto the bodies of Black and Indigenous women. The revenant of rape follows his female protagonists—and Díaz as he travels back—into the rows of cane fields at night. While my focus on Díaz's experience with sexual violence is not an attempt to excuse, rescue, or celebrate Díaz, the themes of Díaz's work map his embodied trauma onto the history of genocide and the Middle Passage. For Díaz, sexual violence, being fucked, and the fukú are tropes for the way in which the Middle Passage, Indigenous genocide, and slavery cracked the world open. He likens his own rape—being fucked and abused—to a cosmic crisis, confessing, "That shit cracked the planet of me in half, threw me completely out of orbit, into the lightless regions of space where life is not possible. I can say, truly, que casi me destruyó."[28] One way to frame Díaz's trauma, as well as his alleged sexual predation and how it shows up in his work, ethically is to think about it structurally and as a legacy of conquest.

For example, in "808 and Heartbreak" Alexander Weheliye and Katherine McKittrick frame the transgressions of the rhythm-and-blues singer and songwriter R. Kelly not as excusable but as a possible result of his sexual victimization, which is a legacy of racism.[29] Of the various traumas that subjects of racism experience, according to Weheliye and McKittrick is "the extreme susceptibility to many different forms of sexual violence and violation."[30] As descendants of the enslaved, Kelly, Díaz, and the women they abuse live lives that are structured by conquest and sexual violence. To describe this terrible inheritance, Weheliye and McKittrick argue that "perhaps not being able to elude sexual violence is the ghost in the machine of this particular version of kinship, to emulate Saidiya Hartman's memorable aphorism."[31] Further, Weheliye and McKittrick ask, "What structures and repertoire must be in place in order for acts of sexual violence to occur and what acts of violation (of trust, of corporeal boundaries, of confidence, and so on) precede physical/sexual violence?"[32] Far from excusing Kelly (and I, in turn, am not excusing Díaz), Weheliye and

McKittrick ask important questions that make one consider the ways in which both men were able to find themselves in the heart spaces and gain the trust of fans and even critics. Was it their ability to bear, embody, articulate, and violently act out a familiarity and intimate knowledge of the pain of what Spillers calls the "female within" that gave them an audience? Is it how they continue to struggle with finding a language, a beat and or a riff that sounds and feels like the intramural violence that is also a relentless legacy of conquest? Díaz's quest for the language and courage to speak his trauma, as well as his own transgressions as an abuser, is an unending labor, like the work of finding a grammar for conquest. He must now contour the ways that the horrors of conquest made him a predator, and he must linger in the process of healing the individuals he has harmed. This healing and accountability is also a grammar of conquest that Native and Black artistic and intellectual endeavors continue to birth.

This project of naming is never done, because the relations of conquest continue right through this very moment, shaping these very thoughts. Conquest must be perpetually elaborated and interrogated with all of our existing faculties, as well as the ones that have yet to be developed. Incorporating the work of creative writers such as Díaz provokes an important discussion about the limits of realism, as well as the existing conceptual and theoretical tools we currently use to think about genocide, slavery, Blackness, and Indigeneity. In an interview with Bill Moyers in 2015, Díaz argued that the genre of science fiction often does a better job of describing the quotidian yet surreal vicissitudes of Black and Indigenous experiences under conquest.[33] Because conquest ushered in such a world-altering rupture, it is almost impossible for the human imagination to fully conceive of the reach of its violence. Beyond the unfathomability of the scale of conquest's historical violence, the fact that its violence does not cease makes it even more difficult for the critical imaginaries that produce critical social theories to contain it or find the appropriate level of abstraction or texture to make it legible. Conquest is always changing and in flux. It is in continual need of new language and new conceptual tools, which often exist at the margins of reason and require methods found in artistic and creative production.

Because conquest exists both within the realm of the visual and "sayable" and outside of it, it always needs new terms of engagement and requires new epistemic systems. It is for this reason that I can now appreciate the fukú, or the "fuck you," of Díaz's conquest. It is fungible and changing like Black life and haunts us like Native ghosts.[34] The fukú lives on — is a revenant—and is always remaking itself in new ways. As Díaz writes, "But the fukú ain't just ancient history, a ghost story from the past with no power to scare. In my parents' day the fukú was real as shit, something your everyday person could believe in."[35] Díaz uses the rhetoric and grammar of those who suffer under the relations of conquest within his fiction and literary criticism as a creative and conceptual device to give readers the feel of conquest's everyday life force. The fukú represents how conquest lives on the tips of the tongues of the descendants of Indigenous and Black folks who are a part of the Dominican and African diaspora in the Americas. In the ways that conquest remains a terrorizing imaginative and conceptual device in the work of Díaz, it also continues to function as an expansive grammar of Black cultural and expressive life.[36]

Díaz's fukú could not have emerged without the inheritance he received from Morrison, whom he claims as his literary muse.[37] In *Playing in the Dark*, she writes about how historical and contemporary humanist criticism has violently dictated what can be considered knowledge or a part of the realm of reason and rationality. Morrison's literary criticism in *Playing in the Dark* is an immense endeavor as it seeks to challenge Western intellectual domination: "More interesting is what makes intellectual domination possible; how is knowledge transformed from invasion and conquest to revelation and choice; what ignites and informs the literary imagination, and what forces help establish the parameters of criticism?"[38] In speaking about what the artist and critic must do to reinscribe the literary imagination, Morrison uses the image of a map and invokes the field of critical geography: "I want to draw a map, so to speak, of a critical geography and use that map to open space for discovery; intellectual adventure, and close exploration as did the original charting of the New World—without the mandate for conquest."[39]

I have seen several scholars quote this pithy and profound passage from Morrison. Coming across it and reflecting on it again in the context of this project, I attend to the date of its publication, a year before the quincentenary of Columbus's voyage and the literary company that it keeps. One of the books Morrison said she "was glad . . . existed" was Leslie Marmon Silko's *Almanac of the Dead*, also published in 1991.[40] The epic novel traces the palimpsestic and ghostlike nature of death and its impact on the Yaqui and southwestern Indigenous nations that in their own ways were attempting to bring about a cosmic and global shift. The fact that Morrison's invocation of conquest to critique humanist criticism in the early

1990s emerged as the five hundred-year anniversary of the Columbian "exchange" was slated to take place is significant. Morrison's call for a different kind of mapmaking and practice of critical geography outside the "mandate for conquest" represents an important act of critique, given the impending historical juncture and marking of the start of the modern era.

Several artists responded to the world's acknowledgment — and, to a large extent, celebration — of five hundred-plus years of the modern age. Sylvia Wynter's essay "1492: A New World View" would be published in 1992 and circulate within a larger conversation that was emerging within Black and Indigenous women's literature and critical commentary. Morrison, Silko, and Wynter were having related and connected conversations about how disciplines, epistemic systems, and everyday enactments and commemorations of historical violence such as genocide and slavery were linked to the violence of fifteenth-century conquest.[41] I situate Morrison's text and her discussion of conquest and mapping as part of an intellectual tradition that speaks directly to the instantiation and spatialization of Whiteness and humanness that the Columbian voyage inaugurated.

These Black and Indigenous intellectual genealogies that collectively speak of and "back to" conquest and the Columbian era create a shoal that slows the momentum of a mode of critical and social thought that would too quickly move toward the twenty-first-century vessel of settler colonial studies. A return to Morrison, Silko, and Wynter and, more specifically, to the ways that they attend to fifteenth-century conquest redirects attention to the ongoing violence of genocide and captivity that continue to animate social relations in the twentieth and twenty-first centuries. I situate Morrison's, Silko's, and Wynter's quincentenary works as speaking for and representing the stories and critical theories that continue to be thrown overboard for newer theoretical paradigms and turns, such as settler colonialism.[42] When their voices come together or are curated as a Black and Native literary tradition marking the Columbian rupture, as they are here, they gather to form a shoal that slows the momentum of the twenty-first-century vessel of settler colonial studies.

Conquest can also be traced as a mode of speech and thinking within the work of a number of Black scholars. Understanding the mechanizations of conquest from within Black studies requires placing an emphasis on the making and remaking of the human (religious, political, bio-economic) as an object of study. According to Weheliye, Black studies has "taken as its task the definition of the human itself":[43]

Given the histories of slavery, colonialism, segregation, lynching and so on, humanity has always been a principal question within black life and thought in the west; or rather, in the moment in which blackness becomes apposite to humanity, Man's conditions of possibility lose their ontological thrust, because their limitations are rendered abundantly clear. Thus, the functioning of blackness as both inside and outside modernity sets the stage for a general theory of the human, and not its particular exception.[44]

As in Weheliye's project in *Habeas Viscus*, in this project the works of Spillers and Wynter model how Black intellectual traditions have scrutinized the making of the human through the relations of conquest. While Spillers and Wynter home in on how the human is created through a process of negating Black and Indigenous life, they ultimately do not leave us in this space of bloody abjection. In their work, they trace Black and other ways of doing humanity—Spillers's "ungendered female flesh" and Wynter's "plantation plot"—that often emerge through spaces of abjection and on terms that might be otherwise unintelligible to the order of Man.[45] Spillers's and Wynter's urgent questions about how the human is made require an interrogation of how conquest shapes the processes of self-actualization in relation to Black and Indigenous peoples, and the Cartesian concept of land as other than human.

Spillers and Wynter theorize the emergence of the hierarchy of the human species as an epistemological order that is able to appear only as a result of the human Other and the captive body. For Wynter, the European Christian can rise to the apex of humanity only through the invention and subjugation of the Native and Black as the heathen Other and then, eventually, the irrational, sensual abject muck in which the last link of the great chain of being hangs. A part of Weheliye's exploration of Wynter's and Spillers's bodies of work entails an in-depth exploration of the ways they expound on the bloody and always ongoing process of crafting and recrafting Man.[46] In addition to the violent and mutable procedures that reproduce Man, Weheliye locates these processes in the swampland of slavery and colonialism, specifically genocide.

What is particularly fruitful about thinking with Wynter and Spillers at the same time is that the work of both scholars reorganizes the geo-temporal dimensions of conquest in ways that expand its spatial and temporal frames beyond the conventional time-space and coordinates of 1492 and the New World. In Wynter's body of work, the shores of West Africa during the 1440s become the inaugural moments of conquest.[47] In a similar adherence to the space and time of Wynter's conquest, Spillers situates conquest on the shores of Guinea.[48] According to Wynter, the fifteenth century through the eighteenth century gave birth to a number of epistemological revolutions within Europe (secularism, the Enlightenment, planetary vision) that make conquest imaginable and executable and that subsequently render the birth of the human as an exclusive category—Man—possible. Man demands the invention and negation of the Negro and Native to know the self. In 1492: A New Worldview," Wynter proposes a "triadic model" (White-Native-Black) rather than a dyadic model (White-Native) to understand the antagonisms that would bring forth the notion of the modern human and inform conquest.[49]

This triadic model is echoed in Spillers's text canonical "Mama's Baby, Papa's Maybe" (1987). As Spillers plots the unfolding of an economy of signification in which the captive emerges through a series of mutilations, she also focuses on the time-space of the "socio-political order of the New World."[50] This sociopolitical "order[,] with its human sequence written in blood, represents for its African and Indigenous peoples a scene of actual mutilation, dismemberment, and exile."[51] The human and its "sequence," or repetition and arrangement for its continuance, is a mode of being that requires genocide, mutilation, displacement, and the negation of Black and Indigenous peoples and their ways of living. Conquest is constituted by a violence formidable enough to encompass both chattel slavery and Native genocide as it extends across Spillers's, Wynter's, and Gilroy's Atlantic.

While Spillers does not explicitly take on Native genocide in the essay, a reparative reading could view this text as a possible point of departure for thinking about Blackness and Indigeneity (as flesh) in relationship to the human's process of self-actualization.[52] Black and Native flesh is certainly a space of engagement in the work of Frank Wilderson. In Red, White and Black (2010), Wilderson, who also uses a triadic frame (Red, White, and Black), reworks and alters Spillers's conceptualization of flesh to elaborate on how the making of the human requires the unmaking of Black and Native bodies into nonhuman matter. Wilderson's nontraditional deployment of Spillers's "body" and "flesh" engenders the human with a body. Conversely, the nonhuman (slave and savage) is fleshly matter that exists outside the realm of the body and, thus, humanity.[53] Perhaps because flesh both exists outside the entrapments of humanism and moves (and is touched) through the experience of captivity, Wilderson reads "flesh" as an experience that is also a part of the hold. Like Wilderson, I stretch the meaning of Spillers's flesh beyond the more conventional reading that posits the body as captive and the flesh as the pre-ontological and liberated space outside of enslavement. I read Spillers's flesh as a not-yet form of Black freedom that exists in the immanence of slavery (and anti-Black violence) and not only in the transcendence of/or before slavery and its afterlife.[54] The flesh is a form of (Spillerian) Black life that finds liberation in the freedom of having "nothing to prove."[55]

Similarly, under the political economic worldview, Wilderson argues that the Native is ontologically rendered nonhuman "flesh." The Black/slave is rendered nonhuman flesh under both "political" and "libidinal" economies. Although Wilderson does not identify Black and Native bodies as ontological equivalents, Native (the savage's) and Black (the Black's) grammars of suffering do share the urgent concerns of the flesh. Wilderson sets forth the conditions of possibility that could result in the making of Black and Native flesh:

> The Middle Passage turns for example Ashanti spatial and temporal capacity into spatial and temporal incapacity — a body into flesh. This process begins as early as the 1200s for the Slave. By the 1530s, modernity is more self-conscious of its coordinates, and Whiteness begins its ontological consolidation and negative knowledge of itself by turning (part of) the Aztec body, for example into Indian flesh. In this moment the White body completes itself and proceeds to lay the groundwork for the intra-Settler ensemble of questions foundational to its ethical dilemmas (i.e., Marxism, feminism, psychoanalysis). In the final analysis, Settler ontology is guaranteed by way of negative knowledge of what it is not rather than by way of its positive claims of what it is.[56]

In exploring the set of negations at work in the making of the human, Wilderson momentarily identifies a moment of interlocution for which, I argue, the discourse of conquest, and its production of flesh, serves as passage. When speaking in terms of the flesh, a space of possible dialogue emerges under rare conditions in which Wilderson argues that the "genocidal modality of the 'Savage' grammar of suffering articulate[s] itself quite well within the two modalities of the 'Slave's' grammar of suffering, accumulation and fungibility."[57] For Wilderson, both of these grammars of suffering and agony find it difficult to assume narrative form within the lexicon made available by humanism, of which, I argue later, the field of White settler colonial studies is part. It is virtually impossible for the Native or the Black to speak through registers of intelligibility that are predicated on their very deathlike settlement, space, and labor (see chapter 3).

Native feminism's theorizations of conquest, genocide, imperialism, and colonialism linger in fleshy matters of death in ways that draw attention to the limitations of causal models that reduce colonialism to Marxian discussions of labor, space, and even settlement. Within Native feminism, one finds another unflinching interrogation of how the conquistador human produces "flesh." Flesh in the form of the "scalp," "the squaw," and the Indigenous woman's womb becomes space that confronts the violence of murder and conquest every day. The flesh and the violence of making flesh is a grammatical system that circulates within both Native feminist decolonial thought and Black studies.[58] Through the contemporary age, Native women's political campaigns and struggles, such as the Missing and Murdered Indigenous Women movement, have had to contend with the ways that Native and Indigenous women, as well as Two Spirit and trans people, are rendered "flesh."[59] In 2014, Marlene Bird of Saskatchewan was beaten, sexually assaulted, and set on fire by her male assailant, Leslie Black. The court transcript reveals that after Black set Bird on fire, he walked to the 7-Eleven convenience store, bought candy, and then walked back past Bird as she lay burning on the ground.[60] In February 2018, the White man who allegedly murdered and dumped the body of fifteen-year-old Tina Fontaine in the Red River in Winnipeg, Manitoba, was acquitted of all charges, even though he was heard implicating himself in her murder in police recordings.[61] The report *Red River Women* by the British Broadcasting Corporation (BBC) tells grisly tales of the severed limbs (arms and legs) of the Native women who have been murdered in Winnipeg.[62] Native feminist thought, speech, and action must always speak back to the gratuitous violence that is perpetrated against Native women to render them flesh. Attending to the lingua franca of conquest and flesh will enable a different perspective from which to attend to the ways that Black and Native studies continue to be in conversation about and struggle against the project of the human.

NATIVE AND NATIVE FEMINIST STUDIES OF THE FLESH

Often the fields and disciplinary concerns of Native studies and settler colonial studies are conflated. However, within this particular Black studies mode of attending to the discourse of conquest and the making of flesh, a distinction is made between Native studies and settler colonial studies.[63] Wilderson discerns a sense or feeling of abandonment within Native studies (specifically in the works of Silko, Ward Churchill, Gerald Taiaiake Alfred, Vine Deloria, and Huanani-Kay Trask) that resonates with the sense/feel of abandonment in some of the work of Afro-pessimists.[64] This same sense and feel of abandonment, however, is not an affective or onto-logical structure shared by settler intellectuals specifically within the field of "White" settler colonial studies, which emerged in the late 1990s and continues to garner credibility and currency in the academy. One Native scholar whom Wilderson references and regards as reluctant, and perhaps unwilling, to invest in or broker an "eventual articulation between" over-lapping elements of Native sovereignty and elements of settler ontology is Huanani-Kay Trask.[65] Although there are resonances present within the constituent parts of sovereignty and White civil society that are antagonis-tic to the possibility of Black life, Wilderson reads Trask as someone who is likely to recoil at the idea of this negotiation. Wilderson argues that Trask "will not countenance" this kind of affinity or alliance.[66]

Some key features of Trask's work mark her scholarship as distinct from that of settler colonialism, although it is still within the discourse of colonialism. In her *From a Native Daughter: Colonialism and Sovereignty in Hawaii* (1993), painful and sustained attention is given to the brutal nature of genocide in a way that does not reduce genocide to mass death or a hor-rific (human) body count as a result of a conflict between humans.[67] Geno-cide — and the making of the Native body as a less than human, or flesh — remains the focus and distinguishing feature of settler colonialism that is worth defining and analytically parsing for readers. While this chapter criti-cally examines how White settler colonial studies becomes the preferred discourse for examining coloniality in North America, it is not a call to move beyond settler colonial studies, particularly because the term "settler colonialism" emerged from the work of Trask. Maile Arvin continues to argue the point that letting go of or turning our backs on settler colonialism would in effect bury or enact a forgetting of settler colonialism's theoretical beginning in the works of Native feminists.[68] In *From a Native Daughter*, Trask deploys and homes settler colonialism to maximize its explanatory power without letting it subsume a larger discussion of Native genocide and conquest. Painful and sustained attention is given in the book to the brutal nature of genocide in a way that does not reduce genocide to an epi-phenomenon of settler colonialism. In addition, when Trask invokes settler colonialism (as one of the first scholars to do so), she uses "settler" in its descriptive mode. For Trask, James Cook's, the British Empire's, and the United States' forms of genocide remain the focus and the distinguishing feature of settler colonialism.

Native feminisms in particular have a way of holding in tension discussions of conquest, imperialism, colonialism, and settler colonialism. For example, the active, animating, and meaningful portions of Trask's prose describe the genocide of Native peoples. She writes, "Modern Hawaii, like its colonial parent the United States, is a settler society; that is, Hawaii is a society in which the indigenous cultures and people have been murdered, suppressed, or marginalized for the benefit of settlers who now dominate our islands."[69] While Trask uses settler(s) in an illustrative capacity, they are just modifiers working descriptively. The quoted sentence is put into motion and animated by the naming of the kinds of violence committed by settlers for their benefit or self-actualization. Far from a "damage-centered" statement, the sentence uses the verbs "murdered, suppressed or marginalized," which direct our attention to the methods and processes of genocide that settlers/conquistadors use to self-actualize.[70] Genocide is theorized as a relational process in which Indigenous peoples experience multiple (and ongoing) kinds of death for conquistador/settlers to live.

Much like Trask, Andrea Smith focuses on the logics/logistics of genocide and conquest in *Conquest: Sexual Violence and American Indian Genocide* (2005) and, by drawing on a vast range of Indigenous women's and feminists' scholarship, brings the gendered and sexualized nature of conquest into full view.[71] Patriarchy as an organizing structure of colonial power creates nonnormative (Othered) bodies that it can target for genocide. Smith chooses to use the term "colonialism" throughout the book and does not take the time to provide a genealogy of settler colonialism or mark the "settler" modifier as particularly special or salient; the time that she spends on theorizing the gendered and sexualized nature of genocide is the distinguishing feature in *Conquest*. Similarly, in her essay "The Three Pillars of White Supremacy" (2006), Smith names as the second pillar of White supremacy the logic of genocide, which holds that Indigenous people must disappear.[72] While Smith does not talk about settler colonialism specifically, she does give colonialism the feature of genocide. It is important to note that the defining and distinguishing aspect of the colonization of the Americas and other settler states is genocide, not settlement or settlers. This text's emphasis on genocide should be kept in a holding pattern and considered fertile ground for the elaboration of a "grammar of suffering in the genocidal mode."[73] During the particular era in which the text was published, the rubric of violence served as a shared point of departure for the organizing of women and people of color. The work of Smith and Trask that deploys colonialism in an expansive and intersectional way functions to facilitate a coalitional politics (Smith and Trask's professed goal) among racialized people and postcolonial subjects.

Trask and Smith are also featured alongside Sarah Deer and Stormy Ogden in *The Color of Violence*, edited by INCITE! Women of Color against Violence, an anthology committed to drawing connections among various forms of racial and gendered violence — and reading them through White supremacy — to foster coalition. The broad term "colonialism" works well to achieve this coalitional sense of mutual identification, though it proves awkward for Black people in the Americas — specifically in the United States, and at times in Canada. While coalition as an imperative is the inflection in which most of the essays in the anthology were written, if read reparatively, or in a way that looks for what is possible (if we are committed to this when it pertains to Indigenous women's work), we might find openings for conversation. Reading these texts in the reparative mode could create dialogue about how they can be critiqued, revised, and reengaged in a way that gives them a different political force and utility.[74]

More recently, Jodi Byrd's *Transit of Empire* (2011), which does not necessarily profess an intention to foster Black and Native coalition, provides a corrective to hegemonic leftist readings of racial and colonial domination in the United States. Specifically, Byrd critiques how Americanists such as Amy Kaplan (and perhaps some tendencies within Black studies) privilege the rubric of slavery and racism as the fulcrum of conquest and U.S. imperialism. Byrd's own intersectional analysis in response to Kaplan, who posits that conquest "cannot be understood separately from the expansion of slavery and the struggle for freedom,"[75] argues, conversely, that "slavery cannot be understood separately from the colonization and theft of indigenous lands."[76] While I agree with Byrd's corrective, I would also argue that the colonization and genocide of Indigenous bodies, cosmologies, and ways of being is as important as the "theft of land" in Black studies. In fact, to move Black and Native conversations closer to a discussion of the production of the human through Black and Native flesh, there must be a sustained discussion of the genocide and colonization of Native bodies and cosmologies. Perhaps by reading Byrd's notion of the Indian as a site of transit for multiple forms of imperial power alongside theories of Black fungibility by Hartman and others in Black studies, scholars can begin to develop new grammatical and conceptual frames for thinking about how the relations of conquest structure Black and Indigenous life.

In 2006, Trask developed an analysis of colonialism that renders the relationship among racism, genocide, and colonization bare. Specifically, she states that "colonization was the historical process, and genocide was the official policy."[77] Thus, for Trask, colonialism is a larger structure or formation that becomes particular and specific to Indigenous peoples when it appears in its genocidal form. What distinguishes the form of colonialism in Hawai'i and the United States from other, nonsettler forms of colonialism is Native genocide. "During the course of little more than a century," Trask writes, "the haole onslaught had taken from us 95% of our Hawaiian people."[78] Again, genocide is the defining feature of this form of colonization, not settlement, and when settlement is invoked, it is always tethered to the violence of genocide.

Colonialism is invoked as a unifying frame in ways that the historical specificities of slavery and Blackness can also emerge and be articulated. Trask states, "Today, the United States is the most powerful country in the world, a violent country created out of the bloody extermination of Native peoples, and the enslavement of forcibly transported peoples, and the continuing oppression of dark-skinned peoples."[79] Further, in Trask's work, particularly in her essay "The Color of Violence," in the INCITE! anthology, settler colonialism, colonialism, and genocide are specific yet supple and agile analytical foci that are not bracketed off from one another in the ways that Edward Cavanagh's and Lorenzo Veracini's definition of "settler colonialism" makes the term irreducible and incommensurate.[80]

Native feminists' individual and collective works in the 1990s into the 2000s created opportunities to think about conquest and colonialism as fundamentally constituted by slavery as much as they were constituted by genocide. This is an example of a reading practice that foregrounds an emphasis on genocide and slavery rather than coloniality and sovereignty as reigning discourses. Prior to the debates and discussions about the necessity to parse and make distinctions among imperial, colonial, settler colonial, and post- and neocolonial forms of power, Native feminist literature such as Silko's attempted to think about the annihilating and death-dealing power of conquest in the Americas. Throughout *Almanac of the Dead*, as Indigenous and Latinx characters trace the origins and significance of an ancient text, Silko provides the reader with an unflinching meditation on gratuitous violence. Her own grammar throughout the novel names the subjects who have committed genocide from the fifteenth century to the present "butchers," "destroyers," and, at times, "sorcerers":

> In the old days the Twin Brothers had answered the people's cry for help when terrible forces or great monsters threatened the people. The people had always feared the Destroyers, humans who were attracted to and excited by death and the sight of blood and suffering. The Destroyers secretly prayed and waited for disaster and destruction. Secretly they were thrilled by the spectacle of death. The European invaders had brought their Jesus hanging bloody and dead from the cross; later they ate his flesh and blood again and again at the "miraculous eternal supper" or Mass. Typical of sorcerers or Destroyers, the Christians had denied they were cannibals and sacrificers.[81]

Rarely (if ever) does Silko refer to White perpetrators or their descendants as "settlers" in the text. She uses "harsher terms" — terms that, Joanne Barker says, are called for to replace "settler" and its etymological and connotative origins in sentiments of "reconciling," and "making friends" while the settler nation-state continues to enact violence and disavows political commitments to the return of land and reparations for slavery.[82] In this way, Silko's grammar of violence becomes the point of suture, or the connective tissue that brings Indigenous and Black flesh and life into the same frame.

Because of Silko's sustained meditation on the gratuitous, world-making violence of the "Destroyers" and Wilderson's reference to Silko's work in *Red, White and Black*, I read the discussion of slavery and Blackness through her character Clinton as anticipating some of Wilderson's discussion of the White libidinal economy's need for Black fungible bodies. Clinton is one of few Black characters in *Almanac*, and the only one who possesses a narrative arc (though small); he is a Black veteran who is working in the book to organize a People's Army of the Dispossessed. Similar to Wilderson's critique of White leftist politics that rely on "exploitation" as a human grammar of suffering, Clinton sustains a critique of Marxism: "Swears he is no Marxist. African and other tribal people had shared food and wealth in common for thousands of years before the white man Marx came along and stole their ideas for his 'communes' and collective farms. 'White man didn't even invent communism on his own,' Clinton said, wiping his mouth on the sleeve of his shirt."[83]

Rather than as a "gift" to the Black and Indigenous peoples of the Americas, Clinton views Marxism as just one of the available tools that can be used in the revolutionary struggle of the dispossessed. Throughout *Almanac*, Black and Indigenous characters and their attendant revolutionary politics name the limitations of various forms of White radicalism. Clinton's revolutionary politics and his analysis of how "anti-Black racism" work are outlined during his radio show. In an episode titled "Clinton's Slavery Broadcast," he explains his theory of the relations of slavery, delivering the thirteen aspects he has identified of the slave-to-master relationship as Bob Marley, Jimmy Cliff, and Aretha Franklin play in the background.[84] Clinton parses dimensions of slavery that sound strikingly similar to Frantz Fanon's appropriation of the Hegelian master-slave dialectic, four of whose features contain overtones that resonate with contemporary Afro-pessimist thought. Clinton cites, for example,

#6. Slaves may serve as laborers, but slaves exist primarily to satisfy sexual and ego needs of the master.

#7. The Master craves the pulse of the cruelty and pleasure the slave arouses in him again and again.[85]

As Clinton describes the sixth and seventh mandates of the master-slave dialectic, the elements of the libidinal economy emerge as a primary structure of the relationship. While Black slave labor and other forms of exploited labor are constitutive of the political economy, the slave is essential as an object of negation for the construction of the master's notion of self. As what Wilderson would describe as an "accumulable" and what Hartman would call a "fungible" object, the slave is a Spillerian open space of sensual pleasure to be used indefinitely. In a Fanonian-Lacanian fashion, Clinton ends the broadcast with an elaboration of the psychosexual dynamics at play in the dialectic:

#12. The slave is offered in Death in place of the Master thus the slave "becomes" the Master if only for an instant as the slave dies.

#13. The slave accumulates power in the realm of the Master's dreams. Gradually, the slave inhabits the Master's idle thoughts during waking hours. The Master's obsession enslaves him. (End of broadcast.)[86]

This recognition on the part of Clinton—and, therefore, Silko—of the totalizing power and pull of Blackness on the psyche and imagination of the master and the organization of the social order is significant. Silko does not relegate the structural position of the Black to the realm of the political-economic as an exploited laborer. Further, Silko's writing of Clinton reveals a profound knowledge of the ways in which the White-human master requires Blackness as a state of nonbeing to imagine his own existence. Silko's *Almanac* represents a form of Indigenous thought and politics that positions anti-Blackness as a world-making and human-making phenomenon. *Almanac* creates a discursive space within Native thought that can consider what Wilderson would call the slave's "ensemble of questions." Silko's meditation on the kinds of social, physical, and ontological death that was required in the making of the Americas creates an ethical space of engagement in which Black people's antagonistic position in the world can surface. These discursive moments that interrupt humanist grammars of suffering, such as labor exploitation and Black subjects as tragic and displaced peoples of Africa, function as disruptions to White settler colonial impulses.

Before settler colonialism was established as a field of study, around 2005–2006, robust yet imperfect discussions were occurring between Black and Indigenous communities.[87] These partial and evolving conversations relied on literature emerging from Native studies and Black diaspora studies.[88] While I do not want to suggest that these texts are sufficient in and of themselves or that the work being done in settler colonial studies is without value, I do want to critically scrutinize how settler colonial studies has become the preferred discourse for examining Indigeneity, relations to land and space, and questions of sovereignty. Why was Native studies usurped and abandoned as the disciplinary lens from which to pursue these questions? Why is Black studies an unlikely place to pursue notions of sovereignty and nation (or the impossibility of sovereignty and nation)? What can be made from shared Native and Black discursive and extradiscursive moments?

Unlike White settler colonial studies, Black studies (particularly Afropessimism) and Native studies sustain a steadfast focus on abolishing genocide and avoid reflexive analogies and detours through humanist modes of thought and expression. Further, settler colonial studies invisibilizes historical and ongoing discussions between Black and Indigenous communities and Black and Native studies.[89] Within existing White settler colonial discourses the extended elucidation of the settler and their concerns interrupts examination of the violence of the slave trader and serial murderer of Indigenous peoples.

In the book *The Empire Writes Back* (2002), Bill Ashcroft, Gareth Griffiths, and Helen Tiffin include a (very) small section that focuses on settler colonies and their literature. In their examination of literary production in settler colonies, the colonized subject is imagined as the White subject writing back to and resisting the colonial power of the metropole.[90] Almost no Indigenous literature is mentioned as a form of anticolonial discourse.[91] In a very short section, the authors define settler literature as White settlers' attempts to distinguish themselves through language and writing from Britain as the United States, Canada, Australia, New Zealand, and South Africa. This method became the frame for thinking about postcolonial thought in the settler colonies. However, *The Empire Writes Back* attends to literary forms and thus does not anticipate the consolidation of settler colonial studies as a specialized field of critical theory. It was too early for the authors to comment on the "settler colonial turn" that was about to take form. However, their focus on White literary cultural production forecasts who would be centered in the emerging discourse of settler colonial studies.[92]

The end of the twentieth century and the beginning of the twenty-first century marked a moment in which women of color scholarship and activism were growing in popularity. Within the academy and social justice organizing, the rubric of violence unified a number of constituents nationally and globally. Organizing against interpersonal and state-sanctioned violence became the suture that connected an international movement of gender, prison abolition, anti-imperial, and anticolonial activists. The World Trade Organization protests, post-9/11 immigrant rights organizing, reproductive justice work, and the 2000 protests of the stolen U.S. presidential election were animated to some extent by the antiviolence movement led by women of color. At the epicenter of this organizing, the enigmatic Andrea Smith emerged as one of the antiviolence movement's most prominent faces.[93]

Prominent Indigenous activists and scholars — such as Madonna Thunder Hawk, Stormy Ogden, Winona La Duke, and Sandy Grande — and their theories of violence became flash points of a movement that centered the ways that imperial and colonial violence continue to perpetuate themselves in multiple forms across the globe. Largely due to the increased attention that women-of-color coalitional work, along with Smith's and Native women's scholarship, was receiving, Native feminist thought began to circulate widely and garner U.S. and international acclaim. The theoretical and discursive axis in the academy—American, Ethnic, Women's, and Gender studies—and in activist circles tilted and rotated around the body of scholarship being produced by Native and women of color in the United States. Texts such as *The Sacred Hoop, From a Native Daughter, Inventing the Savage, Red Pedagogy, Conquest,* and *The Color of Violence,* which elaborated on colonization's connection to other forms of racialized and gendered violence, were the major sources consulted for theorizing the historical and contemporary violence of coloniality in the overlapping scholar-activist circles in the early twenty-first century.[94]

On the heels of the popularity of feminist texts by women of color and Native women, the scholarship of White scholars in White settler states began to gain traction and currency as a countercurrent.[95] The late Patrick Wolfe's book *Settler Colonialism and the Transformation of Anthropology* was published in 1998, and his essay "Settler Colonialism and the Elimination of the Native" (2006) was often the text circulated first and most widely. The essay recycled the book's statement that "invasion is a structure, not an event," which would be quoted and cited widely over the next five to six years and into the present.[96] Wolfe's Foucauldian-influenced theorization (both structuralist *and* poststructuralist) of settler colonialism as a structure (diffuse, omnidirectional, and productive) appeared to have inspired a reanimation of White scholarship on processes of settlement, subject formation, land theft, and colonization in the settler states of Canada, Australia, New Zealand, and the United States. In 2010, Cavanagh and Veracini announced on their blog the need for, and emergence of, a new field of study devoted to settler colonialism as a unique and irreducible form of domination.[97]

According to the origin story that settler colonial studies tells about itself, the body of knowledge that marks it as a distinct area of studies emerges in the 1990s, primarily out of Australian settler scholarship. As an area of studies, it regards settler colonialism as a "distinct social, cultural and historical formation with ongoing political effects."[98] Its genesis is indebted to the intellectual labor of the Australian scholars Wolfe, Cavanagh, and Veracini. In 2010–11, *Settler Colonial Studies* launched its debut issue. With an open-access journal, the field has the infrastructure and capacity to travel transnationally and gain appeal. As a transnational theoretical movement, it travels from Australia and New Zealand to Canada, South Africa, the United States, and other imperial European sites.

Wolfe is regarded as the seminal figure in the field and continues to influence the burgeoning North American field of settler colonial studies. While scholars in Native studies do acknowledge the explicit attempts that Wolfe made to develop the analytics of settler colonialism in relation to "Indigenous thinking and scholarship that exists far longer than settler nations," his work has been used in ways that often end up consolidating settler colonial studies as a White field that displaces Native and Indigenous studies.[99] In 2006, Wolfe made the compelling case that settler colonialism was a more appropriate theoretical frame and structure from which to think about power in settler states. He argued that settler colonialism is larger than genocide and is the best way to conceptualize the elimination of the Native in settler societies. As I mentioned, Wolfe theorized settler colonialism as a "structure" rather than an "event."[100] As a structure, settler colonialism is an ongoing process that can contain other formations; thus, settler colonialism—and its logic of elimination—looms much larger than genocide. Wolfe proclaimed, "To this extent, it is a larger category than genocide."[101] Using a similar logic, my project argues that conquest is a larger conceptual and material terrain than settler colonialism and far more suited for the regional/hemispheric particularities of coloniality in the Americas.

As the unique (and productive) social and theoretical concerns of oceanic settler-Indigenous relations traveled transnationally and landed in North America, some of the particular historical legacies and contemporaneous machinations of relations of conquest were effaced and disappeared. The uncritical adoption of settler colonial discourses from an oceanic context enacts a discursive shift that privileges a theoretical and ethical engagement with settlers, settlement, and settler colonial relations. Together, this works to displace conversations about genocide, slavery, and the violent project of making the human (humanism).

In 2011, in a series of posts that ran through 2017, the Lenape scholar Joanne Barker tried to slow the rapidly moving tide of White settler colonial studies by posting a set of provocations that exposed the limits of the analytic of settler colonialism. In "Why Settler Colonialism Isn't Exactly Right" on her *Tequila Sovereign* blog, Barker expresses concern with the etymology of "settlement" and what it connotes and calls forth as a form of political discourse.[102] She is disturbed by how the term "settle" refers to actions such as reconciling and "making friends." More specifically, the term connotes and encourages a "reconciling of these histories"—of White imperial violence and indigenous death and subjugation—"within the current structure and social formation of the nation-state."[103] Barker contends that settler colonialism does not capture "the current structure or social formation of the U.S."[104]

In fact, Barker prefers to hold on to "harsher terms" such as imperialism and colonialism because they facilitate a more precise understanding of current militarized violence and support people who are strategizing for "empowerment and revolution."[105] Barker sustained and nuanced this analysis, and even engaged in a dialogue with Wolfe and Mark Rifkin in the spring of 2011, over the course of nine blog posts. In 2017, Barker levied another critique of the field for its structuralist rigidity and inadvertent erasure of Black people. In the post "The Analytic Constraints of Settler Colonialism," she works through "a certain analytic within the studies [that] has, however unwittingly, foreclosed and even chilled understandings of Black and Indigenous histories and identities in ways that derail our understandings of U.S. imperialism as a social formation and so our work with one another."[106] Because settler colonial studies — and, more specifically, Wolfe's formulation of invasion as a structure — performs like a "Marxist structuralist" problem for thought, it "rearticulates the problematics of structuralism. It treats society as a fixed, coherent thing that can be objectively described."[107] As a fixed and coherent "thing," the settler state and its structure of invasion are states to negotiate, reconcile with, and reform rather than abolish. Further, due to the structuralist limitations of the discourse of settler colonialism, Barker struggles to think about or situate movements such as #BlackLivesMatter, #SayHerName, #NoDAPL, and #MMIW as contemporary oppositional politics that could be in coalition with one another under a settler colonial regime. More important, she is concerned about the political implications of a settler colonial studies whose decolonial imaginary renders "reparations" and "return" antithetical political objectives without merit.[108]

Informed by a Black studies perspective that continues to be in conversation with Indigenous studies and people, I contend that the danger of the hegemonic hold White settler colonial studies has on the imagination of critical theory is that it actively disavows quotidian forms of anti-Black and anti-Indigenous violence and resurrects the violence of liberal humanism, even as it engages post-Enlightenment thought and poststructuralist critique. The field of White settler colonial studies has yet to truly reckon with the ways that it erases Indigenous knowledge and forms of Indigenous politics of decolonization that require the end of the U.S. and Canadian nation-states as well as the end of Whiteness and the versions of the human that sustain them. The prominence of Settler colonial studies itself as a key analytical turn in the social sciences and humanities performs a form of genocidal violence as it displaces Indigenous and Native studies. Also, the field reproduces a rigid settler-Indigenous binary that erases Black people and anti-Black violence from its analytical frames. When the field attempts to insert Blackness through an applied intersectional rhetoric of inclusion, it makes this "structural adjustment" by incorporating Black people into the analytic as settler-laborers.[109] This misnaming of Black people as both settlers and laborers occurs in part because of the field's reliance on liberal humanist conceptual and theoretical frames inherited from continental theory. Finally, the focus of settler colonial studies on the human rubrics and idioms of land and labor invisibilizes Black political attention and focus on murder, Black fungibility, and the call for the abolition of the deadly terms on which the human and the world were crafted.

DISAVOWING VIOLENCE

Frank Wilderson describes the discursive and material violence that occurs within what he calls the "Settler/Master/Human's grammatical structure."[110] Within this grammatical structure, he argues, there is a disavowal of the violence of genocide in how the settler narrates the formation of the United States. On one level, the disavowal occurs through the settler's preferred part of speech: "clearing" is spoken of only as a noun in the Settler/Master/Human's grammatical structure and never used as a verb. Wilderson draws our attention to this:

> Clearing, in the Settler/"Savage" relation, has two grammatical structures, one [as] a noun and the other as a verb. But the Western only recognizes clearing as a noun. . . . But prior to the clearing's fragile infancy, that is before its cinematic legacy as a newborn place name, it labored not across the land as a noun but as a verb on the body of the "Savage," speaking civil society's essential status as an effect for genocide.[111]

This discursive displacement of violence is reproduced in the very etymological roots of the name of the field that calls itself "settler colonial studies." Like Barker, I argue that key terms and referents such as "settler" and "settlement" are not "harsh" enough. As the primary analytics of the field, they dampen rather than acutely elaborate the kind of violence the field professes to be interested in investigating and eradicating. In 2007, Carole Pateman examined the ascendance of the discursive regime of settlement and the settler contract within British legal discourse. Pateman and Arun Gobin argue that the discourse of settlement emerged in the eighteenth century as a way to conceal for centuries the violence of conquest.[112] In chapter 3, I engage the work of Gobin, who analyzes visual depictions of the British colonies to expose the ways that images of settlement were used to crowd out the violence of slavery and genocide. Similarly, the "settler" in settler colonial studies functions as a ruse and way to distract critical theory from grappling with the relations of conquest, as well as with urgent political and theoretical concerns of Native and Black studies. As Barker attests, "The imperial militarized violence and capitalism of the state sovereignties claimed by the U.S., Canada, Australia, and New Zealand" do not feature as central concerns of the field of White settler colonial studies. As the fervor of White settler colonial studies grows, a form of discursive genocide is performed as Native scholars, texts, and analytics disappear from the conversation. Furthermore, an actual discussion of Native genocide is displaced by a focus on White settlers' relationship to land rather than their parasitic and genocidal relationship to Indigenous and Black peoples.

As #BlackLivesMatter and even #NativeLivesMatter circulate as urgent calls to recognize the sanctity of and protect Black and Native lives, settlement, settlers, and land continue to function as euphemisms that disavow this lived daily violence.[113] Attending to unfinished conversations about Native genocide and Black fungibility moves discussions closer to the possibility of thinking about the abolition of slavery, genocide, humanist notions of sovereignty, and the nation-state. Refocusing on conquest may initiate a conversation that can take up some of the conceptual and ethical work that settler colonialism has left on the conceptual chopping floor. The parasitic and genocidal violence required to make the human or self-actualize as White is hard to conceptualize within the discourse of settler colonialism. Conquest as a grammar and a frame from which to think makes it possible to register the always already intersectional violence of anti-Blackness, slavery and its afterlife, and genocide at the same time.

LAND AS ANIMATING FEATURE

While the interventions by Wolfe and the field of settler colonial studies are important—they should not be dismissed but properly prioritized— it is also important to scrutinize the ways that settler colonial studies becomes primarily preoccupied with the settler's relationship to land, or terra nullius. This focus on terra nullius and land disappears the settler's relationship to violence and the intricate and violent processes of the human's self-making. A focus on settlers and their relationship to land displaces how settlers also become conquistadors/(humans) through Native genocide and Black dehumanization. Further, genocide, or Wolfe's "structural genocide," often becomes a secondary and provisional concern of the field. In Wolfe's own synopsis of settler colonial power, the relationship to land is the privileged site of analysis. He wrote, "In sum, then, settler colonialism is an inclusive, *land-centered project* that coordinates a comprehensive range of agencies, from the metropolitan center to the frontier encampment, with a view to eliminating Indigenous societies. Its operations are not dependent on the presence or absence of formal state institutions or functionaries."[114]

Further, drawing on Cole Harris's work, Wolfe deploys a Marxist analysis to call attention to settler colonialism's "principal momentum," writing, "Combine capital's interest in uncluttered access to land and settlers' interest in land as livelihood, and the principal momentum of settler colonialism comes into focus."[115] Wolfe reduces settler colonialism to a land-centered project, as opposed to a genocide-centered project. Again, genocide and the violent modus operandi of the making of the human and the dehumanization of Indigenous peoples become a mere byproduct. Given that the logic of settler colonialism "transmutes into different modalities, discourses and institutional formations," it has the capacity to deploy other disciplinary regimes, forms of violence, and unlikely bodies and sites for its multiple projects. Moreover, Wolfe's elaboration of settler colonialism's "continuities, discontinuities, adjustments and departures" is a place where other forms of power can reproduce settler relations; however, a preoccupation with these other forms of productive power can also become the space where genocide and Native bodies and people are disappeared.[116]

According to Wolfe, it would not be profitable to read settler colonialism as eliminating Native people in the same way over time (genocide/assimilation); nor would it be productive to think of settler colonialism as a formation that morphs into other forms of colonial dominance (internal colonization, neocolonialism, neoimperialism). This is a deft and important move on Wolfe's part. Genocide can certainly be everywhere and is virtually uncontainable; however, when Native people are removed from the terms of the discussion, genocide is both everywhere and nowhere—and affects no one in particular.

The blog administered by Cavanagh and Veracini argues that settler colonial studies is important enough to justify a field of its own. Cavanagh and Veracini argue adamantly that settler colonialism and colonialism are not the same. They may "interpenetrate and overlap," but they need to be theorized in their own right.[117] White colonists of settler nations need their own theory. In these early definitions, there is not even an obligatory nod to Native studies or Native feminisms. To be fair, settler colonial studies has done a better job of incorporating Indigenous scholars and people of color as it has evolved. Nevertheless, in establishing itself as a new and uncharted theoretical turn, it set in motion a series of appropriations, displacements, and disappearances that make it difficult to engage with Native studies and its conceptual and theoretical terrain. Veracini's definition of "decoloniza-tion" is an example of one of the more troubling displacements that the field enacts. In his essay "Introducing Settler Colonial Studies" (2011), he problematically defines "decolonization"—or states what it is not—on behalf of Indigenous communities. He argues that the settler-Indigenous relationship must continue to end settler colonialism and that demands for the settler to "go away" can be equated with Native genocide.[118] First, Veracini attempts to displace centuries of Indigenous decolonial struggle, praxis, and theory with a White settler theory of decolonization. Second, he constructs a false equivalency and analogy that posits settler migra-tion and redistribution of wealth—that is, the return of stolen land—as a form of genocide and colonization. Settler colonialism in the academy dis-places the project of Native studies and becomes the primary way to talk about—or, rather, avoid—genocide in the United States and other geno-cidal settler states. White settler colonial studies refuses to tarry in death or outside the folds of the human in the ways that Native and Black studies have a tradition of doing.

Land, space, and (White settler) subjectivity become rubrics of analy-sis that are elaborated on and theorized through a resuscitation of Marxist, Foucauldian, queer, and other humanist continental theory.[119] Humanist modes of legibility reassert themselves through Marx's worker, capital-ist, and notion of property and Foucault's analysis of disciplinary power at the level of the individual and governmentality and biopolitics at the scale of populations. Settler colonialism forces its interlocutors into con-versations rife with humanist analogies and discussion of resolutions that Native studies and Black studies (specifically, Afro-pessimism), with their steadfast commitment to abolishing genocide and humanist forms of sov-ereignty, would resist.[120] These analytical and political imperatives within strains of Native and Black studies are important to preserve within discus-sions of coloniality in the Americas.

Settler colonial studies relies on a form of continental theory that has a long legacy of cordoning off the gratuitous violence that gave birth to and continues to structure its intellectual tradition. I argue that this disavowal of violence — specifically, the violent negation of Blackness within humanist thought — is one of the primary reasons that the field has not been able to consider and theorize Black presence. Black studies, Black social movement, and Black frames of analysis often treat the human, as well as the violence of making the human, as an object of study. A White settler colonial studies that refuses to engage this conceptual and scholarly project will be unable to talk to or about Black people.

Resting comfortably within the realm of the human, continental theory has not typically had the stomach for sustaining an investigation of the kind of unspeakable violence that enabled the Marxist worker and the Foucauldian subject as an effect of power, as well as queer and affective theories' subjectless discourses (one can only strive for subjectlessness if you possess subjectivity in the first place), to exist. Continental theories' transgressive moves (affective, sensational, masochistic), even in their post-identitarian and subjectless modes, tend to reinstantiate the White (sometimes queer) male subject that they hope to overcome.[121]

Discourses such as settlement that focus on the bodiless activity of settlement enact a sleight of hand similar to that performed in post-humanist conceptual moves. A focus on Foucauldian-like microprocesses of settlement that erase bodies (most often White bodies) as subjects have been more effective in covering the bloody trail of White/human self-actualization than they have at offering a way around and beyond the entrapments of liberal humanism. While at once disappearing the subject, settler colonial discourses also privilege a linear and coherent narrativity, or what Wilderson and Afro-pessimists might term a "narrative capacity" (even in its affective mode) that delegitimizes the extradiscursive, extra-human, and not always communicable acts of Black and Indigenous survival and ways of knowing, such as haunting. Settler colonial studies represents an internal revolution, critique, and adjustment to postmodern movements within the West and, more specifically, among the people who currently occupy the position of the human. These kinds of shifts in paradigm and thought cannot reckon with the other (than) humanly experiences of those whom Wynter names "Indios, Negroes and native[s]." Moreover, the other and more than human ways that Black and Indigenous people speak are not always legible within settler humanist protocols.

In 1985, during her battle with cancer and as she faced impending death, Audre Lorde once again began reflecting on her relationship to Indigenous peoples in North America. In an entry in her cancer journal, she writes about how she found herself sitting with other Black women and considering the lives and experiences of Native American women:

> Sitting with Black women from all over the earth has made me think a great deal about what it means to be indigenous, and what my relationship as a Black woman in North America is to the land-rights struggles of the indigenous peoples of this land, to Native American Indian women, and how we can translate that consciousness into a new level of working together. In other words, how can we use each other's differences in our common battles for a livable future?[122]

Lorde's journal entry evokes the kind of ethics for which this book holds space. The shoal invokes a material, constructed, and imagined ecotonal space of becoming. In this book, ceremony is also a geography. In her journal entry, Lorde wonders whether a conversation with Native women is possible and asks "how we can translate that consciousness into a new level of working together. In other words, how can we use each other's differences in our common battles for a livable future?"[123]

As Lorde is sitting with Black women from the diaspora, she is compelled to think about Indigenous women in North America. Without being compelled or cajoled by Native studies or chastised by White settler scholars, Lorde, Black women, and Black studies as a field are capacious and ethical enough in their own right to consider the struggles of Native peoples. This is not a conversation that Black people have avoided as an intramural or public dialogue. Lorde's erotic modes that can effectively "absorb chaos," as one of my students, Amy Sarrell, says, is a wonderful way to think about how fugitive and fungible kinds of Blackness use chaos and difference to craft openings and geographies of freedom.[124] Black erotics as a poetics of life and death have the capacity to create a connective force to Black people's deepest selves, as well as to the breath and life force of Indigenous peoples and others.

Whether or not Lorde had her good friend Joy Harjo on her mind during her meditations on the erotic, Lorde's erotic work of imagining more ethical relations already included and, in fact, necessitated a consideration of Indigenous peoples in the Americas. Black and Indigenous creative writers, artists, cultural workers, and invokers of ceremony are often able to attend to the pulse, taste, smell, texture, movement, gestures, and sensations of conquest—the fukú—in ways that connect Black and Indigenous lives through time. It is often through the felt, dreamed, and conjured, as well as through dances and incantation, that the relations, violence, healing, and mutations of the utmost consequence reside. The connections, monstrous intimacies, and portals to new forms of consciousness and connection often evade the capture of narrative. Language and discourse can bring us close but also fail to reveal much about the ways that Black and Native life in the Western Hemisphere are sutured to each other.

The charting of new routes also entails engaging new processes, new forms of mutation and transformation. The performance of defacing Columbus tarries in the repeated scenario of conquest to have us rework it and change its course. Perhaps the defacement and bloodying of a conquistador whose legacy still moves through and shapes everyday life in North America and the Americas is a way to illuminate a path toward a way of life between available language and the space of the "unthought" or, at least, unspoken. These extradiscursive and semigrammatical performances, defacements, and modes of living that confound normative modes of being must coexist with and work on the relations of conquest. Rather than the "BLACK LIVES MATTER" tag eclipsing Native lives and politics, could this recent defacement be absorbed into a longer history of incidents staged by Native and Black people to refuse the narrow and violent conception of the human? Black and Indigenous protests against conquistador ways of life have already been talking to one another in ways that exceed certain forms of humanist narrativity and intelligibility. In the next chapter, Black geographical readings illumine the geographies of Black and Native resistance and fugitivity on an eighteenth-century British map of conquest and settlement that tries to erase Black and Indigenous life.

2

THE MAP (SETTLEMENT) AND
THE TERRITORY (THE INCOMPLETENESS
OF CONQUEST)

On this island things fidget.
Even history.
The landscape does not sit
willingly
as if behind an easel
holding pose
waiting on
someone
to pencil
in lines, compose
its best features
or unruly contours
—KEI MILLER, "What the Mapmaker Ought to Know"

On March 11, 1741, almost two years after the bloody Stono Rebellion led by fugitive slaves seeking to escape to the town of St. Augustine (Spanish Florida), the celebrated South Carolina resident Eliza Lucas Pinckney of Charleston (Charles Town),[1] wrote in her letter book about a "mad" prophet haunted by the specter of Black midnight marauding. In one of her epistles, Pinckney shares the local gossip with a neighbor that a madman in the community had received a prophecy that

> Charles Town and the Country as farr as Ponpon Bridge should be destroyed by fire and swaord, to be executed by the Negroes before the first day of next month. He came to town—60 mile—twice besides sending twice to acquaint the Governor with it. People in general were

very uneasy tho' convinced he was no prophet, but they dreaded the consiquence of such a thing being put into the head of slaves and the advantage they might take of us.[2]

Throughout the eighteenth century, slave revolts rippled across the landscapes of British North America and the Caribbean.[3] On January 7, 1742, Eliza Pinckney reported that she had recently attended the trial of one of her slaves, "Mulatto Quash," who was one of many who had been accused of conspiring to flee to St. Augustine. Frustrating the attempts of White settlers to smooth out and order the landscape in the Low Country, Black and Indigenous insurrection nibbled at the edges of the White psyche, producing a form of chronic anxiety that provoked nightmares and visions of Black insurrection.[4] In fact, Black movement made some Whites go "mad."

Into the mid-1700s, Eliza Lucas Pinckney's community of slave owners and warring Whites (alternately at war with the Cherokee, the Spanish, the French, and Black captives) feared retaliatory violence from all directions. In 1757, the Cherokee Nation raided South Carolinian frontiersmen west of Charles Town. In 1759, Pinckney wrote a letter to a local settler that shared the news of an expedition into the Cherokee Nation to "chastise" the Cherokee for their insolence.[5] The violence that often loomed closest and posed an ever present danger on the plantation landscape (in the house, the field, the bed, the food and drink, the mind) was the movement of Black people.

Pinckney's own family had an intimate knowledge of the kind of danger and fear that Black movement and, specifically, insurrection inspired in the "mad" White prophet. They had fled Antigua when she was a child in response to slave rebellions in that colony. Pinckney's own slaves in South Carolina planned escapes on several occasions. For many British colonists in the Low Country and the Caribbean, Black movement and rebellion lay perpetually unabated and in wait on the horizon. In fact, Pinckney and her community feared that even a mad White man's less-than-credible visions—just the mere thought—of Black rebellion might stir the quivering Black masses. In 1741, the pulsing Black landscape of rebellion consumed the collective imagination of the White body politic.

In this chapter, I argue that White settlers' ongoing anxiety about resistance by Black fugitives and Cherokees animated William Gerard de Brahm's "1757 Map of the Coast of South Carolina and Parts of Georgia." Using a Black geographical reading practice, I offer that Black fugitivity, and what Katherine McKittrick has referred to as "black Atlantic living-ness," created a crisis in representation for White cartography.[6] As a mode of what Denise Ferreira da Silva terms modern writing and a form of auto-poesis — or writing the self into being — eighteenth-century cartography such as de Brahm's map represented an attempt to write the British/Euro-pean subject as a rational, interior self of the mind who exercised domin-ion over irrational and sensual beings such as Black and Indigenous others existing at the margins of humanity. Sylvia Wynter discusses poesis as a process of self-making.[7] Literature, culture, and science (maps) are parts of the orders of knowledge that embed the ideology of the group-self (Us) in opposition to the other (Indios and Negros). These scientific and cul-tural discourses function as a recursive feedback loop that justifies and legitimizes itself while hiding the ways that humans are both produced by (written by) and produce these codes. The notion that humans are exter-nal to — or can gaze on — these natural and self-writing codes is a form of autopoesis. I track this process of autopoesis and self-writing in de Brahm's map. However, I argue that de Brahm struggled to affectively represent Blackness and Indigeneity as states of geographic, cartographic, and onto-logical otherness that could be dominated and relegated to what da Silva calls the exteriority of the "horizon of death." In fact, de Brahm and British settlers' failure to subdue Black fugitivity and Indigenous resistance cre-ated a crisis of representation, or self-making, on de Brahm's 1757 map.

Black and Indigenous movement made it increasingly difficult for de Brahm and the British settlers to depict a linear and stable story of con-quest, settlement, and self-actualization. When examined using a Black geographical reading practice, the map actually reveals an additional or surplus story to that of British conquest and settlement. I read de Brahm's 1757 map in relationship to Eliza Lucas Pinckney's letters to read — or, as McKittrick would say, "notice" — the ways that Black and Indigenous resis-tance to conquest impeded the project of writing and mapping the human as a settled, and therefore finished, project.[8] Fittingly, the Jamaican poet Kei Miller pays homage to Wynter, one of his muses, in a poetic rumina-tion on geography and power in his *The Cartographer Tries to Map a Way to Zion* (2014). In the poem "What the Mapmaker Ought to Know," Miller notices and writes that islands and landscapes "fidget." Speaking back to the colonial violence of mapmaking, Miller warns the cartographer that "landmarks shift" and "slip" from the grip of those intending to fix and dominate people and the earth.[9] Wynter's, McKittrick's, and Miller's geo-graphical interventions ground the readings in this chapter.

Reading the map this way, British conquest, White settlement, and the task of representing British settlers as versions of Wynter's "Man1" through the dehumanization of Black and Indigenous people remains an unresolved and incomplete project.[10] De Brahm's map of the Low Country coastline, settler proprietorship, and Black and Indigenous dehumanization reveals a struggle to gain dominion over Black and Indigenous people and the landscape more than an outright representation of conquest. In fact, Black and Indigenous "livingness" forced de Brahm's and British settlers' cartographic attempts to write themselves into being through anti-Black and anti-Indigenous violence to continually adjust and remain under revision. Finally, and perhaps provocatively, I argue that the representations of Black flutter, kinetics, and flight inspire preliminary and early, or proto-, conceptualizations of Black fungibility, which emerge as an anxious response to Black uncontainability and fugitivity. De Brahm and British settlers attempt to render, and therefore capture, the elusive Black figure by representing it in advance as always already moving, exchangeable, and in flux.

SHOALING THE CONQUISTADOR HUMAN OF 1757

Attending to the morphing nature of the shoal necessitates a supple vigilance. Shoals in the ocean emerge in multiple places. They are also in constant movement and change shape. The first movement of the shoal in this chapter traces how Black and Indigenous life—or, as McKittrick calls it, "livingness"—slows and interrupts White settlement.[11] Black and Indigenous resistance are a continuous presence that prevents any easy settlement and White self-actualization in the mid-1700s.

On a conceptual level, the critical Black geographical reading of the map disrupts how discourses of settlement emerging from White settler colonial studies displace the violence of conquest. In this reading of the map, settlement and cartographic renderings of settlement become technologies of conquest. The map depicts and elaborates the specific ways that "Man1" violently writes and comes into being through Indigenous genocide, Black enslavement, and settlement. Throughout this chapter's analysis of the map, settlement functions as a mode of conquest.

In addition to disruption, the shoal functions as a physical space on the map. There it is represented by the space of the shoreline—where sea and land meet. On de Brahm's map, the shore represents the middle, or interior, space that is surrounded by the exterior spaces of the Black oceanic (chaotic space), as well as the wild abyss of empty Native space (anaspace). As the White human tries to maintain a pure interior space—keep the exterior other out—it is simultaneously produced by what da Silva calls "affectable" others.[12] At the shoal (and shore)—or the in-between space—the White cartographic subject is a byproduct of Black and Indigenous pressure or friction from the outside. The White cartographic subject's conditions of possibilities and of constraint are determined by Black and Indigenous presences. Most important, a focus on the shoal as a process works to reveal the ways in which the attempts to secure White cartographic stability through violence and Black and Native death are tenuous and unstable practices and relations subject to intervention and revision. The shoal functions as a spatial allegory for the moving and shifting space of the human. Rather than a place of safety, the shoreline is an unstable ecozone and nervous landscape where boundaries between the human and Black and Indigenous bodies continually shift.[13]

This chapter's geographical reading practice is animated by the methodology of shoaling, which is distinct from the location of the shoal or shore on the map. As a methodology, shoaling surfaces in this chapter as the disruption of the conquistador imagination and settlement, the intervening in violence and putting texts and objects together or in friction with one another. To slow and interrupt the tendency to read only for anti-Black and anti-Indigenous violence in a map of eighteenth-century conquest, this chapter's methodology uses some of the mathematics and diachronic loops that McKittrick takes to "betray the archive" and to read it for "what else happened."[14] Reading this way requires a willingness to give up a preoccupation to take up another. More specifically, in "Diachronic Loops/ Deadweight Tonnage/Bad Measure," McKittrick asks what would happen if scholars shifted the analytical frame away from the suffering Black body and "toward co relational texts, practices and narratives that emphasize black life."[15] McKittrick argues that this critical shift would create a "transgressive ground of understanding" where new relations between texts are forged and create a space of intertextuality where we can "notice" ruptures and "momentary dislodgings" of normative anti-Black violence.[16] While one might not find liberal forms of "freedom" or the kind of freedom that one imagines and desires, the reader may be able to find a small opening and place to slip through the otherwise closed system of violence.

More specifically, in her reading of James Walvin's legal history *The Zong: A Massacre, the Law, and the End of Slavery* alongside M. NourbeSe Philip's long poem *Zong!*, McKittrick finds a mathematical discrepancy (more people could have clung to life and survived) in the accounting of the dead in the history and finds the Black livingness of the slave ship in Philip's poetics.[17] The variability of the archives alongside the creative texts' holding out for the possibility of Black life enables McKittrick and others committed to a similar project to "notice in the text a place where the data of the massacre" and the macabre "scientific accumulation of black death can no longer tell itself, in the present, through the terms that made it possible."[18] By reading de Brahm's map of settlement together and against Pinckney's anxiety-filled journal, I attempt to create intertextual terrain that reveals the map and its writing of the human as partial and incomplete. Further, I include an analysis of what might be called the provisional, informal, or phantasmagoric details of the map in my reading. In an effort to creatively seek out what McKittrick calls the "unutterable" and "black absented presence," I take seriously the unintended and ghostly reproduction of the Black figures drawn in cartouche.[19] Due to the way the pages of the maps were folded and pressed together, a palimpsestic trace of Black enslaved people working indigo gets reproduced again and again as faded duplication of the original image. I attend to the ways that this image works as a haunting and a reminder of the force of Black life.

Alongside the ways that I read archival material together and with an attention to Black life, I read the map through the theoretical lens provided by Wynter and da Silva. Wynter's body of work has tracked the emergence and evolution of how the human—as an overrepresentation of Man—has been written and rewritten for centuries. Using Wynter's schematics and theorizations of the vicissitudes of the notion of Man, I argue that de Brahm's eighteenth-century cartographic renderings write the human in the tradition of Man1. Writing of Man1, Wynter traces its emergence in the epistemic revolution of secular humanism that transformed the lowly laity into rational man in the fifteenth century. As rational man, the former subject of God and the clergy comes to know himself through establishing a Cartesian boundary between himself and the natural, or sensory-bound, elements of the world around him, including the lands and people of Africa and the Americas. De Brahm, himself a rational man of the eighteenth century, writes the British settler in the likeness of Man1 as a rational and reason-driven interior subject, in contrast to the sensuous and externally, or nature-driven, Black and Indigenous body. I argue that de Brahm and his British contemporaries are inheritors of what I call a "conquistador humanism" that emerges alongside the Christian humanism that transforms into the secular humanism of the Enlightenment. I refer to this kind of humanism as "conquistador" to tether eighteenth-century settlers to the anti-Black and genocidal violence that the discourse of settlement and settler colonialism disavows.

Further, drawing on the work of da Silva, I argue that de Brahm's map attempts to produce a kind of "scientific knowledge" that writes the British/European subject as a transcendent and interior subject by making—or, as da Silva argues, "engulfing"—the Black and Indigenous body as a representation of an outer determined thing.[20] As an outer determined and affectable outside crust or edge of humanity, Indigenous and Black bodies represent a lesser version of humanity. They are the outer edge of humanity in proximity to death and decay. They are incorporated into the category of the human (as others) only to carry the burden and destiny of being lesser beings that live in proximity to genocide and enslavement, or what da Silva calls the "horizon of death." Because Black and Indigenous bodies are buffers between nature and the chaos of exteriority, the transcendent European subject can maintain its interiority and ideal humanness as Man₁. While I render de Brahm's attempt to relegate Black and Indigenous exteriority and death visible, I also attend to the ways that Black and Indigenous life and unruliness surface both on the map and throughout the mid-eighteenth century to disrupt and shoal plans to produce humanity through the death of Blackness and Indigeneity.

DE BRAHM'S ANXIOUS LANDSCAPE

In 1753, the *South-Carolina Gazette* announced the need for a map and commissioned the surveyor William Gerard de Brahm, who had already conducted surveys of the land, documenting property lines, plots, soil types and quality, and the waterways in the area, to make the map.[21] Anxious White settlers hired de Brahm to design a map of their property, as well as a representation of their dreams and aspirations for the region. I visited the four very large quadrants of de Brahm's "1757 Map of the Coast of South Carolina and Parts of Georgia," pieced together like a puzzle in the study of Davidson College's Special Collections Division, in 2015.[22] The map measures 43.5 inches by 48.5 inches, or roughly four feet by four feet. One can imagine the scale of the map tempting a small child to step into it. The massive, arresting, and imposing map is split by a north-south axis represented by the coastline of the Atlantic that hugs the colonies of the southernmost portion of North Carolina, all of South Carolina, and the entire

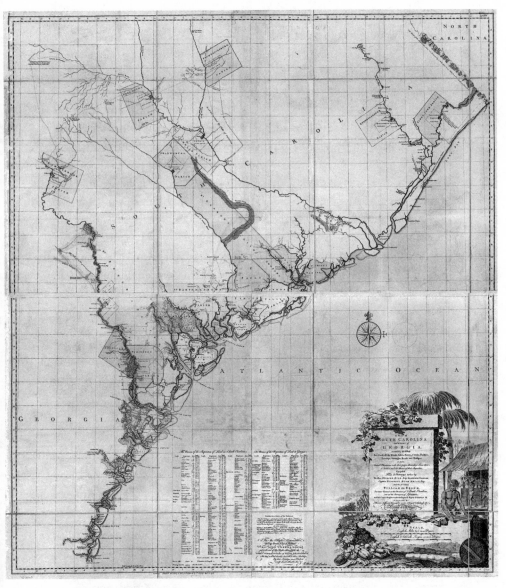

FIGURE 2.1. William Gerard de Brahm's "1757 Map of the Coast of South Carolina and Parts of Georgia." Credit: William Gerard de Brahm, 1757. Map of South Carolina and a Part of Georgia, Containing the Whole Sea-Coast. Courtesy of Archives and Special Collections Division of the E. H. Little Library, Davidson College.

coast of Georgia. The coastline both delineates ocean from land and simultaneously conjoins the coast and the Atlantic Ocean as a coherent system. The land and the sea almost equally shoulder the visual heft of the map.

Reading the map from left to right, or the northwest (quadrant one) to the northeast (quadrant two) and then down to the southwestern (quadrant three) and southeastern (quadrant four) regions, the eye is drawn to the mass of the images at the southern edge or bottom of the map. To the right (or east) of the southern portion of the South Carolina coastline a large ledger that also functions as the legend lists in columns the names of proprietors, as well as the lots that they own. The ledger is centered at the bottom of the map on the vertical axis (y-axis), split between the third and fourth quadrants of the map. The legend is placed in the exact bottom center of the map as the anchor. In the negative space of the Atlantic Ocean, an ornately detailed cartouche pulls the eye toward the southeastern corner of the map. With one side flush against the map's margins and the left edge floating in the ocean, the cartouche features an elaborate engraving (the original in vivid color) of enslaved people processing indigo. Unlike the map of the coast itself, the colorful and detailed cartouche is a large-scale image that zooms in on, or provides a close-up of, enslaved Black people processing indigo amid a lush landscape that abuts the shoreline of the Atlantic Ocean. Ocean vessels are represented in the background docked off the coast. The types of plants, the clothing worn by the enslaved, and even some detailed facial features are visible in the cartouche. The cartouche is a mirror image of the map of the shoreline as it flips and places the Atlantic Ocean on the viewer's left side (or on the map's western region).

On the reproduction of the map held by Davidson's Archives and Special Collections Division there is also a ghostly reproduction of the engraving of the Black bodies processing indigo that appears on the coastline to the west of the legend. For years, the map has been folded and stored in drawers on the sixth floor of the library which has caused a doubling of the image of the enslaved in the cartouche due to pressure, friction, the paper's porosity, the mutability of the ink, the time, and the climate. Although it is not visible in figure 2.1 or in the digital copies in the Library of Congress's digital repository, on the copy at Davidson, a ghostly imprint of the cartouche floats upside down above the original cartouche. The brick and mortar time-space of the archive, including its conservation protocols — which required ritual-like folding and storing of the map over time — thus offers another kind of encounter with the map. I draw attention to how the doubled image of the Black figures engaged in the processing of indigo in the cartouche reproduce, or double, themselves on the map for methodological reasons, as well as to draw attention to the force of Black life.

The palimpsestic image calls attention to the ways that the properties of the map press on, interact with, and remain in relation to one another over time. Methodologically, this palimpsestic quality has led me to enact another doubling or reproduction of the cartouche in chapter 3. There I explore the noxious space of indigo cultivation on the plantation as a Black place of being human on other terms. Furthermore, I call attention to the palimpsestic way in which the image of Black people appears and reappears on the map as way of looking for what McKittrick calls "Black livingness" and how its persistent trace opens up new questions and possibilities.[23] The ghostly doubling of the image of Africans processing indigo in some ways evokes for me the swelling crowd of Africans who poured into the streets during the Stono Rebellion, reportedly with a banner that read "liberty."[24] The doubling of the image also mimics the doubling (and swelling) of Black life that transformed a small gathering of people into a crowd, an army, and a full-fledged rebellion. The map's leaves pressed against one another over time created a substrate with ideal conditions for the image of Black people to reproduce themselves. Attending to the persistence of Black life points to ways of being attentive and open to Indigenous life. The palimpsestic nature of maps also enables a reading of the ways that British settlement was constituted by and depended on Indigenous geographies and patterns of place-making and daily life.

Even within contemporary disciplines such as environmental history, de Brahm's map is written about as a map in motion. In the twenty-first century, historians apply poststructuralist methods that allow for a deconstruction of the images, words, and meanings of the map while reading the map within eighteenth-century power relations. The environmental historian Mart Stewart has argued that maps created by the British empire in the eighteenth century are "imaginative constructions of a place as well as attempts to describe it."[25] Eighteenth-century maps functioned as crucial tools in the increasingly Euclidean organization and conquest of space. Held in high esteem, the 1757 map "has gained a reputation as the first 'scientific' or 'modern' map of southeastern North America."[26] The map became the standard source for geographical knowledge at the time and a model for other British maps during that period of the eighteenth century.[27] Keeping with the tradition of the day, when cartographers depicted social relations in the colonial Atlantic world they generally attempted to depict a single narrative about the struggles and triumphs of the British settlers over the landscape.[28]

In this map, like many others of the eighteenth century, de Brahm depicted British territories as they were "both described and hoped for in an agenda of development."[29] The "agenda of development" that the map reflected was as a vision of how British settlement hoped to change the landscape, as well as render the British subject as a cartographic human vis-à-vis Black and Indigenous human others (or lesser humans). By carefully subjecting de Brahm's map to a Black cartographic analysis, I intend to disrupt discourses of settlement and settler colonialism that attempt to disavow White conquest and violence. Settlement and settler colonialism cannot shake off the extermination of Indigenous peoples and the transformation of Black people into fungible forms of exchange. A countervisual analysis of de Brahm's map argues that conquest is in fact enacted through settlement and settler colonial regimes. More precisely, a form of conquistador humanism remains tethered to the eighteenth-century practices and scenes of British settlement that de Brahm depicted.

Conquistador humanism is the crafting and sustaining of European human life and self-actualization through Black and Indigenous death. Because what I am tracking in de Brahm's map and naming "conquistador humanism" occurred in the eighteenth century, it falls under the period that Wynter theorized as the "emergence of Man1." In that period of conquest and imperial expansion, the European settler represented the ideal self—or Man—and the Indigenous and Black (as well as the insane or "mad" in Europe) were considered "human others."[30] Conquistador humanism expresses itself through a diverse modality of material (political, economic, institutional, military regimes) and discursive (literature, art/aesthetics, cartography) forms. De Brahm, the settlers in South Carolina, and the British Crown enacted their own, unique form of conquistador humanism by cartographically writing themselves onto the landscape of the Atlantic Low Country through renderings of Black fungibility and Indigenous disappearance.

Mapping and cartography are versions of what da Silva has termed "modern text."[31] The cartographic process of rendering the British conquistador-settler as what Wynter calls the overrepresentation of "Man" and order also required the invention, rendering, and (re)mapping of Blackness and Indigeneity as states of nature and representations of chaos. Reading the Low Country landscape in relationship to how Black enslaved people were imagined as "nigger chaos" and Amerindian "chaos" lends itself to a reading of Blackness as a form of liquid chaos and Indigeneity as a chaotic terra nullius.[32] However, a closer look at the attempt to render Blackness and Indigeneity as forms of chaotic and sensuous natural features of the landscape to be tamed reveals an anxiety about the ungovernability of Black and Indigenous people. In other words, the mapping of Blackness and Indigeneity is an attempt to spatially fix and capture forms of Black fugitivity and Indigenous resistance that elude the British and present an existential threat throughout the eighteenth-century Atlantic world. This chapter's reading practice interrupts a single narrative of British triumph over the landscape and Black and Indigenous people in the mid-eighteenth century. Furthermore, this Black geographical reading maps the ways that the eighteenth century's protoscientific practice of cartography in the Atlantic world attempted to spatialize processes of subjectification.

De Brahm's map attempts to represent the human — or, more specifically, Wynter's Man₁ — as form of spatial coherence and logocentric order in relation to Black oceanic chaos and Native absence. Following da Silva, this Black geographical reading tracks how the White cartographic (Cartesian) subject anxiously is written into the map as the interior space of the shoreline. De Brahm's eighteenth-century map attempts to write the British human as an interior subject, or what da Silva calls the "Transparent I" in the face of the external Black and Native threat that haunts and flanks the edges of the map.[33] In terms of philosophical accounts of Man's, or the human's, relationship to reason, philosophers such as Descartes and Hegel imagined two kinds of beings (and minds): the transcendent and the affectable. According to da Silva, distinctions between the two were made according to a specific racial order. The transcendent subject, or "transparent I," that emerged in post-Enlightenment Europe is the kind of mind that is able to know how to emulate and control powers of universal reason.[34] The "affectable I" — in this case, the Black and Indigenous others that emerged in other global regions — possess the kind of mind that is subject to both exterior determination by the "laws of nature" and the superior force of the European mind.[35]

Replicating this racialized schema, de Brahm writes Black and Indigenous life as "affectable" others in the margins of the map, as represented by the sensuous ocean and the vast emptiness of chaotic, unsettled land. Because White cartographic subjectivity, as Man₁, is written through violence — and specifically, a violence that is always contested by the Black and

Indigenous margins—it remains anxious and under duress. Cartography, as a modern mode of writing the self, must grapple with a particular ethno-classes' failures and anxieties as much as their achievements. Of particular importance to this countercartographic reading practice is attending to how the depictions of spatial and symbolic White cartographic coherence—the "cartographic I"—remains an unsettled project. If we read for "Black life," as McKittrick urges us to, it is also possible to read for how de Brahm attempts to quell the anxiety produced by the tenuous and always incomplete project of conquest. The force of the presence of Black and Indigenous life as an existential threat to White life shoals and frustrates traditional readings of this map. Black and Indigenous people throughout the eighteenth century resisted conquistador humanism and its forms of settlement and place-making. Looking at the map with this resistance in mind, one can read it as an incomplete attempt to conquer Black and Indigenous people and settle the territory. The map might reveal that establishing, or writing, the White human as a stable and settled (yet transcendent) individual was not a fait accompli. Black movement and fugitivity, as well as Indigenous resistance and place-making, made the map a nervous landscape and forced the cartographic subject of conquistador humanism to remain a project under revision, or forever anxious.[36]

MAPPING HUMANITY AND ITS OTHERS

De Brahm's map is animated by three illustrative loci of ontological activity and capacity. The anchor of the map is represented by the list and textual representation of White property owners as human. The finely detailed and illustrative rendering of open-ended Black flesh that runs conterminously with the processing of indigo in the cartouche represents the property on the proprietors' list. And, finally, there is the large negative space indexing the "anaspace" of Savage/Enemy, in which the Native is imagined as a space that needs to be kept at bay until it is conquered. The map illustrates a complex story about how the idea of man is conceptualized and established through the production of Indigeneity as synonymous with the chaotic anaspace, or absence of the graphic (discursive) and Blackness as the chaotic open and fleshy material of spatial potential. Reading the ways that the human is violently rendered on this map exceeds the tools readily available in postcolonial and settler colonial methodological approaches and critiques. Conventional readings of colonial landscapes or setter colonial regimes purge this violence and present the transformations to the settled landscape as a natural and at times pastoral descriptions of modern progress. Moreover, if conflict on the landscape is rendered, it is generally depicted as a binary staging of master-slave or settler-Indigenous relations.

Wynter's triad of European-Indigene-Nigger and Wilderson's Settler/Savage/Slave trio guide this ontological reading of de Brahm's map in ways that interrupt the conventional landscape readings. In the context of analyzing de Brahm's map, a triadic model requires a consideration of how Indigeneity and Blackness serve as bookends, or points of an axis, that create a midpoint, or stabilizing point, for the human. Eighteenth-century British settlement, in the context of de Brahm's map, as a technology of conquest, uses mapping—or cartography—as a method of establishing a symbolic system that plots which kinds of humans will live in the regions of affectability, at what da Silva calls the "horizon of death," and which will live in the safety of interiority.[37] When one attends to de Brahm's map in this way, the White "Transcendental I" attempts to produce itself through spatializing Indigenous and Black people as "affectable" others.[38] Nestled in the center at the midpoint is White self-actualized humanity figured as the word or the state of interiority.[39] To be rendered as pure "logos" is to be fashioned as a geographical location of order, language, culture, place, home, humanness, self-actualization, the "Transcendental I," and settlement. Settled and civilized humanity inhabits the ecotonal space of the shore. While buffered by affectable Black bodies represented by the flux of the ocean and Indigenous bodies trapped in the back country of chaotic wilderness, the White "cartographic I" anxiously and continuously has to rewrite and remap the fragile ecozone and shoal of the shoreline as a proprietary and bounded space of logos and order. The production of the White conquistador-settler is an ongoing process of violent autopoesis that must be continually written and revised.

Despite conventional reasoning that would posit that the only humans who appear on the eighteenth-century map are Black ones, I argue that the privileged position of humanity is that which remains beyond the realm of embodied visuality. Rather than appearing as embodied, or not appearing at all, true humanity—or Man1—is made visible and legible through the word and protoscientific coding. The space and place of the White human is established not by embodied and physical representation but through a signification system composed of text, grid lines, and logocentric and geometric symbols that establish subjectivities with cartographic authority through the symbols of property possession.

Legends orient humans. They dictate which way is upright. The visual anchor and center of de Brahm's map, the legend, is located in the middle of its southern border. The chart, titled "The Names of Proprietors of Land in South Carolina," contains four large columns labeled, from left to right, "Lands," "Proprietors," and "Lots." The names of the proprietors are listed alphabetically by last name, which link the individuals listed to stable and, it is hoped, timeless human genealogies of finely pedigreed individuals and families. Both men and women are listed as proprietors; in the context of eighteenth-century colonial property ownership in the Low Country, European (White) human women are also absorbed within the cartographic category of the self-possessed human.

The proprietors are not represented in embodied form on the map. The map was created in the midst of the scientific revolutions and epistemic shifts of the Enlightenment prompted by the planetary migration and exchange of objects, people, and ideas in the era of colonization. Cartesian philosophy, which established the doctrine "I think, therefore I am," aligned thought, order, and rationality with the contours of the natural-rational human. Descartes rendered the axiom open to a spatial representation as he distanced the brain from the body. De Brahm's map also reflects distinctions and separations made between the realm of the sensuous body and the sphere of higher order activity in the brain. The Cartesian regime of representation written into the map becomes a mode of recognizing and understanding the White self (rational human) in relationship to the rest of the less than human sensuous and affectable realm of nature.

In de Brahm's map, the human is largely present as a series of symbolic representations that are largely logocentric and graphically represented through geometric shapes that stand in for places. Places are identifiable locations of activity that attribute role, stature, gender, and relationships among humans.[40] The presence of the White settler as human is established through name and title. The name and the title of the settlers (both men and women are represented) are linked to a plot of property that they own. The map reflects the White human as a possessor of things. In fact, the White human as proprietor possesses the objects and bodies that appear on the map. De Brahm was commissioned to make the map for the very people whose names appear on the ledger of proprietors, and it is from their perspective that the map of territory and possession is viewed. De Brahm made the map for their eyes. More specifically, de Brahm made

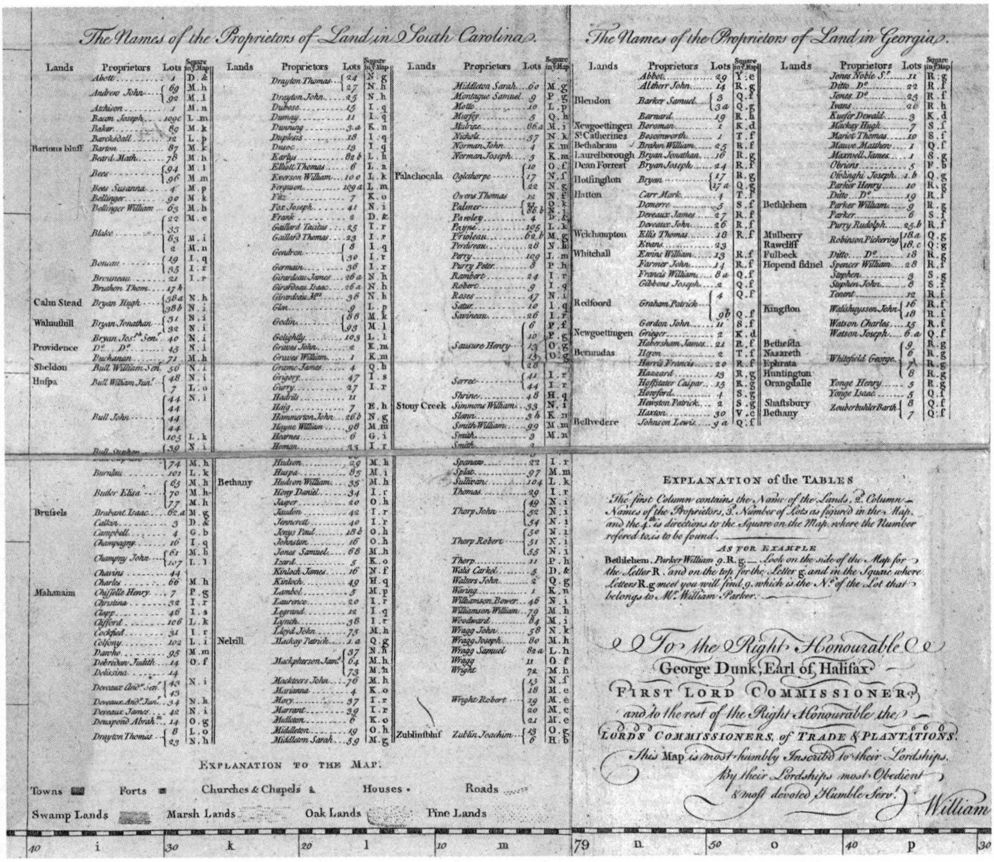

FIGURE 2.2. Legend from de Brahm map, with list of property owners.

the map for the White proprietors eyes to visualize and externalize the space, land, and bodies as territory and property. The map as an inventory, spatialization, and fetishization of possessions does not provide a context within which the White human figure can appear as a body. The reliance on text over the image both hides the White body and, more important, functions to elide the violence enacted by the White body on Black and Indigenous flesh. Even as the White body is excessively and sensuously engaged in the erotics of plantation violence and the horrific acts of genocide, White bodies and violent acts they commit are hidden by the textual representation of Whiteness as order, civilization, and logos.

Humanness, as well as the violence entailed in making the human, appears as an elaborate code with a key on the map. The human and its rational logocentrism becomes a stand-in for the progress of settlement while

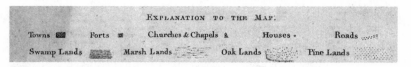

FIGURE 2.3. Key to de Brahm map with symbols for built structures, swampland, and tree types.

hiding the genocidal violence that unmakes Indigenous life and captures Black sentience. The coding system marks the locations of places that define the human world as a space of culture and civilization. If one looks closely, one might notice that the human coding system (only) partially erases traces of Native people's occupancy, use, and settlement and disappears Indigenous peoples' relations to the earth, the water, and one another with eighteenth-century representations of place-making. In palimpsestic fashion, Indigenous relations to the earth and nonhuman ecologies peek or leak through on the map. I discuss the palimpsestic resistance — or resurgence — of the Indigenous on the map later.

On de Brahm's eighteenth-century map, geometric humanist conventions are used to define and mark place as symbols of human and British civilization: towns are dark rectangles; forts are open circles in the middle of shaded squares; churches and chapels are ampersands; houses are dots; swamplands, marshlands, oak lands, and pinelands are equal signs; and roads are parallel hashed lines. While the roads appear to overwrite the entire landscape, their very presence, and their overlapping with Indigenous trails, indicates that White settlement could not exist without the elaborate route and trail system developed by the Cherokee and the Catawba. By covering up and writing over the trails, paths, and travel patterns of the Cherokee, Catawba, and Creek, whose ancestors inhabited the area, de Brahm gives presence to the Indigenous place-making that the violence of cartography seeks to destroy. De Brahm's method of cartographically eliminating Indigenous presence at once works to announce it and, if read with Indigenous life in mind, allows Indigenous movement and geographical relations to speak back through the map.

Another form of the cartographic disavowal of genocide and slavery — and its failure — can be deciphered in the place-naming practices of the settlers. In the column labeled "Land," groups of discrete lots were named in the aggregate "Barton's bluff" and "Calm Stead." It is telling that, during a time of considerable upheaval in the form of slave rebellions, as well as war with the Cherokee and the Creek and with the French and Spanish navies, landowners chose to name property "Calm Stead." Following Stewart's argument that the map reflects settlers' aspirations, one can interpret "Calm Stead" not simply as a disavowal of the violence that was necessary to make conquistadors into settlers but also as an aspiration and, perhaps, a prayer. In other words, the ever present specter of Black and Indigenous rebellion may have inspired place names that spoke of a future free from this existential threat.

Indigenous genocide is also written into the map in the manner in which White space is graphically distinguished from Indigenous space. White humanity has the detail of place, while Indigenous communities are rendered by an unmarking and unmaking of place. The marshes, pinelands, and swamps controlled and put to use by White humans are rendered in greater graphic detail than the spaces in which Indigenous peoples live. According to Stephanie Pratt, in the seventeenth through the eighteenth centuries Native Americans were removed from maps' interiors, which included legends and cartouches, and relocated to the decorative margins.[41] Then they were removed altogether. No humanist geometric symbols for housing, sacred spaces, roads, paths, or meeting places are visible in the empty areas where Indigenous presence is delineated. Although the land of the Cherokees is represented as anaspace void of property, civilization, life, and geo-humanist symbols, the Cherokees' elaborate routes and networks are the templates and infrastructure used to map and construct the roads and passages visible on the eighteenth-century map.

The enormous power of the symbolic economy of the map is dense and ontological. Symmetrical rectangles mark property; inside the rectangles, the names of territories' townships or settlements are written in evenly spaced eighteenth-century British script, with each letter capitalized. Symbols grant life on de Brahm's map. Even the crude graphic symbols for community, activity, organization, and life contain an unending conceptual economy of narrative possibility. Symbols can be filled in with the hopes and desires of Whiteness that represent White people's presence and longevity across time and space. On its face, the symbolic economy of Whiteness on de Brahm's map, while not producing any representations of White bodies, provide Whiteness with a level of graphic and symbolic expression that appears to give it the ability to enact narrativity, futurity, hope, and the possession of space through the word and the modern text. However, when one reads this White logocentric futurity within the context of Black critical cartography, guided by McKittrick's Black practice of noticing, the spare and empty locations of the Cherokee represented as

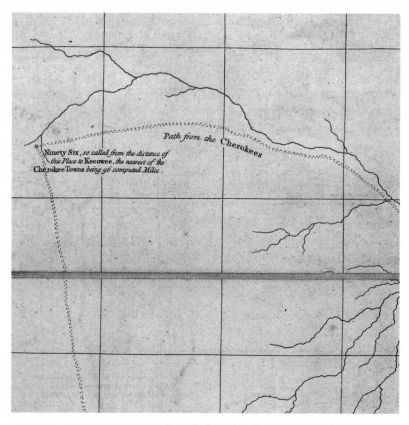

FIGURE 2.4. Northwestern quadrant of de Brahm map, with written directions indicating the "Path from the Cherokees."

crude points—specifically, points from which one needs to retreat (e.g., "Path from the Cherokees")—tell a different story. In the spare and unmarked anaspace of Cherokee camps, the simple directive on the map to the settlers that reads "Path from the Cherokees" indicates that Cherokee presence prevented unfettered movement by settlers into the northwest. In fact, settlers' attempts to move there were stopped. While de Brahm's map attempted to function as a device for foretelling a future of White cartographic domination and self-actualization, this narrative of White mobility and settlement was suspended. More important, the Black and Native subjectivity that the map tries to disavow is the very existence that gives Whiteness its boundaries and limits in ways that require White and human reinvention.

Relegated to the northwestern corner of the map and visually removed from the water, Cherokee, Chickasaw, and Catawba peoples are depicted as fixed, inert forms stuck in a barren and static edge, away from the life-giving movement of the Atlantic. Erasing the presence of other nations and language groups in the region, de Brahm only places and names the "Chikesaw Camp, Catawba Nation and the Cherokees" on the map.

The edge of the map is a space of crude lines, boxes, and open space devoid of symbols that index human activity on the landscape. The Cherokee, Chickasaw, and Catawba spaces on the map represent dying spaces outside the time and space of the oceanic. This is a violent, colonial production of space in that it does not represent the prior relationships the Cherokee, Chickasaw, and Catawba shared with the Atlantic—the banks, tributaries, rivers, streams, inlets, islands, and Low Country watersheds—before they were removed from those areas. The Cherokee, Catawba, and Chickasaw related to the watershed and the ocean in complicated ways.

Native nations and people on the eastern seaboard developed intricate trade and communication routes along waterways. In *The Common Pot*, Lisa Brooks gives an account of the tradition of cartographic representation—*awikhiganak* and wampum—of the northeastern Abenaki, members of the Algonquin language group, both before and after European contact.[42] During the seventeenth century, the Abenaki writing system called Awikhiganak "conveyed knowledge from one person or place to another across the system of waterways that connected them."[43] Rivers and streams were prominent features of Indigenous maps. Brooks argues, "It was along these waterways that messages were carried from village to village."[44] In addition to using the waterways as a system of transit exchange and connection, nations of the Northeast, such as the Abenaki, Yamasee, Cherokee, Chickasaw, Creek, and Catawba used birch bark and other surfaces to make graphic representations of hunting routes, trails, and other important locations. Women's woven wampum beads and belts created another way to represent relationships among nations, as well as communal and spatial narratives.[45]

One of the ways that Brooks excavates Abenaki and other Indigenous people's spatial writing (and mapping) is by reading the colonial archive. Similar to the Black geographical reading practice I employ, Brooks mines the journals of French Jesuits such as Chrétien Le Clercq to "notice" the presence and resistance of Algonquin and Abenaki people. French settlers' diaries such as Le Clercq's contained details about Abenaki space-making practices that included birch maps, petitions (complaints about settlers' aggression and land use), Indigenous footpaths, trade routes, and nation-to-nation communication. French settler colonial archives helped Brooks recover information about the uses of bark maps, the level of a map's detail, denotations related to scale, and complex notions of time. While Le Clercq was on the Wabanaki coast in the village of Kespek in 1677, he noted the "ingenuity in drawing upon bark a kind of map which marks exactly all the rivers and streams of a country of which they wish to make a representation. They mark all the places thereon exactly and do well that they make use of them successfully, and an Indian who possesses one makes long voyages without going astray."[46] According to the Jesuit archives, the making of birch maps was a cartographic method that was passed from generation to generation.[47] Running counter to this French colonial archive of Indigenous space-making, de Brahm's cartographic archive tells a story of Indigenous people out of space or constituting spatial lack.

In de Brahm's representation of space, Indigenous peoples are stripped of a relationship with islands, inlets, rivers, and creeks and the delicate rhythms that needed to be established to coexist with them. Even more important, his map disavows the ways that the water, the inlets, rivers, and land functioned as parts of the Indigenous body, cosmology, and linguistic systems. Mishuana Goeman argues that, through colonialism, European-conceived scales—units of accumulation—have been imposed on the biosphere, turning the environment into separate spaces such as "reservations, nation states, continents, [and] hemispheres," in addition to land and water.[48] To counter this kind of scalar fragmentation, Goeman argues for "indigenous conceptions of land as connected, rather than land as disaggregate," to be centered. Specifically, Goeman references the ways that Pacific Islanders' relationship to water can inform how we map and understand concepts of space. The Pacific Island scholars Vince Diaz and Alice Te Punga Somerville have positioned water as connected with the currents rather than water as that which divides continents, islands, and land.[49] In addition to reorienting one's relationship to the land and water as connected systems in a decolonial spatial practice, exposing the historical and ongoing violence that separated the land and the ocean—and, more important, Indigenous people—from the water is of utmost importance. Coastal Indigenous peoples were removed from the life-giving space of the water through military force and transformed into combatants pushed to the edge of the map in 1757.

As the Native is pushed from the center of the map (the coast) to the lifeless exterior, the exterior (wilderness) is turned into a "horizon of death."[50] The Indigenous region in the northwest is intended as an ana-space, or nonplace, and is marked on the map specifically as a coordinate or point from which to flee. A curved line extends from the point, running almost parallel to the Santee River, with the textual caption below it reading, "Path from the Cherokee." As stated earlier, the untamed interior is depicted as a violent space, representing a geographical and existential limit that humans must escape or avoid.[51] De Brahm's spatial perspective is informed by his participation in wars with the Cherokee and other Native nations. The space where the Indigenous "enemy combatant" lives is also potentially a space of literal death for the British.

The distance from, or how to get away from, the Cherokee is marked as important. For example, in the northwestern portion of the map, a line marking a junction in the upper watershed of the Santee is labeled "Ninety Six, so called from the distance of the Place to Keowee." According to Stewart, "The nearest of the Cherokee towns was 96 computed miles" from the British settlements.[52] Reading the map from left to right — or in the direction of linearity and progress — the line or path "from the Cherokee" maps a movement away from savagery and toward a state of humanity. At the time that the map was commissioned, Eliza Lucas Pinckney resided in the Charles Town area of South Carolina. In her letter book she described life in the late 1750s and early 1760s while living under the threat of violence from the Cherokee, as well as the kind of brutality employed by the settlers to contain them. In a letter to a contemporary dated 1760, Pinckney reports details of a military expedition into Cherokee territory:

The Honorable, Mrs. King

Febr. 1760

Gov. Lyttelton with our army are safely returned from their Cherokee Expedition, where they want to demand satisfaction for the murders committed on our people — the first Army that ever attempted to go into that wild Country. They had been very insolent and commited several Murders and Outrages in our back settlements, nor ever expected white men would have resolution enough to march up their Mountains. Mr. Lyttelton has acted with great spirit and conduct and gained much honour in the affair, and obtained from them what Indians never before granted: such of the murderers as they could then take and Hostages for the rest till they could be taken. If you have any curiosity to know more particulars Mr. Morly to whom I inclose it can furnish you with the Carolina Gazett.[53]

Describing the Cherokee territory as "that wild Country," Pinckney reinforces the notion of Cherokee and Native space as uncivilized. In 1760, the Cherokee were geographically positioned as up in "their Mountains." Again, this reference marks the Cherokee people as a mountain and inland people, with no relation to the Atlantic. They attack Whites in the "back settlements" and the South Carolina frontier, as opposed to the shoreline, from which Indigenous peoples—specifically, the Keowee, Cherokee, Yamasee, and Muscogee—have been removed. A footnote to the letter provides bloody details of one of the British expeditions of 1760:

> Mr. Lyttelton decided to hold twenty-four Indian hostages at fort Prince George until an equal number of trouble making Indians were surrendered to him, an action David Duncan Wallace has called "immoral and stupid." Twenty-three Indian murderers were handed over to Lyttelton. Lyttelton left twenty-one hostages at the Fort until even more Indians were surrendered. When enraged Indians retaliated by raiding settlements along the South Carolina frontier and even attacked Fort Prince George on February 14, 1760 the garrison murdered the hostages. Historians have criticized Lyttelton for his handling of the Cherokee situation, but he received a royal welcome when he returned to Charleston on January 8, 1760.[54]

The White community on the South Carolina coast thus celebrated the slaughter and conquest of the Cherokee.

A number of strategies were used to contain, subdue, and murder the Cherokee. All of these measures and means are a part of an ensemble of activities that constitute genocide and conquest. Taking Cherokee hostages and imprisoning them at the fort and at military prisons in South Carolina is a practice of spatial containment and dehumanization that was also used for Black fugitives and escaped slaves.[55] Imprisonment as an early U.S. spatial formation was a constituent feature of eighteenth-century modes of conquest in what would become North America. Because the Cherokee were not naturalized as slaves (and thus as spatial potential) and commodities in the region at the time, they represented barriers to the creation of space. Representing symbols of anaspace and spatial foreclosure, as well as an existential threat to White settler society, the Cherokee were murdered instead of held captive as slaves.

De Brahm's prior efforts to help the British build forts certainly advanced ongoing efforts to commit genocide against the Cherokee in the mid- and late eighteenth century. These documented accounts of the aggression of the British toward the Cherokee enable a reframing and renaming of the settler as a conquistador. The conquistador-settlers also established this map as a map of Indigenous conquest, as its attempt at disavowal is through tropes and images of settlement. Reading this map alongside Pinckney's diary entries also reveals an era of Cherokee and Indigenous vitality—prior to a portion of their nation's own practice of enslaving Black captives—through their ongoing military campaigns against the settlers. While the Cherokee are read as an ongoing threat and source of anxiety residing at the margins of the map, the White anxiety that they produced in settlers such as Pinckney evoke them as an ever present life force and competing way of life during the drafting of the map.

THE RUSE OF SETTLEMENT

Scholarly effort has been devoted to distinguishing this particular era of settlement as a relatively benign one that preferred nonengagement with the Cherokee. Mart Stewart insists that historians use de Brahm's map to read against the grain of conventional interpretations that depict the British as envisioning an advancing and westward-moving frontier in the mid-eighteenth century. He calls for a more tempered reading of the spatial dynamics and aspirations of the British during the late 1750s. In his fifth endnote, he argues against reading this map in a way that gives too much credence to imperialist or genocidal aims. Stewart cautions readers against too facilely viewing the map as a blueprint for conquest: "It is too easy to read imperialist ambition into the blank open spaces to the west in early maps of the North American coast. Many maps, including this one, were more focused on positioning coastal settlements and the potential for coastal development into a relationship with a larger Atlantic world rather than a North American one."[56]

Stewart attempts to argue against an imperialist (or advancing movement of the British) reading of the map by attributing to de Brahm a capacity for acknowledging Cherokee and Catawba autonomy. He uses de Brahm's textual denotation of Indigenous territories on the map as evidence of a recognition of Native place and, perhaps sovereign borders. "De Brahm's *acknowledgment of Cherokee and Catawba autonomy* on the map was six years before a negotiated boundary, the Proclamation of 1763," he writes, adding that the marking added a clear boundary to western settlement and subverted the assumptions about settlement advance that some readers have identified in the blank spaces in the west of this and other maps.[57] De Brahm makes a point of including on the map the inscription "Path from the Cherokee" that appears as a directive to the contemporary inhabitants, as well as to future ones. If it was a directive, it was certainly one that was not always heeded. As Pinckney's letter to Mrs. King reveals, there were multiple military missions into Cherokee country rather than movement away from it.

The inscription of these eighteenth-century "lines of flight" away from Cherokee territory function as a ruse for the kinds of aggressive and genocidal military strategies that would secure British supremacy, sovereignty, and spatial domination in North America.[58] All forms of European settlement in North America occurred within the context of Western expansion and Indigenous genocide. Since a path "from" these territories exists, there is an implied reference to prior forward movement, or a path "into" into the territories that would require a retreat. The so-called recognized and autonomous boundaries of the Cherokee clearly have been transgressed if an escape route needs to be mapped. While progress appeared to be oriented toward the dynamic and expansive potential of the ocean and oceanic Black bodies, the land in the West could be imagined as space — or frontier — to move into and then fold back into the shoreline. If de Brahm and settlers could imagine the shoreline as moving and advancing west, perhaps the backward wild frontier could become incorporated into the eastern space of the modern Atlantic shore as well.

Eighteenth-century (and all) settlement, including its speculative projections and cartographic sketches and representation, was always violent and embedded in the larger project of conquest. The emergence of "paths from" and "lines of flight" hide the ongoing violence and carnage that resulted from military and quotidian violence committed against the Indigenous people in the southeast. In a remarkably similar fashion to de Brahm, Gilles Deleuze and Félix Guattari engage in a form of disembodied disavowal of the genocidal violence that accompanies White self-actualization. In 1757, that disembodied White disavowal took the guise of a "Path from the Cherokee," or a cartographic misrepresentation of White humanity and settlement as enacting a retreat from and respect for Native life. The ruse of nonengagement, no contact, and bodilessness effectively enacts a disappearing of the militaristic and deadly violence of conquest. This ruse of a benign and bodiless (White) settlement without blood and violence is reproduced in the twentieth century by Deleuze and Guattari's nonrepresentational and rhizomatic lines of flight. In the introduction to *A Thousand Plateaus*, they laud the American, rhizomatic West as an ideal landscape of unfettered experimentation full of connections, ruptures, and unpredictable lines of flight. For Deleuze and Guattari, the rhizomatic frontier is a space where American capitalism and its multiplicative and dynamic movement creates a space of pure open possibility.

Byrd's interrogation of the "colonial nostalgia" latent in Deleuze and Guattari's rhizome is an explicit example of how the violence of White nonrepresentational theory creates an immediate space of impasse for Indigenous, decolonial, Black, and abolitionist intellectual traditions. As Byrd argues, the Deleuzian and Guattarian rhizome assumes its errant, untraceable, and de- and reterritorializing path through Native genocide. The rhizome obtains its metaphorical and theoretical elasticity from the discursive genocide of Indigenous peoples. The ground or territory of maneuver on which the rhizome gains its bearing is unwittingly or perhaps indifferently anchored in the disavowal of Indigenous ancestral claims, history, presence, and ongoing relationship with the land in North America. Deleuze and Guattari covet the free-range and bloody movements in the West, which is described as a land of "Indians without Ancestry" primarily because they do not have to contend with the presence of Indigenous peoples and their prior relationships (ancestors) to the land and space through which they move and clear as nomads. There are no existing people to whom Deleuze and Guattari must be accountable. Therefore, their own and others' self-actualizing, free-form Whiteness can proceed unimpeded: the rhizomatic West — *terra nullius* — is without a people, history, or a cosmology to navigate.

Byrd's reading of Deleuze and Guattari's reproduction or transit of the "Indian" in their book *A Thousand Plateaus* limns some of the methods in which colonialism and modes of conquest are enacted on behalf of the self-actualization of White subjects who produce nonrepresentational theory.[59] In fact, Byrd argues that the "Indian is the ontological prior through which poststructuralism functions."[60] Byrd traces the appearance or deployment of the Indian as a simulation or "present absent" in Deleuze and Guattari's work, which creates space for the White subject and the unending frontier. Byrd also argues that nonrepresentational theory heralded as a liberatory path beyond the subject is colonialist. Byrd indicts Deleuze and Guattari's use of Leslie Fiedler's work in order to invoke the American West and the Indian as exceptional cases that inspire rhizomatic movement through the notion of an ever-receding frontier.[61] It is colonialist on (at least) two accounts: in its need to render the Indian already and inevitably (onto-logically) dead as "it" has no ancestors or living community to whom one need be accountable; and in its invocation of the vanishing "Indian," which opens up the possibility of an ever-receding frontier and inspiration for the metaphor of the rhizome. This logic and mode of conquistador thought undergirds the Deleuzian and Guattarian ethos of experimental and rhi-zomatic lines of flight. Their nonrepresentational theory of lines of flight is only possible as a form of White self-actualizing posthumanism due to the death of Indigenous peoples and their excision from the Earth/land. White posthumanism and its flows and lines of flight are made possible through Native death.[62]

One of the reasons that the White imagination, the vicissitudes of capi-tal, and the unfettered experimentation and potential-filled settlement can proceed in this way is the landscape of "Indians without Ancestry." Deleuze and Guattari engage in a discursive genocide of Indigenous peoples from the conceptual and philosophical landscape in a manner very similar to de Brahm's erasure of Indigenous life through the elimination of a carto-graphic symbolic system that represented Indigenous people and their an-cestry. Yet counter-cartographies that enflesh flat spaces and embed In-digenous stories and place-making into the map are geographies that need to be used in tandem with archival spatial records to craft more critical cartographies.

BLACK CARTOGRAPHIES OF FUNGIBLE SPACE

On de Brahm's map, the Atlantic is a privileged geographical feature along with the natural and manmade watershed areas that are depicted as spaces of vitality, exchange, and commerce. Water is life and cartographically rep-resents the promises inherent in the changing and flourishing coastal land-scapes of the eighteenth century British Atlantic world. The life, movement, vitality, and speculative futurity of the traffic of Black bodies, commodities, technology, and ideas encapsulates the organizing theme and ethos of the map. Spaces that have a relationship to the ocean become linked indexi-cally to time, space, progress, and civilized colonial space.[63] The move-ment of the Atlantic and smaller bodies of water and natural transitions of the landscape from sea to shore, shore to grassland, grassland to trees, and trees to hills, as well as manmade alterations such as marshlands, swamps, oat lands, pinelands, and agriculture, that set the landscape in a state of flux are privileged as they index the progressive movement of empire. Even the plantation on this map becomes oceanic space (in proximity to water) where Black bodies are used to materialize the space of the plantation and White self-actualization on the shore.

De Brahm's inclination to respect the contingency of nature also made the dynamic movement of the ocean a prominent and central feature of the map. The Atlantic, and specifically what Paul Gilroy refers to as the "Black Atlantic," played an integral role in how de Brahm understood the coast to be a landscape in motion. Like the coasts, waterways, and ocean, the prominent Black bodies in the cartouche work to link discrete and often asymmetrical features of the empire (palm trees from different regions, chemical processes) seamlessly into a coherent whole. More than being embedded within this fluid and water-like economy and system of exchange, Blackness can be read as representing the ebbs and flows, or push and pull, on the power relations in the emergent British Empire and within the larger Atlantic world.

While Blackness and Black people are certainly linked to and metaphorized through the ocean and water, I would argue that Black life and representations of Black embodiment, people, and Blackness exceed frames of liquidity. Stewart notes that de Brahm's theme of change and contingency animates the entire map. This theme of change and transition is perhaps most apparent in the narrative conveyed by the cartouche. As the most vivid, detailed, and prominent feature of the map, the cartouche is the true anchor and cornerstone of this eighteenth-century visual story. Placed in the right-hand bottom corner of the map (in the Atlantic Ocean), it is a large-scale etching that effectively zooms in to feature daily plantation activity on the shores of the Atlantic. The Black forms on the cartouche represent intermediary spaces, temporal shifts, spatial possibility, units of exchange, and instability and doubt. The depiction of Black flux and movement on the cartouche is a symbol of both fecundity and danger.

The cartouche is elaborately detailed and animated by moving "humanlike figures" of the enslaved, a coastline, the sea, ships in the distance, foliage, plant life, and a multistage depiction of indigo processing. It was designed to depict the kind of abundance that was being achieved, and hoped for, within the discrete spaces of the individual plots of property that are marked off with lines on the map. The depth, color, and perspective in which the flora and fauna are rendered on the cartouche try to capture what the "natural eye" might perceive (some day). Lush trees and vegetation in the foreground recede into a sandy, shore-like landscape in the background. Ships are docked just offshore in the ocean. Even farther in the background, in what would be the southwestern corner of the territory pictured, the landscape inclines into a hilltop. In the immediate foreground to the left, or east of the dynamic movement of the Black figures and the chemical processes of fermentation, are "squash, watermelon, pumpkins and leaves."[64] In the cartouche they appear to take on a decorative function that symbolizes the (soon to be) real, yet they also represent an artificial and illustrative border to the large stone stele that holds the map's title. The depictions of harvest and abundance illustrated through the diversity of flora, fauna, and cash crops, both imported and cultivated, indicate a degree of mastery over the land by the colonizer.

Considering this theme of transformation, fecundity and the possibility of continual change are important for interpreting the presence of Black bodies on these scenes of cultivation and speculation. Change, exchange, and transition were cycles and fluctuations on the landscape that also mapped onto the vicissitudes of daily life for White settlers, enslaved Black people, and Indigenous people in the region. Spatially and ecologically, Black figures function more explicitly than Indigenous people as sites of transit, or passageways, in the cartouche and within the larger map. An intermediary kind of spatial work takes place at the site of Black flesh in de Brahm's map. Like the coconut tree that functions in an intercessory role to link to distinct colonial landscapes (India, the British Caribbean, and South Carolina and the Low Country) separated by miles of oceans together, Black bodies function as visual devices and sites of transit that enable diverse ecological forms and cycles to work together rhythmically.

While Black bodies are depicted as extensions of oceanic processes of movement and change, Blackness exceeds the metaphor of liquidity on the map. Blackness, particularly Black fungibility, figures as an important symbolic, conceptual economy and universe of unending exchange and metaphorical possibility. Fungibility is an important analytic and metaphor to consider as it moves and shape-shifts in ways that cannot be predicted; nor is it overdetermined by notions of liquidity and the connotations already attached to the oceanic and fluid. I introduce how fungibility functions in the eighteenth-century Low Country, using Black feminist and trans theories and critical geographies and cartographies. I argue that within the de Brahmian imaginary, Blackness becomes a metonym for process and transition that can be found in every natural and supernatural element.

For example, in the context of indigo and rice production cycle in the Low Country, Black enslaved people meditated the transition between these agricultural processes. Before rice can be processed on fields where indigo previously grew, a time needed to be determined to submerge the soil and bring about or impose an ecotone-like or transitionary phase to the soil. The enslaved bodies depicted within the scene of indigo processing, once done with the cycle of indigo harvesting, transformed the soil into a substrate suited for the production of rice. More than laborers, and as facilitators and initiators of this temporal change—indigo time to rice time—the Black figures in the cartouche both mark and determine these agricultural temporal moments as states of change.[65] Even though this shift was directed by the dictates and temporality of late mercantile capitalism, this very temporality depended on and was thus subject to how and when enslaved Black people enacted "rice and indigo time." Black people become the intercessor, or intermediary figure, between two or more agricultural processes, spaces, and temporalities.

Recently, scholars in the humanities have returned to the environmental sciences and, specifically, to the literature on "ecotones"—or transitionary spaces between different soil types or landscapes (water and shore, plain and mountain)—as a metaphor for mapping power and systems of representation in postcolonial contexts.[66] Black bodies as ecotones (and shoals), or what environmental scientists would identity as transitions in the landscape, function as symbols of liminal, in-between spaces and phases in dynamic processes. Seeing and thinking about this map in this manner enables a way of seeing/imagining Blackness and Whiteness as a set of ecotones, shoals, and processes of becoming. Blackness, particularly Black fungibility, figures as an important symbolic, conceptual economy and a universe of unending metaphorical possibility.

I situate Black fungibility within the theorizations of Black enslaved bodies as unanchored and malleable open signs of what Spillers describes as "territories of cultural and political maneuver" to be arranged and rearranged indefinitely.[67] Within the tradition of Spillers, as well as Saidiya Hartman, the concept of fungibility denotes and connotes pure flux, process, and potential. While Spillers does not explicitly employ the term "fungibility" to talk about the commodity-like status of Black bodies in states of change and exchange, her scholarship does address Black bodies as open spaces of shifting "signification and representation" that humans use to make meaning of their lives.

While conceptualizing Blackness as a commodity is not novel, the exchange of the commodity beyond a one-to-one relationship with similar commodity forms differs from the normative notion of fungibility proffered by economic approaches. In this alternative account, the exchange and circulation of Black bodies becomes an open-ended commodity form that can stand in for other commodity forms and other meanings, an important one being the "raw material" of the human.[68] To annunciate this point, scholars often invoke Spillers's verdant prose describing Black "ungendered" flesh as "territories of cultural and political maneuver" in the New World.[69] Pliable and exchangeable, Blackness is a form of malleable potential and a state of change in the "socio-political order" of the New World. In chapter 3, drawing further on the work of Hartman, Spillers and C. Riley Snorton, I discuss how this flesh becomes a site of radical "rearrangement" and "reorganization."[70]

Hartman appropriates the political-economic term "fungibility" to explain the elasticity and exchangeability of Black bodies, arguing that the enslaved embody the abstract "interchangeability and replaceability" endemic to the commodity.[71] But unlike a strict political economic framework's emphasis on exchangeability as a commodity form, Hartman's Black body has figurative and metaphorical value that extends into the realm of the poststructural slippage of the discursive and symbolic. Like Spillers, Hartman destabilizes the one-to-one exchange ratio that a fungible commodity generally retains in economic theory to posit that Black fungible bodies have unlimited figurative and metaphorical value.[72] Explaining this elasticity and flux, Hartman redefines fungibility's relationship to Blackness by stating, "The fungibility of the commodity makes the captive body an abstract and empty vessel vulnerable to the projection of others' feelings, ideas, desires, and values."[73] Black fungibility is the treatment of the Black enslaved body as an open sign that can be arranged and rearranged for infinite kinds of use. According to Spillers's and Hartman's accounts of the slippages that occur during the transit of exchanges, the Black fungible body and its signs can be made metal, liquid, dust, indigo, and more.

FUNGIBLE FLESH

In stark contrast to the abstract symbolism of disembodied Whiteness as the owner of the map, the Black body on the cartouche is rendered in exquisite detail and precise realism. In some senses, Black bodies are represented in almost ideal symmetry and are the closest to approximating the physical ideal of the human "male" form. However, the humanlike form depicted on the map depicts something other than — and in excess of — the grace, respect, dignity, and sovereignty of the eighteenth-century human

FIGURE 2.5. Cartouche from de Brahm map depicting enslaved people processing indigo.

form. That is, the "humanizing" aesthetics that appear on the cartouche are not ones used to advance the cause of abolition. Rather, the healthy, fit, and idealized bodies convey the slave traders' and owners' desires for the optimal commodity, or the "pieza," described by scholars such as C. L. R. James and Wynter as the standard and ideal body that becomes a unit of exchange. In the mid-eighteenth century, the premium and standard commodity unit would be a young Black man age fifteen to twenty-five.[74] De Brahm's engraver and illustrator enfleshes the unit of exchange with vivid detail on the cartouche.

Why would Blackness, or the Black captive, be represented in such an idyllic way on an eighteenth-century map that sought to impose a racial order in which Blackness represented the bottom rung on the chain of being? If the realistic and humanlike rendering is not intended to depict humanity, how can one make sense of the use of detail, depth, perspective, and even color on the original map? Control is established, in part, by exercising the power to represent the other.

I argue that the ostensibly human form represents and attempts to capture Black errant movement. The rendering is meant in some ways to fix the movement (or flux) of Blackness in place to capture it. Postcolonial scholars who have studied the deployment of the picturesque in eighteenth-century British landscape painting agree that it was used in part to control the narrative about British colonialism.[75] In an attempt to "distinguish their brand of colonialism from the barbarism and militarism of the Spanish," the British and, subsequently, Anglo-American brand of colonialism was invoked and performed as a form of settler colonialism.[76] Settler colonialism, according to Anuradha Gobin, implied that this form of British colonialism primarily "implied alteration of the land only through planting."[77] The picturesque emerged as a visual convention of the eighteenth century that enabled the British, French, and Dutch to distance themselves from the brute and sadistic militaristic violence of Spanish conquest. The aesthetic of the picturesque functioned as visual technology of disavowal.

In the case of rendering Black bodies, the picturesque certainly functioned to depict slavery as a humane and civilized institution that managed and modernized a primitive other human population through labor. While this is one function of the picturesque, there are other visual conventions that demand attention. The rendering of the landscape and the Black body as ideal and beautiful not only painted a picture of order; it also functioned to announce a particular quality about the artist and observer. The individual who drew and painted the landscape of the enslaved also needed to make a statement about their own subjectivity, as well as the character of the society from which they emerged.[78] Gobin argues that the perspective and vivid details used in these eighteenth-century performances of the picturesque were also used to make a statement about the community of landowners regarding their taste and sophistication.[79] The artist as conquistador settler and the one possessing the beholding eye is projecting one's position in the world through demonstrating that they are able to access and indulge in the artistic practice of attending to the fine details of the beauty of the picturesque. The unique viewpoint of the picturesque was also intended to convey to the elite back in London that landowners in the colony possessed a "high art sensibility."[80] This particular vantage point was also an exclusive one often shared by the community of explorers and colonial landowners and slave masters. This is the vantage point and the visuality of the possessor.

The proprietors listed on de Brahm's map would have shared this perspective and desire to proclaim their standing in British society. To be able to have such an intimate perspective of the landscape and the Black bodies that populated it, one would have to be an owner of land and slaves. The picturesque is also an aesthetic expression of proprietorship over the images, figures, objects, and people rendered. While the plantation is certainly situated within this schematic and ideology of linearity, progress, and modernity, this does not mean that the Black bodies depicted on it are also modern human subjects. The attention and detail given to the Black body is without equal on this map. The illustrative cartouche contains design elements that incorporate curve, depth, light, and shadow, in contrast to the rest of the map, which uses a uniform and flat, two-dimensional kind of coding and symbol system. This kind of ornate attention was often given to plants and natural objects in the eighteenth century.

The Linnaean perspective and its particular kind of attention to form, detail, and racial categorizations are a part of the modern technology that enabled the "will to knowledge" that undergirded the objectification of nature and bodies.[81] Linnaean perspective (or looking) and depiction could be turned into a systematic process of surveillance and capture. Aestheticizing nature and Black bodies as elaborate and intricate systems did not redeem them from their ontological position as sub- and other humans. Through a beautiful depiction of an otherwise inferior or grotesque other (the wildness of the natural world and the horror of the fugitive slave), one can project their human position and authority through capturing the other as a beautiful and knowable thing.

Seeing up close, knowing through touch, examining and capturing in the delicate details of a painting or drawing established domination over a thing or a body, particularly a moving and unpredictable thing. The slave masters, as well as the artists commissioned by them, made the Black enslaved body an object of knowledge to establish dominance.[82] Black bodies and the New World landscape in the eighteenth century were imagined as spaces of change, potential, and contingency.[83] De Brahm, British settlers, and other artists who attempted to render, and therefore capture, Black bodies and the landscape through maps and visual art were, in a sense, hoping to exert scopic domination over bodies and terrain that could not be fully tamed.

The geographer Denis Byrne argues that colonial landscapes are nervous, meaning that they are always contested landscapes that are dynamic and capable of being manipulated (or used in anticolonial ways) by the colonized to resist the domination of the colonizer. Within this context of colonial instability and contingency it makes sense that otherwise unruly Black slaves who may, in reality, have taken part in (or are descended from) the Stono Rebellion were depicted as orderly and docile working bodies, as the cartouche was also a visual device that worked to "confirm the spatial story of the map."[84] It is here, within the elements of the map, its cartouche, and legend, that a narrative is told about flows of power, relations of possession, property, and the order of human agency. Another spatial story that needs to be attended to is that the map was also a reflection and record of White settlers' fears.

The cartouche representing Blackness as captured matter, coupled with the legend of control and ownership, represents the desired social order and a set of yet to be realized aspirations. The control and management of Black bodies was something to be aspired to and not a given reality that could be confidently depicted. Indeed, the rule and domination of Black bodies was a contested and tenuous process that had to be managed daily. As the Stono Rebellion and the waking nightmares of mad prophets evinced, the enslaved could be unpredictable moving figures on the landscape. I argue that this anxiety seeped into representations of the tenuously ordered landscape in the cartouche featured on de Brahm's map.

I posit that the unpredictable movement of Black bodies, or Black fugitivity, inspired the depiction of Blackness in the cartouche as unstable, moving bodies and in a state of unpredictable flux. Because Black rebellion, fugitivity, and errant movement was so hard—in fact, impossible—to contain, the White imagination continually had to invent and rewrite a strategy of capture. Making Blackness fungible or always on the move (fugitive and criminal) in advance is a way of attempting to anticipate or get in front of Black movement. Black movement, errancy, and fugitivity become part of the repressed White unconscious (libidinal economy) that at times, as indicated by the "deluded" man in the introduction to this chapter, produced madness.

In response, and as a way to assuage this anxiety, Black movement must be reimagined as a somewhat "capture-able" form of chaos that can be harnessed (but not fully controlled) for White self-actualization. The detail and precision of the cartouche represent an attempt to discipline Black errant movement by visually depicting it—specifically, Black rebellious bodies that participated in (or have the potential to participate in) the Stono rebellion. Anne McClintock makes a similar argument in *Imperial Leather* about the "technologies of representation" that the upper class developed in an attempt to discipline the working-class "crowd," or rebellion in the nineteenth century. In late nineteenth-century Britain, the degenerate working-class crowd "occupied a dangerous threshold zone" that, if transgressed, threatened to undo the public and private worlds of the propertied class.[85] Drawing on Freudian psychoanalysis, McClintock argues that as an exemplary threshold image (on the verge of bursting through), the crowd entered the realm of fetish. "The fetish image of the crowd as degenerate," she explains, "was a measure of very real ruling class anxieties about popular resistance, as well as a crucial element in legitimizing the policing of militant working class communities." For upper-class citizens to maintain a sense of control over the crowd or discipline it, the crowd "first had to be represented."[86] Thinking about the unstable, unpredictable, and ever fluttering and Black rebellion as a threshold object, I argue that de Brahm and the settlers of the area needed to gain "scopophilic power" over Black fugitive slaves by representing them as fungible.

More than a formula representing the exchangeability of the commodity, fungibility, in the context of de Brahm's and White settlers' eighteenth-century map, is also a manifestation of White anxiety. Black fugitivity and fungibility emerge through a kind of imperfect dialectical relationship. In *Black on Both Sides*, C. Riley Snorton eloquently offers the term "fungible fugitivity" to elaborate the ways in which "captive flesh figures a critical genealogy for modern transness."[87] Said another way, Snorton works with and on Spillers's notion of Black flesh ungendered to articulate how Black gender indeterminacy, as a form of fungibility, becomes an opportunity for Black rearrangement, maneuver, and fugitivity.

Snorton argues that the global shift marked by the early nineteenth century's transition from the transatlantic trade in slaves to the domestic slave trade staged the ground for fungibility to emerge "as a legal intercession intra- and internationally."[88] Snorton periodizes fungibility and fungible Blackness as emerging during the end of the transatlantic trade in African slaves. In 1818, Henry Colebrooke's definition of "fungibility" enters the economic vocabulary of mercantile capitalism. While fungibility undoubtedly emerges discursively through abrogations, debates, and shifts during the specific era of the end of transatlantic trade, I offer that Black fungibility—or the unending capacity of Black exchangeability—could have emerged as a cognitive, conceptual, affective, and material possibility prior to the moment that Colebrooke gave it a name.

I also argue that prior to the ways that Afro-pessimism inflected fungibility with social death and incapacity, Spillers's and Hartman's theories of fungibility allowed for more flexible and generative use. Like Snorton, I argue that fungibility, its infinite exchangeability, can be used as a resource by fugitive Black people, like Spillers's notion of flesh as a site of radical rearrangement. Black fugitivity's use of Blackness made fungible is evidence of Black ingenuity and invention under conditions of capture, the hold, and social death. Further, I reverse the presumed power dynamic and propose that ideas of Black fungibility emerged as a response or reaction to the unrelenting pulse of Black fugitivity and the White anxiety it causes. In the context of de Brahm's map, I posit Black fungibility as a response to Black movement and errantry. Building on Snorton, I posit that Blackness remains a moving, quivering live field that, enfleshed as "fugitive fungibility," creates anxiety for the White master who tries to contain it.

Like the crowd as a fetish in McClintock's nineteenth-century Britain, the horde of Black rebels "on a move" must also be represented as fungible—in flux—to be controlled and disciplined. However, Black fugitivity can respond to and exploit Black fungibility as a resource to find always opening loopholes of retreat and escape. In chapter 3, I explore how fugitivity and fungibility are tethered to each other by looking at Julie Dash's cinematics of indigo-stained flesh in the film *Daughters of the Dust* in tandem with Black errant embodiment pictured in de Brahm's cartouche. Viewed together, the pores of indigo flesh and pores of the cartouche create a new punctum point and shoal that tempers the axiomatic logic of Black labor.

3

AT THE PORES OF THE PLANTATION

This black urban presence—black life—uncovers a mode of being human that, while often cast out from other official history, is not victimized and dispossessed and wholly alien to the land; rather it redefines the terms of who and what we are vis-à-vis a cosmogony that, while painful, does not seek to inhabit a location closer to that of "the fittest" but instead honors our mutually constitutive and relational versions of humanness.
—KATHERINE MCKITTRICK, "Plantation Futures"

Around 2011, the hue "indigo black," or indigo-stained Black skin, pierced my cornea and grafted itself onto my eye. While I had viewed the film *Daughters of the Dust* countless times before 2011, it was in the context of reflecting on conquest and the relationship between Black enslavement and Indigenous genocide that I found the stained hands of Nana Peazant and her kin who worked the indigo plantation arresting. From 2011 until now, the very idea that the cultivation of violet plants and the crude chemistry involved in their conversion into indigo dye could have an afterlife on the skin, and perhaps across generations, has inhabited a small corner of my mind.[1] In *Daughters of the Dust*, which was released in 1991, Julie Dash tells the story of the Peazant family, descendants of the Gullah people who live on the Sea Islands off the coast of Georgia. The film depicts the twenty-four-hour period before several members of the Peazant family leave the Sea Islands to become modern Black subjects on the shores of Savannah, Georgia; Harlem; and Nova Scotia. Throughout the film, the family tensions, secrets, histories, and dramas climb and reach their own crests as departure from the Sea Islands draws near. As the viewer observes the narrative arcs, the screen captures images of Black people whose hands are stained blue. In an interview with Houston Baker that I elaborate on later,

Dash calls the indigo-stained hands the scars of slavery. Since 2011, I have been haunted by these scars.

While we were in Charleston, South Carolina, in the spring of 2011, my mother and I took a Gullah tour with Alphonso Brown, the local historian who curates the tour, acts as docent, and facilitates commercial exchanges between tourists and Gullah artisans.[2] After traveling to a number of different sites on the tour, I asked Brown about indigo plantations. I wanted to know whether there were any extant sites where indigo-processing vats and materials were preserved. Brown shared that, for the most part, indigo processing had been suspended in the region in the early 1800s because it caused premature death in the enslaved populations who worked it. According to Brown, slaves who processed indigo were susceptible to diseases and illnesses that contemporary medicine would refer to as cancer.[3] Indigo processing was a noxious and potentially fatal endeavor on eighteenth- and nineteenth-century plantations in South Carolina and the Low Country.

Historians have described the region of the plantation cordoned off for indigo processing as "insalubrious."[4] In Dash's filmic depiction of the nether regions of the indigo plantation — a place located both deep within and at the edge of — a dense and haptic scene encloses the lens of the camera with thick, murky clouds of smoke and fog that obscure the people and objects just beyond. So thick and liminal is the gaseous visual scape created on-screen that it might allow a viewer to imagine a rank and putrid stench of rotting plants and weeds potent enough to choke a person.[5] For almost two full minutes about an hour and three minutes into the film, the sights and sounds of indigo-making saturate the visual field. The murky and noxious ecozone has a surreal visual- and soundscape. Microphones pick up the sloshing sounds of liquid being stirred. Soft, faint drums and human chanting create a background layer of sound for the sloshing. An unborn child, a future member of the Peazant family, is depicted as a ghostly figure in a white dress and narrates the scene, which explains that these workers are "the ones who chose to survive."[6] The low, haunting music that plays in the key of A (for Elegba) at the end of the scene is the theme that often plays when the members of the Peazant family are on the beach.[7]

Contrasting the smoky and dark landscape are bright blue fabrics. Three women in the foreground are stirring liquid in large vats with a tall stick. The indigo that has spilled over the lip of the vats stains the sides of the deep wells. The unborn child appears at the vat in the foreground and sticks her hand into one of the poisonous vats and mimics the women's stirring.

One old man is also stirring a vat of liquid, and a woman is hanging the cloth on a line. The camera later frames the unborn child while she holds a square mold for the indigo paste. The camera moves away from the unborn child and frames a young boy watching an elder count the indigo molds. The elder chants as he stacks the molds, and the camera moves back into the dark smoke that billows around the young boy's face. The foggy smoke hides portions of the young boy's body.

As described in historical literature, the area of the plantation marked off for indigo processing was a fly- and insect-infested contact zone, rife with the potential for the transmission of disease. The smoky, hot, rank, and infested zone was often deemed uninhabitable, even for animals.[8] Yet like the hold of the ship, it also contained life that fostered alternative modes of survival, existence, and perhaps even pleasure. The nether region of the indigo plantation is a liminal place that represents a space that is at once both inside and at the very edge of the plantation. It is also a place teetering on the edges of death and life. As a transitional space, the indigo plantation could be called an ecotone—a region of transition between distinct ecological, social, and ontological systems. This chapter tracks the production of ecotonal and liminal spaces at the site and space of the pore. The indigo plantation and the body represent different scales of porosity and illumine the ways that Black embodiment and place disrupt and reorganize humanist representations of bodies and inhabitable space. The indigo plantation represents the edge of one kind of plantation sociality and the beginning of another. Similarly, the pores of the hands of enslaved Black people working indigo function as the edge of the body and as a portal into other kinds of human and nonhuman relations.

In this chapter, I use the metaphor of the pore to make space for alternative readings of representations of Black life in plantation landscapes as open spaces of transit, flux, and exchange through which a number of symbolic economies move and collide. By overlaying or creating a bricolage of the speculative work of Julie Dash and William Gerard de Brahm at each of the images' pores—or openings—I reread the cartouche featuring Black figures processing indigo on the shore in de Brahm's map through Dash's filmic depictions of porous, "indigo-stained" Black hands.[9] I want to pause here to "notice" and again write about the haunting work done by the ghostly doubling of the cartouche on the copy of the map at Davidson College, in which the palimpsestic nature and, more specifically, porosity of the materiality of papyrus/paper maps has enabled the cartouche's Black figures to have a kind of play and errancy that de Brahm did not intend. The paranormal doubling here harkens to Katherine McKittrick's "something else" of Black life as a surplus of anti-Black violence. This bricolage or shoal functions as an alternative geography that represents Black embodiment as states of flux, openings, and portals that include and exceed the rubric of labor. Because the analytic of labor often crowds out other analytics, such as porosity and fungibility, and tends to dictate how Black bodies on plantation landscapes are viewed and perceived, it is particularly challenging to reorient practices of looking in ways that can also facilitate viewing Blackness as something other than labor. The two speculative texts — de Brahm's, which attempts conquest, and Dash's, which depicts "otherwise" ways of being human — work as overlays on each other to create a new ecotonal site of possibility for Black embodiment and place-making. At the pores of Black embodiment, a new scale of the plantation and it various socialities can be perceived. Throughout the chapter, I rely on theorizations of fungibility by Hortense Spillers, Saidiya Hartman, Jennifer Morgan, and, more recently, C. Riley Snorton to situate my analytic of porosity as a frame that exceeds labor. Finally, drawing on McKittrick's work on plantation futurity, I read for Black life in the depths of indigo plantation degradation. Far from reducing on-screen Black figures and porous flesh as abject objects, this chapter reveals the ways that all bodies are always already embedded in and run conterminously with nonhuman life. The kinds of epistemic and ontological openings that appear in Dash's aesthetics and in Black interdisciplinary scholarship align with notions of "all my relations" in conceptualizations of the body's relationship to land and nonhuman life in Native studies. The Anishinaabe poet and scholar Leanne Betasamosake Simpson argues, "Our bodies are embedded in the ecologies and in our intimate relationships with the land."[10] Indigenous insight into the land-body connection, or the land possessing the body, offers a different way to think about and regard the Black hands that are entangled with or stained by indigo. Far from being rendered objectified bodies, they are visual reminders of the ways that the human body is always embedded in the ecologies that surround us. In fact, all bodies are a part of the ecology.

THE SHOALS OF THE PLANTATION

In this chapter, I frame the shoal in four distinct yet related ways. First, the visual analysis of Dash's images of Black-blue hands is read against and with de Brahm's map to methodologically produce a tension and friction. Shoaling as a form of encounter and friction is made more explicit in the counterreading that Dash makes possible in her images of alternative forms of Black embodiment and relations on the indigo plantation. Dash's images disrupt singular narratives of death. Second, fungibility as an analytical frame shoals the impulse to rely on the Marxian regime of labor and other inadequate forms of political economic analysis. A shared Black and Indigenous critique of labor functions as another shoal, or gathering space, that unsettles normative Lockean and Marxist notions of who can be human and on what terms. When the onto-epistemic terms of labor and its modernizing, humanizing, and disciplinary power on Indigenous and Black subjects are rejected, frames such as fungibility, fugitivity, and porosity provide other ways to discuss human relations to the land and nonhuman life-forms. Third, porosity is explicitly engaged as a way to theorize entanglement and interconnection as a part of all human relations. While the focus is on the Black bodies' pores as a space of connection—or shoal—to other nonhuman forms of life, ultimately I theorize this "reality" of human porosity and connection as an attribute of all forms of life. Various forms of life are ecotonal, or hybrid spaces like the shoal; however, our current Cartesian epistemes do not enable an exploration of this reality of entanglement. Fourth, and finally, the indigo-processing zone is theorized as the outer limit, or pore, of the plantation. As a pore, it is both a limit space and a buffer from the abject zone, yet it also keeps the body and social connected to that which is abject. I connect the metaphor of the shoal to the pore as it also functions as an ecotonal and in-between space like the pore.

Porosity and fungibility are elusive and difficult to visualize because they cannot be captured through traditional modes of seeing. Dash, for instance, had to use creative license and stain her actors' hands blue (a stain that would not appear to the human eye offscreen) to depict the "scars" left on Black bodies from indigo processing. I interpret these stained blue hands as other kinds of human bodies that are open and porous sites of transit that index alchemy, radical alterity, and transformation. Labor alone does not sufficiently relay or explain the Black body's significance to the altering of the landscape and its transformation into a process under eighteenth-century relations of conquest and settlement. Further, labor alone does not capture all of the relationships that Blackness has to slavery, genocide, settlement, and capitalism. If we think through Snorton's idea that fungibility and fugitivity are two sides of a "Janus-faced coin," fungibility—particularly, for Snorton, gender openness and capacity for rearrangement—can become a resource and a site of possibility. To overcome this conceptual and visual gap, I argue that new kinds of speculative tableaus, visual practices, and archives need to be created.

Through creating this bricolage (and shoal), the speculative work of both Dash and de Brahm—especially the ghostly, paranormal image of the cartouche that duplicates its image over time—remap and reimagine new kinds of geographies that defamiliarize traditional plantation scenes while creating new landscapes that can depict both bodies and plantations as sets of relations and processes in the making rather than as fixed and already knowable plantation spaces that always already contain laboring Black forms. These new landscapes stretch beyond the humanist narratives of labor and development that privilege settlement, productivity, and human domination of the land. Linking Dash and de Brahm's cartouche at the porous space of the indigo plantation creates an original interdisciplinary and multimedia map that explicitly focuses on the speculative and imaginative nature of colonial mapmaking. Rendering these sites— the film and the map—as porous lends to a reading of the open-ended nature of both speculative mediums. For example, the porosity of the de Brahm map enables a palimpsestic reproduction of the image of the Black figures in the cartouche; because of the map's porous nature, the image of the Black figures could, in the sense that Christina Sharpe introduces in *In the Wake*, annotate it.[11] The Black figures exhibit this paranormal annotation by duplicating their image over and over—a swelling of the crowd— which leaves cartography as a modern form of writing (Man) open to revision. When one reads the map this way, an archive of conquest becomes a site of Hartman's critical fabulation and a way to connect texts to make, as McKittrick argues, human geographies of domination "alterable."[12] Specifically, by mapping de Brahm's eighteenth-century renderings and Dash's twentieth-century images simultaneously, they can be read relationally as speculative and imaginative works that tell multiple stories. In this way, de Brahm's map becomes another spatial imaginary rather than an inscrutable scientific document that holds irrefutable truth. Likewise, Dash's rendering of the porous fungible body helps us destabilize the governing frame of labor for understanding Black embodiment on plantation landscapes. Read together as a practice of critical fabulation, this new map (or these new maps) renders a depiction of the Atlantic and Low Country coast as a volatile and unstable landscape in which Blackness functions as a symbol of transition, flux, and uncapturability in a period in which the British colonies needed to put the landscape in motion to transform and conquer it.

As speculative texts, Dash's 1991 filmic images of the porous, penetrable, and stained hands of former slaves who worked indigo on noxious landscapes and de Brahm's 1757 map depict open-ended representations of Black bodies as states of instability, change, and transition.[13] De Brahm's motives were to control and dehumanize while Dash manages to point to other ways of living in, through, and beyond abjection. But both of their works enable a glimpse of Black bodies (and ideas of Blackness) as suspended states of boundarylessness, gender ambiguity, and intercessory spaces necessary for the completion of chemical processes such as indigo fermentation. De Brahm's and Dash's boundarylessness moves in very different ways: while de Brahm's moves toward a form of dehumanization and Black sensuousness, Dash's moves in a direction of a Black uncontainability that is impossible for de Brahm to contain. Both de Brahm's understanding of the landscape as a dynamic and unstable process and Dash's depiction of pores on Black bodies that function as openings and entryways of connections to larger nonhuman ecosystems resist reducing Black bodies to merely laboring bodies.

While labor is surely depicted, de Brahm's and Dash's visual fields refuse conventional analyses that would collapse multiple and intricate processes into the governing logic of labor. By allowing the eye to maintain chemical processes and pores of the body in a holding pattern, these images can depict Blackness as coterminous with a series of chemical reactions and as porous bodies that exceed the humanist ontological boundaries that would separate plant, objects, and human flesh from one another. Reading de Brahm's and Dash's images of Black embodiment as potentially porous through and against one another works to disrupt conventional interpretations of Black bodies as merely labor while also creating space for other kinds of spatial readings. Further, it opens up possibilities that allow for more agile and generous readings that can bring notions of Black fungibility and fugitivity into closer proximity while also looking at Black people's bodies more ethically and scrupulously.

Combining, merging, and creating new images of Black embodiment—particularly, errant Black bodily forms—also pushes at the limits of what is conventionally construed as the human body. De Brahm's and Dash's depictions of the outer edge of the indigo plantation and the skin affect liminality at different scales. However, at the scale of the pore—whether it is the pore of the plantation or the pore of the skin—the images overlap. As pores, the indigo plantation and the skin function as entrances and exits, openings and closings. The space of the pore represents a multiscale geography that connects the cartouche's depiction of the indigo plantation and Dash's outer region of the plantation to the Black pores of Dash's actors' indigo stains. The tiny pore gives way to an opening onto the edges and depths of the plantation as a process and shifting set of relations. As spaces of passage, pores face both inward and outward, on the inside and on the outside, at the edge and at the beginning of the human, or as something outside of and more than the human. The pore of the body is the shallowest place on the skin/epidermis, acting as the first surface that interacts with other, ostensibly nonhuman matter.

BEYOND THE ICONICITY OF BLACK LABOR

While labor is important, when it is used as the exclusive governing analytic in the scholarship on U.S. slavery and U.S settler colonialism, it hides more than it reveals.[14] Specifically, labor as a governing frame obscures other processes, relations, locations, and symbolic economies that Black bodies and representations of Black embodiment produce and sustain within New World spatial expansion and geography's attendant project of human-making. Labor, though one particular and useful frame of analysis for analyzing colonial and subsequent capitalist contexts, imposes its own, totalizing regimes of reason and visuality. While this chapter, and book, by no means jettison the historical fact that Black people have served as various forms of labor, I argue here that when we look at and contend with the fact or experience of slavery, the enslaved Black body presents a remainder and something in excess of labor.[15] The Black enslaved body is always something more—a fungible, expanding, and becoming-fugitive state. Further, a focus just on the Black laboring body may preclude thinking about the ways that Black bodies are imagined within other symbolic economies, such as conquest, Native genocide, the Cartesian notion of nature, colonial taxonomies, and ecological destruction.

As a flexible analytic, Black fungibility also functions as a mode of critique and an alternative reading practice that reroutes lines of inquiry around humanist assumptions and aspirations that can pull critique toward incorporation into categories such as labor(er). While fraught, considering Black fungibility as an analytical frame forecloses celebratory discussions of Black labor as evidence of Black contributions to Western "settlement" and investments in humanist forms of modernity. Shona Jackson argues in *Creole Indigeneity*, for example, that the analytic of labor as an onto-epistemic system inherited from Enlightenment thought is widely circulated within Caribbean and "postcolonial" thought. Jackson draws attention to the trappings of what she describes as the "metaphysics of labor," which rely on the logic that labor is a disciplining and civilizing process through which Blacks can travel to become human. To become civilized through labor, Indigenous relations to land and Black resistance to labor exploitation must be disavowed.[16]

Considering Black fungibility instead of labor as an analytical frame creates an opportunity to reflect on other kinds of cosmologies—more specifically, Indigenous and Black ones—that radically reimagine the body's relationship to life forms that have been taxonomized as plants or nonhuman. Further, critiques of labor (and Marxist forms of humanism) that emerge from Black studies, such as Hartman's notion of fungibility, align with critiques of labor within Indigenous studies, such as Glen Coulthard's. Thinking with and privileging Marx's notion of primitive accumulation instead of labor exploitation, Hartman is able to focus on the ever expanding use of Blackness beyond labor, and Coulthard is able to center the murder and colonization of Native people and land.[17] I find this shift of attention and emphasis in both Black studies and Native studies important. It does not assume or center a laboring figure that works itself into humanity through alienation—that is, by separating itself from other life-forms that it must denigrate, such as land, water, and animals. These challenges to the worker as a privileged genre of the human—or what Sylvia Wynter would call Man2—can open space to consider what LaMonda Stallings calls an "anti-work politics and postwork imagination."[18] In *Funk the Erotic*, Stallings challenges the very notion of work and the attendant idea that it makes one worthy of life, protection, and dignity.

Moreover, theorizing Black bodies as forms of flux or space in process rather than as human producers, stewards, and occupiers of space enables at least a momentary reflection on the other kinds of (and often forgotten) relationships that Black bodies have to plants, objects, and nonhuman life-forms. A focus on the fungible flux of Blackness can temporarily arrest the tendency to assume that Black life always already orients itself around the human as the center of space and life. As an open and porous state, Blackness possesses various openings, entry points, and ways of orienting itself to social and organic constellations. To break with a totalizing regime of labor, Black porosity is considered as an analytical shoal and alternative reading practice to disrupt the visual regime and iconicity of Black labor.[19]

In part, Black fungibility in this chapter reimagines Black bodies' relationship to the spatial processes that make seventeenth- and eighteenth-century plantation landscapes—both actual and imagined—possible. As Morgan argues in *Laboring Women*, in the seventeenth and eighteenth centuries Blackness (Black bodies and symbols of Blackness) as a form of expansion and spatial possibility became a constituting feature of the spatial imagination of the conquistador-settler rather than a mere technology or tool of expansion. Specifically, Morgan argues that Black women's bodies on plantations in the seventeenth and eighteenth centuries functioned as more than productive and reproductive laboring bodies. Morgan's archival excavations and analyses reveal that Black women's bodies also functioned as symbols and, indeed, the conceptual fodder that made spatial expansion and settlement possible for British settlers. As an analytical framework, Black fungibility illumines the ways that British colonial conceptions of Blackness mediated the ways in which the natural world could be imagined as malleable and an open landscape of flux.[20] I argue that Black bodies, in their fluttering, stretching, and changing states, became a symbol of unstable borders, processes, and the shifting power relations that inspired key renderings of eighteenth-century British plantation landscapes.

Morgan's Black feminist historical analysis of the enslaved Black female body as an open and pliable form that could also represent spatial expansion resonates with both Spillers's notion of "flesh" as a territory of culture and political maneuver and Hartman's theorization of how accumulation and fungibility define Black captivity as a state of perpetual exchange-ability. I anchor the theoretics of fungibility in the scholarship of Spillers, Hartman, Morgan, and Snorton to attend to its origins in Black feminist theorizing, as well as to acknowledge more open-ended readings of Black fungibility that do not necessarily run along the "always already" death-bound inflections of its Afro-pessimist connotations. Spillers and Snorton specifically enable a theorizing of the "rearrangement and reorganization" of Black flesh toward or for a practice of freedom, even as it exists within unlikely noxious and dark zones of the plantation and captivity.

While Spillers's and Snorton's notions of the flesh and fungibility depart from Afro-pessimism in their pursuit of freedom and Black life, the productive set of refusals and lack of faith in liberal humanist forms of social redress found in Afro-pessimist scholarship is retained and expanded beyond its current capacities. However, the generative nihilism and disavowals are harnessed in these rereadings of colonial archives and used to produce a new, speculative tableau in which Black fungible forms can also operate as sites of deferral or as escape from the current entrapments of the human. These Black fungible, porous, and fugitive forms create new experiences, feelings, and possibilities. Relevant and material to the study of geography, Black fungibility even becomes a symbol for space.

As the self-actualization of Man1 and Man2 is linked to the production of space through conquest, I identify Black fungibility as a form of raw material and an expression of spatial expansion used for hu(Man) ascendancy under conquest.[21] This particular spatial treatment of fungibility (for the service of White self-actualization) explores Blackness as an abstract, always moving process that enables human geographical projects. In this way, Black spatiality is imagined as both outside of (ejected from living within) human space and necessary (in its negation) for the production of human places. This is a tension yet to be resolved in our current discussions of human geography. Admittedly, this application of Black fungibility as a spatial methodology tracking the production of humanist space positions Black space as outside liberal geographies of humanity. With this in mind, the making of Black place necessarily occurs on different terms — terms that McKittrick would call "painful" but also that honor "our mutually constitutive and relational versions of humanness."

Following McKittrick, who follows Wynter into the rarely explored corners of the plantation plot to anticipate Black life, my approach to Black fungibility recognizes the violence of the plantation and its afterlife while simultaneously acknowledging the ongoing capacity for the making and remaking of Black life in the midst of plantation violence.[22] In "Plantation Futures," arguably the space that the phantom figures of the cartouche inhabit, McKittrick insists that a necessary double reading of the plantation is urgent. Thinking with Wynter's "Novel and History, Plot and Plantation" (1995), McKittrick argues that the approaches and methods for reading for resistance require a creative and less conventional search for and understanding of other modes of resistance:

> Analytically, the simultaneous rather than dichotomized workings of the plot and plantation, understood alongside the creative work of the fiction plot, recast the politics of resistance. Wynter's essay suggests that plantation futures can go two ways at once: first, where the basic system is left untouched and we are left to defend and justify it and, second, where the awareness of the workings of the system are engendered in a (creative and geographic) plot-life and, at the same time, challenge this long-standing logic. The latter future offered, I suggest, cannot withstand inevitable black-death because it asks that we imagine black-life as anticipatory.[23]

Like McKittrick, Snorton follows Harriet Jacobs's flight to a garret—a loophole of retreat—in a house on the plantation in which she is enslaved in order to think about the ways that the enslaved could alter and manipulate the plantation plot. Snorton follows and accompanies Jacobs off the plantation and into the snaky swamps of North Carolina. While in this uninhabitable, snake-infested swamp, Jacobs was able to transform captivity and its terrain of Black exclusion into conditions "that would allow fungibility to become fertile ground for flight."[24] Very much like the swamp that offered Harriet Jacobs a fugitive and unthinkable geography for a "performance for" escape, the nether regions of the indigo plantation and the chemical process of changing the plant into a dye in the film *Daughters of the Dust* provided Black people with an unexpected loophole of retreat and a geography of life on other terms.

Using the speculative work in *Daughters of the Dust*, I focus on Dash's representation of Black porous flesh stained indigo to visualize Blackness as an open state of possibility with the capacity to transform conditions of subjection. The blue, porous hands of the characters in the film function as shoals and sites of transit that reconfigure Black flesh at the threshold of Man and index possibilities for other kinds of humanity. In the film, Black people refashion abject conditions and noxious spaces into Black places of life that exist outside normative conscriptions of what it means to be human and where that humanity can take place.

BLACK EMBODIMENT IN SPACE

Existing outside the borders of liberal humanism's stable individual, the porous and fungible form is an always unfolding space of possibility. Blackness, as a symbol of fugitivity and fungibility, rather than simply of labor, disorients a number of theoretical approaches.[25] Slavery and its afterlife are animated around the severing of Blackness from human contemporaries and human relations. In *Red, White and Black*, Frank Wilderson attends to how Afro-pessimists "have gone considerable lengths to show that, point of fact, slavery is and connotes an ontological status for blackness; and that the constituent elements of slavery are not exploitation and alienation but accumulation and fungibility."[26] Under slavery and conquest, the Black body becomes the ultimate symbol of accumulation, malleability, and flux existing outside human coordinates of space and time. Instead, Blackness is the raw dimensionality (symbol, matter, kinetic energy) used to make space. As space, Black bodies cannot also occupy space on human terms.

According to Wilderson, Blacks do not share the "spatial and temporal capacity" of the human.[27] While they are used for the production of human geographies of possession, inhabitance, and self-actualization, Black bodies do not exist as human cartographers, inhabitants, or stewards of space and property in eighteenth-century mappings of empire and within human geography writ large. Black bodies are the spatial and temporal coordinates that make human orientation to space possible. Black bodies are, in fact, the spatial coordinates that the human can manipulate and inhabit. Early geographical imaginaries posited "space as outside of human existence."[28] Black bodies, one with nature, take on the coordinates of space within Western thought. Black bodies mark the outsides of humanness.

Conversely, and more in line with McKittrick's Black geographical subjects, I argue that Black bodies negotiate time-space configurations on different terms. Running conterminously with McKittrick's "protean" plantation, the unanchored Black body in flux is at the center of modernity.[29] In fact, the Black body thrown into a state of flux becomes a symbol of process, transformation, expansion, and space under relations of conquest. While under relations of conquest, Black people must imagine and inhabit place in ways outside humanist configurations of geography. I attempt to reread the paranormal "liveness" of the rendering of Black figures processing indigo in a Dashean and McKittrickian tradition that presumes Black endurance and the pursuit of life, pleasure, and other ways to exist in the meantime. Like the volatile landscape depicted in de Brahm's map, Black bodies are porous sites of instability and transition between states. The three bodies in the cartouche represent states of change and fugitive potential. The tremors of muscles in action are at once motions under captivity and debasement, as well as maneuvers and contortions escaping totalizing violence. Akin to the way Darieck Scott rereads Frantz Fanon's "tensely quivering muscles at the junction of the split," I read the Black muscles in de Brahm's map through Dash, Fanon, and Scott as both restrained and resistant in ways that cannot always be predicted and therefore contained.[30]

Reading this map at its pores (overlaying Dash and de Brahm at the indigo plantation and the body) and alongside scholarly interpretations of environmental historians who incorporate how the White surveyor de Brahm was attuned to the volatility of the landscape, enables a rereading of Black bodies on plantation landscapes as shifting, moving, and unstable figures that elude full knowability. While de Brahm's cartouche may appear to capture the Black body in a precarious and unstable state, the same

Black bodies can be viewed as ever changing and unruly forms that are impossible to contain. The decolonial optics of Julie Dash are an example of a more liberatory image of fugitive fungibility.[31] When one focuses on images of Dash's characters whose hands are stained indigo, what becomes evident is how the porosity of Blackness can direct our sight and attention toward the ways that Black modes of living require rethinking human gender and sexual categories, Cartesian separations of human from nonhuman life-forms, and traditional notions of habitable zones of life. When Black fungibility can be perceived — or translated within — the realm of the scopic, it radically transforms the terms of dominant visuality.

Speculative work depicting what is possible enables an examination of both the limits of the White conquistador imagination and the possibilities created by Black imaginaries.[32] Speculative readings also offer a mapping of the limits of the imagination and the epistemological systems that the conquistador-settler relied on to create spatial representations of empire. This visual analysis catalogues and considers the speculative labor and imaginative work required of conquest. Specifically, this analysis tracks the ways that the Cartesian landscape in de Brahm's map and the Black figures on it had to be thrown into a state flux or made fungible (movement, process, and boundarylessness) before they could be imaged as inert and capturable forms that could be fixed in space.

Paradoxically, de Brahm's need to visually and conceptually render human and nonhuman life-forms as discrete, knowable, containable, and fixed also required them to be represented as unstable and changing. The fixed boundaries of Cartesianism are a colonial ruse that obscures how boundaries continually needed to be made malleable and thrown into flux to be reorganized and reconstituted with new humanist boundary markers.[33] Moreover, focusing on process and states of change (things that cannot be pinned down) introduces a way of exposing the colonial ruse of empiricism by illumining the "Black" phantasmic — or uncapturable nature of Black fugitivity — within hegemonic visual regimes. This analysis's scrutiny of the imaginative and speculative nature of eighteenth-century cartography reveals the fiction of empiricism and its production of the idea of truth through an accounting of the "real." The imaginative landscapes of this eighteenth-century map expose that there was not necessarily a discrete, inert, and visible catalogue of "real" bodies, nature, and land that could be truly captured and "known." Therefore, Black bodies, nonhuman life-forms, and the ways that they were categorized through humanist forms of Cartesianism can be continually called into question.

The categories of human and nonhuman "laborer," plant, land, animal, and other forms of life and the boundaries between them all become suspect "political projects."[34] What is important about this denaturalization of humanist boundaries is that if the Black figure on the plantation landscape is something that is obscure and not yet known, it can elude certain forms of representation that attempt to fix it in space and time. Black forms on the landscape are something yet to be understood rather than always already known.

INDIGO-BLACK

In de Brahm's cartouche, Black bodies functioned to connect and cohere small, and even micro-level, chemical changes such as those that occurred during indigo processing. A closer examination of the schematic rendering of the indigo-processing phases in the cartouche reveal how Black fungible bodies merged with and became coterminous with or symbols for colonial chemical processes. Contextualizing de Brahm's cartouche within what Nicholas Mirzoeff periodizes as the modern mode of plantation visuality (1660–1860), I argue that de Brahm's map is a part of the tradition of rendering the landscape as a schematic, or a process in motion.[35] The schematic as a vantage point or perspective enabled the cartographer, surveyor, and artist to reveal the process, such as nature, as a system that is generally assumed to be static.

For example, Mirzoeff uses the plate illustrations of the missionary Jean-Baptiste Du Tertre, who rendered the complex process of indigo cultivation in the Antilles in 1667 in a plate titled "Indigoterie," in *L'histoire général des Antilles habitées par les Français* (The general history of the Antilles inhabited by the French). "Indigoterie" features eleven stages of the indigo production process. The overseer—the eyes of the French Empire—is placed in the center of the drawing in a way that gives him a view of all of the slaves in every phase of the process. Mirzoeff draws our attention to what the rendering attempts to achieve: "This incongruous scene is not a literal depiction of indigo production[,] although it depicts each stage of the necessary work and its resultant division of labor, *but its schematic representation, which makes visible both the process and the power that sustained it.*"[36] The schematic view, which focuses on "the process and the power," makes it possible to view the Black body as more than a slave or laboring body. While it is certainly not self-evident or automatically apparent to any viewer of "Indigoterie," or de Brahm's map, I argue, the sche-

FIGURE 3.1. Cartouche from William Gerard de Brahm's
"1757 Map of the Coast of South Carolina and Parts of
Georgia." Credit: William Gerard de Brahm, 1757.
Map of South Carolina and a Part of Georgia, Containing
the Whole Sea-Coast. Courtesy of Archives and Special
Collections Division of the E. H. Little Library,
Davidson College.

matic in the era of plantation visuality (1660–1860) creates a momentary scopic opening in which one can get a glimpse of when and how the Black figure exceeds that of a laborer and can become a body embedded in or part of a process.

The actual processing of indigo, which carried great aesthetic and symbolic importance for the British empire, is featured prominently in the cartouche. Mart Stewart muses, "In this context, the cartouche might also be read a little more speculatively as emphasizing not just the production of an imperial commodity but as an exaltation of one of the chemical processes—in this case, the fermentation process that turned a plant into a dye and a glorious color."[37] Attending carefully to the chemical process of indigo dye production reveals the Black figures depicted in the cartouche as dynamic and active states of the phases of indigo processing.

When one looks closely at their movements and progressive placement in the cartouche, the three ostensibly Black male bodies appear to mimic modern scientific movement through the stages of a chemical process. In the right background, the slaves' movements depict the rudimentary and elemental processes of stirring. The fermentation of the indican plant is presented as the beginning stage of indigo processing in the cartouche. The figures are also drawn at angles that almost mimic ethnographic and scientific renderings of objects that are shown as vertical sections or as profiles to illustrate their position in a prior and primitive stage. Their bodies and activities represent the moments in which the plants, water, lime— and, perhaps, even muscles due to strain and fatigue—break down to their most basic chemical elements. Indican plants, water, and lime lose their unique elemental properties and are reassembled into an oxidizing solution. Moreover, the Black bodies paddling in the background are rendered repetitive, standardized, and symmetrical replications of one another, depicting a process under way.

As the eye moves to the foreground and toward the little bit of negative space near the left margin, it traces the path of the progression of linear time represented in the drawing. As linear time moves from the background and to the left, the eye travels along and through the more advanced phases of the chemical process. In the final stages of indigo production, the solution of chemical elements is transformed into a deep blue solid. The mass of indigo needs to be subjected to a more sophisticated process, requiring sharp attention to detail, an eye for discerning uniform measurement, and good timing.[38] At this stage, the body is drawn with more precision. The figure in the foreground is shown in a frontal view and at a scale that renders facial features visible. To be a marketable and sellable commodity, the dye blocks need to be measured, weighed, and packed by a skilled eye. A process of chemical breakdown, fluidity, and boundary loss must be converted into discrete economic units and a linearly progressive "scientific" process to be replicated. In this context, Black bodies represent elaborate processes of chemical breakdown, reassemblage, and states of transition on the colonial landscape. When one reads de Brahm's map this way, Black bodily movements can exceed the logics of labor and render the Black body an opaque space that confounds already available frames of legibility. To cause an additional unfurling that engenders rethinking and revisualizing the humanist categories of labor and "male" bodies, I move a few scales down to the skin and then further to the pores.

BLACK POROSITY (AND FUNGIBILITY) AS RESOURCES

Daughters of the Dust depicts the drama that unfolds on the occasion of the Peazant family's migration from the Sea Islands to the mainland territories on the Georgia coast. In the film, formerly enslaved people who process indigo appear on-screen with hands dyed blue. The images in Dash's movie are certainly gendered. Yet germane to my argument is that, at the location of the stained pore, gender distinctions collapse. As Spillers has explained, "Men of the black diaspora . . . had the opportunity to understand something about the female that no other community had the opportunity to understand and vice versa."[39] At the scale of the pore, Black bodies are sensual, non–gender-specific, penetrable, sexual, fecund, and boundless.

In the moments in which the camera's lens focuses tightly in on the fingers, skin, and pores, the hand becomes a space where boundaries among nature, plant, culture, gender, and flesh break down. The hand becomes more than a hand; it becomes something else. Dash's image of a hand stained indigo serves as my *Ur*-text for crafting a visual vocabulary, and now a language, to reorient the Black fungible enslaved body in space. The indigo-stained hands of Nana Peazant create an image of bodily subjection that exceeds a number of conceptual frames used for thinking about Black bodies and slavery. In an interview, Houston Baker asked Dash why she chose to stain the skin of her actors blue, to which she responded, "It was important for me to show these indigo-handed people as a reminder, that these were the scars of slavery, this blueness. I needed to physically show the scars in a different way, because film is like poetry. You want to say something that has been said before, but in a different way."[40] Dash's

FIGURE 3.2. Screen grab from Julie Dash's film *Daughters of the Dust* showing an indigo-stained hand holding a piece of red fruit.

poetics are important, as they are able to exceed the limits imposed by realism and puncture the frame of labor that the limits of realism may leave undisturbed. The actors' indigo-stained hands are also what Nicole Fleetwood calls "counter-iconic" images of slavery.[41] These images do not trap the Black body within the sign of labor. As porous and stained bodies, they break the iconicity of the "Black laboring body" and open up other possibilities for viewing, interpreting, and imagining Black bodies on plantation landscapes.

More than metaphors, these indigo "scars" index forms and orders of violence that exceed both the capacity of the human eye and traditional ideations of slavery as labor.[42] Dash's image of the scarred hands pushes our sight into the realm of fungibility. The boundaries of the slave body are broken or, better yet, do not exist within cognitive orders of Enlightenment humanism. The Enlightenment posits bodies that are stable, autonomous, bounded, and separate from nature. The indigo-stained hands of Nana Peazant transgress Cartesian dualisms and notions of who can be human.

Given Cartesian, dualistic, Enlightenment conceptualizations of space, Dash's hybrid body exists outside the realm of the bounded liberal human. That which is outside of humanness may be considered a part of nature and space. Gillian Rose describes Enlightenment notions of humanity upholding strict boundaries between outsides and insides, noting that "the civilized body was one with limited and carefully controlled passages between its inside and outside."[43] As fungible bodies, Black bodies are porous and can merge with indigo—or nature—and make new kinds of flesh. Black porous flesh and its connections with plants and nonhuman forms of life confound Enlightenment orderings of the world. Indigo-stained pores, or blue-Black flesh, represent an alternative orientation and relation to objects, plants, and human and nonhuman elements in the world. As a speculative artist and filmmaker, Dash *pushes against* liberal notions of the human as separate from nature. Thus, in the film Black bodies and plant molecules are intimately and inexorably interdependent. Dash's image of the hand stained over time by its ongoing subjection to a molecular process of a body becoming both flesh and indican represents the space where the flesh becomes more than a human hand. The pores of the hand become part of an ecological constellation that includes both flesh and plants.

According to Clyde Woods, who writes about the kind of African American representational structure that emerges in opposition to the "totalizing practices of plantation institutions," the world that the enslaved people inhabited on the indigo plantation could have been organized by a "blues epistemology."[44] Reading Woods's notion of the "blues epistemology" alongside Dash's blue-handed people and their more intimate relationship with and knowledge of the porosity of the human and nonhuman world gestures toward a form of Black, or African American, realism that should be noted. Woods argues that the blues culture was, in part, made up of "cosmologies derived from African and Native American traditions, which were populated by known and unknown human, animal and plant spirits, and by the forces of nature."[45] I situate Dash's film and its representation of a radical Black embeddedness and connection to multiple worlds as a part of what Woods names a blues tradition. This blues epistemology tells a different story about what it means to be human. What emerges is a hybrid story of mutual coexistence and relationality with nonhuman, animal, and plant life that radically respatializes the body and notions of the self.

Dash's intervention in the visual realm to depict human skin and indigo dye as one also represents an example of the kind of African American realism—a worldview that takes into consideration everyday life—that must rely on speculation and creative invention to reveal the truth of Black life.

The indigo stain is knowable only at the molecular level (slaves are poisoned and die) and perceptible to the human eye only through decolonial art such as Dash's. The regime of colonial visuality also hides aspects of conquest such as genocide. Specifically, the colonial regime of visuality obscures and makes invisible the genocide of the Yamasee and Indigenous people of the Sea Islands through the rubric of labor. More to the point, once Native bodies are eliminated, they are removed from and no longer visible on the landscape of the plantation where slaves labor. Dash, however, makes it possible to bring into the frame the genocide of the Indigenous people through her depiction of the Cherokee people and the transformation of land/plant life to property vis-à-vis the fungible body (not only the laboring body) of Nana Peazant.

To "see" the genocide of the Native on Nana Peazant's body, her pores need to be spatialized within the context of fungibility. If Nana Peazant's hand represents a scale of the violence that makes the plantation and settlement, which also produces her as a fungible body, then her palm renders visible multiple kinds of violence. The plantation and the clearing were made through the making and unmaking of bodies such as Nana Peazant, the Cherokee Nation, and Indigenous people. Nana Peazant's hand functions as a scale of a new geographical unit: the clearing-plantation-settlement. The clearing, plantation, and the settlement emerge simultaneously through mutually constituting forms of violence. McKittrick argues that the plantation is reintroduced (again and again) as a "protean" and mutable spatial formation that "fostered complex black and non-black geographies in the Americas and provided the blueprint for future sites of racial entanglement."[46] McKittrick's theorization of plantation space as a place in which differently racialized people and different racial projects encounter each another aligns with Dash's geography of the indigo-stained pore as a scale of Black subjugation, Indigenous genocide, and conquistador-settler becoming. Attending to what occurs in the pores of Nana Peazant's hands offer us a new kind of sight. Her pores, as an analytical unit of space embedded in the visual landscape that also features the "lone" surviving Cherokee person on the islands, narrate a story of conquest where the multiple violence of enslavement and genocide merge.

For Nana Peazant's hands to become scarred blue, indican had to bleed into her cuticles and pores. Before that, the indigo plant had to be broken down and reduced to separable chemical components in the form of indican. Before that, indigo plants had to be domesticated and harvested on the plantation-settlement plot. The plantation plot had to be fenced off. And preceding these acts, the land had to be cleared. Before the land could be cleared, the settler had to kill and remove the remaining Yamasee/Cherokee Nation residing there. The presence of Dash's character, St. Julien Lastchild, the lone surviving member of the Cherokee Nation in the film, evokes and makes visible the absences produced by genocide. Nana

Peazant's palms tell a story of multiple kinds of racial violence as well as the new kinds of subjectivities that produced new modes of life on the plantation. Nana Peazant's palms, as well as St. Julien Lastchild's presence, work to bring into the field of vision forms of violence that are excised from the plantation landscape when labor becomes our sole lens for sight. While Nana Peazant's palms represent a scale of the violence of conquest, they also represent ecotones or transitional spaces on the landscape.

BLACK FLUX

In the nether regions of the indigo plantation, Black bodies may merge/mate with plants and create the commodity dye. Black bodies as hybrid plant bodies assume another level of nonnormative and nonhuman sexual excess when situated within the context of the emergence of modern sexuality. Black open, porous bodies both traffic within discourses of sexuality as slippery, wet, and always open and transgress the purview of the sexual. The Black enslaved body embedded within ecotonal processes that tropicalize the landscape of the plantation present new racial and sexual coordinates of human alterity. Black bodies (at the place of the pore) are genderless, sensual, penetrable, sexual, fecund, and boundless in ways that queer theory cannot give an account.

Attending to flesh/pores at their encounter with the pores of indican moves into proximity with the ways that Spillers "breaks" the gender specificity of Black flesh under enslavement. The ostensibly male slaves who participated in indigo processing were susceptible to the same kind of staining, abjection, and sometimes death (likened to cancer) related to toxic exposure as "female flesh unprotected." At the level of pores, the Black bodies in Dash's movie and those working the indigo on the map are ungendered by their capacity for porosity and functioning as sites of transit for chemicals. In fact, gender ambiguity and genderlessness (or the ungendering of the captive) is part of the reason that Blackness gets scripted out of coherent human genres.[47] These indigo Black bodies are also sites of open and unbounded exchange and entry at their pores. These kinds of fluid and open bodies become signs of sensuality, movement, and exchange and often metaphors for the sexual.

While the stained Black pore as a sign of sensuality, movement, and transit runs alongside the sexual, its penetrability is not solely linked to the genital-anus complex. Nor do Black bodies achieve nonnormative status primarily through sex and the sexual metaphors proffered by queer

FIGURE 3.3. Screen grab from *Daughters of the Dust* showing an indigo-stained hand playing a game.

theory. Homosexual/queer subjects (contemporary LGBT individuals) and theory begin in and with the new genres of the human that emerged in late nineteenth-century sexology. During this era of White sexual differentiation and particularity, Dash's characters contend with the generational poisoning and staining of their pores as sensual and, therefore, deselected beings.

I stress this point for a few reasons. One reason is that mainstream queer theory does not do an adequate job of conceptualizing how Blackness reconfigures Western gender and sexuality. Furthermore, queer theory arrogantly assumes that Western gender and sexuality — and their modalities of nonnormativity — can be mapped onto the corporeality of Blackness. For example, Kathryn Bond Stockton's assertion in the introduction to *Beautiful Bottom, Beautiful Shame* that the work of antiracist Black literature has led to a congealing of Blackness is an example of this kind of arrogant misreading. Moreover, Stockton argues that Blackness truly becomes a contagious and spreadable matter only on the back of queerness. When considering the speculative and imaginative work of Dash and of other Black diaspora scholars (particularly those focusing on the Atlantic, oceanic, fungible, and the fugitive), I question Stockton's reading of Black literary and cultural production. If anything, Blackness enters Western modernity from a place of spreadability and boundarylessness made possible by the Middle Passage and various processes that render it outside of coherent and contained human coordinates. It is also from within this place of spreadability, diffuseness, abjection, and nonhumanness from which Black people seek an alternative mode of being human.[48] As Spillers suggested in 1987, as captives turned into malleable "territories of political and cultural maneuver," the community of ex-slaves had "nothing to prove."[49]

Stockton attempts to establish the foundations for an argument that the Black literary and cultural imagination needs to be queered and made a spreadable contaminant. Before Stockton can have White queer theory make this intervention or augment the Black antiracist literary tradition, she must read Blackness as congealed. Stockton confidently reads Black antiracist and queer literature as rigid or solid(ly) afraid of its own spreadability as a contagion.[50] In contrast, queer (read White) activists and theorists (e.g., Lauren Berlant, Judith Butler, Carolyn Dinshaw, Lee Edelman, Joseph Litvak, Eve Kosofsky Sedgwick, and Michael Warner) "have worked to restate 'queer' as 'strange,' to break against any scripted identities for 'gays' or 'homosexuals' — to break with congealment, as it were. And yet, in a sense, they would willingly, gladly, spread contamination. They would make supposedly 'normal' sexualities confess their strangeness and, therefore, their queerness, lending 'normal' sex a whiff of their slang."[51]

Celebrating the queer and contaminating nature of White queer strangeness and its embrace of the nonnormative, Stockton juxtaposes Blackness as conservative, normative, and fearful of leaking out of bounds. Stockton observes, "As for 'black' there's a different dynamic. A dynamic nearly opposite. . . . The range of contaminating significations sticking to 'black,' even so, has led, in rather remarkable fashion, to politically sensitive forms of congealment on the part of some anti-racists advocates."[52] Rather than rehearse the "antiracist" traditions that have refused the politics of respectability and used Black otherness and nonhumanness as a resource, I challenge Stockton to make this claim stick. Stockton is clearly reading outside the interdisciplinary tradition of Black studies that has already embraced Black deviance and nonnormativity as a mode of life outside liberal humanity.[53]

Before Black queer theory emerges, Black literary criticism already construes Black diasporic movement, migration, cultural production, and self-making as boundaryless. Black cultural studies in particular traces Black diasporic lifeways among Paul Gilroy's rhizomorphic oceanic flows of the Black Atlantic that exceed and spread beyond normative units such as the nation-state. Gilroy traces this history of Black oceanic and spreadable cultural flows even before the nineteenth century. Black spreadability was an

essential, if not constitutive, part of Black diasporic and Atlantic epistemologies before the advent of White queer theory. Black studies has not
had to reach for or enact spreadability and contamination in the way that
nonintersectional queer theory has had to exert itself to take up the contamination of nonnormativity.

In fact, Black studies, as a social field both within and beyond Black
queer theory, has argued that both LGBT identity claims and queer theory
work from a space of normative identity. Greg Thomas traces how the "beyond" in Wynter's work takes us beyond humanist aspirations and the internal epistemic revolutions of the West and how Wynter attributes the
"specific articulations of both heterosexuality and homosexuality to the
Darwinian reinvention of Man (2) in 19th century Europe."[54] As Wynter
tracks the emergence and reproduction of Man, she scrutinizes how the
reconfiguration of the nineteenth-century human reshapes itself through
the inclusion of queer or homosexual diversity. Marx's worker as subject
in the nineteenth century can also be a rational wage-earning homosexual
(or female) proletarian. The laborer as woman or homosexual knows itself
as a free wage laborer (with the choice of sexual expression and identity)
through the captivity of the fungible slave who also labors. The European
White proletarian who has achieved sexual liberation and identity (hetero-
and homosexual) through the individuating power of the wage becomes
an intensified Foucauldian individual and subject in relation to the enslaved, nonwage work of Blacks, who are expelled from the boundaries of
the rational human wage worker and sexual subject.

In addition to moving beyond the categories of rational human sexuality, Wynter attempted to move beyond the explanatory frame of labor. In
"Beyond the Categories of the Master Conception: The Counterdoctrine
of the Jamesian Poiesis," she uses C. L. R. James's fiction and autobio-
graphical writing to provide historical, material, cultural, and more pluri-
conceptual frameworks to explain the European bourgeois mode of domination and accumulation that includes and exceeds labor exploitation as
a way to explain global oppression. Wynter defines James's theoretical
framework through the figure or unit of the pieza, stating that the pieza
served as a general equivalent of value for the variety of groups whose labor
could be exploited with the capitalist world system.[55] "Pieza" was the name
the Portuguese gave to the African who functioned as the standard measure of exchange during the slave trade in the sixteenth century. "He" was
a man approximately twenty-five years old, in good health, and calculated
to give a certain amount of physical labor. He served as the general equiva-

lent of physical labor value against which all the others could be measured. For example, three teenagers and older men and women thrown into a job lot as refuse could equate to one pieza. In the Jamesian system, the pieza becomes an ever more general category of value, establishing equivalences among a wider variety of oppressed labor power. Wynter focuses on the pieza as a way to introduce and focus on the "trade in African slaves" as having seminal importance for James and his anticolonial, Pan-African, and anticapitalist politics. James's pluri-conceptual and pieza framework explained the bourgeois mode of accumulation and domination as a system of aesthetics, language, and culture. The pluri-conceptual framework approached the bourgeois mode of reason, property, and accumulation as a larger system that absorbed the mode of production.[56] This system and mode of domination cannot be reduced to labor. In "Sylvia Wynter: What Does It Mean to Be Human?," Walter Mignolo calls this mode of domination and accumulation a cultural, aesthetic, and linguistic statement about man in the sixteenth century. The mode of production and labor exploitation were but forms of oppression that could occur under the larger global system of domination and accumulation. Labor exploitation and the mode of production do not lead or determine global patterns and systems of domination. For Wynter, in her rereading of James, labor exploitation and the mode of production are just one of the many ways that global oppression is organized.

For Wynter, this global model of accumulation, which was established during the sixteenth century through the slave trade, is a more expansive explanatory model that can "encompass both the proletariat and the multiple groups and groupings whose mode of coercion and oppression are outside of the explanatory power of labor."[57] Wynter's postulation represents a shift in focus from labor to accumulation. For Wynter, James enables this displacement and reordering of liberal and Marxist hegemonic explanations of the social order. Hartman enacts this same kind of reordering in *Scenes of Subjection* through her focus on Marx's notion of primitive accumulation. Hartman privileges the analytics of accumulation and fungibility over labor in her configuration of the making of enslaved and free Black subjects. The pieza forged through the transatlantic slave trade of the sixteenth century, according to Mignolo, set in motion what we call capitalism.[58] He explains the pieza as a "sensibility," a system of measure and mode of representation and exchange. As a sensibility, it enabled merchants, traders, and Europeans to make "certain human lives dispensable vis-à-vis different categories of value."[59] I turn now to the image of the "male" in the foreground of the cartouche. More than and exceeding the sign for labor, this "young ostensibly adult male" figure is also a stand-in for other enslaved bodies not represented. Because a lot of slaves who were perhaps too young, too old, or too disabled to labor could be assessed, grouped, and exchanged against or in relation to the pieza, the pieza marked much more than productive labor. The pieza could also stand in for the lot of slaves who represented what Wynter called the "lower categories of human lives," who could not be accounted for within labor's explanatory frame but could still be accumulated.[60] The pieza, whether blue-handed, infirm, or mute, could stand in for the "non-norm," or what Wynter names the "symbolic inversion of norm value" under the global mandate of accumulation.[61]

Conversely, the rational wage worker also has access to human sexuality and sexual identity as a heterosexual or homosexual subject. In "Beyond Miranda's Meanings," Wynter argues that human sexuality, "True Heterosexuality (like True Homosexuality) are human forms of sexuality only reserved for 'the colonizer.'"[62] The nineteenth-century homosexual (twentieth-century LGBT/QUEER) worker can claim rights to humanity through the wage, a unit of economic rationalization and competition that makes the laborer as human different from the Black fungible and sensuous and irrational slave. There is no wage, or unit of economic rationalization, through which to humanize the slave as a human yet exploited worker. The slave's sensuous and nonrational, fungible body is of an order of sensuality and abjection so contaminating that its excess oozes outside of the boundaries human sexual coordinates. Wynter argues that the "birth" of "homosexuality" and "heterosexuality" proper is concurrent with the "rebirth" of Man, also known as Man2, in the economic and Darwinian code of evolution in the nineteenth century. The sexual subject of the nineteenth century who will emerge as the subject of queer theory in the twentieth century does so through the normative process of dehumanizing enslaved Black and nonwaged bodies as forms of sensuous and nonrational flesh.

The maneuvers of fungible and fugitive Black bodies from within the space of debasement do not mimic the itineraries of feminist and queer subjects and theory. Black porous pursuits of freedom take routes less traveled. They are bodies with ever developing entry points subject to infinite lust and endless possibility. Bodies stained blue invoke this boundarylessness, which fungibility requires. Dash's image of indigo blue hands serves as the nineteenth-century punctum point (created in the twentieth century) that further throws into flux de Brahm's eighteenth-century stadium

FIGURE 3.4. Screen grab from *Daughters of the Dust* showing the region of the plantation where indigo is processed.

of Black transition and movement fluctuating conterminously with the landscape. Far from evoking tranquility, the idyllic eighteenth-century scene in the cartouche, the site where indigo was fermented in vats, was a space of literal and social Black death. It was a place on the plantation where it was hard to breathe and a zone many avoided.

Because indigo processing produced a noxious ecozone and abject space on the plantation, the enslaved toiling there were not always within the master's immediate field of vision. Given this relative seclusion, is it possible that this area of the plantation could also function as a space of Black solitude, if not pleasure and freedom? Clyde Woods has argued that the plantation bloc inadvertently produced a subversive blues bloc with counter-epistemologies and modes of resistance. He explains, "To ensure the autonomy of thought and action in the midst of constant surveillance and violence, African Americans constructed a highly developed tradition of social interpretation."[63] The figures in the cartouche evoke the secret societies that momentarily emerged during the intermittent moments when the master blinked their eyes and when they decided to avoid the stank place of indigo processing.

Like the volatile landscape depicted in de Brahm's map, Black bodies are sites of instability. The tremors and movements of muscles in action are at once motions of laboring bodies, captivity, and debasement, as well as possible maneuvers and contortions that escape totalizing violence.[64] Muscles in their suspended state between recoiling and responding hold a potential for action in ways that cannot be predicted and, therefore, always contained.[65] Darieck Scott's focus on the tensed muscle of Black male bodies under duress and abjection enables an understanding of abjection as a means of producing a "break" in "gender and sexuality" in ways that provide an "opportunity for different configurations of gender and sexuality."[66] Following the Black quivering itineraries of Scott, who reads for the ways that the specificity of Black vulnerability and penetrability create opportunities for transgressing the Western gender order, I read de Brahm's indigo-processing scene on new terms.

Perhaps the scene in the cartouche could be reimagined as an erotic scene in which the enslaved enjoyed one another's "indigo" and porous flesh outside the sightline of the master. Imagine that in even more secluded locations, such as under the cover of or behind the shed, a therapeutic massage or amorous touch on a forearm might open up possibilities for sexual or healing encounters. In this context of other Black possibilities, I also reinterpret the countenance of the figure in the foreground. The visage is in a state of continual movement. For example, the mouth is in motion. The mouth's muscles seem to be moving from a neutral expression almost to a smile, which typically signals docility; however, I read the not-quite smile as holding other kinds of affective meanings.

Could the mouth in motion be affecting an expression of contentment due to the lack of immediate White surveillance, the simple pleasure of Black solitude, the anticipation or replaying of non–work-related interactions, or perhaps satisfaction with the making of preliminary plans for rebellion? These dynamic, unstable, and therefore opaque Black figures are beyond full knowability and containability. Yet as it exists in the thick, humid, and noxious indigo ecozones of the nonhuman, Blackness refashions life where human life is not supposed to thrive, or within what Alex Weheliye, drawing on Wynter's notion of the demonic, calls the "liminal precincts" of the current configurations of the human as Man.[67]

POROUSLY FUNGIBLE FUTURES

As a way to conclude this section, I focus on the kinetic energy that is not explicitly depicted but is certainly alluded to in the rendering of the cartouche's foregrounded figure. The kinetic energy can be discerned in the item that seeks to contain it: the figure is wearing a light-colored head wrap. The wrap certainly could have functioned to keep the sweat out of the person's eyes. In addition, given what Stewart has indicated about how the quality of the dye could be compromised by "other elements" that could be introduced into the mixture, such as insects, dirt, and even sweat, one could surmise that the head wrap also worked to protect the dye blocks from the dye cutter's sweat during these final and crucial stages of the process.[68] Here it is possible to read Black errant bodies' continual kinetic energy as a threat to the ongoing practices and regimes of property-making that constituted slavery. Black fungibility as a state of continual movement, change, and exchange, enacted to make Black bodies accumulable and fungible, can also work against the colonial regime's aims. If it is necessary for eighteenth-century visual and plantation regimes to throw Black bodies into a state of continual movement, that very movement becomes a threat to attempts to stabilize and fix Black bodies as inert, docile, and marketable commodity forms.

On a micro level, Black moving, leaky, and sweaty bodies pose a threat to successful indigo processing. The dye cutter's kinetic energy produces sweat that could ruin the dye. Black bodies in motion and Black errant kinetics (sweat) pose various kinds of threats. Rendered as fungible and perpetual states of change, Black bodies also have the capacity for unexpected and unanticipated movements that upend proprietors' or slave owners' claims to them as property. Black bodies on the move—or, as LaMonda Stallings describes them, "transitional bodies"—not only sweat but also flee like the Black fugitives during the Stono Rebellion.[69]

As Black fungible and fugitive figures, Black bodies in flux are dynamic, kinetic sites that the slave owners and proprietors listed on the map truly had only tenuous claims to when considering how porous and fungible Blackness easily morphs into errant fugitivity. As a somewhat tragic yet equalizing and humanizing footnote, in 1793, while seeking medical treatment, Eliza Lucas Pinckney, the famed South Carolinian "conquistador-settler-master" and indigo cultivator, succumbed to breast cancer. While human in all of her capacities as proprietor, socialite, woman of leisure, and reader of philosophy, she could not escape her own affectable, porous body. All bodies—Black, Indigenous, White—that produce the plantation as a living and porous social organism are subject to exposure to nonhuman elements. All bodies, though not equally, are hybrid assemblages and cumulative effects of multispecies entanglements. The affectability that Pinckney and other eighteenth-century cartographic subjects sought to disavow and displace onto the pores of the Black body eventually met up with them at the very horizon of an indigo-induced death that they sought to evade.

4

OUR CHEROKEE UNCLES

Black and Native Erotics

If I lose you, I will lose myself.
—ST. JULIEN LASTCHILD, in *Daughters of the Dust*

The erotic functions for me in several ways, and the first is in providing the power which comes from sharing deeply any pursuit with another person. The sharing of joy, whether physical, emotional, psychic, or intellectual, forms a bridge between the sharers which can be the bases for understanding much of what is not shared between them, and lessens the threat of their difference.
—AUDRE LORDE, *Uses of the Erotic*

St. Julien Lastchild has had a particular appeal to cisgender, heterosexual African American women (and to other African American viewers attracted to his masculinity), as well as to other viewers of *Daughters of the Dust* (1991) who root for forbidden love. In October 2011, the Avery Research Center in Charleston, South Carolina, hosted a symposium on the twenty-year legacy of the film. On the concluding day, the afternoon plenary featured Julie Dash; Vertamae Grosvenor, a Gullah cultural worker and anthropologist; Alva Rogers, who played Eula in the film; and other actors and members of the crew. Folks enthusiastically welcomed Dash and the crew members; however, the cast member who received a noticeably different response was the Chickasaw-Choctaw actor M. Cochise Anderson. When Anderson was introduced, the audience of primarily Black female attendees erupted. While there were primarily Black women in attendance, there were male attendees and possibly queer folks and those gendered outside the cis binary. While I cannot be sure who was cheering, I am sure that a cacophony of applause, catcalls, whistles, cheers, and other forms of adoration were directed toward the actor. I remember hearing an "All right now, Cochise!" and "Git it, St. Julien Lastchild!" as the adoration continued unabated for at least fifteen seconds.[1]

In fact, Anderson's reception demanded that he speak to his erotic power in his remarks. He seemed similarly to enjoy the erotic attention and appeared comfortable amid all of the erotic and perhaps lustful energy in the room.[2] In his remarks, he commented on how the film had greatly enhanced his love life in 1990s. He noted specifically his appeal among Black women while he was living in New York and pursuing an acting career after the release of the film. When I reflect on this exchange of mutual pleasure between the Black audience members in admiration of Anderson's Native and ostensibly hetero masculinity, as well as his playfulness and acknowledgment of the attention from the Black folks in the room, I am aware that there are multiple ways that this erotic exchange can be interpreted.

Although all of the ways that this moment could be read are not attempted here, the erotic and sexual energy is important to examine. The fact that this Black-Native erotic energy has been sustained over a span of twenty years is significant. The duration of the energy begs the question: What kind of work is it doing? The erotic encounter in the film and the afterburn (or afterlife) of that encounter provide a means for rethinking the potential of the erotic and the sexual under conditions of conquest. A normative reading of this erotic current might narrowly project onto St. Julien Lastchild an embodiment of the hetero-patriarchal fantasy of the shining prince riding in to rescue his Black lover Iona Peazant and love itself. While this is a possibility, there is also a possibility for other registers of meaning.

In Tiya Miles's novel *The Cherokee Rose: A Novel of Ghosts and Gardens* (2015), another Cherokee character, Jennifer "Jinx" Micco, captivates Ruth Mayes, an African American writer, into a love affair. Jinx, a Creek-Cherokee tribal historian, is drawn to the Hold House; Ruth, who is also beckoned to the Hold House for an assignment, finds herself drawn to the red-high-top-and-T-shirt wearing Jennifer/Jinx for reasons that she cannot quite explain. Ruth and Jennifer's love affair seems to be set in motion by another force: the ghost of the ancestor Mary Ann Battis, who has summoned them to the property to sort out a series of historical dramas. As a historian-cum-novelist, Miles revisits the violent legacy of plantation relations at the Cherokee Chief James Vann's plantation house at Diamond Hill, Georgia, that she started in her 2010 work of public history, but this time Miles changes genre and creates a fictional account of the history.

Miles confesses that her motivation for writing the novel was that "as a scholar, I was not happy with how the real story ended for enslaved women and Cherokee women on the Vann plantation. But as a novelist, I had the opportunity to write my own ending."[3] In the continuation of story lines from Dash's film *Daughters of the Dust* and in new endings to troubling histories at Diamond Hill, Dash and Miles create stories of erotic attachments between Cherokee (and Creek-Cherokee) and Black characters.

To finish or alter stories, both Miles and Dash had to become students again to learn about the form and aesthetics of the novel. Dash was approached by a publisher to create a sequel to her film in novel form and attests that the process of learning the structure and process of writing internal dialogue was "humbling" and "different from a screenplay form."[4] Dash's novel, which bears the same title as the film, returns to the story of the Peazant family twenty-four years later and starts in Harlem, where members of the family have migrated after leaving the Sea Islands. In the novel, Dash fleshes out the narrative arc of St. Julien Lastchild in a way that connects him with his relatives. Dash's depiction of St. Julien's kin depicts the Lastchild band of the Cherokee as a migratory people who move seasonally with the cycles of the watershed of the Low Country and the ocean.

Rather than read this depiction as inaccurate or as a conflation of the Cherokee and the Yamasee, I read Dash's acts of speculation and creative license as an erotic practice of writing Cherokee people — in the words and spirit of the Cherokee scholar Daniel Heath Justice — "queerly" and in relationship and rhythm with Black diasporic people.[5] I argue that Dash and Miles turn to other genres of creative storytelling to build worlds where Black and Indigenous people have a future. More specifically, Black and Indigenous people make a future, or worlds, for one another by drawing on the power of the erotic. In this chapter, I extend the theme and analytic of porosity while bracketing and discussing some of the problems with the frame to elaborate on the erotic Black and Indigenous subjectivities of Dash's and Miles's characters. Porosity provides an analytical opening to bring bodies of literature about Black and Native erotics, sexuality, and decolonization together to have a conversation about Black and Indigenous relationality that can exceed the notion of coalition as a conceptual and political space of impasse.

Thinking with Dash, Miles, and Lorde alongside Billy-Ray Belcourt and Daniel Heath Justice, who pursue queer readings of Indigeneity, I consider how cinematic and literary depictions of Black and Indigenous erotics challenge traditional notions of sovereignty and selfhood. I argue that the ways that Dash and Miles depict the force of the erotic between St. Julien Lastchild and Iona Peazant and Jennifer/Jinx and Ruth, respectively, represent acts of decolonial worldmaking and create opportunities to rethink contemporary notions and discussions of sovereignty and coalition in Black and Indigenous studies and political spaces. Within Black and Native thought, the space of the erotic often figures as a liberatory space.

In the context of this chapter and this project, "liberatory" means a space of possible futurity for Black and Indigenous people. LaMonda Stallings, in conversation with Ariane Cruz, Amber Musser, and Jennifer Nash, discusses the possibilities that Black kink/perversion and Black erotics offer Black studies and Black people in a moment in which the public sphere — particularly digital space — is saturated with images of Black death and suffering. Similar claims could be made about the daily occurrences of Indigenous death, though they do not saturate digital space with the same frequency that hypervisible Black death does. In a conversation about the potential of Black erotics, Stallings offers that "the erotic maintains a sense of futurity that compels many to resist unilateral and linear thinking about black life that may be dominated by death, suffering, trauma, and pain."[6] While notions of the erotic as discussed by Stallings and her interlocutors engage, take up, and ultimately differ from Lorde's initial elaborations of the erotic in the late 1970s and early 1980s, Lorde remains a touchstone for thinking and feeling through erotic frames that affirm Black life.

By drawing on Lorde's notion of the erotic — specifically, how its power functions as a kind of bridge that can lessen the threat of difference — I reread Iona's, St. Julien's, Ruth's, and Jennifer's desire for one another through a Lordean form of eros that throws them into a productive state of chaos. In "Uses of the Erotic," Lorde speaks about the erotic as a "measure between the beginnings of the sense of self and the chaos of our strongest feelings."[7] The space of the "measure between the beginning of our sense of our self and the chaos of our strongest feelings" is a place of immense transformative power.[8] In the context of these fictional relationships, I posit that the erotic space between what Lorde calls "the beginning of our sense of self and the chaos of our strongest feelings" is a fraught and mixed space.[9] In this erotic in-between space, St. Julien Lastchild, Iona, Jennifer/Jinx, and Ruth experience joy and pain and are forced into states of ecstasy, or chaos, where they are unmoored and must reconstruct new notions of selfhood (and nationhood).

Lorde's form of erotic power can lead one into chaos and into the act of sharing in the other person's journey through darkness and chaos to another side. While chaos can represent a dark and scary space, perhaps the reality of Indigenous genocide or Black suffering that the other has to become aware of and confront, it has the potential to move us closer to knowledge and transformation.[10] Lorde talked more extensively about this descent into chaos in her address to conference participants at New York University in 1979. In her address, titled "The Master's Tools Will Never Dismantle the Master's House," she provided a strident critique of the racism and homophobia that excluded Black and Lesbian women from feminist conversations and organizing in the 1970s. Arguing for the productive tension of difference, Lorde challenged the conference participants to allow themselves to take a plunge into the depths of chaos, saying: "Within the interdependence of mutual (non-dominant) differences lies that security which enables us to descend into the chaos of knowledge and return with true visions of our future, along with the concomitant power to effect those changes which can bring that future into being."[11]

Erotic chaos is a concept that is crucial to decolonization. The power of the erotic is its capacity to take one into the space of chaos, where it can radically disorient one. Disorientation forces new vantage points on people, as well as different perspectives and desires that make space for other people's desires and pleasure. I argue that St. Julien Lastchild and Iona Peazant take a route through Lordean erotics to acquire a chaotic form of transformative knowledge about each other's suffering to make the world a future place of pleasure for each other. The iconic love story of Iona and St. Julien evokes the kind of eros that Lorde defines in her attempt to rescue the erotic from the entrapments of "pornography" and "plastic" notions of love, marriage, and conjugal union in Western humanism. The stakes of their love are poignantly articulated when St. Julien writes to Iona, "I fear that if I lose you, I will lose myself."[12]

St. Julien Lastchild's words to Iona Peazant in the poetic letter that he writes reminds me of the kind of unmoored subject about which the Cree poet and scholar Billy-Ray Belcourt writes. From the space of queer Indigenous studies, in "Indigenous Studies beside Itself," Belcourt thinks and writes about sex and, more broadly, the erotic as a way to interrogate the limitations of notions such as sovereignty, self-determination, and peoplehood and, more importantly, free Indigenous people of the terms' constraints. Belcourt's poetry and prose probe the question of "how sex talk enables us to inspect the constraints that magnetic worlds such as sovereignty, self-determination and peoplehood place on Indigenous studies."[13] While speaking specifically about the discourse surrounding sex, Belcourt works in the tradition of Indigenous scholars who imagine the space of the erotic as a space of decolonial possibility.

I would also situate Belcourt within the tradition of Lorde, who does not want the erotic to be reduced to sex because of the ways that sensuality and relationship uniquely gesture toward bridge-building. Similar to Lorde's claim that the erotic is more expansive than normative notions of marriage, God, and an afterlife that organize and delimit human experiences with ecstasy in the West, Belcourt recognizes the power of sex—and the erotic—to transcend the confines of "political speak."[14] Political discourse and, more specifically, its grammars of sovereignty "stomp some of us into the rut of social death vis-à-vis the genre and form of political speak."[15] Belcourt's lush and sensuous poetics invite the reader to consider the ways that the realm of the sexual incites a kind of unmooring. Belcourt pulls us through erotic prose beyond the space of the sovereign self. This lovely unmooring caresses the cheek of the notion of the erotic as a form of deep sharing that invites one into the space or "measure between the beginnings of the sense of self and the chaos of our strongest feelings," or what Belcourt would describe as the experience of unmooring.[16] For him, "Sex talk makes us talk about states of fragility. Unlike sovereignty, it engenders a discourse about the future that hinges on the tenuousness of being beholden to others in determining one's sense of a livable life."[17] Belcourt's sex and erotics resonate with the ethics that guide this project, which seeks out a space where Black and Indigenous people are beholden to one another or, as Christina Sharpe puts it, can practice an "ethics of care." Belcourt's poetic ruminations on the capacity for sex to move people to a future in which they are beholden to one another play in the chord of the love songs that animate the relationships of Iona Peazant and St. Julien Lastchild and Ruth Mayes and Jennifer Micco. Belcourt's sex and erotics of unmooring push back on the narrowness of notions of both Victorian and, to some extent, queer theory. In speaking back to queer theory—specifically, its application or attempt to queer Indigenous literature and thought—Belcourt makes a distinction between his articulation of being beholden to another from Mark Rifkin's notions of intersubjectivity and vulnerability. Belcourt speaks of this distinction by giving the following caveat: "Like me, Rifkin is set on adding words like 'physicality,' 'intersubjectivity,' and 'vulnerability,' to our rhetoric of protest, but unlike him I refuse to allow sovereignty to swallow these words up. For as I see it, to speak of an 'erotics of sovereignty' is to cloud the constitutive non-sovereignty of the sexual, how it entangles us in the breath of others and intensities of the fragilities of the self."[18]

Belcourt's emphatic claim that the sexual is a space of the nonsovereign provides an important interruption in conventional discourses within Native studies that privilege the notion of sovereignty as the fulcrum and locus point of decolonial ethics and practice. Shifting attention to the sexual and privileging it over the constraining discourse (perhaps not the same as the spirit and practices) of sovereignty acknowledges the critiques of Black studies scholars who argue that the grammar of sovereignty is not something that Black people can access. More specifically, Belcourt's unmoored subjects are in conversation with Jared Sexton, who argues that the most radical elements of Black politics emerge from a space of "baselessness."[19] They refuse to (and cannot) make claims to anything. They cannot utter reclamation, recovery, or the resurgence of their personhood or land. While Belcourt also troubles sovereignty, it is through a space of sensation and sex and on very different terms than Sexton's theoretical critique. For Belcourt, "sovereignty" is too abstract a term for the kind of sensual, material and lived experience of the sexual.

Further, and more controversial within the context of discussions of unmooring, unbecoming, and ecstasy is Belcourt's revelation that "love does not simply rescue us from pain, love plunges us into it."[20] Lorde, who also mines the space of the sensual toward movement into the space of the chaotic and the kind of connection, understanding, and transformation that it can engender, does not cordon off pain from the erotic. Belcourt chastises the use and perhaps even the concept of sovereignty because it "too recklessly banks on good affect. It strains the terrain of affective potentiality and cherry-picks feelings that will get held up as national sentiment. In contrast, sex talk makes us talk about multitudinous forms of brokenness."[21] This form of brokenness is something both Iona Peazant and St. Julien Lastchild, as inheritors of intergenerational trauma, know intimately. To coexist and love each other, they must confront and understand this profound generational trauma and form of brokenness to find ways to heal themselves and each other. The erotic is a powerful space in which, Lorde suggests, we engage the threat and our fear of difference to come to a place that allows us to be with and for one another. For Belcourt, "To talk about sex, to make it an object in Indigenous studies, would require that we do something like an Indigenous studies beside itself."[22] Belcourt asks about the ecstatic moment, how we get "beside" and "beyond" ourselves.

Lorde is similarly demanding in her honoring of processes of deep sharing and connection as a way to joy, completeness, and a "this feels right to me." It requires a radical engagement with another.

Lingering with and in the erotic is a generative way to enter into conversations about sovereignty, coalition, and ethics on different terms. Belcourt's poetic and erotic intervention in the political speak of sovereignty shoals discourses of sovereignty and critiques of sovereignty that frustrate Black and Indigenous dialogue. His troubling of discourses of sovereignty through sensation, erotics, and sex probe similar questions that Sexton asks of Indigenous sovereignty in "The Vel of Slavery: Tracking the Figure of the Unsovereign" (2014). Turning to the space and feel of the erotic in Dash's and Miles's novels, I home in on the descriptive and particular narratives of Black and Indigenous people that, as Barbara Christian argues, creatively "theorize" Black and Indigenous futurity.[23] Stretching its neck past the abstract and toward the smell, taste, and feel of the other, this chapter moves with and pushes through abstract theoretical impasses between Black and Native studies in the hopes of identifying different methods and modes of talking to one another.

While moving toward a new erotic way of theorizing and doing relations, I also hope to provoke a discussion about how the word "coalition" has become "cooked," or associated with impasse and Black and Indigenous loss—political compromise—over time.[24] Perhaps "coalition," as Belcourt argues about "sovereignty," has been weighted down in political speak. I contend that discourses of coalition often foreclose conversations about sex, erotics, and Black and Indigenous futures. The kinds of interracial erotic and sexual relationships that Black and Indigenous people are having with non-Black and non-Indigenous people (particularly White people) are often cordoned off from the political space of coalition talk. Scholars and activists often attend to and trouble coalition politics while neglecting to scrutinize interracial erotic, sexual, and, in turn, political alliances and affinities, particularly their own. Conversations about coalition in the contemporary moment often happen in the abstract and avoid embodied and particular conversations about who people choose to love, have sex with/fuck, build a life with, and bring into the work toward a decolonial future. Coalition as a form of political talk can impede or frustrate important conversations about how sex and erotic relationships are a mode of working through—or getting beside and beyond ourselves—or addressing the legacy of conquest in everyday life. Scholars and activists committed to decolonial and abolitionist work must be open to discussing how their erotic lives—often who we trust to work out survival (and futurity) with—that move along interracial lines (with non-Black or non-Indigenous people) can be folded into what we know as coalition, alliance, solidarity, and ethics. These erotic relationships might offer clues to how relationships with one another—across race—function in ways that reveal some of the problems, constraints, and promises of these erotic forms of solidarity-work. How people fuck, who they choose to marry, and who they decide to spend their lives fighting with is an important terrain of political life. This erotic space is perhaps a more accurate and reliable snapshot of how people work out (or do not work out) day-to-day struggles to affirm Black and Native life in relationship to or in conflict with the political demands of their White or people-of-color lovers. These decisions can no longer remain private in our political lives. While this chapter privileges and takes seriously the liberatory potential of the erotic, it does not argue that sexual politics are automatically models for decolonial politics. However, exploring the potential of Black and Indigenous erotics opens to scrutiny the often private space of who people connect with romantically (and politically) and makes it possible to interrogate transformative and harmful dynamics.

EROTICS OF SOVEREIGN AND UNSOVEREIGN SELVES

Native studies, more than any "oppositional" field in the academy, has grappled with the notion of sovereignty along its multiple political and philosophical valences. Although Native studies has spent a great deal of its scholarly and interdisciplinary effort defining the term, there are multiple notions of sovereignty in play at any one time. Acknowledging the term's roots in Western political and philosophical discourse, Michelle Raheja argues that "sovereignty is additionally an English language placeholder term structuring a vast number of ways that Native people have for tens of thousands of years conceived of their relations to human, non-human animals, the land, ecology."[25] Native sovereignty is a living and dynamic concept in constant flux. While the recognition of Native land claims, treaties, and systems of governance; the fight for cultural sustainability; and the right to self-determination anchor many struggles for sovereignty, the definition of "sovereignty" continues to be contested. Leanne Simpson emphasizes that "sovereignty for indigenous people is not an abstract political concept, it is an intimate lived concept."[26] Native movements for sovereignty are diverse, plural, and often in tension.

Taiaiake Alfred and Glen Coulthard, for example, have each argued that framing Indigenous struggles in terms of sovereignty leads Indigenous politics to cooptation by the state.[27] These two scholars adopt the notion of resurgence instead of sovereignty. In light of this critique, Native people have not fully rejected the term "sovereignty" but refined it (time and time again) to distinguish Indigenous sovereignty from state and patriarchal power.[28] Native feminist claims of sexism and misogyny have also posed challenges to how "sovereignty" has been defined by Native nations. Native women's activism within Native communities and nations that have challenged the "internalization of colonial gender norms" is a form of sovereignty that forced other, older forms of sovereignty to change.[29] As Stephanie Teves, Andrea Smith, and Michelle Raheja write, "Many Native activists are envisioning what sovereignty would look like if it were based on principles of justice for all peoples and care for all of creation."[30] These debates around the meaning of "sovereignty" demonstrate the extent to which it is an open-ended term. As Joanne Barker notes, "Sovereignty is historically contingent."[31]

Teves and her colleagues acknowledge that Indigenous movements for self-determination and sovereignty have always been porous and informed by other movements. For instance, the Red Power movement was informed by the "strategies and tactics of the Black Power movements. . . . This exchange helped facilitate broader support for Native struggles and enabled other groups to integrate and understanding of settler colonialism into their struggles."[32] Discussions of the malleability and porosity of the Native notion of sovereignty are perhaps the space where it is most capacious.

This is often the test that Black studies scholars apply to the politics of Native sovereignty. Is Native sovereignty a pliable and ethical enough space to acknowledge the specificity of anti-Black racism? While Native sovereignty as a concept has stretched and changed due to the stress of internal pressure, can it change in relation to Black people's needs and desires? This is a question that is particularly pertinent when discussing Black and Cherokee relations, specifically Cherokee practices of slavery. Sexton recently called into question the notion of Native sovereignty from Black studies as an interpretive frame, critiquing settler colonial studies and, to some extent, traditions within Native studies for relenting to notions of "resurgence, recovery and recuperation," which have what Wilderson calls the "capacity for coherence" and are therefore intelligible within liberal humanist frames of recognition.[33]

In contrast, what Sexton defines as a "politics of abolition," which calls for the end to slavery (and its afterlife), is a call for the radicalization of Indigenous sovereignty, as well as every radical movement.[34] For Sexton, the radicalization that abolition exerts is a "radicalization through the perverse affirmation of a deracination, an uprooting of the natal, the nation, and the notion, preventing any order of determination from taking root, a politics without a claim, without demand even, or a politics whose demand is too radical to be formulated in advance of its deeds."[35] His articulation of abolition's "baseless politics" sets the stage for a renunciation of the self and, more specifically, a self that can even claim sovereignty.[36] As this critique has been engaged and carefully considered, an important critique of Sexton's position is that it is too abstract and functions outside a specific and material context.[37] For example, it does not adequately attend to the question, "For whom is sovereignty important and in what moment?"[38]

The "who" and the "what moment" illumine how sovereignty is being enacted when the discourse and practice of sovereignty come face to face with Black abolitionist projects. Andrew K. Frank argues that the sovereignty of Muskogee Creek villages in Florida during the eighteenth century protected fugitive slaves and other absconders from Spanish and British colonies.[39] Can sovereignty, particularly a sovereignty that can expand and even dissolve the borders of the self to invite the other—Black fugitive slaves in this occasion—in and then consolidate those same borders to prevent British slave catchers from penetrating its space function as an ethical enactment of sovereignty? If at its core Indigenous sovereignty morphs along its axes of relationality and "interconnectedness," can Native sovereignty function as a malleable analytic that Black and Native erotics can bend, curl, and reshape toward a mutual futurity?[40] More specifically, can Native sovereignty bring about a porous notion of self that opens itself to accepting the erotic potential of the other—in this case, Black, flight, porosity, and chaos. While erotically working on this erotic space, could a new space emerge that exceeds and no longer fits within the discourse or the "placeholder" currently called "sovereignty"? Might a new grammar emerge at the erotic shoals of Black and Native porous futures?

ST. JULIEN AND IONA

In Julie Dash's film and novel *Daughters of the Dust*, erotics set the stage for a majority of the Black and Cherokee encounters. In both the film and the book, circa 1902, St. Julien Lastchild of the Cherokee Nation marries Iona

Peazant. In a sense, he marries into the Peazant family, who are descended from both Ibo people enslaved on the Sea Islands and Ibo people who decided to walk back home through the ocean. This chapter interprets the now iconic love affair between Dash's filmic and literary characters as an ethical encounter and alternative form of erotics that require a mutual and reciprocal kind of Native and Black "self-making" that is not easily incorporated into a frame of coalition or sovereignty.[41] St. Julien Lastchild and Iona Peazant each embrace one another's forms of what Wilderson would call "grammars of suffering" to ensure the other's survival and futurity. This Dashean erotic is an ethical frame that exceeds the terms of coalition and aspires toward a different kind of Black and Native future.[42]

By rereading the "love story" between Iona Peazant and St. Julien Lastchild with questions posed by Afro-pessimism about the ontological position of the Black/slave and Native/savage, I attempt to tease out how Iona Peazant's grammar of fungibility and St. Julien Lastchild's grammar of genocide — ongoing states of death — transform the erotic and disfigure Victorian notions of eros. I argue that St. Julien Lastchild and Iona Peazant rework the Western notion of the erotic by deferring normative humanist notions of love and kinship such as blood, family, nation, and citizenship to embrace or surrender to the erotics of "chaos" in the Lordean sense, which enables new forms of desire, as well as new ways of being Native, Black, and human. In this chapter, I extend or riff on Afro-pessimism's theorization of the ontological difference that Blackness and Nativeness represent to argue that their desire for one another exceeds the Victorian or even the queer. Here I use an Afro-pessimist reading, not to argue for or against coalition, but to reveal the stakes of the erotic for those who are deemed to be of outside human sexuality and erotics (queer or heteronormative) within relations of conquest.[43] Both Iona Peazant and St. Julien Lastchild emerge from and forge kinship structures that are strange and incoherent within humanist and queer erotics. Marked as death-bound subjects under relations of conquest, they do not need to embrace Lee Edelman's "no future." Because Iona Peazant and St. Julien Lastchild represent figures outside of human coordinates, their attempts at sociality and "love" exceed the normative frames for making sense of interracial love, coalitional politics, and queer utopias. Iona and St. Julien make new and "other worldly" Black and Native erotics and ethics possible. They are always already partial and porous subjects susceptible to the annihilating violence of conquest. The stakes of their relationship or erotics are different. They must work out their survival with and through one another. This is a clear premise of both the film and the novel. Their lives and love are under constant assault. There is no pretense of nuptials for upward mobility, citizenship, and incorporation into or fortifying the nation as a family that can be woven into the social fabric.

Parsing out the ways that Iona Peazant's and St. Julien Lastchild's, and Black and Native, forms of pleasure and pain are tethered to each other under conditions of conquest, I expound on Wilderson's analysis of *Daughters of the Dust* and situate the characters' filmic and literary performance of eros as one that is also always already murmuring what Wilderson calls the "grammars of suffering" of the Black and the savage. When St. Julien Lastchild (the only Indigenous character in the film and the film's last remaining member of the Cherokee people) and Iona Peazant (a descendant of the formerly enslaved Black and Gullah community) seek each other out and express their desire for each other, their particular experiences with genocide and Black fungibility are also articulated. Inevitably moving toward pleasure is also a desire to move away from pain and affective states that counter pleasure.

According to Saidiya Hartman, even displays of joy by the enslaved (and descendants of the enslaved) are performed under duress and are coercive for the slave estate.[44] St. Julien Lastchild's "grammar of suffering of genocide" and Iona Peazant's "grammar of suffering of accumulation and fungibility" haunt, shape, and help annunciate their specific forms of desire and need for each other. Their attraction to, or draw toward, each other's realities of actual and social death both foreclose the possibility of the usual human comforts and protections of romantic coupling and offer new modes of self and worldmaking. As a speculative artist, Dash imagines and depicts an erotic and ethical encounter between Black and Indigenous people that works to counter conquest's modes of genocide and Black social death without reproducing humanist notion of sovereignty, selfhood, and nation.

While Wilderson does not analyze the on-screen relationship of Iona Peazant and St. Julien Lastchild, he does provide a frame for rereading the characters and the arc of the film within *Daughters of the Dust* as situated within the landscape of the slave estate and settler colonialism. Within Wilderson's Afro-pessimistic hermeneutic, Black and Indigenous people who utter or attempt to live out a way of life that seeks to ward off or defeat Black fungibility/accumulation and Native genocide operate within specific grammatical structures. These "grammars of suffering" and the alternative forms of life they impose also point to the kinds of epistemological systems and governing structures — building blocks — of the human, or Man's, order, such as "love," kinship, and blood, that need to be reordered.[45]

I want to think with Wilderson for a moment about how the notion or conception of the erotic is taken up by the dead. If the savage and the Black are without the body, are without human gender and sexuality, then what does "erotics" mean in relationship to Iona Peazant and St. Julien Lastchild? How might their relationship be categorized if we do not have the normative and "living" categories of bodies, gender, and sex/sexuality to rely on? Their unconventional and death-bound love requires alternative frames of interpretation to understand its true stakes, as well as its unique appeal to certain Black viewers of the film. Iona Peazant and St. Julien Lastchild form bonds under the impending reality and future of social and actual death. Unlike queer or futureless subjects, as proffered by Edelman, Iona and St. Julien do not have to seek or pursue death to establish new and antinormative modes of sociality and futurity. Black and Native communities under relations of conquest and in the United States are already death-bound and are impossible and tenuous formations, at best.[46] Therefore, their love and erotic bond pursues different goals and pleasures that are not necessarily described by bourgeois, proletarian, feminist, and queer modifiers. Iona and St. Julien experience something different from — either short or in excess of — eros, sex, romance, family, race, nation, and sovereignty.

THE WHERE OF IONA AND ST. JULIEN'S DESIRE

In *Red, White and Black*, Wilderson lauds the unique capacity of Dash and the LA rebellion to depict the Black's or slave's structure of feeling amid the everyday brutality that constitutes and shapes Black life. Dash and others are able to bring to bear on cinema what living a fungible and accumulative existence looks like in the everyday.[47]

Wilderson analyzes the films produced by the filmmakers who were a part of the LA rebellion as "cinematic prisms." Rather than strictly reading for what the Black filmmakers Charles Burnett, Haile Gerima, Dash, Ivan Dixon, and Jamaa Fanaka may have intended as their political or aesthetic messages, Wilderson reads for and finds a collective structure of feeling or ensemble of questions as threads that connect them. He finds something similar and profoundly powerful in how the slave's revolt was able to be registered as structure of feeling in each film. Speaking of *Daughters of the Dust* specifically, Wilderson observes:

The descriptive register can be imagined as an ensemble of questions through which cinema and political discourse face without blinking in unflinching analysis of the Black's "absolute dereliction," a complete abandonment by the cartography of civil society. Witness Julie Dash's *Daughters of the Dust*. What prevents this film from having the life sucked out of it by some grandiose pabulum proclaiming its "universal" message (e.g., the "universal" message of immigration and all its trials and tribulation) is that *Daughters of the Dust* makes the spectator painfully aware that what is essential about the journey being contemplated and argued over by various members of the [Peazant] family is the impossibility of reducing it to an analogy. Certainly, all immigrants all over the world leave one country (or one place) for another. But only Black folks migrate from one place to the next while remaining on the same plantation.[48]

Wilderson's assertion that Black life, suffering, and movement are incommensurable with other experiences of human migration is a useful hermeneutic for examining Iona and St. Julien's "love affair." To interpret their love affair outside the analogies of universal love, heteronormativity, or queer futureless, each character and her or his particular grammars of suffering or death-bound structural position in the world needs to be parsed.

I-O-N-A'S SYNTAX

About ten minutes into *Daughters of the Dust*, the camera focuses on a young woman, creating a tight frame around her profile, which is punctuated by dark, short, and lush, individually twisted locks that frame a medium-brown face. Her face is turned toward a set of windows and curtains that allow the sunlight to peak through the darkness of the morning in the sleeping quarters in which she stands. She holds a letter close to her chest/heart that she reads while wearing a white lace gown. The sweet words from a lover in a Victorian epistle dense with chaste prose speak of adoration, affection, and longing.

As the young woman reads the words, "Iona, with the greatest respect for yourself and the Peazant family, I beg that you stay by my side here on this island,"[49] the scene cuts to a medium shot of an outside space and a light-brown-skinned man unclad from the waist up, wearing blue pants held up with suspenders that run vertically up his chest and reach over his naked shoulders. As his laboring body moves from standing to clearing moss on a large oak, both the camerawork and audio, which match his movement, and the voiceover reveal that he is the author of the letter. The young man, whose dark hair falls below his shoulders, is finally framed by the branches of a massive oak tree as Iona reads his sign-off: "Iona, as I walk towards the future, with your heart embracing mine, everything seems new, everything seems good, everything seems possible. Signed St. Julien Lastchild. Son of the Cherokee Nation, Son of these islands we call Dataw, Coosa, Edisto, Sapelo, Dafuskie, Ossabaw, Kiwa, Wassaw, Paris, and Santa Helena."[50]

Throughout the film, the affective registers of erotic tension, heartache, and forbidden, impossible love are brought to the screen. Most of the scenes that feature the two characters together are marked by stealth and secrecy. In the context of her family's impending migration and the expectation that she will travel with them, Iona is a fugitive making her own route to love. To an extent, St. Julien becomes the desired, as well as necessary, avenue to her erotic and personal freedom. Iona's very name bespeaks the roots of the captivity that both she and her family seek to flee. Early in the film, members of the Peazant family who have already migrated to the mainland make a trip back to Ibo Landing to assist the Peazant family members who remain on the island with their first journey to the mainland. On the boat to the island, Viola Peazant, a mainlander, explains the origins of the unconventional names held by Peazant family members to a photographer, Mr. Snead, who has been hired to photograph the family and their last days on the island. "It's fifty years since slavery, Mr. Snead," she says, "but here, we still give our children names such as 'My Own' (Myown) and 'I Own Her' (Iona), 'You Need Her' (Unita)."[51]

Iona's mother, Haagar, has named her daughter the subject-verb-object conjunction "I Own Her" to stake a possessive claim over the child. In a twisted, yet earnest, attempt to establish bonds of human kinship, Haagar redeploys the relations of property set by the institution of slavery, but on her own terms. She takes ownership of her children through their names and her constant surveillance and regulation of their lives. Iona's sister Myown, Haagar's oldest child, ends up leaving the island and traveling to New York with her mother. Myown and Iona are representations and constant reminders throughout the film of how slavery haunts and shapes the Peazant family's present. As Haagar tries to work against the legacy of Black enslavement, she unwittingly, yet lovingly, reimposes the order of possession and ownership through an attempt to own and control her daughters.

Iona becomes a reminder of the ways that Blackness is reproduced as fungible and accumulable on the slave estate that is the United States.

In the film's final frame, in which Iona and St. Julien appear on-screen, St. Julien rides in on a stallion, his long black hair trailing in the wind, and pulls up near the shore. There, a boat is docked and holds passengers headed for the mainland. Iona's mother and sister sit in the boat that Iona is preparing to step into herself. However, she sees her lover atop a horse, turns toward him, and runs as her mother yells out her name. Iona runs, jumps, and is lifted onto the horse by St. Julien Lastchild. She wraps her arms around his waist and lays her head on his shoulder, wearing a painful expression that captures the depth and consequences of her choice. Her decision to remain on the island with her lover has been interpreted by many as a moment of radical self-love and agency. In an interview with bell hooks, Dash talked about the significance of the scene, asking, "When have you ever seen an African American woman riding off into the sunset for love, only, and not escaping?"[52]

In the exchange between hooks and Dash, the love affair and Iona's choice are understood as an act of Black women's sexual agency in a time that Black women were resisting the perception that they were all "ruin't," or without sexual agency.[53] hooks confessed to celebrating Iona's choice to stay on the island rather than leave with her family as a rare moment in which a Black women is depicted following her heart or simply pursuing what makes her feel good. This kind of agency is incredibly important to illuminate, given the specter of sexual violence that, through Eula's rape, haunts the film. Unlike many of the characters in Dash's film and novel, racial miscegenation as performed and written through Iona Peazant becomes a choice, not a byproduct of violence. While Dash and hooks narrate a particular kind of Black feminist agency through the character Iona Peazant, Iona's decision to leap onto a horse with her lover and gallop away does not fully escape Victorian sentimentality and its attendant notions of romance, true love, and heterosexual conjugal unions. While the potential for reading against the grain is possible through a 1990s Black feminist cultural lens, there are other ways to read against a normative interpretation.

What might wrench this scene from the entanglements of "African American" Victorian erotics is a consideration of how Iona's choice to remain on the island with St. Julien may further frustrate incorporation into modern and Victorian prescriptions for being human. For example, Dash creates a character who is engaged in an act of radical self-making through

FIGURE 4.1. St. Julien racing to meet Iona before the Peazant family departs for the mainland.

FIGURE 4.2. Screen grab from Julie Dash's film *Daughters of the Dust* showing St. Julien Lastchild and Iona Peazant on horseback.

affiliations that stretch outside of her racial group and resist any inclusion into the nation-state or aspirations to become a modern subject. Unlike her mother, Haagar, and sister Myown, who migrate to Harlem, Iona stays in the dark nether lands of the Sea Islands. When Amelia, the protagonist of Dash's novel *Daughters of the Dust*, visits her Aunt Iona, who in the novel lives with her husband St. Julien and their children, she must travel "back into the swamp where her Aunt Iona lived."[54] One could not walk there, and the voyage on water was not easy. Amelia "could not imagine how her Aunt had lived back here"; Iona and St. Julien's union could only take place back in the swamp, a "place of unusual beauty and mystery."[55]

Forfeiting the geographical and regional accouterments of mainland and cosmopolitan Harlem, Iona fails to strive to become a modern Black subject. Part of the process of (attempting) modernization includes a geographical and psychic displacement that effaces Gullah (nonnational) ways and embraces urban life. Further, Iona lacks the desire to continue on an upwardly mobile, northern journey to Harlem and the place of Black cultural, political, and economic renaissance. Movement up North also indexes a teleological movement toward Black Enlightenment that included certain forms of Black diasporic urbanity and cosmopolitanism. Further, Iona turns her back on burgeoning separatist and Black nation-building movements such as Garveyism and the Nation of Islam, which require adherence to a form of sexual respectability politics of nonmiscegenation and racial solidarity.[56] By staying on the island, Iona also foregoes the possibility of taking part in some of the future integrationist projects of the Civil Rights Movement, which will attempt to produce Black Americans as modern subjects and citizens. Instead, she chooses to cling passionately to a form of love tethered to a Black and Native decolonial struggle that resists consolidating the U.S. nation-state.

When speaking about her relationship with St. Julien Lastchild to Amelia, Iona says:

> It only natural. Dat me an Julien be together. It de way de ancient people an de captive live with each other from de very first. De old stories tell bout how de buckra come cross de water wit captives, gonna make de ancien people captives. How de anciens and de captives share what lil dey got, learn each odder ways, take de good from both. How de buckra rain down so much misery an sickness dat de captive took to run and de ancien show dem de way. Dey look for safe place an fight til de dead to keep de buckra from stealin dem back. De ancien an de captive build

dey life together, clear de land, plant de crop, raise de children to be strong. An when de buckra send de army to chase de ancien from de land, de ancient an de captive run to Florida, some escape to Mexico, an some wind up out dere in Oklahoma. But Julien family never quit de lan.[57]

Resisting the impulse to reduce Iona's relationship to its romantic and sentimental veneer, I concede that Black and Native interdependence and cooperation are always fraught. Historically, Black people more often than not have been compelled (by violence) to become citizens and try to settle the land and make a place for themselves while pushing the genocidal machine along. Native people often find it necessary and strategic to seek recognition from the nation-state by practicing anti-Black racism (and slavery in the case of the Cherokee nation) and elaborating a discourse of nationhood that African Americans find impossible to access.[58] When interdependence and cooperation do occur, they often happen in zones and territories that are hard to travel to and are often forged under conditions of duress. As evinced by Iona and St. Julien's life together, love also takes place in the nether places of the swamp and under exilic conditions that resist incorporation into violent national formations.

In the novel, Haagar never speaks to her daughter Iona again and refuses to rest eyes on Iona and St. Julien's mixed-breed children. For Iona, love requires relinquishing attachments to normative notions of kinship and citizenship and an embrace of erotic forms of chaos that necessitates the making of the self on new terms.

LAST OF THE CHILDREN, ST. JULIEN

In the film, the loss of sovereignty, or even the impossibility of a sovereign self, is evoked in both the names of both Iona Peazant and St. Julien Lastchild (of the Cherokee Nation). Within Dash's etymological system, these names mark the characters' ontological positions in ways that are hard to ignore. The very name "St. Julien Lastchild" indexes the genocide of his people; he is a walking reminder of Native genocide and the Trail of Tears, as well as of the members of the Cherokee Nation who decided not to enslave Black people to gain recognition within the Eurocentric discourse of nationhood, sovereignty, and civilization. What is so radically different about the depiction of St. Julien Lastchild from other filmic depictions of Native Americans and Indigenous peoples is that he does not articulate a need for the recovery of land or a Cherokee people through a nation.

St. Julien Lastchild does not seek to become civilized through adopting slavery. He does not seek a coherent cartography of the human. Instead, he marries a Black woman and becomes part of the Black community of the walking dead. St. Julien Lastchild, in a sense, becomes Black. Wilderson contends, "In allowing the notion of freedom to attain the ethical purity of its ontological status, one would have to lose one's Human coordinates and become Black. Which is to say one would have to die."[59] Reading the film and the novel within the context of U.S. racial formation and "blood algebra" of blood quantum and the "one drop rule," St. Julien Lastchild's race, nation, and sovereignty are potentially annihilated by "Black blood" and its expanding hypo-spatial and temporal logic of hypo-descent. According to the anthropologist and history of science scholar Kim TallBear, "The history in the United States of racial assignment by hypo-descent and the black-white binary that has resulted in U.S race relations has made it difficult or impossible in practice to have one's race legitimated as white when one has recent African ancestry. On the contrary, it is the norm to identify as black even while clearly also having recent European or Native American ancestry."[60] The American calculus of Native American blood quantum and Black hypo-descent, or the one-drop, rule function as diametrically opposed racial and temporal-spatial logics.

Native American blood is a vanishing commodity that is in threat of being diluted through absorption into Whiteness and, in this case, annihilated by Blackness. By contrast, Black blood travels across space and time like a stain that pollutes all blood (even White) that it seeps into, turning everything Black. Certainly, the logics of conquest inform the particular kinds of calculus that produce ongoing Native annihilation and the production of Black surplus accumulations of property. TallBear speaks of the persistence of blood as an enduring metaphor (and proto-science) used in the United States to discuss and evoke kinship, property, and evolution. She asserts that, "since its inception, 'Indian blood' has enjoyed a unique place in the American racial imagination, and tribal communities are managed (by others or by us) according to the precise and elaborate symbolics of blood. Considered a property that would hold Indians back on the road to civilization, Indian blood could be diluted over generations through interbreeding with Euro-American populations. Indians were seen as capable of cultural evolutions (unlike Africans) and, therefore, of cultural absorption into the white populace."[61]

In one reading of the film, St. Julien Lastchild could be as interpreted as abandoning or losing his Indigeneity, tribe, race, and nation—and, therefore, claims to sovereignty—to experience futurity. By choosing a Black lover and reproductive partner under the regime of U.S. blood logics, he must, in a sense, surrender to Blackness or become Black. In this reading of the film, St. Julien chooses Blackness as a kind of otherwise futurity.

St. Julien Lastchild defers the conventional form of Native sovereignty determined by narrow notions of nationhood and engages instead in an act of remaking the self and "a people" through the choice to find a future in the space of social death embodied by Iona and the Peazant family. To allay his greatest fear, expressed in his appeal to Iona, "If I lose you, I will lose myself," St. Julien seeks out Iona, the Peazant family, and Blackness as space in which to find and secure a self. In the context of Native American and Indigenous "blood policing," this kind of choice might represent an "anti-national" or queer form of self and community-making in that it seeks out "Black blood." Within the logics of conquest, "Black blood" carries an annihilating power in a single drop of its ever expanding spatial property and death-conferring capacity. For St. Julien, a space of social death becomes the site of another kind of futurity.

Putting St. Julien Lastchild's act of self-possession in conversation with queer Indigenous theory, his desire and masculinity mark a queer performance of Cherokee identity-making. During an interview in 2011, Daniel Heath Justice spoke about his relationship to the terms "queer" and "Two Spirit" with Qwo-Li Driskill, remarking on Cherokee existence as an anomaly that resists normative ways of being. Justice stated, "There's a lot to being Cherokee that is really exciting and powerful and disruptive and beautifully quirky and weird and anomalous. So, I'm very happy with queer."[62] Situating Cherokee identity formation within queer acts offers one way to reread St. Julien Lastchild's erotic and "reproductive" choices that would produce anomalous queer Black-Cherokee progeny who do not constitute proper Indigenous nations. Lastchild does not possess an erotic-reproductive ethos that moves toward Native sovereignty as (racial purity) defined by Western logics of "blood quantum."

Under the early twentieth-century notion of race, St. Julien and Iona would produce Black children with Native blood but with perhaps no guaranteed claims to a Cherokee Nation. Iona's womb is constructed as place that produces social death. It is at once an open, passive, and receptive space of death, however, with the potent and penetrative capacity to overwhelm White and Indigenous blood. Under the legal doctrine of *partus sequitur ventrem*, Iona and St. Julien's children will, as Christina Sharpe so eloquently states, "live in the wake of slavery" in which Black children inherit the nonstatus of the Black mother.[63] St. Julien is an Indigenous person who has shown up for "wake work" in the afterlife of slavery.[64] His limb on the tree of ancestors in the Peazant family is a strange blood story.

St. Julien Lastchild's bloodline is particularly confounding and contentious within conventional notions of how Cherokee blood, lineage, and identity are supposed to cohere within normative stories of Cherokee nationhood. Speaking about how the Cherokee Nation and identity have had to confront their "anomalous position" in relation to the rest of Native/Indigenous America, Justice said:

> I'd be a little hesitant to say that to be Cherokee is to be queer, but I think that we are in an anomalous position in a lot of ways in broader Native America. I mean, we're hated in Indian Country 'cause we're supposedly not Indian enough, but it's been our transformative Indian-ness that has made us survive. And I find it really troubling that there are so many people in the nation who would want to take away that transformability out of some weird misguided fear about cultural purity, when we've always been inclusive, we've always been adaptive. Not always *happily*. I think that's an important point, too, but that would be queer. That's also about being queer. That's survival. And not just surviving, but *thriving*.[65]

To both survive and thrive, St. Julien Lastchild must desire, embrace, and hone an erotic structure and sensibility that is both, as Justice describes, "anomalous" (distinct from queer) and transformative.[66] St. Julien must embrace a lack of cultural purity, or reject the sanctity of Cherokee cultural and "blood purity," to both survive and thrive. Moreover, within liberal humanism at the turn of the twentieth century, St. Julien and Iona Peazant would produce children without a nation and without humanity. To live another kind of life and on otherwise terms, St. Julien must reject rigid notions of Cherokee nationhood and sovereignty that rely on cultural homogeneity and anti-Blackness.

In the film, St. Julien Lastchild's relationship to the Cherokee Nation is ambiguous, at best; in the novel that functions as a sequel to the film, however, his relations with the Lastchilds are restored. In response to the film's alleged treatment of Indigenous people, Caroline Brown argues that Dash silenced St. Julien Lastchild and rendered him a voiceless prop that functioned to serve Iona's storyline.[67] Brown has responded only to the film, not to the film and the novel. While *Daughters of the Dust* is still a story centered on the Peazant family, in the novel Dash chooses to reacquaint the reader (and film's audience) with St. Julien Lastchild's extended family, who move around the Hiwassee Valley and the Low Country throughout the year. At this point, St. Julien is far from being the last child of the Cherokee Nation, as Dash creates a moment in which generations of Lastchilds return to the land they call Chicora. At an evening ceremony, they tell their migration story: "We have gone in many directions to seek our own way, but always we return to this land for our renewal. Once again we are together in this season of cold to send prayer and thanks to our ancestors who brought us this land. Let us join together to tell the story of our people, and may you draw strength and courage from this land we call 'Chicora.'"[68] While I have found no evidence that the novel functioned as a corrective to the film's possible invisibilization of a Cherokee community outside of St. Julien Lastchild, it does attempt to give pronounced presence to Cherokee sociality. In the time span between the film and the novel Dash enacts a reversal of the Trail of Tears and attempts to resist the genocide of the Cherokee. This adjustment is important to note: because Dash's depiction of the Lastchilds rests in a place balanced between the discourse of nationhood and people, it does not fully succumb to traditional notions of nationhood and nationalism; nor does it make Cherokee people completely amorphous.

Justice discusses the potential dangers of a discourse of Cherokee openness and malleability in *Our Fire Survives the Storm*, arguing that "Cherokee identity is often seen as conveniently porous and easily appropriated, diluted from an ideal Indigenous purity."[69] He pushes back on depictions of Cherokee porosity, and considering the ongoing genocide of Indigenous people and his "firm belief that Indigenous nationhood is a necessary ethical response to the assimilationist directive of imperial nation-states," he might push back against both Dash's fictional and this book's depiction of Cherokee people.[70] While I would not read Dash as either protective or adversarial toward Cherokee nationhood, she does appear to depict a Cherokee peoplehood that is open and supple enough to incorporate Black blood, people, and life in ways that alter and sustain Cherokee identity. Dash could be characterized as embracing what Justice calls "peoplehood, the relational system that keeps the people in balance with one another, with other people and realities, and with the world."[71] I would hesitate to characterize Dash's embrace of peoplehood as a denial of Cherokee nationhood. I would, however, risk speculating that Dash does not valorize or move toward a nation in her depiction of Cherokee life because, as an African American (of the United States), neither she nor Gullah people have access to the possibility of a Black nation in this hemisphere.[72]

Dash's work of speculative fiction, however, engenders an unusual depiction and geography of Cherokee identity and their relationship to the land. More specifically, Dash imagines a Cherokee band that has moved farther east to the coast, into the land of the Yamasee nation. Rather than construe this as an inaccuracy or error, this respatialization of the Cherokee could be read as a merging with the Yamasee and Gullah people. In this depiction of Cherokee identity, the Cherokee Nation seems to take on a migratory or diasporic form that resonates with Black movement. They move around the southeastern Atlantic and hug the waterways. This kind of movement and connection to the Atlantic, or oceanic, resembles and resounds with the Black diasporic experience and metaphors privileged in much of the literature and critical theory in Black studies. In a movement toward the Yamasee and Black people, the Lastchilds remake themselves amid the violence of conquest.

St. Julien Lastchild's arc in Dash's compendium (film and novel) certainly contributes to the production of what Justice would call a Cherokee practice of *ayetl* (nation), or a center that remembers other stories and histories. The ayetl is inclusive and grounded in counterstories that contest "versions of Cherokee history, sovereignty, and nationhood that seek heteronormativity."[73] St. Julien Lastchild and his Cherokee relations are reminiscent of how Qwo-Li Driskill theorizes Cherokee subjectivity. In the essay "Stolen from Our Bodies," Driskill argues that "many Cherokee stories deal with characters considered outsiders, who live in liminal spaces, help bring about change and aid in the process of creation."[74] As Driskill states, "Cherokeeness is one of the most flexible or queer indigenous modes of life."[75]

In a similarly queer fashion, by writing the novel Dash rewrites U.S. "blood fictions" of hypo-descent and blood quantum to make it possible for Blackness and Indigeneity to coexist in ways that do not need to annihilate each other. St. Julien and Iona's children as described in the book are a perfect amalgam of Black and Indigenous physiognomy. Whether this is an adjustment made on the part of Dash to preserve Indigeneity and Cherokee heritage in the *Daughters* saga, this kind of physical representation of Blackness and Indigeneity is far from one that annihilates Native tribes. Nativeness and Blackness find a way through blood and genes to coexist in the body and in future generations in the novel in a way that is not necessarily apparent in the film. Neither Nativeness nor Blackness has to eclipse the other. In the novel, Iona and St. Julien's children are Black and Native. Hypo-descent does not rule and does not become the racial and spatializing logic of the conquistador nation. Blackness becomes an element that indexes life and counters Blackness as increase, space, expansion, and property. The children speak a hybrid language made up of a combination of Gullah and Cherokee. They are able to produce new grammars and idioms.

The story of the Lastchilds in the novel enables us to meditate on the choices that many Cherokee faced, particularly when it came to relating to Black people. St. Julien, the Lastchild of the Cherokee Nation, inhabits a space of death and possibility that moves toward dialogue and, perhaps, coalition with Blackness. I imagine that a part of St. Julien Lastchild's erotic appeal among heterosexual African American women (and perhaps others) registers on an affective level that is not always perceptible to or effable for African Americans and for Black people in general. St. Julien Lastchild offers a depiction of a Native person betraying the possibility of recognition through sovereignty and a notion of the "nation" that betrays the slave. On some level, whether accessible to cognitive processing or not, St. Julien Lastchild fulfills many long-held hopes for Black and Native alliance. In the novel, it is at the ceremonial space where a fire is burning that Amelia, Iona's niece, is able to take in her aunt's kin — the Cherokee people, her uncle Saint Julien's relations. The Cherokee people, who have at times reflected themselves through the inspirational phoenix, invite a descendant of slaves, Amelia, into the fire, where they acknowledge and celebrate their survival. Justice names this fire a will to survive "through catastrophe, chaos, and change" and a "fire that survives the storm."[76]

JENNIFER/JINX AND RUTH:
EROTIC HAUNTING AND POROUS SUBJECTS

In *Black Slaves, Indian Masters*, Barbara Krauthamer argues that the ways that Indian removal and slavery intersect makes it even more difficult for scholars to build coherent historiographies and narratives. "Delving into the history of black slavery and indigenous removal," she writes, "yields moments that illuminate the fundamental ways in which the history of slavery defies scholarly logic and remains unimaginable."[77] Slavery remains only a partially articulated historical process that has shaped Indigenous genocide and colonization. What the archives of slavery and Indigenous genocide and removal have in common is that they are almost impossible to retrieve. These holes in the archive inspired how Miles came to the story of Jennifer and Ruth in *The Cherokee Rose*.

Tiya Miles spent the time and resources afforded her by the MacArthur "genius" award to tarry with her dissatisfaction with the historical archive. Engaging in the practice that Hartman calls "critical fabulation" to give Black and Indigenous girls other kinds of possibilities—or what Katherine McKittrick calls a telling of "what else happened"—Miles betrayed the archive.[78] Her experiences with the archive, particularly the story of the enslaved Black woman Pleasant on the Cherokee Chief James Vann's plantation in Georgia, led her "to want to create a fictionalized ghost at the historic plantation site that undercut the romanticization of slavery and embodied the need for justice." She says, "My plantation-house ghost represents history in the story, serves as a vehicle for the contemporary characters' connection to the past, and stands as an indictment of the abuse of black women in slavery."[79]

In *The Cherokee Rose*, Miles draws on the late Cheyenne tribal historian John Snipes, who advocated for a method "that combine[s] oral and written sources and [is] responsive to community needs." Snipes was compelled to pursue his topics as a historian "when he kept feeling prodded toward it in intangible ways."[80] Miles's character Jennifer Micco, who is on a quest to clear up a story about a missing Black and Creek girl named Mary Ann Battis, who has been accused of being a traitor to her Creek Nation, was influenced by Snipes. Much like Snipes, who remained open to a prodding or the intangible, Jinx Micco's porous and open Native female masculinity and her curiosity as a historian is constructed as equally open to the prodding of the intangible or the erotic. Jinx's love interest, Ruth Mayes, was inspired by Miles's "family and friends who have suffered domestic violence, as well as by a brief time that [Miles] spent working at a domestic violence shelter on an Indian reservation after college."[81] Miles brings these lovers together through the slave girl Mary Ann Battis. Mary calls Jennifer, Ruth, and Cheyenne Cottrell, an upper-middle-class "Black American Princess," to the Hold plantation. Over the course of the novel, the women discover a ghost, retrieve a Moravian missionary's diary, learn a history of plantation violence, and accept the charge to appease Mary's ghost through addressing their own individual and collective traumas. In the midst of attending to the collective task of reckoning with the violence of slavery and its afterlife as it appears in each of their present-day lives, Jennifer and Ruth enter into a relationship, finding love, companionship, and ways to heal with and through each other the generational trauma that has origins in genocide, conquest, and slavery. For a first-time novelist, constructing and sustaining the narratives of three women and ghost is a difficult task. Rather than write the story in multiple first-person accounts, Miles uses an omniscient narrator, Mary Ann Battis, through whose eyes the reader witnesses the book's opening scenes of construction trucks' shovels overturning Cherokee and Black graves at Hold House.

Miles spends the first half of the book introducing us to the three central characters—Jennifer/Jinx, Cheyenne, and Ruth—and creates layered and complex backgrounds for each. Reviewers have noted that aspects of the novel seem rushed. Jesse Peters, for instance, wrote that Miles's plot "sometimes feels contrived, and the dialogue can seem stilted and merely functional. It is indeed convenient for Jinx to stumble across a history book with information about Mrs. Gambold on her way to Georgia."[82] However, one could also attribute the pace, serendipity, and momentum of the novel to the force and power of Mary's and another realm's unseen hand. The guiding force of an ancestor meddling in romance and guiding people to thresholds of buried secrets aligns with Black and Indigenous cosmologies and stays true to Miles's historical method inspired by the intangible. Furthermore, as it pertains to the flickering movement and quick shift of motivations and desires, and to erotic desire, diasporic Black gender and sexuality studies offer explanatory and theoretical frames for Ruth's and Jinx's capacity to catch or be possessed by feelings of love so quickly in the novel.

West African cosmologies such as Winti and Voodoo that figure the human as porous and subject to the power of the loa could explain the characters' behavior. The likelihood of people changing their desire, attraction, and even gender performance or sexual practice like the "wind," is explained by the Afro-Surinamese anthropologist Gloria Wekker. In *The Politics of Passion,* Wekker describes the cosmologies of working-class Afro-Surinamese women who practice Winti and engage in *mati* work, which can take the form of same-sex, opposite-sex erotics and transactional sex. Mati sexual and social practices happen in the context of how survival is intimately tethered to the erotic in postcolonial conditions of poverty. Within the Winti cosmology, much as in Voodoo, the human is posited as a porous and open subject who is always at the mercy of the spirits, or the loa. Drawing on Erica Bourguignon's analysis of the functions of Voodoo in Haiti, Wekker elaborates on a human porosity that sets the stage for spirit possession, arguing that "the characterization of the human self-implied in the [Voodoo] cosmology as vulnerable, powerless, porous to all kinds of negative forces, in need of protection and of divine intervention to bring about a desired change, whether in the sphere of illness, love, success in work or conflicts in the family, goes right to the heart of how Afro-Surinamese working-class women perceive themselves."[83] The loa (or Mary in the case of Miles's novel) can make a person desire someone (want someone's soul), take on another gender, or engage in a mundane task. What appears to the reviewer to be a quick or convenient storyline, particularly in the case of the erotic charge and connection that Jinx and Ruth feel, could be a function of their porosity and susceptibility to the erotic power of Mary within.

In fewer than twenty pages of the novel, and over the course of perhaps an hour within its timeline, Ruth and Jennifer meet, are mysteriously drawn to each other, and find themselves kissing; they remain connected until the end of the novel. On page 92, Ruth notices Jinx get out of the car parked next to her Volkswagen Beetle: "Ruth glanced back at the woman, who had slung a messenger bag over her shoulder and was loping on long, lean legs toward the house, a look of purpose on her face."[84] Jinx is described by the narrator as having a "purposeful look [that] had given Ruth an inner jolt. Something about the woman's stance, the ease of her limbs in motion, made Ruth want to know more."[85] Throughout the novel, Jinx is clad in wrinkled cargo shorts, red high-tops, and old T-shirts that her long braid rides the length of throughout the novel. When Ruth is finally in close quarters with Jinx, she describes her scent as clover-like.

Jinx comes face to face with Ruth in the threshold of the door to the historic Hold House. She will find herself at the threshold of doorways time and time again with Ruth; this inside-outside transitionary space is a recurring symbol and literary device in the novel. The narrator describes Ruth as "generously figured" with "tight, animated curls spilling over a cloth headband" that "loop[s] around the top of her ears." As Jinx looks at Ruth, she takes in her "rich powdery cinnamon" skin; what Jinx finds most arresting about Ruth are her "semisweet chocolate-brown" eyes framed by tortoiseshell glasses that "[sit] off-kilter on the bridge of her nose." The narrator makes us aware that "Jinx looked a second too long at those eyes, deeply dark and withholding."[86] Two short pages later, Jinx has already given Ruth the nickname "Chocolate Eyes."[87] Jinx waits eagerly for Ruth to speak and finds "herself focusing on the woman's lips, wondering what her first words will be."[88]

Jinx will spend time trying to make eye contact with Ruth, who tends to look away and withhold sustained eye contact or touch. She will also notice that Ruth smells like cherries. Ruth tends not to "gravitate to people, not socially or romantically [and] never lets them close enough to discover there [is] a hole inside her," Miles writes. "But Jennifer Micco was down-to-earth, direct and smart."[89] Ruth is startled by how quickly she responds to Jennifer's request to accompany her on a walk to the garden. In a very short period of time, an erotic connection is secured.

Miles has provided a foreshadowing of their union by the time Jennifer and Ruth head out to the old kitchen. As a historian and scholar of cultural landscapes, Miles attends to how physical structures are also the sites of Black and Indigenous union, conflict, violence, love, and healing. During their walk through the garden, Jennifer and Ruth approach a small, round structure. They are uncertain about its history and function and discuss its possible origins. It appears to be a small, spherical house from the eighteenth century. Ruth thinks that "it could be African-influenced. . . . West African houses were round. Some of the slaves here might have remembered how to construct them."[90] Jinx adds, "Or it could be an early Cherokee winter lodge. . . . They were round houses, too. In fact, it could be a hybrid form."[91]

Jennifer's acknowledgment of and desire for Black and Cherokee hybridity evokes the kind of queer erotics that, Justice argues, characterize the anomalous nature of Cherokee people. Justice argues that this capacity for survival (of Native genocide, forced removal, enslavement) through a kind of adaptive hybridity in part constitutes the Cherokee as queer.[92] Ruth and Jennifer move from structure to structure, space to space, and story to story as they remap the history of the Hold estate and Black and Cherokee/Creek relations in northern Georgia. As they move and speak about the structures and the spaces, they enact Indigenous and Black practices of space-making that rely on breath, speech, and utterance. The critical Indigenous geographer Mishuana Goeman argues that "stories are a narrative tool that must be part of Native feminisms; they serve as fertile grounds wherein the layers of geography are unfolded, explored, and expounded upon."[93] Similar to Goeman's, McKittrick's body of work recounts the ways that Black geographies of resistance emerge from speech and poetics. Goeman asserts that in the work of the Diné poet Esther Belin, "The power of 'breath' to reconfigure spatial and gendered relationships through speech and prayer is emphasized, while the 'words' or discourses of colonialism that impose borders on Diné are unsettled through the 'air we breathe.'"[94] Jennifer and Ruth reconfigure the space of the Hold plantation through what Goeman refers to as the power of breath and what McKittrick would refer to as the "sayability" of geography and place.[95] This remapping is also inspired by Jennifer and Ruth's erotic cartography, partially drawn by Mary Battis in what Cherokee and other southeastern tribes' cosmology would call the Upper World.[96]

After passing the mysterious hybrid round house, Jennifer and Ruth find themselves in the kitchen cabin, the very place that Mary Ann Battis needs them to be for them to find the Moravian missionary's diary. The diary entries tell the stories of the Black, Cherokee, and White women on the plantation. They also tell the story of Battis's captivity and abuse at Hold House. It is the archival evidence and story that clears the record and exculpates her from the indictment of the Creek community. It proves that she is not a traitor to her Muskogee Creek mother and did not convert and thus become part of the catalytic wave of Creek assimilation into Christianity. Jennifer's aunt, who has died before the novel opens, is the Creek historian who passes down the role to her niece, as well as the myth that Black Creek people succumbed to colonial European religion and culture. In the cabin, Jennifer/Jinx and Ruth can clear Mary's name and enact a ceremony on the behalf of the Black and Indigenous women who suffered at Hold House. They can also find healing for themselves in this space.

Jennifer/Jinx and Ruth once again find themselves, Mary, and a brutal history in the threshold of the kitchen door. The most intense cresting and climaxes of their erotic connection take place in this doorway in the novel. The threshold operates as a space of transition, a liminal space that is neither fully outside nor inside but in-between, a portal to different times and spaces. Approaching the cabin, "Jennifer pushed through lopseed stalks to enter the low-slung doorway. Ruth tripped over a threshold warped by the elements, righted her clog and stumbled behind her."[97] Both Ruth and Jennifer/Jinx will be unmoored by an encounter with the erotic, palimpsestic swirl of the collapse of the time and space of upper and middle worlds.[98] Ruth and Jennifer/Jinx sit on the ground in the cabin, which smells like a pine forest after the rain, and Ruth inhales Jennifer's sweet clover smell: "In the silence, she could hear the sound of Jennifer's breathing—steady, rhythmic, alive."[99] In an intense yet soft collision and converging of time and space, Ruth and Jennifer/Jinx enter into what Lorde describes as the "measure between the beginnings of the sense of self and the chaos of [their and their ancestors'] strongest feelings."[100] A rush of forces tear open a number of borders (emotional, temporal, spatial) and portals to historical trauma and love and healing. New knowledge, new sight, and new senses are gained to make new relationships with oneself and others possible. Miles writes:

> Sitting on the floor of the cabin, Jennifer tells Ruth, "Mary Ann Battis, the girl I'm looking for, could have sat where we're sitting now, some year, some day, in the 1880s."
>
> Ruth looked at Jennifer for a long moment, at her dark thoughtful eyes. She was suddenly aware of the sweet clover smell of Jennifer's skin. In the silence, she could hear the sound of Jennifer's breathing—steady, rhythmic, alive.
>
> "The girl you're looking for," Ruth replied.
>
> "Well . . ." Jennifer paused, her eyes questioning. "One of them.
>
> Jennifer was looking at [Ruth], flirting with her, leaning in close to her. Ruth didn't know what to do, and so she closed her eyes. When Jennifer kissed her, the touch was tentative at first. Ruth fell into the softness, the clover-scented warmth. She slid her glasses off and placed them on the dirt floor beside her. She eased her arms back, resting her weight on her palms. *Shh, shh*, the river cane whispered from the hillside. *Shh, shh. Come. Go back. Come. Go back.* The rustling echoed in her ear drums, sounding like a voice that had traveled across a great distance. Ruth snapped open her eyes, pulled her cheek from Jennifer's hair, and peered over Jennifer's shoulder.
>
> "What's wrong?" Jennifer asked.
>
> And that's when Ruth saw the girl.[101]

In the doorway, Ruth sees Mary Ann Battis, the enslaved Black Creek girl as she looked at age fourteen or fifteen. After Ruth is visited by Battis, she and Jinx find the diary of a Moravian missionary who lived on the plantation. They are forced to address both the anti-Black racism of the Creek community in Oklahoma that has elided and misrepresented Battis's story in their histories and the trauma that Ruth experienced as a child victim of domestic abuse. Jinx is forced to contend with the incomplete and racist history of the Creek community and to confront both her own fears about completing her doctorate in history and her previous choices to remain "romantically" unpartnered. Ruth opens herself up to the love of Jinx; leaves Minnesota, which has represented a space of isolation and deferred dreams; and moves to Oklahoma. The novel ends with the Hold House property being returned to Adam Battis, a descendant of Mary Ann Battis and Chief Hold, the Cherokee slave master.

More than a neat and "convenient" tale of an act of small redress for colonial genocide—for theft and the sins of the Cherokee band who participated in enslaving Black people—Miles's novel, like Dash's work, creates opportunities to rethink and reimagine Black and Indigenous entanglement through a frame of the erotic. Dash and Miles create alternative narratives for Black and Indigenous subjects that move against the grain of conventional modes of redress and resolution. For example, Iona rejects and Ruth does not appeal to the violent U.S. nation-state (or her violent White father) and their promise of "Black citizenship" and kinship that requires the annihilation of Indigenous people and their Black selves. St. Julien Lastchild and Jennifer/Jinx Micco yield to a particular kind of porosity that reimagines what it means to be Cherokee and Creek people and nations. Dash and Miles offer other possibilities through the erotic as a space of otherwise relationality.

In addition to painting a horizon of Black and Indigenous futurity through Black and Indigenous erotics, Dash and Miles rework notions of selfhood and subjectivity in ways that both honor and challenge Black diasporic and Cherokee modes of survival. As a way to end this chapter, I return to the theme and metaphor of porosity that has run through three of the chapters of this book. While not valorized, porosity is a shared and historically and violently imposed historical condition—or ontology—that Black and Indigenous people have resisted and adapted to in order to produce new modes of life.

Furthermore, the ways that Dash and Miles depict Cherokee masculinity—and, in the case of Jinx Micco, Cherokee and Creek female masculinity—as nonnormative or errant (and queer) pose meaningful challenges to normative notions of Cherokee nationhood and belonging. The errant and queer masculinities of St. Julien Lastchild and Jinx Micco are porous, malleable, and open to being shaped by their Black lovers and, by extension, Black life. The Indigenous masculine subjects depicted in Miles's and Dash's novels invite into their lives a Black companion who rejects inclusion within traditional patriarchal family relations and Black citizenship frames that perpetuate anti-Indigenous violence. Further, the Black and Indigenous erotics in the novels function as relationships that are mutually invested in Black and Indigenous futurities. In fact, the Indigenous and Black erotic subjects create and live lives that make both Black and Indigenous futures possible. Dash's and Miles's erotic models are hopeful, at minimum, and potentially gesture toward the kind of erotic work that can redefine Black and Indigenous relations and politics in ways that exceed the current constraints of coalition and alliance. I end this chapter at the warm light of the Lastchilds' fire that warmed the face of Amelia at a ceremony celebrating St. Julien, Iona, their fully Black *and* Cherokee children, and all of their relations. The next chapter honors the practice of ceremony through a Black diasporic artist's sculptural celebration of Black and Indigenous futures.

5

A CEREMONY FOR SYCORAX

I met Charmaine Lurch through Jin Haritaworn in April 2015.[1] Charmaine and her creative partner, Mosa McNeilly, had just completed their two-woman performance, "Refusing the Imaginary of Fungibility: The Black Female Body in Flux," that spring. Without my knowledge, they had invited me into their creative process and relationship. "Refusing the Imaginary of Fungibility" transformed themes from my dissertation, "In the Clearing: Black Female Bodies and Settler Colonial Landscapes," into dance, song, poetry, sketches, paintings, and murals that ended up taking shape as an elaborate ceremony that celebrated the generative and life-giving flux of Blackness made "female," or of Black femininity, in the African diaspora. I was more than humbled. Although I was far from an artist, a trained art historian, or a scholar of aesthetics and visual analysis, I was invited into a dialogue and relationship with Lurch, a Toronto-based painter, sculptor, and arts educator. More important, I was invited to partake in the process of learning a different way to see, think, and perceive.

Rather than pull away, I decided to be led by the tide toward the final shoal of this book. The final sandbar and archipelago appears off the shores of a kind of Black "exilic thought" that I encounter in the work of Lurch and Black Canadian scholars such as Dionne Brand, Katherine McKittrick, and Rinaldo Walcott. Using Lurch's work "Revisiting Sycorax" as a point of departure, I trace a through line in the Black aesthetics, poetics, and intellectual production of Brand, McKittrick, and Walcott that unsettles hegemonic, and often congealed, national and regional hegemonies within Black diaspora studies. Lurch's sculptures take up Sylvia Wynter's adaptation of the notion of the demonic in physics through the ways that she molds and manipulates space in her wire sculptures. Lurch ruminates on, fingers, conjures, and shapes space with her sculptures, which are inspired by the tesseract, a mathematical formulation that describes a fourth dimension. Lurch's wiring manipulates the tesseract to move among dimensions (e.g., from three-dimensional to four-dimensional space) and even between realms that are not yet knowable.

In Lurch's *Conversations in Flux: Visible Presence Unfolding in Time and Space* show, three multimedia and multidimensional paintings and sculptures "animate" the often invisibilized Black presence in North America.[2] They are "Blueprint for a Mobile and Visible Carriage," "Revisiting Sycorax," and "The Phenomenal Henrietta Lacks." All three works give scale, presence, and a haptic quality to the Black people and figures in the African diaspora. "Blueprint" honors Thornton and Lucie Blackburn and their multiple, shifting geographies as travelers to Canada from Detroit and owners of Upper Canada's first cab company. Henrietta Lacks is also honored as an ancestor who has the indomitable distinction of always being present and with us and yet unseen, since her cells were stolen and used for scientific and medical research. Finally, there is "Revisiting Sycorax," the wire sculpture of the absented Black and or dark (Native, Indigenous, Other) presence in Shakespeare's *The Tempest* (1611).

Lurch's wire sculpture of Sycorax, an Algerian woman and the deceased mother of Caliban, is an arresting and airy piece that bends modernist form and sculptural conventions in ways that open up public space and participation.[3] For me, Lurch's "Sycorax" became a new interlocutor for this project and a kind of antimonument or cenotaph to the statue of Christopher Columbus with which I opened chapter 1. Both Lurch and Sycorax pursue a conversation about the human in the Americas.

When I sat down with Lurch in Toronto in July 2015, she joyfully explained the movements involved in making space using the tesseract in her sculpture. With her hands moving and stirring the air, she described working with, or working, the tesseract as a way to "perform a kind of mapping and claiming that can disrupt, trace anew and place black lives":[4]

CHARMAINE: And so, there is a mathematical formula that moves us from 3D to 4D called a tesseract. I really love that idea of the tesseract, because I work in, I create in space. And so I'm always thinking about the space. And the tesseract is a four, a four-dimensional, um, shape that you can't see. And so I'm saying the Black body will move and does move in different ways.[5] Henrietta Lacks moves in different ways that we can't see.

TIFFANY: You made me think of Sylvia Wynter then with the demonic, and she's an artist and a philosopher—like, you're going to those spaces. It's amazing.

CHARMAINE: Thank you. How I'm thinking about the tesseract is to imagine early people and their understanding of the world as flat. Until we could actually move outside and take a picture of the world that was round, we had only imagination and ideas to work with. So I'm saying we're at that point with fourth dimension where we can't see it until something in our brain or someone is able to show us—kind of understanding in the present [and] trusting in the future that we're going to be able to know this fourth dimension.... [M]aybe we are in the fourth dimension in the way that we imagine things and make things out of air and create things that didn't exist before. The tesseract is a shape, and I will show it to you, that is always moving and changing. So for me, the tesseract is a, a wonderful analogy of flux; of, you know, motion and change and future. So that's kind of how I go from a point of a pencil to imagining a different future for Black people.

TIFFANY: That's amazing, what you just said. And I don't know—this analogy will not do justice to it. But as you were talking about this dimension we can't yet see, ... that we need some other kind of capacity [to see], it has to happen in a certain time. You made me think of ... my ability to see the Blackburns. I've never seen them before. I've never seen images, but you sharing their particular journey with me, me being at this physical location, ... gives new breath to talk about them and to talk about the archaeological site. I can conjure an image that might be in this moment. I can see two figures. I might not be able to see it again outside of my exchange with you, but that's what I'm thinking about when you explained the, is it the tesseract?

CHARMAINE: Tesseract.

TIFFANY: Tesseract. I was just thinking about this fleeting moment where it requires a relationship with you and requires space, right? A particular coordinate on the planet to invoke a particular image of people who are in the past, but you can visit now and that can perhaps move someone later in the future to share that story.... [Y]ou're talking about time and space in a way that we can't wrap our heads around, right? And it also, most importantly, requires a relationship, and I think that's what I'm trying to get to in my work.

I was inspired that you had used my work as a point of departure, and I was, like, I want to use what Charmaine is doing as a point of departure to get me somewhere else.... [I]t's not just a kind of, "Oh I'm going to look up someone's work . . . in a museum." . . . I want to know who they are; I want to do that extra kind of labor to really understand that process. So that was amazing what you just explained to me. That is so amazing.

CHARMAINE: That is how I felt when I . . . read your work. How we can move each other's work through . . . these interactions, through these conversations, and through reading. You know, we're all thinking a little differently, and, yeah, I think's it when we come together that real change can happen. You've been so generous, you know, when we said, "We're doing your work," and I thought, "Oh, I hope she understands [that] we credit [her] research with helping us think about our work in new ways."

Lurch's ability to move inside, outside, and alongside, as well as to re-interpret, academic scholarship in Black studies is astounding. An astute student of Wynter, she works with Wynter's use of the demonic and its unknown Black coordinates as a muse for manipulating her own lines into the fourth and fifth dimensions and beyond through the mathematics of the tesseract. Often imperceptible, this movement among dimensions, or from one dimension to another, creates an errant and demonic movement in space. When Lurch's figures come into form in her sculptures, they create alternative kinetics, motions, dimensions, and space. Lurch's Black diasporic sculptures enact an unruly dimension of aesthetic space that represents a break in the theoretical, geographic, and aesthetic conventions that orient Black diaspora studies and, more specifically, attempts within the discipline to represent Black and Indigenous relations in the Anglophone Americas.

I argue that Lurch's wire sculptures in *Conversation in Flux*, like the Black exilic thought of Brand, McKittrick, and Walcott, slow the vessel of Black diaspora studies, particularly the navigational course and speed dictated by a U.S.-centric Black studies. Walcott's Black exile thought and politics, Brand's gospel of "no nation," and McKittrick's notion of "wonder" and embrace of Wynter's demonic interrupt the hegemonies of U.S. Black studies and a diasporic flow that can at times trace the shape of the nation within Caribbean studies. At the offshore shoal of Black "exilic studies/thought," a new kind of Black geographical form emerges. Lurch renders the diasporic, exilic, and errant movements of Black life in particularly poignant ways through "Revisiting Sycorax." Figured as Black and Indigenous feminine forms, Black and Indigenous people represent the exiles of conquest and settler colonial nation-states. Sycorax's line of exilic thought wrinkles narratives of conquest and Black and Indigenous relations because of its wayward and, perhaps, tesseract-like relationship to the nation-state and the hemisphere.[6]

"Revisiting Sycorax" is a multidimensional, porous sculpture made of black and copper-colored wire that evenly distributes its weight across its balance of positive and negative space.[7] While the scale of the sculpture reproduces the stature of a life-size human, its asymmetry, multiple openings, and web- and netlike patterns belie the monumental heft of Western cenotaphs that monumentalize the ideal human form. In stark contrast to the Columbus statue that towers over visitors on the shores of Boston's waterfront, Lurch's Sycorax stands a little over six feet tall.[8] Having emerged more than a hundred years after the itinerant sailor's voyage to the Caribbean, Sycorax arose from the imagination of Shakespeare as an unseen figure in the play *The Tempest*. Sycorax is reconstructed in the play as a series of memories and a haunting idea; Black and Indigenous artists and scholars have pondered the meanings, location, and significance of the enigmatic figure of Caliban's mother in narratives of discovery and the birth of modernity.

Black studies — specifically, Caribbean studies and the Negritude movement — has established a tradition of transforming *The Tempest* into a decolonial allegory. Primarily through a strategic and decolonial disidentification with Caliban, Black artists and scholars have found ways to subvert the scene of conquest and have the Black or Indigenous colonial subject speak back to Prospero, the West, and imperial power writ large. In these reinterpretations of the play, little, if any, attention is paid to Sycorax. Dead when the play begins, Sycorax is figured as an Algerian witch who was banished to the deserted island and gave birth to Caliban. While Sycorax is largely ignored by more masculinist and nationalist reworkings of the play, Black female literary scholars and artists have taken her and her absence seriously. The Black literary critic Abena Busia, whose body of work has contended with how the "master texts" of colonial regimes such as the British Empire render Black, and specifically African, women voiceless, wrote one of the canonical postcolonial critiques of Western literature: "Silencing Sycorax" (1989).[9] In it, she argues that the "symbolic laryngectomy" of Sycorax in *The Tempest* and of "native women" generally

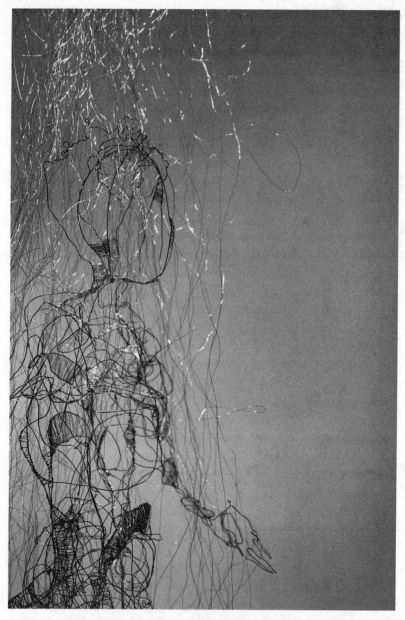

FIGURE 5.1. Midrange photograph of Charmaine Lurch's wire sculpture "Revisiting Sycorax." Courtesy of the artist.

is pervasive in colonial texts. While Prospero invokes Sycorax as a specter and a curse throughout the play, Sycorax does not have her own voice or embodied presence. Furthermore, Sycorax is depicted as a subject without language, and therefore without humanity, who passes on her aporetic, or language-less, state to her son Caliban.[10] Caliban is taught to speak/curse by Miranda and Prospero.

Examining various colonial texts and dominant discourses, Busia finds that it is difficult and sometimes impossible to retrieve — or recognize — the African/Black woman's or Sycorax's voice within colonialism's discursive terrain. Drawing on Gayatri Spivak's essay "Can the Subaltern Speak?" (1988), Busia argues that Black women cannot continue to look to colonial texts to find Sycorax's and Black women's voices.[11] Inspired by Spivak's revolutionary ancestor Bhuvaneswari, who committed suicide while menstruating, Busia directs the reader's attention to the kinds of alternative narratives that the "native" woman's and Black women's bodies can tell. Busia urges Black and postcolonial literary critics to look to narratives of the body that are "not always and only, or even necessarily, a speech act."[12] Similarly, looking for Sycorax beyond the realm of normative modes of narrativity, Kinitra Brooks argues that the power of Sycorax lies in her ability to haunt the characters of Shakespeare's play. Although she has no embodied or sonic presence in the play, Sycorax functions as a haunt, or a haint, that refuses to be excluded.[13] The very idea of Sycorax produces "fear and suspicion" in the characters of the play.[14] This haunting presence, while lacking embodiment, voice, and conventional subjecthood, has an otherworldly power in the play that classical literature and the Black literary tradition have overlooked.[15]

In "Who Cuts the Border? Some Readings on America," Hortense Spillers, much like Busia, argues that Sycorax passes down an aporetic and laryngitic state to Caliban.[16] In a sense, Caliban is overdetermined by his mother and her lack of language. Spillers opines that "even though Sycorax is given no script in *The Tempest*, as we recall, her 'absence,' except in commentary provocation, confirms the 'unrepresentability' of Caliban, the mothered-womaned, to a spectator-audience."[17] Caliban and all of Sycorax's kin (Black and Indigenous) are rendered language-less, and therefore unrepresentable. When I asked Lurch about interpretations of Sycorax as silence, she suggested that Sycorax used other, perhaps poetic, forms of communication that were illegible to Western narrative forms.

Indigenous scholars have staked their own claims and investments in figuring Sycorax as an Indigenous mother of Caliban. Pushing back against

Caribbean reinterpretations of the play that reimagine Caliban and, by extension, Sycorax as creole (mixed) subjects of what will become Black nations in the Caribbean, Indigenous scholars such as the Pacific Islander Vicente Diaz has challenged the "creole" subjectivity of the Caribbean basin. Diaz wonders whether there is space within narratives of "creolization" for an "aboriginal indigeneity" to exist in the Caribbean.[18] The scholars Shona Jackson and Melanie Newton also pose these questions to Caribbean philosophical and literary traditions that figure Caliban and Sycorax as enslaved Black subjects in the Anglophone Caribbean.[19] Irene Lara, working within Latin American and Latino studies, attempts to reclaim and construct a "literacy of Sycorax" as a decolonial third space in the Americas. She argues that within both colonial and masculinist decolonial texts there is a silencing of Sycorax. As the dark "black, native, mestiza, and mulatta" Other, Sycorax represents the monstrous difference of sexual and spiritual alterity.[20] Lara asks what it would mean to position oneself "alongside Sycorax." Doing this, or positioning oneself in this way, she says, works to make Sycorax's absence present even in the conventionally nationalist anticolonial discourses that tend to restage a Hegelian struggle between the master Prospero and the slave Caliban that tends to crowd out other actors. Drawing attention to the androcentric or masculinist limits of "the School of Caliban," Lara argues that decolonial scholars such as Aimé Césaire and Roberto Retamar deploy Sycorax in their reworkings of *The Tempest* in ways that supplant her with the Yoruba figure Eshu, or in the case of Retamar, relegate her to an indigenous or mestiza "Earth mother."

Further, even among Black, Latina, and women-of-color feminist attempts to disidentify with the play, decolonial feminists have reworked the narrative in ways that produce affinities and alliance with Miranda (in the case of Coco Fusco) or have created a new tradition that feminizes Caliban for feminist purposes. Lara cites the emergence of a "Calibana positionality," in which female decolonial feminists have staked claims to Caliban's subjectivity and become daughters or female versions of Caliban to become revolutionary anticolonial agents of change. In these feminist revisions of *The Tempest*, Sycorax is still forgotten. In a similar vein, though not taking up Caliban's positionality, Wynter argues in "Beyond Miranda's Meanings" that "Caliban's woman" or mate (a counterpoint to Miranda) occupies the position of unthought, or the demonic, and is disappeared from the play and colonial forms of writing."[21] Wynter cautions Caribbean and Black American women, inclined to proclaim a space for themselves as "Caliban's woman" or womanists, to resist too quickly claiming a womanist position and instead to continue interrogating the terms of their erasure from Western gender and its modes of writing the human. Wynter's analysis of *The Tempest* draws attention to how the violent logics of conquest, and specifically genocide and slavery, exclude Indigenous and Black women of the Americas from the category of the human.

Lara's pushback to the tradition of Chicana and Caribbean feminists' "Calibana" positionality is incisive. She argues that feminizing Caliban or taking up Caliban's voice risks creating a subject that is intelligible and can be "interpellated into a patriarchal nation-state framework."[22] However, to remember Sycorax, a subject who is without an "audible voice," "an exile without a nation," and accused of being a witch, is an act of a whole different order. Occupying Sycorax's position overturns the order of Man and refuses the aesthetics, orders, and structures of the violence of conquest. Lara asserts that it is Sycorax's "resounding silence that creates an alternative counterhegemonic positionality for social change."[23] From Sycorax's positionality, or third space, one will not uncritically take up "the master's tools" (whether in language, the pen, the gun, or elsewhere) in an attempt to "dismantle the master's house," as Audre Lorde describes.[24] For Lara, the silence surrounding Sycorax should not be reduced to "lack" but points to something else. It signals the existence of a powerful epistemology that loves and lives alongside of, "yet reaches beyond, the disenchanted secular modern nation."[25]

What is significant about and resonates with Lurch's sculpture is that Lara insists that fostering a literacy of Sycorax requires the "creation of more artistic and theoretical works that focus on Sycorax."[26] Attending to the ways that building this literacy requires creativity, Lara shifts aesthetic form at the end of her essay and writes a poem fittingly entitled "Ceremony of Sycorax's Soul." The poetics give voice to Sycorax and craft a language of compassionate encounter and healing that shuns the "structures that occasion the cursing."[27]

Working within Black and decolonial feminist traditions of finding the "demonic" and unpredictable grounds from which to conjure Sycorax's presence, Lurch works with dissident Black diasporic form to create a space for Sycorax. As a creative response to building what Lara calls a "literacy of Sycorax," Lurch uses a nonmodernist form that provides a new grammar along the axes of morphology and shape. She plays in and shapes the space of Sycorax's "resounding" silence in a way that honors what Lara would call the "something else" that is beyond the narrativity, order, and form of the secular nation-state. Lurch's aesthetic as a Black diasporic subject in *Conversations in Flux* explores themes of migration and exile. Like Brand, McKittrick, and Walcott, who interrogate and at times reject the nation, Lurch sculptures Sycorax outside the claims of any one nation, race, or people. Working in this tradition of diasporic exile and drawing on the Wynter's work, Lurch sculptures toward the space of Wynter's (and Mc-Kittrick's) demonic through manipulating dimension and lines into the space of the tesseract. Lurch's adaption of the notion of the tesseract is what Wynter names the "demonic model outside of the consolidated field of our present mode of being/feeling/knowing."[28] Lurch takes up the fifth and other dimensions of the tesseract and what Wynter would call the demonic of Sycorax and "Caliban's woman" who are disappeared from *The Tempest*. Prospero speaks of Sycorax as a "hunchbacked foul witch" (1.2.258) who is filthy, obscene, discolored, and "physically loathsome." In a kinetic response, the movement of Lurch's Sycorax evokes a dancing grace and beauty encased in gold and black that counters the insults and curses of Prospero. Lurch's sculpture also contrasts sharply with the crude form of Robert Mallary's sculpture "Sycorax" (1962), which attempts to play at the nexus of the grotesque and the human. In the tradition of Shakespeare, Mallary produces Sycorax as a crude and raw form that is close to nature and its abjection. Lurch's scale of Sycorax is life-size and scaled for human engagement, as opposed to being scaled as a larger-than-life figure that inspires terror. It counters the demonic of sorcery and black magic with the demonic of the tesseract and the lines that disappear into dimensions and planes that are hard to see. Lurch's Sycorax is a kind of antimodern "form." It speaks or communicates in modes outside colonial speech, discourse, and narrativity. Lurch figures ideas and form in ways that words cannot quite replicate. The form that Lurch gives Sycorax is porous and holey. Its form and "wholeness" remain incomplete — or, as Lurch offers, "complete in a different way" and in constant formation.[29] Lurch's dimensions resist a closed and linear narrative or form. They work in opposition to the Columbian monuments and cenotaphs defaced in chapter 1.

Lurch molds her own version, or ensemble, of questions about the "whereabouts" of Sycorax by interlacing air and wire in ways that perforate and displace air to rearrange the space around and within it. Lurch's refigured and newly interpreted reinvention of Sycorax critiques Western sculptures, monuments, and notions of the human. As I approached "Revisiting Sycorax," I was tempted to reach out and touch the sturdy yet fragile sculpture.

FIGURE 5.2. Lurch completing the wiring on "Revisiting Sycorax."
Courtesy of the artist.

The multiple open spaces produced by the spiderwebbed and netlike mass of strings of black and copper wire are buttressed by thicker black wire that appears to function as the outline and skeleton of Sycorax's physique. A vertical axis of cascading wire mimics water; defines air; and spans a space ten feet from ceiling to the floor. The wiring from the ceiling enters the space of the sculpture's head and functions as an appendage of the body reaching into the sky (another dimension); it is also part of the architecture and scaffolding that supports the body of the sculpture. Sycorax's body is kept upright by braided wire; around the braid that extends down from the ceiling, thinner wire strands cascade and fall over the sculpture like a rain shower or a net. Sycorax does not present herself/themselves as a freestanding and autonomous form. It is visibly attached to both the ceiling and the floor. A mass of wire that mimics the ruffles at the hem of a dress, or a patch of high grass, or perhaps even the sand of an island, covers the sculpture's feet.[30] Lurch's rendering of Sycorax is a rupturing and shoaling of the form and narrative of modernism. As a counterpoint to the Columbus statue in its celebration of the instantiation of modernism and the human, Sycorax is a figure that is porous and full of holes.

Heavier wire is used to outline the frame, or exoskeleton, of the body, while smaller, more irregular, jutting, curving, bending, smooth, and broken "almost lines" crisscross, break, wrap, and tangle themselves with the air to suture together an interior figure of a female form. The intertwined bends, curls, and unfurlings of the wire memorialize the Black and Native female in the Americas. By representing Sycorax as copresences for each other and as a singular entity in mid-motion, Lurch successfully pays homage to the often forgotten Black and Native feminine (and maternal) energy and presence in the Americas. Sycorax is a relational entity and figure that stands alongside, and conterminously with, another rather than a figure that is made by negating the Other. In the wire sculpture, Lurch renders Indigeneity and Blackness indistinguishable as they are both represented by the color black or the dark feminine. The copper wire and black wires meld into one another like skin.[31]

As a form of flesh, Sycorax reclaims the fleshy and liberated materiality of Black and Native peoples that conquest disavowed.[32] What conquest turned into meat, the "squaw," and the Black cunt, Lurch bends and twists with the movement of her own fleshy wrists into what could be interpreted as a dancing figure.[33] The simultaneous upward movements of the left arm and left leg work against the physics, kinetics, and normative proprioception of walking or running. Another kind of movement altogether is occurring. The upward thrust of motion both moves and suspends the figure in an off-center and off-balance motion. All of the weight is forced onto the right side and downward into the ground, while the kinetic energy on the left side pulls the weight of Sycorax upward. The movements of the figure compelled me to wonder what the context was/is for this kind of leaping or dancing. Is she dancing between the fourth and fifth beat, a tesseract beat? Are the two figures — in one — in the midst of a ceremony with each other? Are they in a trance? Whatever kind of movement the form and forms are engaged in, the Black and Indigenous feminine forms recognize each other and are in motion with each other.

Their motion together and the new kind of kinetic energy that the forms produce create a shift in perspective. This is the kind of ritual and ceremonial work that M. Jacqui Alexander would call "sacred." The sculpture's invocation of ceremony is important as it comes close to and touches the kind of ceremony Wynter tracks or looks for in her work. As Wynter moves with John Bishop's fallow longing for a ceremony for Othello and Desdemona (which still remains unimaginable for him), Wynter pursues a way to mark a ceremony or ritual act that can usher in the heretical, the unthinkable, and the unfathomable without trapping it/them once it is/they are conjured. How does the ceremony and the rupture and the movement toward the unthinkable — a more just notion of the human — continue without end?

Lurch's ritual of twisting and wiggling points, lines, and planes in a way moves close to Wynter's conception of the demonic and its unpredictability and openness. Lurch scrunches, stretches, and disfigures normative notions of time, dimensionality, and space. She spent a great deal of time speaking with me about the mathematics of the tesseract and its potential to subvert normative notions of dimension and aesthetic form. During the interview, I asked Lurch, the arts educator, to break down how time-space works through her use of line and form:

TIFFANY: I like how you talked about using the points . . . as a point of departure, but also using wire as another form of moving a line, and that helped you think about time and space differently, . . . since we're working it through these. So what were you thinking about as far as time was concerned in this piece?

CHARMAINE: So time moves through your work ["In the Clearing"] a lot in that you reference the . . . early clearing of the land — you know, how the Black body moves. In my work, you know, . . . [I am]

referencing Thornton and Lucie Blackburn as the past and then Henrietta Lacks as the future. So for me, visually with materials, once I put my pencil down, that's a point. As soon as I move [the pencil], it's past. It's in the past, and I am always moving towards a future and the present—in the present moving towards the future. So, you know, if you were a mathematician, you would extrapolate, or you know point. The first point of the pencil is A, if you move from A to B, that's a line. What I do is I wiggle my line all over until it creates something. That's what I'm doing.[34]

"Revisiting Sycorax," "Blueprint for a Mobile and Visible Carriage" (Thornton and Lucie Blackburn), and "The Phenomenal Henrietta Lacks" are an extension of Lurch's wiggling of the line, transcending the incrementalization and ordering of time—past, present, future—until they "create something" new. Ceremonies, like prayer, dance, and wiggling a line, reorganize space-time and, as Alexander explains, bring "the self in intimate concert with the Sacred," or an/Other.[35] As a meditation on Black and Indigenous flux, Sycorax symbolizes a space of flux, indeterminacy, and possibility all at the same time.

On a more representational level, the intertwining of Black and Indigenous "flesh" reflected by the black and copper wire makes the viewer contend with the ways that Black people and Indigenous people in North America/on Turtle Island and the hemisphere remain shaped by one another's presence. The open and malleable wire form of Sycorax evokes the ways that Black diasporic subjects and Indigenous people remain porous and edgeless in relationship to one another. This open edgelessness and lightweight wire bending also reference the Caribbean influences of creolization in Lurch's aesthetic. Lurch says that she bends wire in a style "kind of [like] that Trinidadian, carnivalesque intervention; [it is] very different, but that's also in my mind as I'm doing that wire work." As an example, she cites the work of the multimedia Trinidadian artist Christopher Cozier who creates memory-scapes of Caribbean colonial and contemporary life through mixed-media sketch and sculpture installations.[36] As a first-generation Jamaican Canadian living in Toronto, Lurch contends with the ways that Blackness and anti-Blackness are always embedded within practices of Indigenous genocide throughout the hemisphere. The Black cul-

---

FIGURE 5.3. Close-up of "Revisiting Sycorax," showing dense and entangled wiring. Courtesy of the artist.

tural and political imagination is always in a state of flux as it considers the lives of Indigenous peoples in the Caribbean and on Turtle Island. The lines of Lurch's, and her family's, movement and routes around the Caribbean basin and Turtle Island can also be traced in the multiple, intersecting, and shifting planes of perspective that the sculpture offers. The multiple and moving points, blending of points on the chromatic scale, and open-ended spaces of "Revisiting Sycorax" are meandering and confounding. One is forced to move or dance around Sycorax in an attempt to trace an ever elusive point of departure or arrival. Sycorax initiates a thread through the tradition of a Black exilic thought that asks Black diaspora studies to interrogate some of the enclosures it erects.

OFFSHORE ERRANCIES: IN THE SYCORAXIAN LINE OF BLACK EXILE

I inherited the project of this book from a particular form of Black diasporic politics and a unique intellectual genealogy established through centuries of political struggle and Black creative invention that I encountered in Toronto. I admit that I arrived late to the scene and experienced only a portion of Black Canada's vast political and intellectual geography. On the Tuesday that I arrived in 2006, I stumbled into a crowd of Black and Indigenous people demanding the return of land in Caledonia to the Six Nations. Black people and members of the Six Nations blocked off a section of Dundas Street in front of City Hall. I had never witnessed such a swelling and heaving crowd of protesting Indigenous nations as a Black person growing up in the tristate area of the Delaware River Valley, where radical people-of-color groups and collectives rarely included Indigenous peoples.[37] I immediately felt the violence in the land surge up through the concrete and permeate every molecule of air/space. The Black folks in the city also acknowledge the funk and residue of ongoing genocide. Resisting the Canadian project of Indigenous genocide and colonialism is a part of the pulse of Black radical politics in Toronto.

Alongside Black folks' acknowledgment of colonialism and Indigenous genocide was an acute diasporic sensibility of being in exile. In space after space—whether among Black teachers and parents organizing around the Toronto District School Board's zero-tolerance policy targeting Black youth, Black trade unionists, Black LGBT and queer folks, Black prison abolitionists, or Black artists and community folks—I witnessed a brand of Black diasporic politics that did not seek a comfortable resting space in the Canadian nation-state. Articulated best by Rinaldo Walcott in *Black Like Who? Writing Black Canada*, Black Canadian's diasporic politics can be thought of as "located between the U.S. and the Caribbean, Canadian Blackness is a bubbling brew of desires for elsewhere, disappointments in the nation and the pleasures of exile—even for those who have resided here for many generations."[38] This restlessness was reflected in a range of Black diasporic experiences with exile that ranged from the specific loss of kin associated with legacies of enslavement in the Americas to the devastation of knowing home but not being able to return to the African continent due to the legacies of colonialism. Arriving in Canada in the 1880s, the 1950s, or in the twenty-first century, Black people rarely docked in a place they could call home. Canada inspired in Black people what Walcott might call a longing for "elsewhere," or what Dionne Brand sought to call forth in the title to her novel *In Another Place, Not Here*.

This sense of disappointment or being perpetually out of place in Canada is felt by Black people descended from ancestors who were enslaved in the Americas, as well as by Somalis, Black Muslims, and other Black diasporan people criminalized and killed by the state. Many, like Brand, even professed that they "d[id]n't want no fucking country" before they arrived in Canada.[39] This particular kind of rejection of the nation-state not only makes the refusing "Black Canadian" subject surprising and unexpected, but it also produces an orientation to the nation that troubles the fields of African diaspora and Black studies. The specific kind of Black exilic relationship to a notion of home in settler nation-states is particularly acute for Black people in North America. Saidiya Hartman's claim to statelessness and homelessness as a productive state of being—or ontology—orbits alongside Brand's and Walcott's gospel of no nation in Canada.[40]

For Black Canadian subjects, home remains a changing place in the making and always in flux. Walcott captures this stretching and morphing sense of home when he muses, "Home, in the diasporic framework is an ethical place, not a narrative of containment."[41] This pliable and unproprietary sense of homemaking was an ethic I experienced as a flexible praxis and at times a ceremonial labor that was continually performed by the Black people in the Canadian nation-state. In a similar movement toward land and sovereignty as kinds of Indigenous processes of making home, Mishuana Goeman defines land as a meaning-making process rather than "a claimed object."[42] Similarly, Leanne Betasamosake Simpson recognizes the relationship to self and others as key and rejects sovereignty as something that is recognized by the settler state.[43]

While I was in Toronto I was fortunate enough to meet three Black women and an Anishinaabeg woman—Larissa Cairncross, Abi Salole, Marika Schwandt, and Christine Luza—committed to Black and Indigenous healing while living on Turtle Island. Our encounters and relationships were cultivated through the enactment of ceremony with one another. The sacred rituals honed a sense of being with one another and being present in a place we created amid the rising smoke of sage on to which we could never really hold. The rituals inspired in Larissa, Abi, Marika, and me an ability to relinquish our hold on the notion of a Black nation or nation-state as a sanctuary. For Christine, it troubled her understanding of Native sovereignty as a rigid notion of territory, peoplehood, and nation that was tethered together by a Western notion of governance. Home increasingly had to do with how those of us in the circle amid the rising smoke make peace with one another again and again. Home would become an open-ended Black practice of seeking out a place in the vein of Wynter's demonic while in Toronto.

Returning to Toronto in 2015 represented an opportunity to remake home through different Black diasporan ceremonies with Charmaine Lurch. Even as a mere viewer of Lurch's work, one is participating in a ceremony, whether one knows it or not. Lurch's sculptures and paintings from *Conversations in Flux* exhibit a through line between the diasporic figures and exilic movements of Henrietta Lacks, Lucie and Thornton Blackburn, and Sycorax. Through form, Lurch connects the escape of Lucie and Thornton Blackburn from slave traders across the Detroit River to Upper Canada, to Henrietta Lacks's life and the extraction of her cells in Baltimore that dispersed her genetic material across time and space, to the always morphing geographies of Sycorax. Through her sculptures and paintings, Lurch creates and crosses Black geographies in ways that mimic the unusual terrains of Black exilic thought and aesthetics.

Lurch's errant and disappearing point and lines reinvent Black geography on what McKittrick calls demonic grounds. Her tesseract movements meet up with the demonic musings of Wynter that gesture toward otherwise ways of being human and McKittrick's errant engagement with the discipline of geography. Both Lurch's use of form and McKittrick's blackening of geography are hard to contain and slip in and out of place. Their Black diasporic interventions into modernist form and the disciplinary constraints of geography both slow traditions' momentum and throw traditions into flux. While Lurch's and McKittrick's geographical location in Toronto matter, I avoid overwriting their geographies as belonging to or the property of any specific (Canadian) nation. Instead, I respect the ways that their engagement with Toronto and the Canadian nation-state also remain in flux and resist national, regional, and supranational enclosures.

In this vein, the ways that Walcott remaps Black Canada in *Black Like Who?* is important. Walcott rearranges conventional maps and places Black Canada "between the U.S. and the Caribbean."[44] The betweenness of which Walcott speaks, or this space of displacement, rearrangement, and suture, forces a rereading of the map of the Americas as well as a rereading of Black diaspora studies. Walcott's rearrangement is an explicit challenge to the traditions of centering either the United States or the Caribbean in the field by establishing Black Canada as a crucial nexus. When Walcott rewrites the geography of Black diaspora studies by situating Black Canada as a meeting point, he "attempts to formulate some conceptual ground for thinking about the relationships between pre-Confederation Black people and more recent arrivals. In particular, [Walcott] suggested that the politics and sensibilities of diaspora could work well to invent traditions that bought these two groups into conversation."[45] The conceptual ground that Walcott so eloquently achieves in his remapping resonates with what Lurch depicts and invokes so powerfully in her sculptures and paintings. Practicing a cartographic and geographical rearrangement of her own, Lurch manipulates and shapes a new map of Blackness in the Americas, as well.

Lurch invents her own diasporic ceremony of shaping new encounters and new spaces through sculpture. In essence, she invents traditions that create conversations among the Blackburns (escaping the United States), Sycorax (traveling between the Caribbean and North Africa), and Lacks (whose cells are dispersed across the galaxy) as diasporic subjects that traverse, produce, and undo the spaces of the United States, Canada, and the Caribbean. These Black diasporic subjects touch in time and space in Toronto while also remaking what we know as Toronto through Lurch's art. While Lurch's and Walcott's work produce a conceptual, analytical, and creative center (albeit temporarily and shiftingly) in the space of Black Canada, I argue that Lurch sculpts and shapes Black Canada into a nodal point that also functions as a shoal. Lurch pulls Black "American" (of the Americas) subjectivity, politics, and aesthetics away from the mainland of the United States and the shorelines of the Caribbean to the shoals of exilic movement. Lurch uses various Black diasporic subjects' movement at the level of genes, bodies, transit systems, and colonial specter away from nation-bound approaches and rigid scales of analysis. In this way, Lurch practices an undisciplined and radical form of Black place-making.

McKittrick has described Black Canada or Black presence in Canada as a sort of "wonder."[46] Her work in *Demonic Grounds* forces a reckoning with the where of Black Canada. As the Black Canadian subject is often written out of the Canadian nation-state, as well as a portion of Turtle Island, artists such as Afua Cooper, Dionne Brand, and Charmaine Lurch must reassert the presence of the Black subject. This reassertion—or presencing—and act of making Blackness visible are not projects that seek a claim to citizenship. In fact, they expose the ways that the Canadian nation-state must script Blackness out of its national origin story to know itself as innocent—particularly untouched by the stain of slavery—and unique within the Americas.

In an interview with Peter James Hudson, McKittrick elaborates on the contributions of Black Canadian thought that, for her as of 2014, remained an "un-fielded" endeavor of study. Of Black Canadian scholars in particular, McKittrick says, "They offer what I consider a conceptual frame that brings black Canada into view and, at the same time, discloses the racialized workings, and thus failures, of the nation-state and the attendant unmet democratic promises of modernity. This kind of frame situates black Canadian thought within the context of diaspora—the intellectual and creative and historic narratives that are always locally outer-national."[47] As a diasporic and outer-national formation, the Black subject writing, creating, and living from within the space of Canada is a witness to the "unmet democratic promises of modernity" and of the nation-state itself.[48] The Black subject is also a representation of the uncanny and the specter of the disavowed racial terror that haunts the Canadian landscape.

For the average White Canadian, the practice of slavery in Canada is and was ostensibly covered up. Slavery remained a surprise in the historical (and contemporary) imagination until Marie-Joseph Angelique lit Montreal on fire and burned the city to the ground in 1734. Similarly, the flight of Lucie and Thornton Blackburn from slave catchers in the United States, and their subsequent establishment of a taxi service that lay the groundwork for the Toronto Transit Commission's trolley line, disrupts the White Anglo-Saxon enclosures placed around the White Canadian nation and its story of becoming. Black arrivants from the Caribbean and Africa from the 1950s on have continued to rearrange the space of the city through the practice of Caribbean Carnival at events like Caribana and Pelau's Masqueerade, and Black Lives Matter protests continue to interrupt the mundane flow of colonial terror by re-creating the "de road" when and wherever necessary.[49] These traditions that remap the landscape of Canada also remap the space of the United States and the North American continent.

Black Canada produces another scale of Black life and Black cultural formations to which Black studies must attend. The ways that Black people are able to re-create regions and traditions in the United States and Canada is a practice that transgresses borders and even calls them into question. For example, Alissa Trotz has tracked itineraries of Caribbean travelers between West Indian shopping centers in Toronto and New York who create home and the space of the Anglophone Caribbean in North America through their consumption and travels back and forth across the border. An alternative site of Caribbeanness is created in a different "spatial terrain" from which to experience "home."[50] Trotz's travelers, Blokorama, Black Lives Matter, and Caribana, as well as other diasporic market and cultural exchanges, produce what Walcott theorizes as North American Blackness.[51]

North American Blackness presents a challenge to some of the nationalisms and nation-bound analytics within Black studies. North American Blackness as a supranational formation is kin of and akin to the Black Atlantic as an analytic and methodological approach for attending to Black cultural and political configuration that exceeds the nation-states of Canada and the United States. More expansive and inclusive than U.S. Black, Black Canadian, and Caribbean studies, North American Blackness emerges from the experiences and struggles of Black people who live in, move through, and negotiate the white supremacist—and white majority—nation-states of the U.S. and Canada. This Black North American frame also functions as a critique of the ways that the U.S. and Canadian nation-states sustain the relations of Native genocide, slavery, and anti-Blackness through forms of state violence that attempt to secure the respective states' national borders. Lurch's work attends to the ways that North American Black life contests national borders and respatializes Black life by connecting the experiences of exile of Lucie and Thornton Blackburn, Henrietta Lacks (and her cells), and Sycorax at Walcott's in-between space of Canada. By wiggling points and lines, Lurch transforms the exhibit spaces in Toronto into a demonic site that takes on the dimension-scrambling characteristics of the tesseract.

By situating Sycorax in relationship to North American Blackness in the space of the Toronto Centre for the Arts gallery, the Caribbean can also momentarily fold into place as a central node. This kind of simultaneity is embedded within the twists, bends, and wiggling lines of Lurch's sculpture

"Revisiting Sycorax." Sycorax's formation is possible only through the tangling together and intertwining of black and copper wire. Black femininity is dependent on the existence and persistence of Indigenous femininity for its own survival. In addition to tying Black and Indigenous existence together, Lurch's Sycorax rearranges geographies of conquest. The spatial implications of her corrective to and transporting of Sycorax, as a symbol of the figurative and historical erasure of Black and Indigenous femininity that occurs within Shakespeare's account of discovery, to Canada from the Caribbean produce a geographical rupture. Lurch's sculpture enacts a geographical shift or her own respatialization of conquest by transferring the landscape and the sites of conquest that are the bodies of Black and Indigenous female bodies to the Canadian landscape.

Within both Indigenous (Taíno/Arawak) and Black diasporic (Caribbean) hermeneutics and interpretations of *The Tempest*, the Caribbean becomes the space of encounter. While the two communities tussle with each other over the racialization (or representation) of Caliban, and therefore of Sycorax, as Indigenous, Black, or Mestizo, some semblance of consensus emerges about the where of the epic narrative of the inaugural events of New World discovery. As several Black studies scholars have argued, the story of modernity and the New World begins in the basin of the Caribbean. The violent rupture that created the time, space, and people of the Caribbean also created the Americas, including Canada.

Thinking about the Caribbean as the birthplace of the New World and the Americas renders Canada a child of the Caribbean. To imagine Canada, we thus must first imagine the Caribbean; we must first imagine the place from which Lurch and her family traveled. We must imagine the genocide of the Taíno people and the enslavement of African people in the Caribbean before we can even imagine the birth pangs of Canada. The Caribbean basin begat Canada. Similarly, Indigenous and Black women's bodies make the Americas, North America, and Canada possible. Sycorax could be interpreted as the mother of Canada returning. Situating the figure of Sycorax and the Caribbean in the nation space of Canada also enacts a flipping of the map of the Americas. It turns the map of the Americas — specifically, Canada, the United States, North America and its supposed archipelagos of the Caribbean — on its head. Through recognizing the Caribbean basin and its islands as geological forms or shoals themselves, an island epistemology breaks through the surface and is brought to bear on the epistemologies and cartographies that have produced what we now know as the United States and Canada. Rather than repeating islands or island territories as units of possession, the Caribbean archipelagos and shoals of 1492 that Lurch transports north to Canada and centers through the figure of Sycorax reproduce Canada as another island.[52] Sycorax's presence, as an island subject or subjectivity, transforms the mainland territory or space of Canada into another island territory. If the Black Canadian subject is deconstructed and imagined as a moving and rootless geographical subject emerging from the diasporic space of enslavement and the Caribbean, its Canadianness is radically upended. Further, if Blackness's and Sycorax's island subjectivity has to be accounted for, so does the U.S. and Canadian mainland's taxonomization and geological categorization as nonisland space. Lurch's remapping of the Americas resonates with Walcott's exilic thought and Brand's gospel of no nation. Walcott's work calls for a reimagining of the Black diaspora in North America or a Black North American studies that is less bounded.[53] These kinds of respatializations of Canada and North America begs a question: what kind of shoaling or disruption does the Black and Indigenous Caribbean cause to Canada and the Americas?

Black exilic geographies of flux, interfacing with Indigenous geographies of relationality, produce a kind of hemispheric thought that embraces the ways that First Nations peoples' Turtle Island evokes the archipelagos of Indigenous cosmogonies and geographies. Like the islands of the Caribbean—or the shells of turtles—that can also be imagined as spaces where the sea floor rises up and breaks the surface of the water, at the space of Lurch's Sycorax, Black and Indigenous geographies become a conceptual and geographical shoal and a place to foment a more radical Black and Native studies.

Rather than imagine the Columbian moment as a form of modern geographical and scientific rupture that "Man" and men such as Columbus instantiated, Lurch imagines the rupture of the tesseract as a moment of flux that people have always been imagining and inventing and enacting through ceremony. Further, people will continue to produce these creative and spatial ruptures on new terms. Unlike Columbus, however, Lurch accesses the space between dimensions as a space of ethical possibility. As a sculptor, Lurch wiggled, bent, and altered the line and other geo-humanist epistemologies in ways that did not require Black or Indigenous death for Sycorax to take form. This form of creation as a relational process counters the monumentalization of the itinerant soldier Columbus on Boston's North End waterfront.

In a ceremony of resistance to the exclusive and violent writing of the human, the supporters of "Black Lives" disrupt older ceremonies—of stone and concrete—to make space for black and copper-wired futures. Lurch's initiation of the ceremony between Black and Indigenous feminine forms ritualizes an instantiation of humanity on new terms. Her wire tribute "Revisiting Sycorax" pays homage to Black and Indigenous peoples who seek out the ceremony to be moved by, affected by, and render themselves open and available to one another. For it is only when Sycorax is open to her twoness that she can buck against kinetic normativity and lift her left arm and left leg on the beat/dimension of the tesseract. In this new ceremony, she is with herself and them at the same time.

CEREMONIES

Ending with a meditation on ceremony returns to the ways that this book opened. Wynter's protracted engagement with the metaphor of the ceremony—specifically, the rituals that instantiate Man and other restrictive genres of the human—stands as a powerful critique of the ways that governing systems of knowledge enter into and form the social order. My reading of Wynter's invocation of ceremony is unconventional. Departing from more theoretically robust and faithful interpretations, I engage Wynter's ceremony at the level of embodied, quotidian, and transformative practice. I want to bring her moments of transformation—talked about in her interview with Greg Thomas in 2006—throughout her scholarly career into conversation with the personal moments of transformation discussed by scholars such as M. Jacqui Alexander, Audre Lorde, and Leslie Marmon Silko. Wynter's metaphor of the ceremony extends beyond a mode of critique, doubling as a praxis and space where the order of knowledge and being can be ritually disassembled. Wynter opens the essay "A Ceremony Must Be Found" with an epigraph that features John Peale Bishop's poem "Speaking of Poetry." In the poem, the narrator cannot fathom the possibility of a ceremony that can sufficiently mark the unthinkable and heretical union between Desdemona and Othello.[54] Like Bishop, William Faulkner, and others who cannot imagine, yet attempt to call forth, a ceremonial event that could mark the illicit breach of the barrier between Man (European) and the other human (Black), Wynter appeals to the unprecedented and transformative ceremony—however, on radically different terms. Heretical epistemic revolutions—or ceremonies—such as those that occurred in 1968, in the Black Arts Movement, and in the language of cosmogonies such as Rastafarianism that emphasize the "over/turn," have the potential to break open the enclosures embedded in multiple forms of knowledge systems that erect enclosures around the category of the human.[55]

Ceremonies carry potential for transformation. However, ceremonies as understood, written, and performed by Bishop, Faulkner, and Wynter are very different. I also argue that ceremonies as constructed events for Indigenous and Black people as New World subjects are different from those for conquistador subjects. For Bishop and Faulkner, the ceremony or event of the wedding nuptial is a bounded temporal moment that is composed of a set of discrete actions that emerge from a particular tradition. For example, the wedding as a sacred event that is sanctioned by God, the state, and a witnessing community of humans marks a juncture and shift in time and social status through a set of discursive acts. The culmination of bodily comportment, dress, ritual, and an oral pronouncement by an official constitute a form of juridical force that has authority. According to Judith Butler, these performative acts instantiate heterosexual desire and, in essence, normalize heterosexual binaries, the biological construction of man and woman, and gendered personhood.[56] The wedding is an authoritarian performative act of humanism. The wedding, in and of itself, constitutes the two parties involved as humans. For Bishop and Faulkner, a ceremony or wedding does not yet exist to unite Desdemona, or white womanhood, to Othello the Moor, or Blackness. The wedding, as it is imagined within humanism and as a function of instituting the human, has no protocol or performative act that can yet announce Othello as a man. It leaves Bishop and Faulkner wanting.

Ceremony is also an important collective metaphor, process, and repertoire of Black and Indigenous flesh seeking to rearrange life. Wynter's notion and practice of ceremony spans more than thirty years across her immense body of work. Wynter has been speaking and writing about ceremony since the 1980s. Wynter's notion of ceremony emerged during a moment in which she felt that she was "crossing a frontier." In the interview with Thomas, Wynter recalled writing the piece just as she was beginning to use a personal computer. At this particular technological frontier, she revealed, she felt as if she was at the "most heretical" point in her development as a scholar. Referring to "The Ceremony Must Be Found," Wynter states, "In that essay, I think that you can see where the crossing begins."[57] The heresies that Wynter commits in her work take place in the very ways that she breaks and creates emancipatory openings in a cognitive order that overrepresents man as the genre of being human that functions as the apex or proper performance of humanity (i.e., Man1 and Man2). Breaking each cognitive and epistemic shift at its seams to reveal the construction and naturalization of its overrepresentation is a radical ritual through which Wynter lays bare the innards and mechanisms of Man's invention. Her overturning, shoaling, and interruption of the ways that humanity is imagined remains a foundational hermeneutic for Black studies, Black aesthetics, and Black politics.

Attending to the break, the shift, the transgression, the overturning, and the mutation, Wynter teaches her readers that the hegemonic order of knowledge and inventing/writing the "self" are brittle and bendable processes that can be altered. Her own ceremonial acts of heresy—rupture, overturning, and emancipatory openings—have also changed over time. Wynter confided to Thomas that it was when she retired in the early 1990s that she "began to really push to see that it was the system of knowledge itself, it's not a matter of what you can do inside it. You really had to come to this. That's when I became, I would say, heretical." Her retirement coincided with a planetary shift in consciousness around 1992: the quincentenary of the Columbian rupture and exchange. Wynter shared that the lecturing and preparation she did to mark that anniversary induced another opening or crossing in her work.[58] It was in 1992 that Wynter wrote the essay "1492: A New Worldview." This planetary moment was not just significant for Wynter's work, but for other Black and Indigenous women in the Americas as well.

NEW CEREMONIES: DISTINCTIONS WITHOUT EDGES

The hum of the chorus, the interweaving of textiles, the shared drum skin that beats out a new dance and the praising and calling forth of shared gods offer some of the most poignant moments, utterances, knots, kinetics, gestures, and modes of thinking about how the relations of conquest bring Black and Indigenous death and life into each other's folds. In the passages of the novels of by Díaz and Silko, and within the accounts of Alexander's own haunting by Kituba, the lives, deaths, and spirits of Black and Indigenous peoples gather as tapestry, as current, pulse, and a collective force. I argue that Indigenous genocide and slavery—and, ultimately, the abolition of both—while distinct and particular types of fabrics when threaded through and around conquest, stitch a textile whose patterns do not have edges. While each form of violence and the Native and Black responses to them have irreducible stress points and textures, they can never be bracketed off or sequestered from one another in North, South, or Central America or the Caribbean.

Conquest—or, more specifically, the violent bloodletting of Indigenous genocide and slavery—created a shoal. The shoal's very materiality emerges as a result of the accumulation and sedimentation of solid matter offshore. As a location offshore or in the middle of the sea, the shoal is an amalgam of sea and not sea. Like the ensemble of materials at the ecotonal space of sea and land, the bodily matter of Indigenous and Black people met in the sea due to the violence of conquest. Speaking from what Wynter and McKittrick might call a "demonic ground" of haunting, memory, witness, and convening with the ancestors, Alexander narrates—or chants—in *Pedagogies of Crossing* the affective itineraries of the Middle Passage. Speaking from an unidentifiable place and using multiple voices, Alexander writes:

> Not only humans made the Crossing, traveling only in one direction through the Ocean given the name Atlantic. Grief traveled as well.
>
> The dead do not like to be forgotten, especially those whose lives had come to violent end and had been stacked sometimes ten high in a set of mass graves, the head of one thrown in with the body of another, male becoming female, female becoming male, their payment for building the best stone fortress that hugged a steep hill, reputed to be the most well secured in the Caribbean. Secure for the British, that is, who buried their antipathy for the French for one brief moment and killed off three hundred Indians in one day in the hope of proving ownership of the country.
>
> For months after the massacre, Indian blood usurped the place of mud and ran into the narrow channel that led to the Caribbean Sea, but not before depositing layers of bloody silt thick with suffering at the bottom of the river's floor. The bloody river took the story to the Sea, the Wide Sargasso Sea, which absorbed the grief, folding it into its turquoise jade until it assumed the color of angered sorrow. It spun into a vortex, a current in the Caribbean. The Trade Winds. North, pushing clear to Guinea, close to the shores of the Old Kongo, Kingdom of the Bantu. Cabinda. Down, down Benguela. Angola. Forced upward again. Dahomey. Trade Winds South. Brazil. Nago. Candomble. Jeje. Swept into the Cape Horn up to Peru, Colombia, Ufaina. Spitting. Descending in the drift of the West Winding, climbing just underneath the dividing line that rests in the imagination. Equator. Kalunga.

It joined the grief of those who had just died emaciated, gasping for air in the two-storied house locked shut for months by the man who believed he could own flesh.[59]

The flowing blood of Black people down the hill from the fortress ran over and seeped into the soil of the "clearing" where Indigenous people were massacred. This blood and flesh that intermingled on the land and spilled into the sea no doubt changed the composition of the ocean and created a shoal.

Christina Sharpe's meditation on the Black captive bodies carried in the hold of the *Zong* and spilled/poured/thrown over its sides considers the matter of their flesh and how it changed the ocean. The body and the blood turned flesh and then turned salt remains. In the midst of her wake work, Sharpe considered the "residence time" of the nutrients, salt, and substance of the flesh of those emptied into the ocean.[60] She asked her colleague Anne Gardulski about the chemical and atomic life of their matter, their salt. Gardulski assured Sharpe that the atoms, the blood and the salt of the people thrown overboard, "are out there in the ocean even today."[61]

Through the temporality of residence time, the blood, matter, and salt of Black and Indigenous flesh have their own way of contaminating, haunting, touching, caressing, and whispering to the other in the ocean. Alexander's and Sharpe's invocations of the spirit energy and flesh of those who inhabited and resided in the depths of the ocean further animate the metaphor of the shoal. Thinking with Sharpe's poetic-scientific and Alexander's ceremonial renderings of Black and Indigenous flesh and energy as living nutrients and components of the ocean, along with the shoal metaphor, enables a way to picture the process of solid ocean matter accumulating on the sea floor and rising up and breaking through the skin of the ocean like a pimple. Alexander's and Sharpe's incantations and poetics perform the capaciousness of Black diaspora studies.

Alexander's cartography of crossings that traces the itineraries of Middle Passage grief and flesh that commingled with Indigenous blood is a new kind of critical geography—made from conquest but not replicating it—that traces the edgelessness of genocide and slavery. Alexander's and Sharpe's methodologies, pedagogies, poetics, and ceremonies—or tarrying with spirit—birth new modes of New World knowing and knowledge production. In fact, surviving New World violence creates new epistemic processes and formations. In their novels, Silko and Toni Morrison attend to the psychic and trans-temporal portals that the rupture—of New World violence—opened for new kinds of knowledge, ceremony, and life for African-descended and Indigenous peoples in the Americas. For Silko, the ceremony as an embodied ritual in *Almanac of the Dead*—as a practice of worship, prayer, flight, healing, and dance—is a sacred space of becoming, rebirth, and new beginnings. As if she were writing to Alexander and, more specifically, to the other side of Alexander's Middle Passage, Silko includes a narrative of ceremonial reclamation and healing through a remaking of old African gods on new terms and new terrain:

> From the beginning, Africans had escaped and hid in the mountains where they met up with survivors of indigenous tribes hiding in remote strongholds. In the mountains the Africans had discovered a wonderful thing: certain African gods had located themselves in the Americas as well as Africa: the Giant Serpent, the Twin Brothers, the Maize Mother, to name a few. Right then the magic had happened: great American and great African tribal cultures had come together to create a power-ful consciousness within all people. All were welcome—everyone had been included. That had been and still was the greatest strength of the Damballah, the Gentle. Damballah excluded no one and nothing.[62]

In Silko's novel, the African gods had also made the journey or the cross-ing. The gentle Damballah who "excluded no one and nothing," read in the context of Wynter's and the Black diaspora's search for a shift in con-sciousness or a mode of knowing that includes everyone and everything, represents a new ceremony. The process or ritual act of accepting old gods on new terms—a new consciousness—that is always open to revision rep-resents the kind of ceremonial practice that reconciles abolitionist Black diasporic thought with decolonial Indigenous thought in both Wynter's and Silko's work.

Later in the novel, in an attempt to further elucidate the making of a new Black and Indigenous people who were melded together through the on-going labor of surviving conquest, Silko presents the Mardi Gras Indian. While critics may read the depiction of the Black Indian as a deracina-tion of African people through an imposition of Indigeneity, I interpret Silko as writing and affirming the making of a new diasporic and Indige-nous people. Silko writes that the "Black Indians dance with wild aban-don. The dances are tribal."[63] When the Black Indians dance or enact the ceremony of dance, "No outsider knows where Africa ends and America begins."[64] Lurch's dancing Sycorax also enacts the ceremonial blurring of lines of which Silko speaks. Lurch's sculpture prevents the viewer from being able to discern where Blackness ends and where Indigeneity begins. Ceremonies such as Lurch's "Revisiting Sycorax" bring to fruition things that cannot yet name (or escape signification) because they do not emerge from the grammar of humanism.

Unlike the humanist ceremony of the ritual of marriage that constitutes and instantiates the human through linear time—a before and after—and marks one as human through bourgeois hetero- and homonormative monogamous sexuality, there is no pronouncement in Sycorax's dance. It is not a performance for the state; nor is it recognized by the state as a performance of a discrete and normative identity. Sycorax makes humanity a state of flux, change, and transformation. Or, in other words, to be human is to be in a state of ceremony, or to be ceremony. According to Wynter, "Being human is always a doing, a praxis."[65]

For Wynter, the ceremony "found" is a continual overturning and heretic-like disruption of the overrepresentation of knowledge systems that narrowly inscribe the human as man. Ceremony is the continual disruption of the formation of the structural opposition that creates an us and a them or the geo-epistemology of "the Line."[66] Ceremony in its other-than-liberal humanist vein is open, malleable, repeatable, and unending. Ultimately, Wynter is in search of a ceremony that is "able to reenact Renaissance humanism's original 'heresy' without performing or enacting a 'them/ourselves' split."[67]

As a way to track this heretical ritual or ceremony of flux, I attend to Lurch's aesthetic practice of wiring Sycorax as an open state of Black and Indigenous relationality. To some extent, Lurch's practice references and pays homage to the kind of ceremonial work in which Black and Indigenous women have engaged to know one another and, thus, the self. Ceremony unsettles the body, Western epistemologies, and notions of time and space. The labor of ceremony requires a simultaneous reclamation and surrender of the body to a collective agreement to enter into chaos. Chaos allows us to enter into a Lordean space of erotic possibilities, where bodies transfer experiences and come into contact with the sacred together.

Throughout Lorde's body of work on the erotic, the transformative space of the chaotic emerges time and time again. In her keynote speech at the National Third World Gay and Lesbian Conference in 1979, Lorde told the audience, "The ignorance will end when each of us begins to seek out and trust the knowledge deep inside of us, when we dare to go into that chaos which exists before understanding and come back with new tools for action and change. For it is from within that deep knowledge that our visions are fueled, and it is our vision which lays the groundwork for our actions and our future."[68]

Chaos is a productive space. It inspires new action and new space. Within the chaotic and renewing space of ceremony, Black matters and issues and Native matters and issues temporarily lose their boundaries and at times merge and appear anew. Ceremony is a space-making practice of Black and Indigenous women. In 2006, the Black and Indigenous women of Toronto INCITE! Women of Color against Violence conjured a new geography through ceremony. This Black and Indigenous space in flux represented a place outside the nations and states of the imaginaries and recognition of the United States, Canada, Trinidad, Ethiopia, and South Africa. This new space forged through ceremony created a shoal where the grammars of decolonization and abolition came together and uttered a possibility of doing humanity off the shores of the mandates of conquest.

The ceremonial and sacred work of Lurch's sculptures, Lorde's willingness to approach the chaos of the erotic, and INCITE!'s ceremony work create new epistemologies and ways of being with one another and the self. Within the context of ceremonial work, I imagine and theorize the sacred as knowledge gained or a way of knowing—epistemology—that recognizes an intimate connection to the other people with whom you are conducting the ceremony. In other words, it is a form of ethics. The sacred in the context of Lurch's and INCITE! Toronto's work functions as the knowledge or knowing that your survival as a Black person is inseparable from your and their (your-their) survival as a Native person. This knowledge of interconnection is not a process that can be accessed alone. Sacred knowledge is coproduced and requires other bodies—or another body—to be accessed.

The ceremony that Wynter seeks is a process that must be performed again and again and again. The ceremony also, and most important, depends on the collective movement, thoughts, vibrations, and pulses of the people gathered. The beauty of a metaphor such as the ceremony is that it is a ritual embedded in and that makes up the social realm into and out of which we can move, think, pray, and work. New and old ceremonies come in from the ether and invite us to become heretics, make a break with the old and initiate the new. Some ceremonies are violent, and some are invoked to make things right with ourselves and another.

For instance, the ceremonial work in this book came about as a result of bodily and emotional discomfort with the new ways conquest touched me when I arrived in Toronto in 2006. The ritual that this book project has invited me to engage was a larger ceremony of healing. Part of this book's task aspires to get close to the catastrophic violence of conquest and the ceremonies that made the unthinkable possible. Understanding and naming the ceremonies that institute violence helps us determine how we name ourselves and our roles in the violence. Part of the ceremony includes acknowledging that the ways that we make claims to and perform our humanity often—and more than likely—requires the death of the other.

The #BlackLivesMatter ceremony in chapter 1 disrupted the aesthetics, logics, and genre of the conquistador human that require anti-Black and anti-Indigenous regimes of violence. In chapter 2, ceremonies of Black and Indigenous resistance produce geographies of life that counter the violence of settlement, as well as the cartographic subject and its map of conquest. In chapter 3, rituals of caressing, caring for, and acknowledging Black embodiment and its pores and points of connection to life marked as nonhuman invite new world-making practices. In turn, new world-making practices require pores, skin, bone, touch, erotics, and new haptic modes that change our relations to notions of the human as an ordered sovereign, bounded, raced, and settled individual. The Black and Indigenous eros explored in chapter 4 reorients conversations about "coalition" by grounding them in struggles to experience life with one another in the midst of being unmoored. Finally, Charmaine Lurch's sculptural spatialization of the tesseract, the wiggling and distortion of the line create new aesthetics that invoke the human ceremony on new terms that invite us to shape what it means to be alive. The protests, cartographies against the mandate of conquest, Black-blue embodiment, Black and Native erotics, and Black aesthetics initiate ceremonies that break with violent anti-Black and anti-Indigenous modes of being human. They create new and shifting grounds.

Yemaya, that broad expanse of Ocean, who lives on sea and on land has pushed past modernity's mode of reason and taken up temporary sojourn on the insides of this artificial enclosure, come to accept, to cleanse, to bless, to remind us that in the same way the breaking of the waves does not compromise the integrity of the Ocean, so too anything broken in our lives cannot compromise that cosmic flow to wholeness. The body cannot but surrender in order to make way for this tidal flow. And this, too, necessitates practice.

—M. JACQUI ALEXANDER, *Pedagogies of Crossing*

Land is not the traditional element used to analogize Black flux or think about dynamic, fluid, and ever moving Black diasporic subjectivity. Rarely does land evoke the kind of flexibility, elusiveness and trickster-like qualities that Black diasporic life symbolizes in the Western Hemisphere. Water, most often the ocean, has been Black studies' most faithful metaphor.[1] Throughout this book, I have been thinking about these questions: What becomes of Black metaphors of flux when their waves hit the shore? What happens when Blackness docks, gets twisted, and entangled in genocide and, encounters the Native/Indigenous subject? What grows, takes shape, and emerges at this place? This project has been a conjuring of these co-ordinates.

Black life at the space of the shoal becomes complicated and at times unfamiliar. The old woman of Caribbean history engaged in the morning ritual of sweeping who walked on water with sand in her toes caused Kamau Brathwaite to pause and consider the mysteries of Black diasporic life. Like Brathwaite, I am forced to pause and consider how Black existence at the shoals takes on new shape and meaning. Black life at the shoals, much like Jacqui Alexander's writing of Yemaya, who inhabits both land and sea, "pushes past modernity's mode of reason."² Charmaine Lurch's renderings, depicted on the cover and in the sculpture "Revisiting Sycorax" (see chapter 5), bear witness to the ongoing ceremonies, praxes, and reworkings of what it means to be Black and human, or otherly human existence outside what Toni Morrison calls the mandate for conquest. I concluded the book with Lurch's wire sculptures of Sycorax as a counterpoint to the statue of Christopher Columbus that opens chapter 1. Its defacement by ostensibly Black or Indigenous actors is a ceremony of its own that attempts to put a long-lasting conception of the human under pressure. The ceremony of defacing conquistador Man is also a space where Black and Indigenous speech touch. More than anything, I have attempted to listen to how Black and Indigenous people speak to one another.

I keep listening for this dialogue as two of the most visible mobilizations and standoffs with U.S. state violence and state-sanctioned corporate violence, the Movement for Black Lives and the Standing Rock Sioux's camp of Water Protectors, coincide with the writing of this book.³ Both movements have reignited mobilizations around the world that directly and explicitly confront anti-Black and anti-Indigenous violence. Both of these movements demand and pose these ethical questions: "Whose lives matter?" and "Who can be considered human?" Further, the ethical demands that tether themselves to these inquiries require that nation-states reflect on how their very existence depends on and is made possible by the death of Black and Indigenous peoples.

The refusal of both movements to accept the United States' and other nation-states' notions of the human has the capacity to implode the very foundations of the United States as a project. This book ultimately argues that the most radical of Black and Indigenous projects — abolition and decolonization — exceed the horizons of freedom currently imagined by a White leftist imaginary and discourses of settler colonialism. I have argued that White settler colonial studies as a "leftist" mode of critique refuses to interrogate the violent orthodoxies that continue to write the White progressive — worker, queer, trans, antiracist — subject as the ethical center of the human. Black abolition and Native decolonization are radical imaginaries and ongoing ceremonial spaces that drag the left offshore and into the space and horizons of the shoal. In this book, I have attempted to honor Black and Native thought and politics that challenge the essential assumptions, practices, and daily performances of what it means to be human. Black and Native struggles that call for the acknowledgment and honoring of forms of life that exceed the human as written by Marxist, anarchist, feminist, and queer social movements cannot continue to fight for space within the leftist discourse of human (or posthuman) freedom. Abolitionist and decolonial movement offshore drags liberal humanist (and posthumanist) discourses of freedom to the shoals to contend with Black and Native demands that Man give an account of its violence. In this book I have interrogated normative aesthetic representations of the human (as conquistador), challenged the necessity of a cartographic self, questioned the sanctity of labor as the anchor for one's humanity, and refused notions of sovereignty that cannot account for the porous and open-ended engagements with another.

As the reascendency of violent white supremacist fascist regimes and their normalization of relations of conquest have surfaced (again), the political reawakening that Black Lives Matter and Lakota Sioux struggles for water and life has reinvigorated a discussion about coming together or creating a collective groundswell. On the heels of vigorous and contentious conversations initiated by Afro-pessimists and activists committed to Black struggle about how anti-Blackness shapes the coalition politics of the left and of people of color, I hope more than anything that this book provokes a conversation about how Black and Native communities can "end this world" and remake reality and its relations on more just terms. It may also be time to create some new grammar and an erotic politics rooted in the everyday that does not reproduce the problems of coalitional work for Black and Indigenous people.

Perhaps "coalition" carries too much baggage. Another kind of speech might be better suited for the kinds of intimacy, connection, conflict, debate, self-collective reflection, and support — or backup — we desire from one another. But even if our current terms leave us wanting, we cannot stop our pursuit of ethical connection to one another. I believe that our yet-to-come notions of connectedness and relationality are capacious enough to yield something more than coalition in the end. A new relationality can imagine new kinds of Black and Native futures. I believe that the stakes of this conversation are so high because of the capacity for Black abolition and Native decolonization to remake life in all its expansiveness on new terms. Just as Black and Indigenous life, struggle, and joy are forged off the shoreline in the space of the shoal, so must the new worlds we desire and make for one another.

PREFACE

1 Shanna Louise Smith, "'Tell Me Your Diamonds' Story Bearing in African American Women's Life History Narratives" (Ph.D. diss., University of Maryland, College Park, 2014).

2 Eve Tuck and Christine Ree, "A Glossary of Haunting," in *Handbook of Autoethnography*, ed. Stacy Holman Jones, Tony E. Adams, and Carolyn Ellis (Walnut Creek, CA: Left Coast, 2013), 639–58.

3 Throughout the book, I use "Native" and "Indigenous" to refer to the people and the descendants of the people who lived — and now live — on the territories now known as North America, Central and South America, and the Caribbean prior to the fifteenth century and, more specifically, contact with Europeans who came to the Americas in the fifteenth century. At times I use the terms interchangeably.

4 From 2006 to 2008, Marika Schwandt, Christine Luza, Abi Salole, Larissa Cairncross, and I formed a Toronto chapter of the International INCITE! Women of Color against Violence organization. The large majority of our work consisted of relationship building. A part of that relationship-building work included ceremony.

5 Turtle Island is the name given to the landmass currently known as North America — specifically, Canada and the United States — by Iroquois-speaking nations and people in the territory before European settlers arrived. The name is from a common creation story that emerged among Chippewa, Anishinabek, and other Iroquois language groups that explains the origins of the landmass as created by Sky Woman. According to Duane Champagne, "A great female turtle is a central feature of the Chippewa [and Iroquois-speaking nation] creation teachings. The land created by Sky Woman is held above the water on the back of a female turtle. Turtle Island is the name given to the land": see Duane Champagne, *Notes from the Center of Turtle Island* (Lanham, MD: AltaMira, 2010), viii. In addition, drawing from my own personal experience working with the group INCITE!

Toronto, as an act of solidarity with the Anishinaabe and Native women activists who were part of the INCITE! Toronto chapter (2006–2008), members of INCITE! Toronto began referring to North America as Turtle Island. We did this to acknowledge the name that the Original or First Peoples of the region of the Great Lakes (Ontario, Michigan, Minnesota, Wisconsin) had given the landmass. This deliberate use of an Anishinaabe name for the landmass helped the INCITE! group enact a form of decolonial politics by changing our language in a way that denaturalized the linguistic link between the colonial name "Canada" and the landmass located in the northern region of the Americas: see Tiffany Jeannette King, "In the Clearing: Black Female Bodies, Space and Settler Colonial Landscapes" (Ph.D. diss., University of Maryland, College Park, 2013).

6 Originally recorded around 1977–80, the song "Buffalo Solider" was released on the album *Confrontation* in 1983 on the Tuff Gong/Island Label. Producers included Bob Marley and the Wailers, Errol Brown, and Rita Marley. The following lyrics appear in the fourth verse of the song: "I'm just a Buffalo Soldier/In the heart of America/Stolen from Africa/Brought to America/Said he was fighting on arrival/Fighting for survival/Said he was a Buffalo Soldier/Win the war for America."

7 The term "Five Civilized Tribes" emerged in the nineteenth century to describe the eastern bands of the Cherokee, Chickasaw, Creek, Choctaw, and Seminole Indigenous peoples who were able to maintain and shifting and uneasy equilibrium with European and, eventually, U.S. powers through their adaption of practices such as slavery, private property, and Christianity.

8 Here, I introduce the term "conquistador-settler" to connote the ways that the subjectivity of the conquistador persists into the current moment. The conquistador is also a subjectivity that is tethered to the contemporary figure of the settler. Currently, Indigenous studies and the field of settler colonial studies, as well as activists on the left, tend to refer to descendants of the White colonial settling population as "settlers." This moniker generally references the settlers' relationship to land and to an extent Indigenous people. I argue that "settler" does not explicitly name its relationship to the ongoing violence of genocide that continues to be enacted on Indigenous bodies. The term "settler" also entirely disavows the relationship that White settlers have to the institution of slavery, its afterlife, and ongoing practices and regimes of anti-Black violence. "Conquistador-settler" invokes both the violence enacted on the Indigenous and Black body and the possession of land.

9 See Rey Chow, *The Protestant Ethnic and the Spirit of Capitalism* (New York: Columbia University Press, 2002), 3; and Jasbir K. Puar, *Terrorist Assemblages: Homonationalism in Queer Times* (Durham, NC: Duke University Press, 2017), 2.

10 My use of "on a move" is a play on the greeting used by members of the

Philadelphia-based Black liberation group who used to greet each other with the saying, "On the move!"

11 Robin D. G. Kelley, *Freedom Dreams: The Black Radical Imagination* (Boston: Beacon, 2002).

12 I cite and honor my own Black radical genealogies as emerging from and extending traditions that advanced Black freedom alongside Native/Indigenous freedom. Examples of this political commitment can be found in the political rhetoric and campaigns of the Black Panther Party, the Black Liberation Army, and activists such as Assata Shakur and Angela Davis. Further, contemporary Black femme, queer, and trans activists such as Mary Hooks and Toni Michelle, who make up the Atlanta chapter of Black Lives Matter, proclaim that they "leave no one behind" as they fight for Black freedom and Black joy.

13 Ralph David Abernathy was a civil rights leader from Atlanta whom the city has recognized by renaming Interstate 20 in his honor.

INTRODUCTION

Epigraph: "Shoal," *Oxford English Dictionary Online*, accessed December 12, 2017, http://www.oed.com.ezproxy.gsu.edu/view/Entry/178378/.

1 See Sylvia Wynter, "1492: A New World View," in *Race, Discourse, and the Origin of the Americas: A New World View*, ed. Vera Lawrence Hyatt and Rex M. Nettleford, 5–57 (Washington, DC: Smithsonian Institution Press, 1994), 9.

2 See Gomes Eanes de Azurara and Charles Raymond Beazley, *The Chronicle of the Discovery and Conquest of Guinea*, no. 95 (London: Hakluyt Society, 1899), xcviii.

3 See the work of John Henrik Clarke and Sylvia Wynter, who use archival sources to place Columbus off the coast of West Africa in the 1430s and 1440s prior to landing in the Caribbean in 1492: John Henrik Clarke, *Christopher Columbus and the Afrikan Holocaust: Slavery and the Rise of European Capitalism* (Brooklyn, NY: A&B, 1992); Sylvia Wynter, "1492: A New World View," in *Race, Discourse, and the Origin of the Americas: A New World View*, ed. Vera Lawrence Hyatt and Rex M. Nettleford (Washington, DC: Smithsonian Institution Press, 1994), 5–57.

4 The New World in the fifteenth and sixteenth centuries referred to a wide expanse of global space that included territory newly recognized as habitable. European geography and worldviews posited most of the territory south and east of it as a torrid and uninhabitable zone. Caribbean scholars such as Wynter and Elsa Goveia mark a rupture in this closed geographical system, when the exploratory and imperial missions of Portugal and Spain made contact with people on the coasts of West Africa and Amerindian peoples on the continent that would become the Americas: see David Scott, "The Re-Enchantment of Humanism: An Interview with Sylvia

Wynter," *Small Axe* 8, no. 120 (2000): 173–211. Later, in the eighteenth-century expeditions, the British would expand into Oceania (the Pacific) and around the globe. While all of these spaces function as New World spaces in relationship to Europe, this project focuses on the Western Hemisphere and the Americas (North, Central, and South).

5 See G. W. Littlehales, "On the Improbability of Finding Shoals in the Open Sea by Sailing over the Geographical Positions in Which They Are Charted," *Annals of Mathematics* 9, no. 1/6 (1894–95), 163.

6 Littlehales, "On the Improbability of Finding Shoals in the Open Sea by Sailing over the Geographical Positions in Which They Are Charted," 164.

7 Littlehales, "On the Improbability of Finding Shoals in the Open Sea by Sailing over the Geographical Positions in Which They Are Charted," 164.

8 See Sylvia Wynter, "Beyond Miranda's Meanings: Un/Silencing the 'Demonic Ground' of Caliban's 'Woman,'" in *Out of the Kumbla: Caribbean Women and Literature*, ed. Carole Boyce Davies (Chicago: Africa World Press, 1990), 355–72. In the essay, Wynter cites the work of physicists in defining the space of the demonic. She informs the reader that the demonic model is one "posited by physicists who seek to conceive of a vantage point outside of the space-time organization of the humuncular observer." Wynter describes it as a vantage point. In the essay, Wynter is appealing to Black women to go beyond womanism as a discourse of representation and move toward a space "outside the consolidated field" of our present mode of "being/feeling/knowing," which would include discourses (feminism), epistemes, and "specific modes of being" that continue to exclude people: Wynter, "Beyond Miranda's Meanings," 364. Katherine McKittrick also deploys Wynter's use of the demonic to invoke the geographical practices of Black women and Black diasporic subjects: Katherine McKittrick, *Demonic Grounds: Black Women and Cartographies of Struggle* (Minneapolis: University of Minnesota Press, 2006).

9 While ecotone literature has been evolving since 1965, scholars in the humanities in the late twentieth century and early twenty-first century have been appropriating this literature from the environmental sciences to think through and articulate relations of power in the social realm: see Paul G. Risser, "The Status of the Science Examining Ecotones," *BioScience* 45, no. 5 (1995): 318–25. See also the conference "New Ecotones," held in 2015, http://pays-anglophones.upv.univ-montp3.fr/files/2014/12/Programme-New-Ecotones-2015-definitif.pdf.

10 See Michael LeVan, "The Digital Shoals: On Becoming and Sensation in Performance," *Text and Performance Quarterly* 32, no. 3 (2012): 211. LeVan describes shoals as underwater formations, usually composed of sand or silt, in which waters become shallow (or correlatively, in which the floor of a body of water becomes elevated). Often, shoals emerge and submerge with the changing of tides, rhythmically breaking the surface.

11 LeVan, "The Digital Shoals," 211–12.

12 Throughout the book, when I use the terms "Black studies" and "Native studies," I am referring to specific intellectual and political projects within two broad interdisciplinary traditions that explicitly focus on challenging the epistemic truth claims of Western intellectual traditions. Both Black and Native studies emerged from community and student struggles — some for inclusion, some for a redistribution of resources — in the late 1960s and early 1970s. More specifically, Black studies in this book references an intellectual tradition that interrogates forms of positivism, modes of interpretation, traditions of citation, and scholarship that defines the human against or in opposition to Blackness. Similarly, Native studies in this book refers to an intellectual tradition that contests "colonial constructions of truth" that attempt to produce and depict Indigenous peoples as dead: see Audra Simpson and Andrea Smith, "Introduction," in *Theorizing Native Studies*, ed. Audra Simpson and Andrea Smith (Durham, NC: Duke University Press, 2014), 5.

13 Antonio Benítez-Rojo, *The Repeating Island: The Caribbean and the Postmodern Perspective* (Durham, NC: Duke University Press, 1996); Edward Kamau Brathwaite, *ConVERSations with Nathaniel Mackey* (Rhinebeck, NY: We, 1999); Paul Gilroy, *The Black Atlantic: Modernity and Double Consciousness* (Cambridge, MA: Harvard University Press, 1993); Édouard Glissant, *Caribbean Discourse: Selected Essays* (Charlottesville: University Press of Virginia, 1989); Hortense J. Spillers, "Mama's Baby, Papa's Maybe: An American Grammar Book," *Diacritics* 17, no. 2 (1987): 64–81; Omise'eke Natasha Tinsley, "Black Atlantic, Queer Atlantic: Queer Imaginings of the Middle Passage," GLQ 14, nos. 2–3 (2008): 191–215.

14 McKittrick, *Demonic Grounds*, xxi.

15 Brathwaite, *ConVERSations with Nathaniel Mackey*, 29.

16 Brathwaite, *ConVERSations with Nathaniel Mackey*, 30.

17 Brathwaite, *ConVERSations with Nathaniel Mackey*, 32.

18 Brathwaite, *ConVERSations with Nathaniel Mackey*, 32.

19 Brathwaite, *ConVERSations with Nathaniel Mackey*, 33.

20 Brathwaite, *ConVERSations with Nathaniel Mackey*, 29.

21 Scholars including Bill Ashcroft, Elizabeth DeLoughrey, and Shona Jackson have also interpreted Brathwaite's tidalectics as a way of entangling or invoking the Caribbean subjects' relationship to the land (multiple places that include Africa and the Caribbean), as well as the ocean: see Bill Ashcroft, "Archipelago of Dreams: Utopianism in Caribbean Literature," *Textual Practice* 30, no. 1 (2016): 89–112; Elizabeth M. DeLoughrey, *Routes and Roots: Navigating Caribbean and Pacific Island Literatures* (Honolulu: University of Hawai'i Press, 2007); Shona N. Jackson, *Creole Indigeneity: Between Myth and Nation in the Caribbean* (Minneapolis: University of Minnesota Press, 2012).

22 Brathwaite, *ConVERSations with Nathaniel Mackey*, 35.

23 Brathwaite, *ConVERSations with Nathaniel Mackey*, 35.

24 Brathwaite, *ConVERSations with Nathaniel Mackey*, 33.

25 Brathwaite, *ConVERSations with Nathaniel Mackey*, 34.

26 Édouard Glissant, *Poetics of Relation*, trans. Betsy Wing (Ann Arbor: University of Michigan Press, 1997), 189.

27 Glissant, *Poetics of Relation*, 190–91.

28 McKittrick, *Demonic Grounds*, xxii.

29 While attending to the usefulness of the oceanic metaphor and the chronotype of the ship, Gilroy's *Black Atlantic* offered a productive geographical and metaphorical site from which to exceed nation bound analytics in British cultural studies, American studies, African American studies, and history. While thinking with the productive linkages of the ocean as a way to think with dynamic and moving diasporic subjects, Gilroy did not reduce Black resistance and aesthetic, intellectual, and political thought to liquidity. His turn to diaspora and the metaphorical capacities of water was intended to help Black diasporic thought wrest itself from totalizing frames such as the nation and, perhaps, even water if its use becomes static in its need to overwrite and trap Black aesthetics and thought.

30 See, e.g., Liquid Blackness, the Atlanta-based research group housed at Georgia State University that takes as its point of departure the premise of "liquidity as a primary aesthetic form in which blackness is encountered in our contemporary visual and sonic landscape." This statement appears on the research group's website, accessed March 9, 2018, http://liquidblack ness.com/about.

31 Liquid Blackness website, accessed March 9, 2018, http://liquidblackness .com/about.

32 Anna Reckin, "Tidalectic Lectures: Kamau Brathwaite's Prose/Poetry as Sound-Space," *Anthurium: A Caribbean Studies Journal* 1, no. 1 (2003): 5.

33 Maggie Montesinos Sale, *The Slumbering Volcano: American Slave Ship Revolts and the Production of Rebellious Masculinity* (Durham, NC: Duke University Press, 1997), 126.

34 In the novel *Praisesong for the Widow*, Paule Marshall tells a story about the Ibo who turned around at the shore and walked back across the ocean to Ibo land. The territory in the Sea Islands on which the Ibo turned their backs is named Ibo Landing. Dash re-creates Marshall's tale and the Black geography of Ibo Landing in the movie and novel *Daughters of the Dust*: see Paule Marshall, *Praisesong for the Widow* (New York: Plume, 1984).

35 See Vincente Diaz, "No Island Is an Island," in *Native Studies Keywords*, ed. Stephanie Teves, Andrea Smith, and Michelle Raheja (Tucson: University of Arizona Press, 2015), 99.

36 Diaz, "No Island Is an Island," 93.

37 Hokulani K. Aikau, Maile Arvin, Mishuana Goeman, and Scott Morgensen, "Indigenous Feminisms Roundtable," *Frontiers* 36, no. 3 (2015): 94.

38 Aikau et al., "Indigenous Feminisms Roundtable," 95.

39 Aikau et al., "Indigenous Feminisms Roundtable," 95.

40 Aikau et al., "Indigenous Feminisms Roundtable," 95.

41 Caribbeanists have engaged Brathwaite's tidalectics as a poetic and analytic to close the geographic gap that has been posited between Black diasporic and Indigenous life in the Americas. See Elizabeth DeLoughrey, *Routes and Roots: Navigating Caribbean and Pacific Island Literatures* (Honolulu: University of Hawai'i Press, 2007); and Shona Jackson, *Creole Indigeneity: Between Myth and Nation in the Caribbean* (Minneapolis: University of Minnesota Press, 2012).

42 McKittrick, *Demonic Grounds*, xxiii.

43 For a discussion of the limits of critique within queer theory, see Eve Kosofsky Sedgwick, "Paranoid Reading and Reparative Reading; or, You're So Paranoid, You Probably Think This Introduction Is about You," in *Novel Gazing: Queer Readings in Fiction* (Durham, NC: Duke University Press, 1997), 1–40, which has informed a mode of reading prevalent in cultural studies and, specifically, affect theory that attends to the possibilities and gaps and openings in what appears to be a closed hegemonic system. Scholars such as Kathleen Stewart and Ann Cvetkovich, who focus their scholarship on affect and public feelings, evince this mode of reading and attending. Cvetkovich describes a reparative mode of reading as a way to focus on the "surfaces" and textures of "everyday life rather than just the putative aspects": Ann Cvetkovich, *Depression: A Public Feeling* (Durham, NC: Duke University Press, 2012), 5. Put another way, Cvetkovich argues for a reading practice that looks for alternatives to critique: Cvetkovich, *Depression*, 132. Looking for alternatives tempers what Sedgewick has named a paranoid tendency within queer studies—particularly seen in critiques of homonormativity—to watch for "how forms of resistance are ultimately coopted": see Cvetkovich, *Depression*, 6. Following Sedgwick, Cvetkovich proposes developing an attention for where it feels like "something else is happening" and strategies for survival emerge. I argue that Black feminist—specifically, Black women's—thought is rarely read in this reparative mode: see Tiffany Lethabo King, "Post-Indentitarian and Post-Intersectional Anxiety in the Neoliberal Corporate University," *Feminist Formations* 27, no. 3 (2015): 114–38. Rather than looking for ways that intersectionality creates small fissures and ruptures within hegemonic fields of power, theories such as intersectionality or Black feminist thought are imagined as already being captured by the state or, in this case, as a closed Black-White binary discourse that cannot account for Indigenous people.

44 See, e.g., Afua Cooper, *The Hanging of Angélique: The Untold Story of Canadian Slavery and the Burning of Old Montréal* (Athens: University of Georgia Press, 2007); Charmaine Nelson, "Hiram Powers's America: Shackles, Slaves, and the Racial Limits of Nineteenth-Century National Identity," *Canadian Review of American Studies* 34, no. 2 (2004): 167–84; Charmaine Nelson, *Slavery, Geography and Empire in Nineteenth-Century Marine Landscapes of Montreal and Jamaica* (London: Routledge, 2016); Charmaine

Nelson, "Slavery, Portraiture and the Colonial Limits of Canadian Art History," *Canadian Woman Studies* 23, no. 2 (2004): 22–29; McKittrick, *Demonic Grounds.*

45 Rinaldo Walcott, "The Problem of the Human: Black Ontologies and 'the Coloniality of Our Being,'" in *Postcoloniality — Decoloniality — Black Critique: Joints and Fissures*, ed. Sabine Broeck and Carsten Junker (Frankfurt am Main: Campus, 2014), 93–108.

46 For examples of more recent, twenty-first-century scholarship that engages the discourse of settler colonialism, see Shanya Dennen, "Occupying Spaces of Belonging: Indigeneity in Diasporic Guyana" (M.A. thesis, University of Texas, Austin, 2013); Sandra Harvey, "Passing for Free, Passing for Sovereign: Blackness and the Formation of the Nation" (Ph.D. diss., University of California, Santa Cruz, 2017); Gerald Horne, *The Apocalypse of Settler Colonialism: The Roots of Slavery, White Supremacy, and Capitalism in Seventeenth-Century North America and the Caribbean* (New York: New York University Press, 2018); Jackson, *Creole Indigeneity*; Robin D. G. Kelley, "The Rest of Us: Rethinking Settler and Native," *American Quarterly* 69, no. 2 (2017): 267–76; Tiffany Jeannette King, "In the Clearing: Black Female Bodies, Space and Settler Colonial Landscapes" (Ph.D. diss., University of Maryland, College Park, 2013); Justin Leroy, "Black History in Occupied Territory: On the Entanglements of Slavery and Settler Colonialism," *Theory and Event* 19, no. 4 (2016); Kyle T. Mays, "Transnational Progressivism: African Americans, Native Americans, and the Universal Races Congress of 1911," *Studies in American Indian Literatures* 25, no. 2 (2013): 241–61; Tiya Miles and Sharon Patricia Holland, eds., *Crossing Waters, Crossing Worlds: The African Diaspora in Indian Country* (Durham, NC: Duke University Press, 2006); Frank B. Wilderson III, *Red, White and Black: Cinema and the Structure of U.S. Antagonisms* (Durham, NC: Duke University Press, 2010).

47 Arika Easley-Houser, "'The Indian Image in the Black Mind': Representing Native Americans in Antebellum African American Public Culture" (Ph.D. diss., Rutgers University, 2014).

48 Easley-Houser, "'The Indian Image in the Black Mind.'"

49 Jackson, *Creole Indigeneity*; Melanie J. Newton, "Returns to a Native Land: Indigeneity and Decolonization in the Anglophone Caribbean," *Small Axe* 17, no. 2 (2013): 108–22.

50 Gilroy, *The Black Atlantic.*

51 Scott, "The Re-Enchantment of Humanism," 194.

52 Scott, "The Re-Enchantment of Humanism," 194–95.

53 See Sylvia Wynter, "On How We Mistook the Map for the Territory, and Reimprisoned Ourselves in Our Unbearable Wrongness of Being, of Desêtre: Black Studies toward the Human Project," in *Not Only the Master's Tools: African American Studies in Theory and Practice*, ed. Lewis Gordon (Boulder, CO: Paradigm, 2006), 124.

54 In her work, which attempts to appropriate Marx's standpoint theory to argue for a feminist standpoint theory, Nancy Hartsock argues that feminism, like Marxism, posits a new theory of the subject: see Nancy Hartsock, "Marxist Feminist Dialectics for the Twenty-First Century," *Science and Society* 62, no. 3 (Fall 1998): 400–413. In the article, Hartsock argues that Marx's theory of the subject resists the pull of liberal humanism, which privileges an individual subject. Instead, Marx advances an idea of a collective subjectivity that is much like Michel Foucault's theory of subjectivity subjected to laboring for the benefit of the other and pouring their existence into an object: Hartsock, "Marxist Feminist Dialectics for the Twenty-First Century," 407. Hartsock attempts to argue that this kind of collective subjectivity—the workers' and women's—is a form of theoretical antihumanism. However, from the perspective of Black studies and, more specifically, the work of Sylvia Wynter, workers and women, or Marxism and feminism, become other kinds of "orthodox fronts" that ending up constituting a universal voice that attempts to speak for all and in the process erases other kinds of experiences and struggles: see Sylvia Wynter "Beyond the Word of Man: Glissant and the New Discourse of the Antilles" *World Literature Today* 63, no. 4 (1989): 640.

55 Tonya Haynes, "Sylvia Wynter's Theory of the Human and the Crisis School of Caribbean Heteromasculinity Studies." *Small Axe* 20, no. 1 (2016): 93.

56 Michelle V. Rowley, "Whose Time Is It? Gender and Humanism in Contemporary Caribbean Feminist Advocacy," *Small Axe* 14, no. 1 (2010): 12.

57 Scott, "The Re-Enchantment of Humanism," 196.

58 Wynter, "1492: A New World View," 5.

59 Spillers, "Mama's Baby, Papa's Maybe," 70.

60 As Clark has argued, Columbus honed his navigational and conquistador skills on the shores of West Africa in the 1460s: see Clarke, *Christopher Columbus and the Afrikan Holocaust.*

61 Anuradha Gobin, "Constructing a Picturesque Landscape: Picturing Sugar Plantations in the Eighteenth-Century British West Indies," *Hemispheres: Visual Cultures of the Americas* 4, no. 1 (2011): 9. See also Carole Pateman, "The Settler Contract," in *Contract and Domination*, ed. Charles Mills and Carole Pateman (Malden, MA: Polity, 2007), 35–78.

62 Gobin, "Constructing a Picturesque Landscape," 9; Pateman, "The Settler Contract."

63 Gobin, "Constructing a Picturesque Landscape."

64 Wilderson, *Red, White and Black*, 207.

65 Wilderson, *Red, White and Black*, 207.

66 Wilderson, *Red, White and Black*, 210.

67 Stefano Harney and Fred Moten, *The Undercommons: Fugitive Planning and Black Study* (Wivenhoe, UK: Minor Compositions, 2013), 94. Moten meditates on the hold as a productive space of Black thought that aspires to a

"not yet" experience of freedom that cannot be spoken because it has not yet been fully realized. The realization of this new world order also exists outside current forms of narrativity and speech.

68 In his autobiography, Frederick Douglass describes the "bloody transaction," or spectacle of the whipping of Aunt Hester, as his initiation into the reality and grim understanding of the brutal relationship between the slave and the master that defined the institution of slavery. This scene is described as the "blood stained gate, the entrance into the hell of slavery"; see Frederick Douglass and Ira Dworkin, "Narrative of the Life of Frederick Douglass, an American Slave," 6. In the autobiography he recounts the ways that his master whipped his Aunt Hester just to hear her scream—screams that he described as "heart rending shrieks." This scene that epitomizes the relations of slavery has been referenced in a number of Black studies texts. For example, in *Scenes of Subjection*, Saidiya Hartman refuses to reproduce the violence of the scene in which Douglass recounts Aunt Hester's whipping: see Saidiya V. Hartman, *Scenes of Subjection: Terror, Slavery, and Self-Making in Nineteenth-Century America* (New York: Oxford University Press, 1997). Fred Moten recognizes the violence of reproduction and instead focuses on the utterance, sound, and performance of Aunt Hester's scream—the object's scream—as a way to theorize Black thought, aesthetics, speech, and performance as outside normative modes of human narrative, speech, and intelligibility: Fred Moten, *In the Break: The Aesthetics of the Black Radical Tradition* (Minneapolis: University of Minnesota Press, 2003).

69 See Jared Sexton, "The Vel of Slavery: Tracking the Figure of the Unsovereign," *Critical Sociology* 42, nos. 4–5 (2014): 10–11.

70 Hartman offered this clarification about what she was attempting as she engaged Marx's work. She found Marx's theory of the value of labor lacking for the enslaved Black subjected to violence, domination, and use as a form of property. Black slaves became the pedestal on which wage labor—often misnamed slavery—was built. To make this adjustment without throwing away the usefulness of Marx's work, Hartman adapted Marx's use of primitive accumulation to theorize the ways that Black bodies were subjected to the violence of racialization, domination, and accumulation to fix them in White imagination and law as forms of property. She made these clarifying statements at the I, Too, Am the Afterlife of Slavery conference, Northwestern University, Evanston, IL, June 1–2, 2017. She also makes this clarification in *Scenes of Subjection*, 99.

71 Hartman, *Scenes of Subjection*, 7.

72 Hartman, *Scenes of Subjection*, 7.

73 Spillers, "Mama's Baby, Papa's Maybe," 67.

74 See Mishuana Goeman, "Land as Life: Unsettling the Logics of Containment," in *Native Studies Keywords*, ed. Stephanie Teves, Andrea Smith, and Michelle Raheja (Tucson: University of Arizona Press, 2015), 77.

75 Glen Sean Coulthard, *Red Skin, White Masks: Rejecting the Colonial Politics of Recognition* (Minneapolis: University of Minnesota Press, 2014), 13.

76 See Jackson, *Creole Indigeneity*, 233.

77 See Sylvia Wynter, "Beyond the Categories of the Master Conception: The Counterdoctrine of the Jamesian Poiesis," *C. L. R. James's Caribbean* 69 (1992): 63–91.

78 Hartman references various Black acts toward freedom as representing "loopholes of retreat" that she defines as "a space of freedom that is at the same time a space of captivity": Hartman, *Scenes of Subjection*, 9. These spaces of freedom and captivity trouble liberal nineteenth-century narratives of the self-possessed individual and freedom.

79 C. Riley Snorton, *Black on Both Sides: A Racial History of Trans Identity* (Minneapolis: University of Minnesota Press, 2017), 84.

80 Snorton, *Black on Both Sides*, 69.

81 Wynter, "Beyond Miranda's Meanings," 364. Wynter cites the work of physicists in defining the space of the demonic. She informs the reader that the demonic model is one "posited by physicists who seek to conceive of a vantage point outside of the space-time organization of the humuncular observer" and describes it as a vantage point. In the essay, Wynter is appealing to Black women to go beyond womanism as a discourse of representation and move toward a space "outside the consolidated field" of our present mode of "being/feeling/knowing," which would include discourses (feminism), epistemes and "specific modes of being" that continue to exclude people.

82 Wynter, "Beyond Miranda's Meanings," 364.

83 Katie Cannon, *Black Womanist Ethics* (Eugene, OR: Wipf and Stock, 2006), 2.

84 Cannon, *Black Womanist Ethics*, 2.

85 Cannon, *Black Womanist Ethics*, 2.

86 Audre Lorde, *Uses of the Erotic: The Erotic as Power* (Berkeley, CA: Crossing, 1978), 88; Audre Lorde, "The Master's Tools Will Never Dismantle the Master's House," in *This Bridge Called My Back: Writings by Radical Women of Color*, ed. Cherríe Moraga and Gloria Anzaldúa (New York: Kitchen Table, 1983), 94–103.

87 Lorde, *Uses of the Erotic*, 88.

88 Lorde, *Uses of the Erotic*, 89.

89 Billy-Ray Belcourt, "Indigenous Studies beside Itself," *Somatechnics* 7, no. 2 (2017): 182, 185.

90 Belcourt, "Indigenous Studies beside Itself," 185.

91 Qwo-Li Driskill, Chris Finley, Brian Joseph Gilley, and Scott Lauria Morgensen, eds., *Queer Indigenous Studies: Critical Interventions in Theory, Politics, and Literature* (Tucson: University of Arizona Press, 2011), 16.

92 Driskill et al., *Queer Indigenous Studies*, 16.

93 Driskill et al., *Queer Indigenous Studies*, 19.

94 King, "In the Clearing," 13.

95 See Miles and Holland, *Crossing Waters, Crossing Worlds*.

96 King, "In the Clearing," 14.

97 Hartman develops the notion and practice of critical fabulation as practiced by Black scholars who must engage the brutal archives of slavery and their gaps. What she describes as the "double gesture" involved in "critical fabulation" explains holding in tension the practice of both straining against the limits of the archive through creating narrative/figurative/speculative work and acknowledging the impossibility or the failure of being able to fully represent the lives of the captives in the archive. In the essay "Venus in Two Acts" and in the book *Lose Your Mother*, Hartman confronts her own process of grappling with hope and the impossibility of being able to know what happened. She must come to terms with the fact that she can never know, "for instance[,] that the two wordless girls on the *Recovery* found a country in each other's arms"; further, she does not want to "place yet another demand" on the girls or the dead: see Saidiya V. Hartman, "Venus in Two Acts," *Small Axe* 12, no. 2 (2008): 1–14; Saidiya Hartman, *Lose Your Mother: A Journey along the Atlantic Slave Route* (New York: Farrar, Straus and Giroux, 2007).

98 Katherine McKittrick. "Diachronic Loops/Deadweight Tonnage/Bad Made Measure," *Cultural Geographies* 23, no. 1 (2016): 3.

99 McKittrick, *Demonic Grounds*; Katherine McKittrick, "Mathematics Black Life," *Black Scholar* 44, no. 2 (2014): 18.

100 McKittrick, "Mathematics Black Life," 22.

101 McKittrick, "Diachronic Loops/Deadweight Tonnage/Bad Made Measure."

102 McKittrick, "Diachronic Loops/Deadweight Tonnage/Bad Made Measure," 10.

103 McKittrick, "Mathematics Black Life," 22.

104 McKittrick, "Diachronic Loops/Deadweight Tonnage/Bad Made Measure," 3.

105 Over the course of her body of work, Wynter theorizes Man as a version of the human that is written and rewritten in ways that make it appear — or are discursively represented — as the only way to be human.

106 Denise Ferreira da Silva, *Toward a Global Idea of Race* (Minneapolis: University of Minnesota Press, 2007), 117.

107 Da Silva, *Toward a Global Idea of Race*, 117.

108 McKittrick, "Diachronic Loops/Deadweight Tonnage/Bad Made Measure," 3.

109 McKittrick, "Mathematics Black Life," 220.

110 To secure the humanist project of conquest, Black and Native bodies become sites of "fixed-flux" that are constantly slipping into death, like the Native, and sliding into zones of social death, like Black fungibility. Within the geographical and humanist (geo-humanist) imagination,

Blackness as a site of flux and change is a suspect and irreconcilable mode of life. The zones of Black and Indigenous social death are also the least interrogated realms of alternative modes of livability. This book therefore stages an extended rumination on the theoretical, methodological, creative, and ethical potential of Black fungibility. It reclaims Black fungibility as an ontological position and project, as well as a state of Black immanence that is worked out and through from moment to moment. Within relations of conquest, Black fungibility indexes the conceptual and actual sites of colonial spatial expansion; Indigenous genocide; the (always moving) inside-outside boundary of the human, gender, and sexual indeterminacy; and unlikely spaces of freedom. I situate Black fungibility within the genealogy of Hortense Spillers's and Saidiya Hartman's theorizations of Black enslaved flesh as unanchored, malleable, and open signs. Throughout, Spillers's "Mama's Baby, Papa's Maybe" is an important touchstone for the text in how it helps the book elaborate on Black fungible flesh that is a "[territory] of cultural and political maneuver" that can be arranged and rearranged infinitely.

As a Black fleshy analytic, I argue, Black fungibility can denote and connote pure flux, process, and potential. In this project, Black fungibility represents the unfettered use of Black bodies for the self-actualization of the human. To be rendered Black and fungible under conquest is to be rendered porous, undulating, fluttering, sensuous, and in a space and state between normative configurations of sex, gender, sexuality, space, and time to stabilize and fix the human category. Black fungibility is an expression of the gratuitous violence of conquest and slavery whose repertoire has no limits or bounds. It operates both materially on the body and produces Blackness (as idea and symbol) as a discursive space of open possibility. As Black fungibility is a form of gratuitous violence that is unending and unpredictable, Black struggle's resistance to and maneuvering within fungibility is as unpredictable and uncontainable. As a Black mode of critique, it elaborates and gives texture to various forms of violence while also revealing unexpected and ever emerging modes of freedom — or what McKittrick would call a "loophole of retreat." In this way, Black fungibility resists more conventional understandings and deployments of fungibility as solely a space of Black death, accumulation, dereliction, and limits. In this volume, Black fungibility also represents a space of alterity and possibility.

111   See Leo Bersani, "Is the Rectum a Grave?" *October* 43 (1987): 197–222; and Lee Edelman, *No Future: Queer Theory and the Death Drive* (Durham, NC: Duke University Press, 2004).

112   For more on Wynter's notion of the "demonic," see "Beyond Miranda's Meanings," 364.

113   Dionne Brand, *Land to Light On*. Toronto: McClelland and Stewart, 1997.

Epigraphs: John Henrik Clarke, "Christopher Columbus and Genocide," presentation delivered on January 12, 1992, posted February 17, 2013, accessed January 7, 2017, https://www.youtube.com/watch?v=vqoTB sgk6gg; Junot Díaz, *The Brief Wondrous Life of Oscar Wao* (New York: Penguin, 2007), 2; Toni Morrison, *Playing in the Dark: Whiteness and the Literary Imagination* (New York: Vintage, 2007), 3.

1 Julia Craven, "Political Activists Throw Blood Back in Christopher Columbus' Face," *Huffington Post*, July 2, 2015, accessed December 22, 2017, http://www.huffingtonpost.com/2015/07/02/columbus-monument-vandalized_n_7716138.html.

2 Craven, "Political Activists Throw Blood."

3 Matt Conti, "Christopher Columbus Statue Vandalized with Red Paint and 'Black Lives Matter' Text," *North End Waterfront*, June 30, 2015, accessed December 26, 2016, http://northendwaterfront.com/2015/06/christopher-columbus-statue-vandalized.

4 Craven, "Political Activists Throw Blood."

5 Bob McGovern, "Vandalism No Way to Make Point," *Boston Herald*, July 1, 2015, accessed December 22, 2017, http://www.bostonherald.com/news_opinion/local_politics/2015/06/pol_vandalism_no_way_to_make_point.

6 Brian Maloney, "Now It's Columbus under Attack: Boston Statue Defaced with 'Black Lives Matter,' Red Paint," Newsequalizer, July 1, 2015, accessed December 26, 2016, http://mediaequalizer.com/brian-maloney/2015/07/now-its-columbus-under-attack.

7 Maloney, "Now It's Columbus under Attack." Susana Morris reminded me that the commenter's name, "Jack Sparrow," is a pirate character (played by Johnny Depp) in the film *Pirates of the Caribbean.* One can only surmise whether the commenter ironically chose a handle or screen name in this instance.

8 Diana Taylor, *The Archive and the Repertoire: Performing Cultural Memory in the Americas* (Durham, NC: Duke University Press, 2003), 28.

9 Taylor, *The Archive and the Repertoire,* 28.

10 Taylor, *The Archive and the Repertoire,* 28.

11 Taylor references Guillermo Gómez-Peña and Coco Fusco's 1992 installation and performance "Two Undiscovered Amerindians," which was staged in multiple colonial centers including Columbus Plaza in Madrid, as an example of what subversion from within might look like: Taylor, *The Archive and the Repertoire,* 65.

12 Taylor argues that the power of the scenario's performativity or theatrics is that it forces us to situate ourselves in relationship to it. As participants, spectators, or witnesses, we need to "be there," part of the act of trans-

fer. Thus, the scenario precludes a certain kind of distancing: Taylor, *The Archive and the Repertoire*, 32.

13 Patrick Wolfe argued that "invasion was not an event but a structure": Patrick Wolfe, "Settler Colonialism and the Elimination of the Native," *Journal of Genocide Studies* 8, no. 4 (2006): 390.

14 Fred Moten, *In the Break: The Aesthetics of the Black Radical Tradition* (Minneapolis: University of Minneapolis Press, 2003), 26.

15 Taylor argues that some acts and performances of resistance in the Americas are "untranslatable": Taylor, *The Archive and the Repertoire*, 13.

16 Rizvana Bradley and Damien-Adia Marassa use Édouard Glissant's notion of poetics to rethink "Black writing" beyond a graphic performance and "modality of alphabetic script but as an ensemble of life practices," throughout the African diaspora. They argue that Black writing is a performance by the enslaved that emerges as a counter-genre to conventional modes of Western "modernist" writing. For instance, Bradley and Marassa argue that the Black writing of formerly enslaved diasporic Black people works against the traditional interpretation of the slave narrative as explained by scholars such as Henry Louis Gates as a form of writing born within the humanist tradition of narrativity: Rizvana Bradley and Damien-Adia Marassa, "Awakening to the World: Relation, Totality, and Writing from Below," *Discourse* 36, no. 1 (2014): 113.

17 Bradley and Marassa, "Awakening to the World," 113.

18 Taylor, *The Archive and the Repertoire*, 13.

19 Taylor, *The Archive and the Repertoire*, 17.

20 Similarly, Black graffiti is not a total or totalizing act within Black hip hop performance cultures. Graffiti is a part of a larger performance ensemble that includes emceeing, breaking, and beat boxing.

21 See Sylvia Wynter, "No Humans Involved: An Open Letter to My Colleagues," *Knowledge on Trial* 1, no. 1 (1994): 69. In this article, Wynter extrapolates from her colleague St. Claire Drake, who makes a distinction between "street tasks" and "intellectual tasks" and argues that there is "street speech" and "intellectual speech."

22 Manu Vimalassery, Juliana Hu Pegues, and Alyosha Goldstein, the editors of the "On Colonial Unknowing" special issue of *Theory and Event*, frame Jodi Byrd's term "colonial unknowing" to explain the ways that settler colonialism performs a forgetting and ignorance about genocide and settlement: see Manu Vimalassery, Juliana Hu Pegues, and Alyosha Goldstein, "Introduction: On Colonial Unknowing," *Theory and Event* 19, no. 4 (2016), accessed April 4, 2018, https://muse.jhu.edu.

23 See Mishuana Goeman's work on Esther Belin's poetry and Coyote and Navajo women "talking that talk" in *Mark My Words: Native Women Mapping Our Nations* (Minneapolis: University of Minnesota Press, 2013).

24 See Frank B. Wilderson, *Red, White and Black: Cinema and the Structure of U.S. Antagonisms* (Durham, NC: Duke University Press, 2010), 5. Wilderson

speaks of a grammar—often unspoken, unheard—as a structure through which the labor of speech takes shape. Film has its own ontological grammar of structure, a particular kind of scaffolding or mold through which only certain kinds of grammars of pain, redress, and conflict can be heard. The grammar of the human is one. Savage (Native/Indigenous) and the Slave (Black) have another structure. The Native's grammar of genocide and the Black's grammar of fungibility generally cannot be depicted in film's closed grammatical structure of the human.

25 Díaz, *The Brief Wondrous Life of Oscar Wao*, 1–2.

26 Díaz, *The Brief Wondrous Life of Oscar Wao*, 1.

27 Junot Díaz, "The Legacy of Childhood Trauma," *New Yorker*, accessed August 3, 2018, https://www.newyorker.com/magazine/2018/04/16/the -silence-the-legacy-of-childhood-trauma.

28 Díaz, "The Legacy of Childhood Trauma."

29 Katherine McKittrick and Alexander G. Weheliye, "808 and Heartbreak," *Propter Nos* 2, no. 1 (2017): 15.

30 McKittrick and Weheliye, "808 and Heartbreak," 16.

31 McKittrick and Weheliye, "808 and Heartbreak," 16.

32 McKittrick and Weheliye, "808 and Heartbreak," 15.

33 See "Rewriting the Story of America: Interview with Junot Díaz," *Bill Moyers and Company*, show no. 151, broadcast December 20, 2015, accessed October 14, 2016, https://www.youtube.com/watch?v=UuOGIPKEgfY. In the interview, Díaz talks about the limits of realism and the ways that fiction and science fiction do a better job of explaining the actual or "real" quotidian violence of this hemisphere. He describes seeing firsthand the stark asymmetries in the quality of life that people in the Dominican Republic and the United States experience, describing his move from the Dominican Republic to the United States as otherworldly and like a scene from a science fiction movie.

34 See Eve Tuck and C. Ree. "A Glossary of Haunting," in *Handbook of Auto-ethnography*, ed. Stacy Holman Jones, Tony E. Adams, and Carolyn Ellis (Walnut Creek, CA: Left Coast, 2013), 639–68.

35 Díaz, *The Brief Wondrous Life of Oscar Wao*, 2.

36 Many of Díaz's works, which center on the lives of characters from the Dominican Republic and the Caribbean, recite the history of the Columbian rupture. Díaz as a public intellectual also discusses the ongoing legacy of colonial violence in his nonfiction writing and public speaking: see Junot Díaz, *This Is How You Lose Her* (New York: Penguin, 2013); Katherine Miranda, "Junot Díaz, Diaspora, and Redemption: Creating Progressive Imaginaries," *Sargasso* 2 (2008–2009): 23–40.

37 On multiple occasions, Díaz has referenced Morrison as his literary muse and the writer who taught him how to write. See, e.g., his introduction of Toni Morrison in his conversation with her on December 13, 2013, at the New York Public Library, accessed April 3, 2018, https://www.youtube.com /watch?v=J5kytPjYjSQ.

38 Toni Morrison, *Playing in the Dark: Whiteness and the Literary Imagination* (New York: Random House, 1993), 15.

39 Morrison, *Playing in the Dark*, 15.

40 Toni Morrison wrote one of the blurbs for Leslie Marmon Silko's *The Almanac of the Dead* (New York: Simon and Schuster, 1991).

41 Morrison, *Playing in the Dark*; Silko, *The Almanac of the Dead*; Wynter, "1492: A New Worldview."

42 The ways that Megan Spencer and Alyssa Hunziker situate Morrison's work—specifically, *A Mercy*—squarely within discussions of Indigeneity and settlement is an example of the kind of reparative readings that attend to Black studies engagements with Indigeneity and settlement outside the normative discourse of settler colonialism: see Megan Spencer [Megan Hamel], "Cartographies of Haunting: Black Feminist Refusal in Toni Morrison's *A Mercy* and Octavia Butler's *Kindred*," M.A. thesis, Oregon State University, 2016; Alyssa A. Hunziker, "Toni Morrison, Indigeneity, and Settler Colonialism," *Settler Colonial Studies* 8, no. 4 (2017): 507–17.

43 Alexander G. Weheliye, *Habeas Viscus: Racializing Assemblages, Biopolitics, and Black Feminist Theories of the Human* (Durham, NC: Duke University Press, 2014), 20.

44 Weheliye, *Habeas Viscus*, 29–30.

45 See Hortense Spillers, "Mama's Baby, Papa's Maybe: An American Grammar Book," *Diacritics* 17, no. 2 (Summer 1987): 67; Sylvia Wynter, "Novel and History, Plot and Plantation," *Savacou* 5 (1971): 95–102; Tiffany Lethabo King, "The Labor of (Re)reading Plantation Landscapes Fungible(ly)," *Antipode* 48, no. 4 (2016): 1022–39.

46 While it may appear to people that the point was to announce the presence of Blackness and specifically the Black Lives Matter movement because spokespeople from the group deny that it was a part of their public campaigns, one cannot know that promoting the formal organized movement work of Black Lives Matter was the intent.

47 See Sylvia Wynter, "Beyond the Categories of the Master Conception: The Counterdoctrine of the Jamesian Poiesis," *C. L. R. James's Caribbean* 69 (1992): 63–91; Sylvia Wynter, "Beyond the Word of Man: Glissant and the New Discourse of the Antilles," *World Literature Today* 63, no. 4 (1989): 637–48; Sylvia Wynter, "Unsettling the Coloniality of Being/Power/Truth/Freedom: Towards the Human, After Man, Its Overrepresentation—An Argument," *CR: New Centennial Review* 3, no. 3 (Fall 2003): 257–337.

48 Spillers, "Mama's Baby, Papa's Maybe."

49 Wynter, "1492: A New Worldview," 5.

50 Spillers, "Mama's Baby, Papa's Maybe," 67.

51 Spillers, "Mama's Baby, Papa's Maybe," 67.

52 See note 41 in the introduction.

53 Spillers, "Mama's Baby, Papa's Maybe," 68. Spillers uses the modifier "cap-

tive" to describe "flesh" under the conditions of captivity. Flesh is described as both a liberated subject position and a condition of Blackness under captivity. This could be the reason that there are multiple readings of body and flesh and competing interpretations that position the flesh in some instances as a condition of captivity, and others as a position/condition of liberation from humanist discourses, such as that of the body.

54 Spillers, "Mama's Baby, Papa's Maybe," 83. I find freedom in Spillers's proclamation that Black people have the benefit of existing outside the constraints of the humanist shackles of gender, sexuality, class, and other coordinates. We other-than-humans are free in that we, in Spillers's words, "have nothing to prove."

55 Spillers, "Mama's Baby, Papa's Maybe," 83.

56 Wilderson, Red, White and Black.

57 Wilderson, Red, White and Black, 28. Further, in two conversations with Wilderson, on July 2 and July 26, 2017, I asked him about his faith in the capacity for the grammars of fungibility and genocide to speak—or be intelligible—to each other. Ten years after the publication of his book Red, White and Black, Wilderson admitted that he had less faith in this kind of Native and Black exchange and referenced Jared Sexton's "The Vel of Slavery" as the text that prompted him to rethink the resonance between genocide and fungibility. I, however, am still invested in Wilderson's initial proposal in 2010 that the Black grammar of fungibility can speak to the Red grammar of genocide.

58 The flesh and the fleshly violent loss of Indigenous life is a grammar of Native feminist studies. For example, Heather Davis and Zoe Todd reference the "fleshy violent loss" of genocide and colonialism as global and apocalyptic crises that Indigenous people understood as human and environmental catastrophes long before the discourse of the Anthropocene emerged in the twenty-first century: see Heather Davis and Zoe Todd, "On the Importance of a Date, or, Decolonizing the Anthropocene," ACME 16, no. 4 (2017): 761–80.

59 Native women in Canada have lobbied to the Canadian crown for an investigation into the estimated 1,200–4,000 women who have been murdered or gone missing in Canada and whose cases have been unresolved since 1980: Her Majesty the Queen in Right of Canada, "Our Women and Girls Are Sacred," interim report of the National Inquiry into Missing and Murdered Indigenous Women and Girls, 2017, http://www.mmiwg-ffada.ca/files/ni-mmiwg-interim-report-revised.pdf.

60 "Leslie Black, Sask[atchewan] Man Who Set Woman on Fire, Is Not Dangerous Offender: Judge," Huffington Post, August 31, 2017, accessed March 1, 2018, http://www.huffingtonpost.ca/2017/08/31/leslie-black-sask-man-who-set-woman-on-fire-is-not-dangerous-offender-judge_a_23192448.

61 Joanna Jolly, "Red River Women," BBC News, April 8, 2015, accessed

March 1, 2018, http://www.bbc.co.uk/news/resources/idt-dc75304f-e77c
-4125-aacf-83e7714a5840.

62 Jolly, "Red River Women."

63 Several Native feminists also make this distinction — in particular, Joanne
Barker, who from 2011 through 2017 has sustained an online discussion
about the distinctions between White settler colonialism and Native
studies, especially the tendency of White settler colonial studies to distance
the analytic from militaristic violence, capitalism, and the political concerns
of "return" and "reparations." See Barker's blog, *Tequila Sovereign*, at
https://tequilasovereign.com.

64 Wilderson, *Red, White and Black*, 12.

65 Wilderson, *Red, White and Black*, 166.

66 Wilderson, *Red, White and Black*, 164.

67 Huanani-Kay Trask, *From a Native Daughter: Colonialism and Sovereignty in
Hawaii* (Honolulu: University of Hawai'i Press, 1993), 25.

68 Maile Arvin has argued on a number of occasions that scholars should not
jettison the term or the analytics of settler colonialism, as the term and
intellectual labor of the field began with the work of Huanani-Kay Trask
and Native feminists. Arvine made this important point at the Otherwise
Worlds: Against Settler Colonialism and Anti-Blackness Conference,
Irvine, CA, April 2015.

69 Trask, *From a Native Daughter*, 25.

70 Eve Tuck, "Suspending Damage: A Letter to Communities," *Harvard Educational Review* 79, no. 3 (2009): 409–28; Trask, *From a Native Daughter*, 25.

71 Smith cites the important contributions of several notable Native feminist
scholars in *Conquest: Sexual Violence and American Indian Genocide* (Cambridge, MA: South End, 2005). See also Chrystos, *Dream On* (Vancouver:
Press Gang, 1991); Chrystos, *In Her I Am* (Vancouver: Press Gang, 1993);
Sarah Deer, "Expanding the Network of Safety: Tribal Protection Orders
for Survivors of Sexual Assault," *Tribal Law Journal* 4 (2003): 1–28; Sarah
Deer, "Federal Indian Law and Violent Crime: Native Women and Children at the Mercy of the State," *Social Justice* 31, no. 4 (2004): 17–30; Sarah
Deer, "Toward an Indigenous Jurisprudence of Rape," *Kansas Journal of
Law and Public Policy* 14 (2004): 121–54; Jennifer Nez Denetdale, "Representing Changing Woman: A Review Essay on Navajo Women," *American Indian Culture and Research Journal* 25, no. 3 (2001): 1–26; Charlene
LaPointe, "Boarding Schools Teach Violence," *Plainswoman* 10, no. 4
(1987): 3–4; Lee Maracle, *I Am Woman: A Native Perspective on Sociology
and Feminism* (North Vancouver: Write-On, 1988); Luana Ross, *Inventing the Savage: The Social Construction of Native American Criminality*
(Austin: University of Texas Press, 1998); Audra Simpson, "Paths toward
a Mohawk Nation: Narratives of Citizenship and Nationhood in Kahnawake," in *Political Theory and the Rights of Indigenous Peoples*, ed. Duncan
Ivison, Paul Patton, and Will Sanders (Cambridge: Cambridge Univer-

sity Press, 2000), 113–36; Audra Simpson, "To the Reserve and Back Again: Kahnawake Mohawk Narratives of Self, Home and Nation" (Ph.D. diss., McGill University, Montreal, 2004); Kim TallBear and Deborah Bolnick, "'Native American DNA' tests: What Are the Risks to Tribes?" *Native Voice* 51 (2004): 3–17; Mililani B. Trask, "Hawaiian Sovereignty," *Amerasia Journal* 26, no. 2 (2000): 31–36.

72 Andrea Smith, "Heteropatriarchy and the Three Pillars of White Supremacy: Rethinking Women of Color Organizing," in *The Color of Violence: The INCITE! Anthology*, ed. INCITE! Women of Color against Violence (Boston: South End Press, 2006), 68.

73 Wilderson, *Red, White and Black*, 27.

74 See Eve Kosofsky Sedgwick, "Paranoid Reading and Reparative Reading; or, You're So Paranoid, You Probably Think This Introduction Is about You," in *Novel Gazing: Queer Readings in Fiction*, ed. Eve Kosofsky Sedgwick (Durham, NC: Duke University Press, 1997); Ann Cvetkovich, *Depression: A Public Feeling* (Durham, NC: Duke University Press, 2012). Sedgwick and Cvetkovich encourage a reading practice that does not lapse into the paranoid negativity that a text will fail to live up to its promise or will politically disappoint but instead reads for what is generative and provides openings.

75 See Jodi A. Byrd, *The Transit of Empire: Indigenous Critiques of Colonialism* (Minneapolis: University of Minnesota Press, 2011), 12. Byrd cites Amy Kaplan, *The Anarchy of Empire in the Making of U.S. Culture* (Cambridge, MA: Harvard University Press, 2005).

76 Byrd, *The Transit of Empire*, 12.

77 Huanani-Kay Trask, "The Color of Violence," in *The Color of Violence: The INCITE! Anthology*, ed. INCITE! Women of Color against Violence (Boston: South End Press, 2006), 81.

78 Trask, "The Color of Violence," 81.

79 Trask, "The Color of Violence," 82.

80 Edward Cavanagh and Lorenzo Veracini, "Definition," *Settler Colonial Studies* (blog), 2010, accessed May 2, 2013, http://settlercolonialstudies.org.

81 Silko, *The Almanac of the Dead*, 475.

82 Joanne Barker, "Why Settler Colonialism Isn't Exactly Right," *Tequila Sovereign* (blog), accessed February 24, 2018, https://tequilasovereign.com/2011/02/28/why-settler-colonialism-isnt-exactly-right.

83 Silko, *The Almanac of the Dead*, 408.

84 Silko, *The Almanac of the Dead*, 427.

85 Silko, *The Almanac of the Dead*, 428.

86 Silko, *The Almanac of the Dead*, 428.

87 In fact, a conference was convened at the University of Toronto, Diasporic Hegemonies: Race, Gender, Sexuality and the Politics of Feminist Transnationalism, on October 17–19, 2006, that attempted to stage a conversation about Blackness and Indigeneity in the hemisphere. Rinaldo Walcott's

presentation focused on Wynter's "1492: A New World View." Jacqui Alexander addressed the participants and attendees on a concluding panel that prompted thinking about mutual harm. Andrea Smith spoke to some of the limitations of reparations as a frame of ownership. Bonita Lawrence introduce the notion that Blacks might be settlers. This conference represents one among many stirring conversations between Black and Indigenous peoples in the Americas.

88 Points of departure for some of these discussions were texts such as M. Jacqui Alexander, *Pedagogies of Crossing: Meditations on Feminism, Sexual Politics, Memory and the Sacred* (Durham, NC: Duke University Press, 2005); Bonita Lawrence and Enakshi Dua, "Decolonizing Antiracism," *Social Justice* 32, no. 4 (2005): 120–43; Smith, *Conquest*; Wynter, "1492."

89 See Joanne Barker, who also argues this in "The Analytic Constraints of Settler Colonialism," *Tequila Sovereign* (blog), accessed September 15, 2017, https://tequilasovereign.com/2017/02/02/the-analytic-constraints-of-settler-colonialism.

90 Bill Ashcroft, Gareth Griffiths, and Helen Tiffin, *The Empire Writes Back: Theory and Practice in Post-Colonial Literatures*, (New York: Routledge, 2002), 15.

91 See Ashcroft et al., *The Empire Writes Back*, 15. A discussion of Indigenous literature is essentially relegated to footnote status, and the White settler's knowledge production remains the site of examination.

92 Joanne Barker refers to the scholars who emerged between 1999 and 2010 and desired to "flush out the specific historical conditions of when, how, and why settlers have claimed sovereignty and territorial rights over indigenous peoples" as marking a unique moment in which momentum and attention began to shift toward White scholars in the field of settler colonial studies: see Barker, "Why Settler Colonialism Isn't Exactly Right."

93 In the early 2000s—and more specifically, during the period in which INCITE! Women of Color against Violence captured the attention of Women of Color activists around the globe—Andrea Smith was known and accepted as a member of the Cherokee Nation. In July 2015, news articles circulated about her, and a community of Indigenous feminist scholars issued an open letter weighing in on the discussion about her identity: see Samantha Allen, "Meet the Native American Rachel Dolezal," *Daily Beast*, accessed February 7, 2018, https://www.thedailybeast.com/meet-the-native-american-rachel-dolezal; "Open Letter from Indigenous Women Scholars Regarding Discussions of Andrea Smith," Indian Country Today, July 7, 2015, accessed February 7, 2018, https://newsmaven.io/indian countrytoday/archive/open-letter-from-indigenous-women-scholars -regarding-discussions-of-andrea-smith-5jTCIy_mHUCCE26kGsH49g. The co-signatories argued that Andrea Smith is not Cherokee and has not been accountable to Indigenous communities. In response, Native activ-

ists and scholars published their own letter of support in a blog post titled "Against a Politics of Disposability," July 7, 2015, accessed February 7, 2018, https://againstpoliticsofdisposability.wordpress.com/2015/07/07/against -disposability. The coauthors—including Native feminists and other supporters—posted letters of support for Andrea Smith. They also drafted statements about how a "politics of disposability" uses identity policing and claims of inauthenticity to attack Indigenous people. On July 9, 2015, Andrea Smith issued her own statement affirming her identity as Cherokee on her blog post "My Statement on the Current Media Controversy," accessed February 7, 2018, https://andrea365.wordpress.com/my-state ment-on-thecurrent-media-controversy/.

94 See Paula Gunn Allen, *The Sacred Hoop: Recovering the Feminine in American Indian Traditions* (Boston: Beacon, 1992); Trask, *From a Native Daughter*; Ross, *Inventing the Savage*; Sandy Grande, *Red Pedagogy: Native American Social and Political Thought* (Lanham, MD: Rowman and Littlefield, 2004); Smith, *Conquest*; INCITE! Women of Color against Violence, *The Color of Violence*.

95 Native American and Indigenous women's work, such as Joy Harjo's poetry, Leslie Marmon Silko's fiction, and Rigoberta Menchú's autobiography, should also be included in this roll call, or list, of Indigenous women's thought that was being read rather widely within and outside the academy and activist circles before the advent of the field of settler colonial studies.

96 Wolfe, "Settler Colonialism and the Elimination of the Native," 393.

97 See Edward Cavanagh and Lorenzo Veracini's *Settler Colonial Studies* blog at http://settlercolonialstudies.org.

98 Penelope Edmonds and Jane Carey, "Editors' Introduction," *Settler Colonial Studies* 1, no. 1 (2013): 1.

99 In 2016, the Seneca scholar Mishuana Goeman dedicated a memorial essay to the late Patrick Wolfe. In it, she attests to the ways that Wolfe approached his scholarship as an ally and lovingly states that Wolfe "engaged our field in a respectful and nuanced manner, far beyond many scholars of this settler stature that perceive Indians/Natives/Indigenous as objects of study. His work became a place to engage Indigenous studies concerns in relations to settler colonial studies that at times leaves out indigenous epistemologies and ontologies, as well as our own political framings": Mishuana R. Goeman, "In Memoriam: Patrick Wolfe (February 18, 2016)," *Amerasia Journal* 42, no. 1 (2016): 141.

100 Wolfe, "Settler Colonialism and the Elimination of the Native," 390.

101 Wolfe, "Settler Colonialism and the Elimination of the Native," 402.

102 Barker, "Why Settler Colonialism Isn't Exactly Right."

103 Barker, "Why Settler Colonialism Isn't Exactly Right."

104 Barker, "Why Settler Colonialism Isn't Exactly Right."

105 Barker, "Why Settler Colonialism Isn't Exactly Right."

106 Barker, "The Analytic Constraints of Settler Colonialism."

107 Barker, "The Analytic Constraints of Settler Colonialism."

108 Barker, "The Analytic Constraints of Settler Colonialism." Barker cites the postulation by Lorenzo Veracini that the settler and Indigenous relation will have to remain intact even under a politics of decolonization because if Indigenous people were to demand that the "settler go away," this demand would reproduce the originary violence of settler colonialism.

109 Wilderson calls structural adjustments the "riders" and kinds of discursive moves which attempt to attach categories like "woman," "man," "feminist," "queer," "trans," and "worker," to Black flesh. Wilderson argues that White humans and "Blacks" use these humanist modifiers to try to incorporate Blackness into the discourse and the grammars of suffering of the human: Wilderson, *Red, White and Black*, 306.

110 Wilderson, *Red, White and Black*, 207.

111 Wilderson, *Red, White and Black*, 207.

112 Carole Pateman and Charles Mills examine the emergence of the settler contract within the legal discourse of the British crown, revealing an attempt at discursive distancing. Pateman's essay marks as significant the ways that Western legal thought shifts from the discourse of conquest (subduing) to a discourse of settlement (which is supposed to index contracts and consent). She reviews literature that illuminates the ways that the British Empire attempted to put a discursive or theoretical gulf between themselves and the "atrocities that accompanied Spanish conquest": Carole Pateman, "The Settler Contract," in *Contract and Domination*, ed. Charles Mills and Carole Pateman (Malden, MA: Polity, 2007), 44. This discursive shift from one of conquest (violence) to one of planting settlements, establishing contracts and consent, was not an indication of British rejection or disavowal of gratuitous violence but a means of concealing the violence of conquest by invoking the discourse of settlement. Settlement becomes a euphemism that invokes a relationship to terra nullius as land or wilderness (including beasts but not people) that needs to be subsumed under the "law of nature." The discourse of settlement also confers the power to engage in private war (or private individual genocide) to the settler from its introduction in the sixteenth century through the early nineteenth century.

113 Stephanie Woodard argues that Native Americans are killed by the police at higher rates than any other racial group in the United States: see her special investigation "The Police Killings No One Is Talking About," *In These Times*, October 17, 2016, accessed January 21, 2017, http://inthese times.com/features/native_american_police_killings_native_lives _matter.html.

114 Wolfe, "Settler Colonialism and the Elimination of the Native," 393.

115 Wolfe, "Settler Colonialism and the Elimination of the Native," 394.

116 Wolfe, "Settler Colonialism and the Elimination of the Native," 394.

117 Wolfe, "Settler Colonialism and the Elimination of the Native," 394.

118 See Lorenzo Veracini, "Introducing Settler Colonial Studies," *Settler Colonial Studies* 1, no. 1 (2011): 7.

119 See Patrick Wolfe, *Settler Colonialism and the Transformation of Anthropology*; Patrick Wolfe, "Settler Colonialism and the Elimination of the Native"; Scott Lauria Morgensen, *Spaces between Us: Queer Settler Colonialism and Indigenous Decolonization* (Minneapolis: University of Minnesota Press, 2011); Mark Rifkin, "Indigenizing Agamben: Rethinking Sovereignty in Light of the 'Peculiar' Status of Native Peoples," *Cultural Critique* 73, no. 1 (2009): 88–124; Mark Rifkin, *When Did Indians Become Straight? Kinship, the History of Sexuality, and Native Sovereignty* (Oxford: Oxford University Press, 2010).

120 See Sexton, "The Vel of Slavery."

121 Amber Jamilla Musser's *Sensational Flesh* offers a critically important reading practice of subjectless discourses such as the affective turn. In her introduction, Musser explains an important intervention of the text: "Throughout this book, I seek to reinvigorate these other ways of reading masochism, particularly because reading it as exceptional reifies norms of whiteness and masculinity and suppresses other modes of reading power, agency, and experience": see Amber Jamilla Musser, *Sensational Flesh: Race, Power, and Masochism* (New York: New York University Press, 2014), 6.

122 Audre Lorde, *I Am Your Sister: Black Women Organizing across Sexualities* (New York: Kitchen Table/Women of Color, 1985), 109.

123 Lorde, *I Am Your Sister*, 109.

124 In my course "Gender and Sexuality in the African Diaspora," we read Lorde's *Uses of the Erotic: The Erotic as Power* (Berkeley, CA: Crossing Press, 1978). In the spring of 2016, we had a discussion in which we tried to understand Lorde's notion of the erotic's relationship to chaos. Does it bound it off? Does eroticism come just shy of chaos? One of my students, Amy Sarrell, offered her interpretation that Lorde's notion of the erotic could absorb chaos and use it as a form of power.

2. THE MAP (SETTLEMENT) AND THE TERRITORY (THE INCOMPLETENESS OF CONQUEST)

Epigraph: Kei Miller, "What the Mapmaker Ought to Know," in *The Cartographer Tries to Map a Way to Zion* (Chicago: Carcanet, 2014), 15.

1 Eliza Lucas Pinckney is memorialized in U.S. history as a heroine who saved the colonial economy of the Low Country. At times, she is also interpolated into the story of the founding of South Carolina and the nation. Her letters, recipe book, and memoir are all archival materials that help historians construct the myth that Pinckney "single-handedly introduced Carolinians to the culture and manufacture of indigo": David Coon, "Eliza Lucas Pinckney and the Reintroduction of Indigo Culture in South Carolina," *Journal of Southern History* 42, no.1 (February 1976), 67. Coon credits

folklorists and historians like David Ramsay, author of *The History of South Carolina, from its First Settlement in 1670 to the year 1808*, for the creation of narratives that attribute the cultivation of cash crops like rice and indigo to sole individuals rather than to the collective and regional efforts of an agricultural community. Pinckney has become an icon of rugged individualism and agricultural competency and a gendered embodiment of American autochthony. Her writings have become enshrined as an example of the essence of an exceptional American Protestant work ethic and temperament that tames and settles the land of the nascent settler colonial nation. Her constitution and achievement is equally important because it resides in the innocence of a teenage girl who represents the hopes, aspirations, and accomplishments of a nation that needs to understand itself as innocent.

2   See Elise Pinckney and Marvin R. Zahniser, eds., *The Letterbook of Eliza Lucas Pinckney, 1739–1762* (Columbia: University of South Carolina Press, 1997), 30.

3   Slave revolts in New York (1721, 1741) and Louisiana (1731), and the throughout the Caribbean in 1791 and 1794, frustrated the attempts of settlers to establish dominion over Black and Indigenous peoples in the British and French colonies.

4   The Stono Rebellion in 1739 was a violent insurrection in which fugitive slaves killed their White enslavers in attempts to flee South Carolina and migrate to Spanish Florida—specifically, St. Augustine. During the rebellion, the enslaved burned several plantations.

5   Pinckney and Zahniser, *The Letterbook of Eliza Lucas Pinckney*, 125.

6   Katherine McKittrick, "Diachronic Loops/Deadweight Tonnage/Bad Made Measure," *Cultural Geographies* 23, no. 1 (2016): 3.

7   See Sylvia Wynter, "The Ceremony Must Be Found: After Humanism," *boundary 2* 12, no. 3; 13, no. 1 (Spring–Autumn 1984): 19–70.

8   McKittrick, "Diachronic Loops/Deadweight Tonnage/Bad Made Measure," 4.

9   See Miller, *The Cartographer Tries to Map a Way to Zion*.

10 Wynter's notion of Man1 and Man2 are elaborated throughout her body of work. Man1 emerges in the fifteenth century through conquest as the normative rational subject (European), in contrast to natural (chaotic) others such as Negros and Indios, whom they subdue. In the nineteenth century, due to the advent of Darwinism and modern capitalism, Man2 emerges as a competitive (selected being) who rationally uses the market to gain an advantage over the dyselected (Niggers, Indians, the insane, and the unemployed). Wynter traces these hierarchies and their adjustments—epistemic ruptures—over time as a way to demonstrate the shortcomings of the adjustments to humanism thus far, but she also highlights the shifts to illustrate the malleability or changeability of the order.

11 McKittrick, "Diachronic Loops/Deadweight Tonnage/Bad Made Measure," 3.

12 Denise Ferreira da Silva delineates the production of two kinds of minds within the body of work of Enlightenment-era philosophers. In the glossary that she provides at the beginning of the book, she defines the "transparent I" as a construction that represents European Man and the subject, the ontological figure consolidated in post-Enlightenment European thought. The "affectable I," by contrast, is the racial other that is posited as affected by and overdetermined by exteriority or natural forces. This subject is placed closer to the horizon of death and subject to the chaos of the natural order: Denise Ferreira da Silva, *Toward a Global Idea of Race* (Minneapolis: University of Minnesota Press, 2007), xv.

13 Denis Byrne introduces and uses the term "nervous landscape" to talk about space and landscape as contested and dynamic processes. Since the landscape is not simply "possessed" by the colonizer but is a process that the colonized are also implicated in making, the colonized can transform the landscape and use it against the colonizer. Thus, the landscape becomes an unpredictable and unstable space that makes the colonizer nervous: see Denis R. Byrne, "Nervous Landscapes: Race and Space in Australia," *Journal of Social Archaeology* 3, no. 2 (2003): 169–93.

14 McKittrick, "Diachronic Loops/Deadweight Tonnage/Bad Made Measure," 3.

15 McKittrick, "Diachronic Loops/Deadweight Tonnage/Bad Made Measure," 16.

16 McKittrick, "Diachronic Loops/Deadweight Tonnage/Bad Made Measure," 4, 10.

17 McKittrick, "Diachronic Loops/Deadweight Tonnage/Bad Made Measure," 15.

18 McKittrick, "Diachronic Loops/Deadweight Tonnage/Bad Made Measure," 14–15.

19 McKittrick, "Diachronic Loops/Deadweight Tonnage/Bad Made Measure," 22.

20 Da Silva, *Toward a Global Idea of Race*, 70.

21 See Mart A. Stewart, "William Gerard de Brahm's 1757 Map of South Carolina and Georgia," *Environmental History* 16, no. 3 (2011): 524.

22 While visiting Davidson College's Archives and Special Collections Division in November 2015, I was able to get a sense of the scale of the map, which was laid out for me by the staff. The entire map covered three-quarters of the large conference table in the viewing gallery of the Special Collections Center.

23 See Katherine McKittrick, "On Algorithms and Curiosities," keynote speech delivered at the Feminist Theory Workshop, May 8, 2017, accessed January 13, 2018, https://www.youtube.com/watch?v=ggB3ynMjB34. In the talk, McKittrick emphasizes the need to reconsider our desires and methods as they pertain to analyzing archives of anti-Black violence, which tend to steer us toward death. Rather than succumb to the reflexive tendency to

lean in to Black death, scholars should consider what "Black life" and "Black livingness" do to "open up new question marks."

24 See the website that accompanies the PBS series *Africans in the Americas*, accessed May 20, 2018, http://www.pbs.org/wgbh/aia/part1/1p284.html, which contains notes and additional resources on the Stono Rebellion. For example, the site provides the following information about the rebellion: on September 9, 1739, in South Carolina, just miles outside Charleston, "a band of slaves marched chanting 'liberty'" and carrying a sign with the word "Liberty" written on it.

25 Stewart, "William Gerard de Brahm's 1757 Map of South Carolina and Georgia," 524.

26 Stewart, "William Gerard de Brahm's 1757 Map of South Carolina and Georgia," 524.

27 Stewart, "William Gerard de Brahm's 1757 Map of South Carolina and Georgia," 524.

28 De Brahm, the surveyor and mapmaker, was also a military fort designer, settler, and owner of land and slaves in the Georgia colony. Though it is not visually represented, this biographical information is essential to analyzing the graphic story told by the map. The various social and imperial roles that de Brahm performs in the colonies indicate that he is an interested party, with his own investments in the processes and relations the map depicts. De Brahm's own investments, desires, and hopes are aligned with those of some of the other parties who commissioned the making of the map. An impetus of progress thus guided the imaginations of de Brahm and others as subduers and enemy combatants of Indigenous peoples, captors of enslaved Blacks, producers of imperial commodity forms in the British Empire, and British subjects with a mandate to expand the empire to the farthest corners of the world. Often the imagination of the cartographers and sponsors of eighteenth-century maps are underexamined aspects of mapmaking. If these imagined landscapes and seascapes are in fact constituting features of a map, the imaginations, hopes, and unmet desires of its creators must become objects of scholarly attention: see Charles Mowat, "That Odd Being, 'de Brahm,'" *Florida Historical Quarterly* 20, no. 4 (April 1942): 325. In the article, Mowat includes biographical information on the cartographer that also reveals that the British government appointed him in 1764 as the "Surveyor General of the Southern District of North America" and "Surveyor General of East Florida." As a member of the British military and part of the imperial officers in charge of military affairs that managed Indian Affairs in the American colonies, de Brahm was a part of the mission to conquer Indigenous peoples in the Americas.

29 Stewart, "William Gerard de Brahm's 1757 Map of South Carolina and Georgia," 524.

30 Greg Thomas, "Sex/Sexuality and Sylvia Wynter's 'Beyond . . .': Anti-Colonial Ideas in 'Black Radical Tradition," *Journal of West Indian Literature*

10, nos. 1–2 (2001): 92–118; Sylvia Wynter, "Unsettling the Coloniality of Being/Power/Truth/Freedom: Towards the Human, after Man, Its Over-representation—An Argument," CR: New Centennial Review 3, no. 3 (2003): 257–337.

31 Da Silva, *Toward a Global Idea of Race*, xv.

32 Wynter, "The Ceremony Must Be Found," 36.

33 Da Silva, *Toward a Global Idea of Race*, xv.

34 Da Silva, *Toward a Global Idea of Race*, 117.

35 See note 12 in this chapter.

36 Byrne, "Nervous Landscapes."

37 Da Silva, *Toward a Global Idea of Race*.

38 Da Silva, *Toward a Global Idea of Race*, xv.

39 Da Silva, *Toward a Global Idea of Race*, xvi.

40 See Ginette Verstraete and Tim Cresswell, "Introduction," in *Mobilizing Place, Placing Mobility: The Politics of Representation in a Globalized World*, ed. Ginette Verstraete and Tim Cresswell (Amsterdam: Rodopi, 2002), 12. Cresswell argues that since antiquity, Western philosophy has enshrined space as universal and abstract. People, bodies, and the particular aspects of mere place did not belong there—that is, until the 1970s, when "humanistic geographers" attempted to repeople space and focus on the "geographical nature of being-in-the-world."

41 See Stephanie Pratt, "From the Margins: The Native American Personage in the Cartouche and Decorative Borders of Maps," *Word and Image* 12, no. 4 (1996): 349–65.

42 Lisa Brooks references the work of G. Malcolm Lewis, who refers to Awikhiganak and wampum as Indigenous writing systems based on carto-graphic principles: see Lisa Brooks, *The Common Pot* (Minneapolis: University of Minnesota Press, 2008), 12.

43 Brooks, *The Common Pot*, 9.

44 Brooks, *The Common Pot*, 9.

45 Brooks, *The Common Pot*, 9.

46 Brooks, *The Common Pot*, 9.

47 Brooks, *The Common Pot*, 9.

48 Hokulani K. Aikau, Maile Arvin, Mishuana Goeman, and Scott Morgensen, "Indigenous Feminisms Roundtable," *Frontiers* 36, no. 3 (2015): 94.

49 Aikau et al., "Indigenous Feminisms Roundtable," 94.

50 Da Silva, *Toward a Global Idea of Race*, xvi.

51 While not all Indigenous peoples were marked as hostile people and spaces to supposedly retreat from the actual movement of White advancement and aggression, all were marked as abstractly as possible on the map. While the Catawba Nation, by comparison, is not marked as a space to avoid, as the Cherokee's territory is, the Catawba space in not delineated in the same representational fashion in which the settlers' plots, cultural life, and flora and fauna are. There are signs of life, activity, cultivation, and growth over

time (or development). The vicissitudes of a dynamic and evolving community are depicted on the settled coast. In contrast, the location of the "Catawba Nation" is simply marked as adjacent to the upper watershed of the Wateree: Stewart, "William Gerard de Brahm's 1757 Map of South Carolina and Georgia," 526. After the Stono Rebellion of 1739, the British settlers of South Carolina commissioned Catawba and Chickasaw members to help them capture escaped slaves who were imagined as a threat to the slaveholding class, as well as to the empire at the time. The British had not secured this kind of alliance with the Cherokee whom they would continue to war with through the 1760s. There are no representations of Native and Indigenous nations or peoples in figurative form. They are either crudely represented or depicted as geographical places from which to flee.

52 Stewart, "William Gerard de Brahm's 1757 Map of South Carolina and Georgia," 526.

53 Pinckney and Zahniser, *The Letterbook of Eliza Lucas Pinckney*, 137–39.

54 David Duncan Wallace, *South Carolina: A Short History, 1520–1944* (Chapel Hill: University of North Carolina Press, 1969), 177–79; M. Eugene Sirmans, *Colonial South Carolina: A Political History, 1663–1763* (Chapel Hill: University of North Carolina Press, 2012), 333–34.

55 See Eliza Lucas Pinckney's notes on the trial and imprisonment of her own Mulatto slave (Mol), who was accused of attempting to escape to St. Augustine in Spanish Florida: "Wrote to my father concerning my brother Tommy, his Nurse, his pretty stile in writing, &c. Inform him of some negroes detected going to Augustine. The accused Mol[att]o Quash. I was at his trial when he proved himself quite Innocent. The ring leader is to be hanged and one Whyped. That we rejoiced in the prospect of seeing my papa this spring. Mr. Geln not yet arrived; 'tis imagined he is detained by p——y. Polly gone to school at Mrs. Hick's at 140 pounds per annum": Elise Pinckney and Marvin R. Zahniser, eds., *The Letterbook of Eliza Lucas Pinckney, 1739–1762* (Columbia: University of South Carolina Press, 1997), 57n73.

He can be identified as the same "Mullatto Quash" listed among the twenty working slaves at Wappoo included in Eliza's dowry, and is also referred to as "Quashy, a Carpenter" (1746) and "Quash, a carpenter, since baptized by the name John Williams" (1749). "Wills and Miscellaneous Records, Charleston County," 100 vols., Charleston County Library, SC: 75A:95–106, 75B:373–74, 78A:250.

56 Stewart, "William Gerard de Brahm's 1757 Map of South Carolina and Georgia," 533–34.

57 Stewart, "William Gerard de Brahm's 1757 Map of South Carolina and Georgia," 533–34, emphasis added.

58 Gilles Deleuze and Félix Guattari, *A Thousand Plateaus: Capitalism and Schizophrenia* (London: Bloomsbury, 1988).

59 Gilles Deleuze and Félix Guattari, *A Thousand Plateaus: Capitalism and Schizoprenia*, 5th ed., trans. Brian Massumi (London: Continuum, 2004).

60 Jodi Byrd, *Transit of Empire: Indigenous Critiques of Colonialism* (Minneapolis: University of Minnesota Press, 2011), xxxv.

61 Leslie A. Fiedler, *The Return of the Vanishing American* (New York: Stein and Day, 1968).

62 For further discussion of Deleuzo-Guatarrian rhizomes and lines of flight as discursive practices of Native genocide, see Tiffany Lethabo King, "Humans Involved: Lurking in the Lines of Posthumanist Flight," *Critical Ethnic Studies* 3, no. 1 (2017): 162–85.

63 The space of the plantation is not just a physical space but a space that is an effect of a set of relationships. The relations among notions of property, masters, and Black fungible bodies can be established or disrupted anywhere in space and time in the eighteenth century. For example, plantation relations can exist on a boat, in the field, or on the shore, as depicted in the cartouche on the shoreline.

64 Stewart, "William Gerard de Brahm's 1757 Map of South Carolina and Georgia," 533.

65 Stewart explains that the indigo and rice cycle was created for efficiency: Stewart, "William Gerard de Brahm's 1757 Map of South Carolina and Georgia," 529.

66 While ecotone literature has been evolving since 1965, scholars in the humanities in the late twentieth century and early twenty-first century have been appropriating this literature from the environmental sciences to think through and articulate relations of power in the social realm: see Paul G. Risser, "The Status of the Science Examining Ecotones," *BioScience* 45, no. 5 (1995), 318–25, as well as the recent New Ecotones conference, held in 2015, http://pays-anglophones.upv.univ-montp3.fr/files/2014/12/Programme-New-Ecotones-2015-definitif.pdf.

67 Hortense Spillers, "Mama's Baby, Papa's Maybe: An American Grammar Book," *Diacritics* 17, no. 2 (Summer 1987): 67.

68 Hortense Spillers, Saidiya Hartman, Farah Jasmine Griffin, Shelly Eversley, and Jennifer L. Morgan, "'Whatcha Gonna Do?': Revisiting Mama's Baby, Papa's Maybe: An American Grammar Book: A Conversation with Hortense Spillers, Saidiya Hartman, Farah Jasmine Griffin, Shelly Eversley, and Jennifer L. Morgan," *Women's Studies Quarterly* 35, nos. 1–2 (Spring–Summer 2007): 300.

69 Spillers, "Mama's Baby, Papa's Maybe," 67.

70 In *Black on Both Sides: A Racial History of Trans Identity* (Minneapolis: University of Minnesota Press, 2017), C. Riley Snorton expands upon Spillers's notion of flesh as a site of rearrangement and, in its ungendered form, a state of gender indeterminacy. In my 2017 Black Feminist Thought course, a presentation on "Mama's Baby, Papa's Maybe" by graduate students Katherine (Kat) Nelson and Melanie (Zalika) Ibrahim made sense of and

explained flesh as a site of radical reorganization outside of liberal humanist frames.

71 Saidiya V. Hartman, *Scenes of Subjection: Terror, Slavery, and Self-Making in Nineteenth-Century America* (New York: Oxford University Press, 1997), 21.

72 Attempting to explain this economy of signification's purchase on Black flesh, Spillers explicates the dynamic by starting with a discussion of Blackness's relationship to the commodity under slavery. A metaphor contains slippage; therefore, the signified and signifier fail to line up squarely at the site of the intended commodity with which it is to be exchanged. "If, as Meillassoux contends, 'femininity loses its sacredness in slavery,' then so does 'motherhood' as female blood-rite/right. To that extent, the captive female body locates precisely a moment of converging political and social vectors that marks the flesh as a prime commodity of exchange. While this proposition is open to further exploration, suffice it to say now that this open exchange *of female* bodies in the raw offers a kind of Ur-text to the dynamics of signification and representation that the gendered female would unravel": see Spillers, "Mama's Baby, Papa's Maybe," 75. For an example of how Spillers's work on the malleability of Black flesh or its capacity for "reorganization," see Snorton, *Black on Both Sides*.

73 Hartman, *Scenes of Subjection*, 21.

74 See Sowande Mustakeem, *Slavery at Sea: Terror, Sex, and Sickness in the Middle Passage* (Urbana: University of Illinois Press, 2016). Mining the maritime archives, Mustakeem discovers in the log of a sailor that in 1753 the South Carolinian merchant William Toliff requested young men age fifteen to twenty-five. This is the specified age range and sex of the Portuguese standard of the ideal African slave. The Portuguese named this gendered and aged category the "pieza," which stood as a standard exchange unit—or the ideal body—in the sale of slaves. In 1752, the South Carolina merchant John Guerard wrote to the slave ship captain Watts, advising him that he wanted "Negroes Suitable for this Place." For the merchant that meant "adult male slaves" with no "Crooked Limbs or other Blemishes": see Mustakeem, *Slavery at Sea*, 44. This preference matches the aesthetic on de Brahm's cartouche and references a New World unit of exchange standard of the pieza.

75 See Anuradha Gobin, "Constructing a Picturesque Landscape: Picturing Sugar Plantations in the Eighteenth-Century British West Indies" *Hemispheres: Visual Cultures of the Americas* 4, no. 1 (2011): 42–66; Krista A. Thompson, *An Eye for the Tropics: Tourism, Photography, and Framing the Caribbean Picturesque* (Durham, NC: Duke University Press, 2006); Amar Wahab, *Colonial Inventions: Landscape, Power and Representation in Nineteenth-Century Trinidad* (Newcastle upon Tyne, UK: Cambridge Scholars, 2010).

76 Gobin, "Constructing a Picturesque Landscape," 6.

77 Gobin, "Constructing a Picturesque Landscape," 6.

78 Gobin, "Constructing a Picturesque Landscape," 6.

79 Gobin, "Constructing a Picturesque Landscape," 16.

80 Gobin, "Constructing a Picturesque Landscape," 16.

81 Gobin, "Constructing a Picturesque Landscape," 16.

82 See J. Douglas Porteous, "Bodyscape: The Body-Landscape Metaphor," *Canadian Geographer/Géographe Canadien* 30, no. 1 (1986): 2–12. Since Medieval Europe and through the Enlightenment the body has stood in as a microcosm for the larger world. The body has been used as a way to perceive and name the world. In European imaginaries, the body and the landscape at times stood in for one another. To make the vast landscape more knowable, the body that was becoming a more familiar territory in science became the landscape's synecdoche. The landscape was anthropomorphized to make it familiar and humanlike and thus more knowable. The body and the landscape were imagined and often configured as a feminine other—and as a pornotopia. The body, and thus the landscape, were the erotic and exotic other of the Cartesian dualism of self and other. The Black body as other and mapped onto the New World landscape as terra nullius became objects that could be possessed through one another.

83 According to Stewart, every landscape for de Brahm "was always in a process of change and transformation, and each statement about it was conditional." When de Brahm, who was described as an alchemist and a mystic, "marked soils by type[,] he was considering the relationship of soil with everything else, and indicating the potential for transformation as well," Stewart writes. "Even rocks could become pregnant, [de Brahm] explains in the Report, about the interactions among soils, vegetation, water and climate, at least if given enough time." As de Brahm's particular vantage point or perspective was as a surveyor and "activator" of the land and the natural processes of moving landscapes, such as the plantation, his commitment to understanding, depicting, encouraging, and exploiting the "infinite volatility of these interactions"—always in process, almost moving, always dynamic"—are rendered in the details of the map, and particularly in the cartouche. The produce, legumes, vegetation, and crops are plentiful and the workflow of the enslaved figures is active, orderly, and fluid: Stewart, "William Gerard de Brahm's 1757 Map of South Carolina and Georgia," 524.

84 Gobin, "Constructing a Picturesque Landscape," 16.

85 Anne McClintock, *Imperial Leather: Race, Gender and Sexuality in the Colonial Contest* (New York: Routledge, 1995), 119.

86 McClintock, *Imperial Leather*, 119.

87 Snorton, *Black on Both Sides*, 57.

88 Snorton, *Black on Both Sides*, 56.

Epigraph: Katherine McKittrick, "Plantation Futures," *Small Axe* 17, no. 3 (2013): 12.

1 I theorize the staining or scarring of the hands of actors in the film in Tiffany Lethabo King, "The Labor of (Re)reading Plantation Landscapes Fungible(ly)," *Antipode* 48, no. 4 (2016): 1022–39; Tiffany Jeannette King, "In the Clearing: Black Female Bodies, Space and Settler Colonial Land-scapes" (Ph.D. diss., University of Maryland, College Park, 2013). Christina Sharpe also thinks about this afterlife of indigo in the film *Daughters of the Dust* and briefly in *In the Wake: On Blackness and Being* (Durham, NC: Duke University Press, 2016).

2 See the website for Alphonso Brown's Gullah Tours at http://gullahtours .com/gullah/about-alphonso-brown.

3 Elizabeth Roberts references the work of Jenny Balfour-Paul, who wrote *Indigo* and reports that many slaves would die anywhere between five to seven years after exposure to the toxic process of processing indigo: see Jenny Balfour-Paul, *Indigo* (London: British Museum Press, 1998); Eliza-beth Roberts, "What Gets Inside: Violent Entanglements and Toxic Boundaries in Mexico City," *Cultural Anthropology* 32, no. 4 (2017): 592–619.

4 Kenneth Beeson describes the plantation as a space in which "the stench of the work vats, where the indigo plants were putrefied, was so offensive and deleterious, that the 'work' was usually located at least one quarter of a mile away from human dwellings. The odor from the rotting weeds drew flies and other insects by the thousands and greatly increasing the chances of spread of diseases. Animals and poultry on an indigo plantation like Whites suffered, and it was all but impossible to keep livestock on, or near, the indigo manufacturing site." Kenneth H. Beeson, "Indigo Production in the Eighteenth Century," *Hispanic American Historical Review* 44, no. 2 (May 1964): 215.

5 Beeson, "Indigo Production in the Eighteenth Century," 215.

6 In this scene in the film a voiceover of the narration of the unborn child describes the people in the scene as the "ones who chose to survive."

7 Julie Dash, ed., *Daughters of the Dust: The Making of an African American Woman's Film* (New York: New Press, 1992). For another discussion of Dash's film as a work of speculative fiction, see Julia Erhart, "Picturing What If: Julie Dash's Speculative Fiction," *Camera Obscura* 13, no. 2 (38) (1996): 116–31.

8 Beeson, "Indigo Production in the Eighteenth Century," 215.

9 Julie Dash, dir., *Daughters of the Dust* (1991); John William Gerard de Brahm, "1757 Map of the Coasts of South Carolina and Georgia," Special Collections Division, Davidson College, Davidson, NC.

10 Leanne Simpson, "Sovereignty," in *Native Studies Keywords*, 20.

11　Christina Sharpe introduces Black visual and textual reading practices that include what she calls annotation and redaction. She argues that "redaction and annotation" move one "toward seeing and reading otherwise, toward reading and seeing something in excess of what is caught in the frame" and imagines that "the work of Black annotation and Black redaction" can move the reader beyond the inevitability of anti-Black violence and death and invite a different kind of looking and seeing that counters the inevitability of death and abandonment: see Sharpe, *In the Wake*, 117. Simone Browne contextualizes and defines redaction in terms of state power and theatrics, writing, "We can think of redaction here as the willful absenting of the record and as the state's disavowal of the bureaucratic traces of Fanon, at least those which are made publicly available. Here Frantz Fanon is a nonnameable matter. Now dead, yet still a 'currently and properly classified' security risk, apparently, as 'the fact of existence or nonexistence' of Fanon's records itself is 'intelligence sources and methods information that is protected from disclosure.' With this, the redaction and Executive Order 13526 could be understood as a form of security theater where certain 'intelligence sources and methods,' if in existence, could still be put into operation, and as such could not be declassified": Simone Browne, *Dark Matter: On the Surveillance of Blackness* (Durham, NC: Duke University Press, 2015), 2. Browne's tracing of redaction as a form of absenting and security theater is different from Sharpe's use, which considers how Black aesthetics blacken out dehumanization and annotate scenes of anti-Black violence where there needs to be an insertion of Black life.

12　See note 97 in the introduction. See also Saidiya V. Hartman, "The Belly of the World: A Note on Black Women's Labors," *Souls* 18, no. 1 (2016): 166–73; Katherine McKittrick discusses how geographies of domination are also spaces to read for geographies of resistance in *Demonic Grounds: Black Women and Cartographies of Struggle* (Minneapolis: University of Minnesota Press, 2006), xxxi.

13　In an interview in 1992 with bell hooks, Dash talks about the film *Daughters of the Dust* as being like a form of speculative fiction. Dash says, "It's interesting that you [hooks] say mythopoetic, because *Daughters of the Dust* is like speculative fiction, like a what if situation on so many different levels. Like what if we could have an unborn child come and visit her family-to-be and help solve the family's problems?": Julie Dash, "Dialogue between bell hooks and Julie Dash," in Dash, *Daughters of the Dust*, 29. See also Erhart, "Picturing What If: Julie Dash's Speculative Fiction."

14　Contemporary literature in the fields of colonial, postcolonial, and settler colonial studies often triangulate Blackness into the Indigenous/settler dyad of settler colonial relations through the rubric of Black labor. Within this scholarship, the White settler is theorized as exploiting Black labor to produce settler space: see Aman Sium, "'New World' Settler Colonialism: 'Killing Indians, Making Niggers'" (blog post), *Decolonization, Indigeneity,*

Education and Society blog, November 22, 2013, accessed May 14, 2014, http://decolonization.wordpress.com/2013/11/22/new-world-settler-colonialism-killing-indians-making-niggers; Eve Tuck and K. Wayne Yang, "Decolonization Is Not a Metaphor," *Decolonization: Indigeneity, Education and Society* 1, no. 1 (2012): 1–41; Patrick Wolfe, "Land, Labor, and Difference: Elementary Structures of Race," *American Historical Review* 106, no. 3 (2001): 894–905, Patrick Wolfe, "Settler Colonialism and the Elimination of the Native," *Journal of Genocide Research* 8, no. 4 (2006): 387–409.

15 See Hartman, "The Belly of the World."

16 There has also been pushback to Hegelian logics of labor and labor's attendant telos and the temporality of modernity within Caribbean philosophy and Black studies: see Shona N. Jackson, *Creole Indigeneity: Between Myth and Nation in the Caribbean* (Minneapolis: University of Minnesota Press, 2012); Sylvia Wynter, "Beyond the Categories of the Master Conception: The Counterdoctrine of the Jamesian Poiesis," *C. L. R. James's Caribbean* 69 (1992): 63–91.

17 See Saidiya V. Hartman, *Scenes of Subjection: Terror, Slavery, and Self-Making in Nineteenth-Century America* (New York: Oxford University Press, 1997); Glen Sean Coulthard, *Red Skin, White Masks: Rejecting the Colonial Politics of Recognition* (Minneapolis: University of Minnesota Press, 2014).

18 See LaMonda H. Stallings, *Funk the Erotic: Transaesthetics and Black Sexual Cultures* (Urbana: University of Illinois Press, 2015), 21.

19 An example of the ways that porosity and other units of analysis are used to think about formerly enslaved and contemporary Black bodies/embodiment is evident in the attention that scholars, such as Vanessa Agard-Jones, have given to the porous and Blackness as key concepts. Jones taught a class titled Porous Bodies while at Yale University in 2015 that was cross-listed in African American studies, anthropology, and women's, gender, and sexuality studies.

20 Jennifer L. Morgan contextualizes Black laboring bodies both in and as the space of settlement in the English colonies during the seventeenth and eighteenth centuries in a way that can move readers beyond the narrow mode of production into the libidinal and symbolic. Although Morgan's tome is titled *Laboring Women*, her analysis of Black women's bodies within the context of New World slavery exceeds the frame of labor and effectively argues that Black women function as the symbolic economy for space-making in the Americas. She explores the construction of the Black female captive as a productive, reproductive, and symbolic body under slavery's mode of production and space-making processes, contextualizing Black women as spatial subjects, as they are essential to the settlement of land during the colonial period in the coastal regions of the what will become the U.S. South and the West Indies: see Jennifer L. Morgan, *Laboring Women: Reproduction and Gender in New World Slavery* (Philadelphia: University of Pennsylvania Press, 2004). In fact, the Black female body must

be discursively constructed to make it possible to even conceive of planting settlements during the "first generations of settlement and slave ownership" in South Carolina and Barbados.

Morgan argues that this historical moment of settlement required symbolic constructions and particular uses of the Black female body: Morgan, *Laboring Women*, 17. The Black female body as a formation is an ever-expanding figure. The very idea of the Black female body in a state of flux and expansion makes imaginable physical expansion across the land into the frontier. McKittrick eloquently argues that transatlantic slavery instantiated a particular kind of Black-gendered geographical process, offering that "more specifically, transatlantic slavery incited meaningful geographic processes that were interconnected with the category of 'black woman': this category not only visually and socially represented a particular kind of gendered servitude, it was embedded in the landscape": McKittrick, *Demonic Grounds*, xvii. I extend McKittrick's argument into the space of conquest and settler colonialism to argue similarly that Black women are already "embedded in the landscape" of settlement and expansion.

During seventeenth-century colonial settlement, the spatial capacity of Black femaleness exceeded its use value as labor (as plower, tiller, planter) on the land. According to Morgan, in early eighteenth-century South Carolina and Virginia, representations of Black women as savages and bodies occupying a liminal position began to emerge: Morgan, *Laboring Women*, 17. While Black bodily liminality was discursively imagined and constructed due to the needs of labor and reproduction, this liminal position was also the result of the new relationship Black women had with the land in the New World. A point often missed by those who equate enslavement with labor is that the Black female body as a new form on the seventeenth-century landscape in the Low Country and the Caribbean had to be *reconciled* with Black women's role as workers on a new and foreign landscape. The Black female body did not axiomatically lend itself to easy comparisons with other working bodies.

21 On Man1 and Man 2, see Wynter, "Beyond the Categories of the Master Conception"; Sylvia Wynter, "Unsettling the Coloniality of Being/Power/Truth/Freedom: Towards the Human, after Man, Its Overrepresentation—An Argument," *CR: New Centennial Review* 3, no. 3 (Fall 2003): 257–337.

22 See McKittrick, "Plantation Futures."

23 McKittrick, "Plantation Futures," 11.

24 Snorton, *Black on Both Sides*, 84.

25 Jaime Amparo Alves, "From Necropolis to Blackpolis: Necropolitical Governance and Black Spatial Pin São Paulo, Brazil," *Antipode* 46, no. 2 (2014): 323–39; McKittrick, *Demonic Grounds*; Katherine McKittrick, "On Plantations, Prisons, and a Black Sense of Place," *Social and Cultural Geography* 12, no. 8 (2011): 947–63.

26 Frank B. Wilderson III, *Red, White and Black: Cinema and the Structure of U.S. Antagonisms* (Durham, NC: Duke University Press, 2010), 14.

27 Wilderson, *Red, White and Black*, 263.

28 Phil Hubbard and Rob Kitchin, "Introduction: Why Key Thinkers?" in *Key Thinkers on Space and Place*, ed. Phil Hubbard and Rob Kitchin (Thousand Oaks, CA: Sage, 2010), 4.

29 McKittrick, "On Plantations, Prisons, and a Black Sense of Place," 2011.

30 See Darieck Scott, *Extravagant Abjection: Blackness, Power, and Sexuality in the African American Literary Imagination* (New York: New York University Press, 2010), 64–65.

31 This is a play on and reversal of C. Riley Snorton's conception and use of "fungible fugitivity"; see *Black on Both Sides*.

32 I particularly appreciate one of my reviewer's comments, which pushed me to challenge or, at least, blunt the implied force and capaciousness of the White imagination in a way that made it appear as inescapable: see King, "The Labor of (Re)reading Plantation Landscapes Fungible(ly)." By no means do I mean to imply that Black life is always and already and forever limited by the violent White imagination. Perhaps it was due to the myriad ways that Black captives found ways to survive captivity, the Middle Passage, and ongoing forms of dehumanization that a flexible and supple notion of Blackness as ever changing was required by the White imagination. More archival and speculative work needs to be done to amass content in which one can imagine and theorize the ways that Black fugitivity and resilience push the White imagination—or what one of my reviewers has called the lack of White imagination. However, my reading does argue that Black fungibility configures Blackness as existing outside current conceptions of the human.

33 This reading situates the production of de Brahm's map in a period in which the British colonies needed to render and transform the landscape into a process to conquer it. Paradoxically, cartographers such as de Brahm actually had to depart from or momentarily breech Enlightenment and colonial regimes and orders of thought/perception, such as Cartesianism, to establish and reinforce them. Sarah Jane Cervenak makes a similar argument about the disinterested rationality of Enlightenment reason. When Enlightenment reason had to contend with racial and sexual difference, its logic or knowledge system paradoxically relied on an irrational and interested form of wandering. According to Cervenak, "The epistemological and moral disinterestedness said to characterize the Enlightenment was formed through an ecstatic, erotic existence, or wandering off the straight and narrow path. Engaging some of the seminal work of the recognized Enlightenment philosophers Immanuel Kant and Jean-Jacques Rousseau, I think about how their encounters with racial and sexual difference undermined the requisite disinterestedness of the Enlightenment itself. Put another way, the straight path of reason was always already troubled by its impossible reach, the

promiscuous maneuvers of an 'epistemic model that takes as its model the colonization of the world (of experience),' according to Willi Goetschel": Sarah Jane Cervenak, *Wandering: Philosophical Performances of Racial and Sexual Freedom* (Durham, NC: Duke University Press, 2015), 15. See also Willi Goetschel, "Epilogue: 'Land of Truth — Enchanting Name!' Kant's Journey at Home," in *The Imperialist Imagination: German Colonialism and Its Legacy*, ed. Sara Friedrichsmeyer, Sara Lennox, and Susanne Zantop (Ann Arbor: University of Michigan Press, 1999).

34 Donna Haraway, "Situated Knowledges: The Science Question in Feminism and the Privilege of Partial Perspective," *Feminist Studies* 14, no. 3 (1988): 575–99.

35 Nicholas Mirzoeff, *The Right to Look: A Counterhistory of Visuality* (Durham, NC: Duke University Press, 2011).

36 Mirzoeff, *The Right to Look*, 52, emphasis added.

37 Mart A. Stewart, "William Gerard de Brahm's 1757 Map of South Carolina and Georgia," *Environmental History* 16, no. 3 (2011): 532.

38 Stewart, "William Gerard de Brahm's 1757 Map of South Carolina and Georgia," 529.

39 Hortense Spillers, Saidiya Hartman, Farah Jasmine Griffin, Shelly Eversley, and Jennifer L. Morgan, " 'Whatcha Gonna Do?': Revisiting 'Mama's Baby, Papa's Maybe: An American Grammar Book': A Conversation with Hortense Spillers, Saidiya Hartman, Farah Jasmine Griffin, Shelly Eversley, and Jennifer L. Morgan," *Women's Studies Quarterly* 35, nos. 1–2 (Spring–Summer 2007): 304.

40 Houston Baker and Julie Dash, "Not without my Daughters: A Conversation with Julie Dash and Houston A. Baker Jr.," *Transition* 57 (1992): 164.

41 Nicole R. Fleetwood, *Troubling Vision: Performance, Visuality, and Blackness* (Chicago: University of Chicago Press, 2011).

42 As a filmmaker, Dash can make the invisible visible on-screen. Dash's consultant, the historian and Gullah expert Margaret Washington Creel, insisted that although indigo would not have remained on the hands of the slaves who worked in the indigo-processing plants, the indigo was still poisonous. The chemical elements that seeped into the pores of the enslaved contributed to slaves' deaths: see Dash, *Daughters of the Dust*.

43 Gillian Rose, *Feminism and Geography: The Limits of Geographical Knowledge* (Minneapolis: University of Minnesota Press, 1993), 32.

44 Clyde Woods, *Development Arrested: Race, Power, and the Blues in the Mississippi Delta* (London: Verso, 1998), 31.

45 Woods, *Development Arrested*, 56.

46 McKittrick, "On Plantations, Prisons, and a Black Sense of Place," 948, 950.

47 Spillers, "Mama's Baby, Papa's Maybe."

48 I think here with Vanessa Agard-Jones who draws on the metaphor of sand as a simultaneously a site of entangled colonial histories of enslavement, a site of diffusion and ambiguity particularly when it pertains to reading

Black diasporic gender and sexual configurations: see Vanessa Agard-Jones, "What the Sands Remember," GLQ 18, nos. 2–3 (2012): 325–46.

49 Spillers, "Mama's Baby, Papa's Maybe," 67, 74.

50 See Kathryn Bond Stockton, *Beautiful Bottom, Beautiful Shame: Where "Black" Meets "Queer"* (Durham, NC: Duke University Press, 2006), 29.

51 Stockton, *Beautiful Bottom, Beautiful Shame*, 29.

52 Stockton, *Beautiful Bottom, Beautiful Shame*, 29.

53 Stockton attempts to make a small qualification that still demonstrates a lack of deep engagement with Black literary or queer theory and attempts to throw a bone to Black queer theory and its burgeoning potential. She quips, "Granted, there are now black queer theorists whom we might interpret as pushing to read 'Black' as a sign for loss of boundaries or the queerness of death. But if 'Black' spreads in these studies — I am not sure it actually does — it does so on the back of queer": Stockton, *Beautiful Bottom, Beautiful Shame*, 29. Stockton goes on to cite Sharon Holland and Robert Reid-Pharr's work as a form of Black queer theory that appropriately uses "black gay" male life to make "black boundaryless." See Sharon Holland, *Raising the Dead: Readings of Death and (Black) Subjectivity* (Durham, NC: Duke University Press, 2000); and Robert Reid-Pharr, *Black Gay Man: Essays* (New York: New York University Press, 2001). While Stockton celebrates this Black attempt to prove itself sufficiently spreadable, it unfortunately achieves this feat only due to the work and malleability of queerness and queer theory. With qualifications, Stockton concedes, "To be sure, 'gay,' in Reid-Pharr's thinking, is making 'black' spread beyond the bounds of normativity. But what is the range of black border crossing? Just how far does 'black boundarylessness' extend itself? Whatever the answer, aside from such thinkers working both terms ('queer' with 'black'), there has not been an obvious move within black American or black Atlantic studies to spread the sign 'black,' with its contaminations, over the general social field": Stockton, *Beautiful Bottom, Beautiful Shame*, 30. Stockton's indictment is confounding for anyone who seriously reads Black literature, literary criticism, or work in Black gender and sexuality studies.

54 Greg Thomas, "Sex/Sexuality and Sylvia Wynter's 'Beyond . . .'": Anticolonial Ideas in 'Black Radical Tradition,'" *Journal of West Indian Literature* 10, nos. 1–2 (2001): 103–4.

55 Wynter, "Beyond the Categories of the Master Conception," 81.

56 Wynter, "Beyond the Categories of the Master Conception," 81.

57 Wynter, "Beyond the Categories of the Master Conception," 78.

58 Walter Mignolo, "Sylvia Wynter: What Does It Mean to Be Human?," in *Sylvia Wynter: On Being Human as Praxis*, ed. Katherine McKittrick (Durham, NC: Duke University Press, 2014), 114.

59 Mignolo, "Sylvia Wynter," 114.

60 Wynter, "Beyond the Categories of the Master Conception," 78.

61 Wynter, "Beyond the Categories of the Master Conception," 77.

62 Sylvia Wynter, "Beyond Miranda's Meaning: Un/Silencing the 'Demonic Ground' of Caliban's 'Woman.'" In *Out of Kumbla: Caribbean Women and Literature*, ed. Carole Boyce Davies (Chicago: Africa World Press, 1990), 355–72.

63 Woods, *Development Arrested*, 29.

64 Scott, *Extravagant Abjection*.

65 Scott, *Extravagant Abjection*.

66 Scott, *Extravagant Abjection*, 129.

67 Alexander G. Weheliye, *Habeas Viscus: Racializing Assemblages, Biopolitics, and Black Feminist Theories of the Human* (Durham, NC: Duke University Press, 2014), 21, cites Wynter "Beyond Miranda's Meaning," and Wynter's use of the term "demonic" from the field of physics.

68 Stewart, "William Gerard de Brahm's 1757 Map of South Carolina and Georgia," 538.

69 Stallings, *Funk the Erotic*.

4. OUR CHEROKEE UNCLES

Epigraphs: The quote is from the character St. Julien Lastchild in Julie Dash, dir., *Daughters of the Dust* (1991); Audre Lorde, *Uses of the Erotic: The Erotic as Power* (Berkeley, CA: Crossing, 1978), 90.

1 Anderson spoke on a plenary at the We Carry These Memories Inside of We symposium, Avery Research Center, Charleston, SC, September 17, 2011.

2 While this chapter intends to celebrate a range of affects described as the erotic, which include agape love, friendship, deep political solidarity, romantic love, and sex/fucking, I acknowledge the ways that Native masculinity has been objectified and sexualized. I am also aware that Black women can participate in this sexualization. Daniel Heath Justice talks about how the iconic cinematic and televisual image of the fierce, noble, wild, handsome Lakota warrior with long black hair and feathers has become the "epitome of savage sensuality." Dash certainly could have relied on this stock image and the way it has been trafficked as an erotic image when imagining her character St. Julien Lastchild. While the power dynamic in the depiction of sensual Indigenous masculinity by Black women is different from the power dynamic involved in Hollywood's creation and circulation of the image, the power dynamics should be named: see Daniel Heath Justice, *Our Fire Survives the Storm: A Cherokee Literary History* (Minneapolis: University of Minnesota Press, 2006), 3.

3 See Tiya Miles, *The Cherokee Rose: A Novel of Gardens and Ghosts* (Winston-Salem: John Blair, 2015), Reader's Guide (hereafter, RG) 1–2.

4 Julie Dash, "Julie Dash Discusses *Daughters of the Dust* on BarnesandNoble .com, African American Literature Book Club, December 19, 1997, accessed April 5, 2016, http://aalbc.com/authors/juliedashchattext.htm.

5 Justice argues that Cherokee people are a queer Indigenous nation as they have had to rely on nonnormative modes of building community and relations to survive conquest. Intermarriage and the reimagining of notions of sovereignty have been practices of Cherokee life. I also draw from the reparative reading practices used in Mark Rifkin's *Settler Common Sense: Queerness and Everyday Colonialism in the American Renaissance* (Minneapolis: University of Minnesota Press, 2014). When Rifkin writes about the works of Nathaniel Hawthorne, Henry David Thoreau, and Herman Melville while acknowledging the limitations and the reification of Indigenous disappearance in their works, he holds space and argues that "rather than dismissing [their] claims as merely putative (they think they are contesting the state but are not really), I take them seriously, arguing that the texts I address develop what might be understood as specifically queer critiques of the state": Rifkin, *Settler Common Sense*, xviii. By situating and rereading these texts in the context of Native presence and resistance, Rifkin is able to read in ways "that open room for thinking other possibilities": Rifkin, *Settler Common Sense*, xviii. I draw on Rifkin's model of reading White settler texts reparatively to argue that Black women's texts that actually attempt to hold space for and write in Indigenous presence should be read generously rather than putatively.

6 Louis Chude-Sokei, Ariane Cruz, Amber Jamilla Musser, Jennifer Christine Nash, LaMonda H. Stallings, and Kirin Wachter-Grene, "Race, Pornography, and Desire: A TBS Roundtable," *Black Scholar* 46, no. 4 (2016): 61.

7 Audre Lorde, *Sister Outsider* (Berkeley, CA: Crossing Press, 1984), 87.

8 Lorde, *Sister Outsider*, 87.

9 Lorde, *Sister Outsider*, 87.

10 See Audre Lorde, "The Uses of the Erotic: The Erotic as Power," *Uses of the Erotic: The Erotic as Power* (Berkeley, CA: Crossing, 1978).

11 Audre Lorde, "The Master's Tools Will Never Dismantle the Master's House," in *This Bridge Called My Back: Writings by Radical Women of Color*, ed. Cherríe Moraga and Gloria Anzaldúa (New York: Kitchen Table, 1983), 96.

12 Julie Dash, dir., *Daughters of the Dust*, film, Geechee Girls, New York, 1991, 00:10:14 seconds.

13 Billy-Ray Belcourt, "Indigenous Studies beside Itself," *Somatechnics* 7, no. 2 (2017): 182.

14 Belcourt, "Indigenous Studies beside Itself," 182.

15 Belcourt, "Indigenous Studies beside Itself," 182.

16 Belcourt, "Indigenous Studies beside Itself," 185.

17 Belcourt, "Indigenous Studies beside Itself," 185.

18 Belcourt, "Indigenous Studies beside Itself," 183.

19 Jared Sexton, "The Vel of Slavery: Tracking the Figure of the Unsovereign." *Critical Sociology* 42, nos. 4–5 (2016): 7.

20 Belcourt, "Indigenous Studies beside Itself," 183.

21 Belcourt, "Indigenous Studies beside Itself," 184.

22 Belcourt, "Indigenous Studies beside Itself," 184.

23 Barbara Christian, "The Race for Theory," *Cultural Critique* 6 (1987): 51–63.

24 Its particular inertia, particularly in the way it has been understood as sometimes dismissing Black and Indigenous claims amid its people-of-color claims, has caused an impasse in this contemporary conjuncture.

25 Michelle Raheja, "Visual Sovereignty," in *Native Studies Keywords*, ed. Stephanie Teves, Andrea Smith, and Michelle Raheja (Tucson: University of Arizona Press, 2015), 27.

26 Leanne Betasamosake Simpson, "A Place Where We All Live and Work Together: A Gendered Analysis of Sovereignty," in *Native Studies Keywords*, ed. Stephanie Teves, Andrea Smith, and Michelle Raheja (Tucson: University of Arizona Press, 2015), 22.

27 See Stephanie Teves, Andrea Smith, and Michelle Raheja, "Sovereignty," in Teves et al., *Native Studies Keywords*, 9.

28 Teves et al., "Sovereignty," 9.

29 Teves et al., "Sovereignty," 13.

30 Teves et al., "Sovereignty," 15.

31 Teves et al., "Sovereignty," 15.

32 Teves et al., "Sovereignty," 5.

33 Sexton, "The Vel of Slavery," 10–11.

34 Sexton, "The Vel of Slavery," 11.

35 Sexton, "The Vel of Slavery," 11.

36 Sexton, "The Vel of Slavery," 7.

37 See Iyko Day, "Being or Nothingness: Indigeneity, Antiblackness, and Settler Colonial Critique," *Critical Ethnic Studies* 1, no. 2 (2015): 102–21; Justin Leroy, "Black History in Occupied Territory: On the Entanglements of Slavery and Settler Colonialism," *Theory and Event* 19, no. 4 (2016).

38 This is a question one reviewer of this manuscript posed that compelled me to think about multiple contexts in which sovereignty is deployed for various reasons, some of which advance Black fugitivity and abolition. I am grateful for the reviewer's prodding and challenging me to go deeper.

39 Andrew K. Frank, "Taking the State Out: Seminoles and Creeks in Late Eighteenth-Century Florida," *Florida Historical Quarterly* 84, no. 1 (2005): 17–18.

40 Maile Arvin, Eve Tuck, and Angie Morrill, "Decolonizing Feminism: Challenging Connections between Settler Colonialism and Heteropatriarchy," *Feminist Formations* 25, no. 1 (Spring 2013): 23.

41 I use the term "iconic" to connote its value as an idealized image of Black and Indigenous coalition, alliance, and kinship for women who are familiar with Dash's film.

42 As a speculative artist, Dash imagines and depicts an ethical encounter between Black and Indigenous peoples — specifically, Gullah and Cherokee — in ways that counter conquest's modes of genocide and Black accu-

mulation and fungibility. Iona Peazant and St. Julien Lastchild's attempts to know and love each other gesture toward—or attempt—new ways to negotiate violent practices of racialization, nation building, modernization, and citizenship projects. Ultimately, I argue for an ethics of erotic encounter as a way to think about how Black and Indigenous people might relate to one another. Different from coalitional politics, the ethics of erotic encounter enables a discussion of the ways that eros forces people to remake themselves in relation to others' desires. Another motivation for exploring interracial erotic encounters rather than coalition politics is due to the way erotics, sex, and desire create space to expose and explore publicly some of the latent, hidden, or unspoken desires and expectations that coalition fails to address or even consider.

43 See Frank B. Wilderson III, *Red, White and Black: Cinema and the Structure of U.S. Antagonisms* (Durham, NC: Duke University Press, 2010).

44 See Saidiya V. Hartman, *Scenes of Subjection: Terror, Slavery, and Self-making in Nineteenth-Century America* (New York: Oxford University Press, 1997), 75. Hartman elucidates what the recuperated slave body can reveal and make possible. This history is illuminated not only by the recitation of the litany of horrors that characterized the "commercial deportation of Africans," but also by performance practices that serve as a means of redressing the pained body and restaging the event of rupture or breach that engendered "the other side." The (counter)investment in the body as a site of need, desire, and pleasure, and the constancy of unmet needs, repressed desires, and the shortcomings of pleasure, are articulated in the very endeavor to heal the flesh and redress the pained body. For Hartman, even moments in which the pained body is being cared for (e.g., Dash's montages of the erotic activity of the hands) draw us back to the underside of modernity. However, when we are able to view violence at the same moment that we are able to see the agency of the slave and the recuperation of the body, we are not destroyed or paralyzed.

45 Wilderson, *Red, White and Black.*

46 See Stephanie Woodard, "The Police Killings No One Is Talking About," *In These Times*, October 17, 2016, accessed January 21, 2017, http://inthesetimes .com/features/native_american_police_killings_native_lives_matter .html.

47 The LA Rebellion refers to the African and African American film students who entered the UCLA School of Theater, Film, and Television in the 1960s in the "aftermath of the Watts rebellion." Over a period of two decades more than twenty-seven Black filmmakers developed a community of support in which to make liberatory films for the Black community. Julie Dash is included in this illustrious list of filmmakers. See more information at https://www.cinema.ucla.edu/la-rebellion. Wilderson states, "I am interested in Black filmmakers of the 1970s, like Charles Burnett, Haile Gerima, Julie Dash, Ivan Dixon, and Jamaa Fanaka, not as auteurs or brilliant indi-

viduals, but as cinematic prisms. I believe that regardless of the political views these filmmakers may or may not hold, their bodies and their aesthetic sensibilities became ciphers for a rather special intense and rare phenomenon of Black people on the move politically. I would like to suggest that the political antagonism that was explained and the insurgent iconoclasm that was harnessed by these filmmakers, in the films' acoustic strategies, lighting, mise-en-scène, and image construction and camera work, marked an ethical embrace of the Slave's ensemble of questions regarding the Slave estate's structure of violence and the Slave revolt's structure of feeling": Wilderson, *Red, White and Black*, 124–25.

48 Wilderson, *Red, White and Black*, 140.

49 See Julie Dash, ed., *Daughters of the Dust: The Making of an African American Woman's Film* (New York: New Press, 1992), 88. The screenplay and script appear in the book. St. Julien Lastchild's lines appear here in the book.

50 Dash, *Daughters of the Dust: The Making of an African American Woman's Film*, 91.

51 Dash, *Daughters of the Dust: The Making of an African American Woman's Film*, 88.

52 Dash, *Daughters of the Dust: The Making of an African American Woman's Film*, 49.

53 In the film and the screenplay, there is a moment in which Eula castigates the respectability politics of some of the Peazant women who judge Yellow Mary and her sexual history. Eula, a victim of sexual assault herself, claims a lineage of coming from enslaved Black women who all had a relationship to sexual violence and, in some respects, could be considered ruined (ruin't) individually or collectively: Julie Dash, screenplay for *Daughters of the Dust* (1991), 74.

54 Julie Dash, *Daughters of the Dust: A Novel* (New York: Penguin, 1997), 161.

55 Dash, *Daughters of the Dust* (1997), 162.

56 See LaShawn Harris, *Sex Workers, Psychics, and Numbers Runners: Black Women in New York City's Underground Economy* (Urbana: University of Illinois Press, 2016).

57 Dash, *Daughters of the Dust* (1997), 173–74.

58 Zainab A. Amadahy and Bonita Lawrence, "Indigenous Peoples and Black People in Canada: Settlers or Allies?" in *Breaching the Colonial Contract*, ed. Arlo Kemp (Dordrecht, Netherlands: Springer, 2009), 105–36.

59 Wilderson, *Red, White and Black*, 23.

60 Kim TallBear, *Native American DNA: Tribal Belonging and the False Promise of Genetic Science* (Minneapolis: University of Minnesota Press, 2013), 131.

61 TallBear, *Native American DNA*, 45.

62 Qwo-Li Driskill, Chris Finley, Brian Joseph Gilley, and Scott Lauria Morgensen, eds., *Queer Indigenous Studies: Critical Interventions in Theory, Politics, and Literature* (Tucson: University of Arizona Press, 2011), 109.

63 See Christina Sharpe, *In the Wake: On Blackness and Being* (Durham, NC: Duke University Press, 2017), 15.

64 This term comes from Sharpe's notion of "wake work" or the labor of sustaining Black life in the context/weather of anti-Blackness: see Sharpe, *In the Wake*.

65 Qwo-Li Driskill conducted interviews with Two Spirit and queer Cherokee Nation/Asegi Ayetl members as a way to renarrate and reimagine the nation. One of his interviewees was Daniel Heath Justice. The interview is in Qwo-Li Driskill, "D4Y DBC (Asegi Ayetl): Cherokee Two-Spirit People Reimagining Nation," in Driskill et al., *Queer Indigenous Studies*, 106.

66 Driskill, "D4Y DBC (Asegi Ayetl)," 106.

67 Caroline Brown, "The Representation of the Indigenous Other in *Daughters of the Dust* and *The Piano*," NWSA *Journal* 15, no. 1 (2003): 1–19.

68 Dash, *Daughters of the Dust* (1997), 187.

69 See Justice, *Our Fire Survives the Storm*, 6.

70 Justice, *Our Fire Survives the Storm*, 8.

71 Justice makes a distinction between "state focused nationalisms" and "tribal nationhood." Justice defines Cherokee and tribal nationhood as "the political extension of the social rights and responsibilities of peoplehood. It is the underpinning of what Jace Weaver calls "communitism," which is something "more than merely "community." It involves a particular way of attempting to live in community as Natives: Justice, *Our Fire Survives the Storm*, 24. Justice also elaborates on the concept of "community" to distinguish it from non-Indigenous and liberal forms of community that tend to be exclusively focused on the human and fail to focus on ecological interdependence and fall back on nation-state notions of the polity and the collective: see Justice, *Our Fire Survives the Storm*, 225n12.

72 A nation for African Americans within the U.S. nation-state, or even under Native sovereignty, is not a foreseeable possibility and therefore not an aspiration for Dash and the Gullah people she writes about.

73 Driskill, "D4Y DBC (Asegi Ayetl)," 109.

74 See Lisa Tatonetti, "Indigenous Fantasies and Sovereign Erotics: Outland Cherokees Write Two-Spirit Nations," in *Queer Indigenous Studies: Critical Interventions in Theory, Politics, and Literature*, ed. Qwo-Li Driskill, Chris Finley, Brian Joseph Gilley, and Scott Lauria Morgensen (Tucson: University of Arizona Press, 2011), 155–71. Tatonetti's title references Qwo-Li Driskill, "Stolen from Our Bodies: First Nations Two-Spirits/Queers and the Journey to a Sovereign Erotic," *Studies in American Indian Literatures* 16, no. 2 (2004): 50–64.

75 Tatonetti, "Indigenous Fantasies and Sovereign Erotics," 168.

76 Justice, *Our Fire Survives the Storm*, 8.

77 See Barbara Krauthamer, *Black Slaves, Indian Masters: Slavery, Emancipation, and Citizenship in the Native American South*, (Chapel Hill: The University of North Carolina Press, 2013), 8.

78 For a discussion of critical fabulation as a resistant act, see note 97 to the introduction above. See also Katherine McKittrick, "Diachronic Loops/ Deadweight Tonnage/Bad Made Measure," *Cultural Geographies* 23, no. 1 (2016): 3–18; Katherine McKittrick, "Mathematics Black Life," *Black Scholar* 44, no. 2 (2014):16–28.

79 Miles, *The Cherokee Rose*, RG 4.

80 Miles, *The Cherokee Rose*, RG 4; see also Miles, *The Cherokee Rose*, 251.

81 Miles, *The Cherokee Rose*, RG 2.

82 Jesse Peters, "The Cherokee Rose: A Novel of Gardens and Ghosts by Tiya Miles (Review)," *Studies in American Indian Literatures* 27, no. 4 (2015): 137.

83 Erica Bourquiqnon, "Spirit Possession and Altered States of Consciousness: The Evolution of an Inquiry," in *The Making of Psychological Anthropology*, ed. G. Spindler (Berkeley: University of California Press, 1978), 92–93; Gloria Wekker, *The Politics of Passion: Women's Sexual Culture in the Afro-Surinamese Diaspora* (New York: Columbia University Press, 2006), 93.

84 Miles, *The Cherokee Rose*, 92.

85 Miles, *The Cherokee Rose*, 92.

86 Miles, *The Cherokee Rose*, 94.

87 Miles, *The Cherokee Rose*, 95.

88 Miles, *The Cherokee Rose*, 95.

89 Miles, *The Cherokee Rose*, 107.

90 Miles, *The Cherokee Rose*, 109.

91 Miles, *The Cherokee Rose*, 109.

92 During a July 2015 interview with Cherokee writer, filmmaker, and activist Zainab Amadahy, she spoke of her own Cherokee ancestors' experiences as slaves alongside Black enslaved people in Greene County, Virginia. The Cherokee have the distinct experience of being both enslaved and holders of slaves.

93 Mishuana Goeman, "(Re)Mapping Indigenous Presence on the Land in Native Women's Literature," *American Quarterly* 60, no. 2 (June 2008): 295. One way or mode of producing more inclusively human and livable space is through the creative act of poetry. The autopoesis of Black and Native geographies are sacred acts. Goeman's poetic muse Ester Belin and McKittrick's poetic inspiration in the work of Dionne Brand have been used by each to unmap and remap the space of Turtle Island and the spatial desires of the Black diaspora. Breath to the poet is life. Goeman makes important distinctions between the breathy verbal acts of Indigenous prayer and poetry that have transformative power as opposed to the words, discourse, and power of logos to separate and taxonomize space.

94 Goeman, "(Re)Mapping Indigenous Presence on the Land in Native Women's Literature," 298.

95 See Katherine McKittrick, *Demonic Grounds: Black Women and the Car-*

tographies of Struggle (Minneapolis: University of Minnesota Press, 2006),
    xxiii.

 96 Justice, *Our Fire Survives the Storm*, 27.

 97 Miles, *The Cherokee Rose*, 110.

 98 Miles, *The Cherokee Rose*, 110.

 99 Miles, *The Cherokee Rose*, 111.

100 Audre Lorde, *Uses of the Erotic: The Erotic as Power* (Berkeley, CA: Cross-
    ing, 1978), 87.

101 Miles, *The Cherokee Rose*, 111.

5. A CEREMONY FOR SYCORAX

 1 I met Charmaine Lurch at the Critical Ethnic Studies conference held at
    York University, Toronto, in April 2015. Jin Haritaworn introduced Char-
    maine to me; Charmaine was enrolled in one of Jin's courses. Jin had
    assigned my dissertation, "In the Clearing: Black Female Bodies and Settler
    Colonial Landscapes," to the class, and Charmaine and another student,
    Mosa McNeilly, opted to engage the text by creating a multimedia perfor-
    mance. Some of what emerged from the performance became pieces in
    Lurch's show *Conversations in Flux: Visible Presence Unfolding in Time and
    Space*.

 2 Charmaine Lurch, *Conversations in Flux: Visible Presence Unfolding in Time
    and Space* website, accessed July 21, 2018, http://charmainelurch.ca/conver
    sations-in-flux.

 3 Lurch explained her intention in an email to me on July 24, 2018.

 4 Lurch, email.

 5 Charmaine Lurch, interview by the author, Toronto, July 21, 2015.

 6 The location of all four artists and thinkers in Canada/Turtle Island—and,
    more specifically, in Toronto—is important to the kinds of interventions
    they are able to make. Later in the chapter, I discuss the specific kinds
    of diasporic thought and aesthetics to which I was introduced while in
    Toronto and discuss this kind of Black diasporic thought in relationship to
    Canada, the United States, the Anglophone Caribbean, and Black studies.

 7 I first saw Lurch's multidimensional sculpture "Revisiting Sycorax" as
    part of the exhibition *Conversations in Flux: Visible Presence Unfolding in
    Time and Space*, Toronto Centre for the Arts, Lower Gallery, October 2015.
    According to the online description of the exhibition, "*Revisiting Sycorax*
    references Shakespeare's classic *The Tempest*. Sycorax is the invisible and
    voiceless woman in the play, recognized in scholarly circles as a metaphor
    for black/indigenous populations. Constructed of wire forms and shapes
    the figure holds space inside and out. Lurch's *Sycorax* is a metaphor for past
    and present, temporal and spatial. The tesseract figure is poised; portraying
    movement and stasis concurrently": "Charmaine Lurch: Conversations
    in Flux: Visible Presence Unfolding in Time and Space," *Akimbo*, n.d.,

accessed February 5, 2017, http://www.akimbo.ca/87048?startDate=&
venue=&city=&type=exhibitions&showDays=30.

8 My former car, plane, and bus travel mate, Milca Fils Aime, a Haitian
   daughter of the African diaspora, is five feet, nine inches tall. When she
   stood next to the statue, her shoulders were a bit higher than Sycorax's, and
   she could easily reach out and hold Sycorax's hand if she desired.

9 Abena P. A. Busia, "Silencing Sycorax: On African Colonial Discourse and
   the Unvoiced Female," *Cultural Critique*, no. 14, Construction of Gender
   and Modes of Social Division II (Winter 1989–90): 81–104.

10 Busia, "Silencing Sycorax," 94.

11 Gayatri Spivak, "Can the Subaltern Speak?" in *Marxism and the Interpretation of Culture*, ed. Cary Nelson (Urbana: University of Illinois Pres, 1988),
   271–313.

12 Busia, "Silencing Sycorax," 104.

13 Kinitra D. Brooks, *Searching for Sycorax: Black Women's Hauntings of Contemporary Horror* (New Brunswick, NJ: Rutgers University Press, 2017), 7.

14 Brooks, *Searching for Sycorax*, 7.

15 Brooks, *Searching for Sycorax*, 7.

16 Lurch adds that another possible reading of Spillers's aporetic is to think of
   aporia in another vein as an act of "raising a doubt or objection" rather than
   silence and speechlessness: Lurch, email.

17 Hortense J. Spillers, "Who Cuts the Border? Some Readings on America,"
   in *Black, White, and in Color: Essays on American Literature and Culture*
   (Chicago: University of Chicago Press, 2003), 325.

18 See Vicente M. Diaz, "Creolization and Indigeneity," *American Ethnologist*
   (2006): 577.

19 See Shona N. Jackson, *Creole Indigeneity: Between Myth and Nation in the
   Caribbean* (Minneapolis: University of Minnesota Press, 2012); Melanie J.
   Newton, "Returns to a Native Land: Indigeneity and Decolonization in the
   Anglophone Caribbean," *Small Axe* 17, no. 2 (41) (2013): 108–22.

20 Irene Lara, "Beyond Caliban's Curses: The Decolonial Feminist Literacy
   of Sycorax," *Journal of International Women's Studies* 9, no. 1 (2007): 80,
   89.

21 It is important to note that Wynter is not so much making a case for the
   representation and humanization of Black/Native heterosexual existence
   as she is stating that there is no possibility for Caliban to reproduce. In *The
   Tempest*, there is no Black or Native equivalent to Miranda. Since Sycorax's
   death, Caliban has no elders, contemporaries, or descendants: Sylvia Wynter, "Beyond Miranda's Meanings: Un/Silencing the 'Demonic Ground' of
   Caliban's 'Woman,'" in *Out of the Kumbla: Caribbean Women and Literature*,
   ed. Carole Boyce Davies (Chicago: Africa World Press, 1990), 360.

22 Lara, "Beyond Caliban's Curses," 90.

23 Lara, "Beyond Caliban's Curses," 90.

24 Audre Lorde, "The Master's Tools Will Never Dismantle the Master's

House," in *This Bridge Called My Back: Writings by Radical Women of Color*, ed. Cherríe Moraga and Gloria Anzaldúa (New York: Kitchen Table, 1983), 110.

25 Lara, "Beyond Caliban's Curses," 90.

26 Lara, "Beyond Caliban's Curses," 92.

27 See Irene Lara's poem, "Ceremony of Sycorax's Soul," published in "Beyond Caliban's Curses: The Decolonial Feminist Literacy of Sycorax," *Journal of International Women's Studies* 9, no. 1 (2007): 80, 89. Seniti Namjoshi created two poem cycles to experiment with the subject matter of *The Tempest*: see Seniti Namjoshi, *Sycorax: New Fables and Poems* (New Delhi: Penguin, 2006).

28 Wynter, "Beyond Miranda's Meanings," 364.

29 See Lurch, email.

30 Depending on one's perspective, Sycorax could also be interpreted as emerging from a plume of smoke or rising from the ground/grass.

31 Lurch says, "I often use wire that I have on hand but specifically chose the black wire as a necessary indication of color/blackness/indigeneity which forms the core of the piece. Copper/brass/are soft metals—introduced a kind of light and life, an aesthetic for imagination, easy to bend. The fact that copper is an electrical conductor is interesting to think about": notes from an email by Charmaine Lurch, drafted February 25, 2017.

32 See Spillers's notion of "liberated flesh," or flesh that is not captured by the humanist discourse of the body and its constraints of race, gender, or ability: see Hortense Spillers, "Mama's Baby, Papa's Maybe: An American Grammar Book," *Diacritics* 17, no. 2 (Summer 1987): 65–81.

33 In the Algonquin and Mohawk languages, the word "squaw" means female genitalia or vagina. However, the word was appropriated by French and English explorers and settlers in the seventeenth century and used to dehumanize Indigenous women. By the nineteenth century, it was circulating among settlers as a racialized and gendered slur. As a derisive term or slur, the word came to be associated with Indigenous women and girls and their reproductive anatomy. For centuries, Indigenous women have organized to prevent the term from being used. In 1992, Susan Harjo (Mohawk) appeared on *The Oprah Winfrey Show* to spread awareness about the kind of violence that the use of the term inflicted on Indigenous women and communities: see Debra Merskin, "The S-Word: Discourse, Stereotypes, and the American Indian Woman," *Harvard Journal of Communications* 21 (2010): 345–66. See also Denise K. Lajimodiere, "American Indian Females and Stereotypes: Warriors, Leaders, Healers, Feminists; Not Drudges, Princesses, Prostitutes," *Multicultural Perspectives* 15, no. 2 (2013): 104–9; William Bright, "The Sociolinguistics of the 'S-Word': Squaw in American Place Names," *Names* 48, nos. 3–4 (2000): 207–16.

34 Lurch, interview.

35 Jacqui Alexander, *Pedagogies of Crossing: Meditations on Feminism, Sexual*

Politics, Memory and the Sacred (Durham, NC: Duke University Press, 2005), 270.

36 For more on Trinidadian artist Christopher Cozier, see his artist page at http://davidkrutprojects.com/artists/9079/christopher-cozier.

37 The Delaware Valley tristate area comprises Philadelphia, southern New Jersey, and northern Delaware.

38 Rinaldo Walcott, *Black Like Who? Writing Black Canada* (London, ON: Insomniac, 2003), 27.

39 Dionne Brand, *Land to Light On* (Toronto: McClelland and Stewart, 1997).

40 Saidiya V. Hartman, *Lose Your Mother: A Journey Along the Atlantic Slave Route,* (New York: Farrar, Straus and Giroux, 2007).

41 Walcott, *Black Like Who?*, 23.

42 Mishuana Goeman, "Land as Life: Unsettling the Logics of Containment," in *Native Studies Keywords*, ed. Stephanie Teves, Andrea Smith, and Michelle Raheja (Tucson: University of Arizona Press, 2015), 73.

43 Leanne Betasamosake Simpson, "Sovereignty," in Teves et al., *Native Studies Keywords*, 23.

44 Walcott, *Black Like Who?*, 27.

45 Walcott, *Black Like Who?*, 14.

46 Katherine McKittrick, *Demonic Grounds: Black Women and Cartographies of Struggle* (Minneapolis: University of Minnesota Press, 2006), xxx.

47 Peter James Hudson, "The Geographies of Blackness and Anti-Blackness: An Interview with Katherine McKittrick," *C. L. R. James Journal* 20, nos. 1–2 (2014): 236.

48 Hudson, "The Geographies of Blackness and Anti-Blackness," 236.

49 "De road" is a term used by fêters and people participating in Carnival. The main activities of dancing, winning, fêting, and partying happen on the road where the bands and dancers process. Caribana is a yearly festival honoring the tradition of Carnival in Trinidad that celebrates the Caribbean community in Toronto. During the annual Toronto Pride celebration a queer contingent of Black and people of color LGBT organizers affiliated with Pelau's Masqueerade in the tradition of Trinidadian Carnival throw a parallel event to celebrate queer Black and racialized diasporas in Canada. In Cassandra Lord's "Performing Queer Diasporas: Pelau MasQUEERade in the Toronto Pride Parade" (Ph.D. diss., University of Toronto, 2015), Lord theorizes "de road" as a process and space-making practice in which national identities become fragmented and even dissolve, particularly for folks who reproduce queer Trinidadian Carnival traditions in diasporic communities such as Toronto.

50 D. Alissa Trotz, "Rethinking Caribbean Transnational Connections: Conceptual Itineraries," *Global Networks* 6, no. 1 (2006): 41–59. Organized by Black LGBTQI people affiliated with the collective Blackness Yes!, Blokorama is a block party and community event held during the Toronto Pride event to support Black queer and trans people. It was organized to address

the exclusions of a largely white Pride event and in recent years has worked with Black Lives Matter Toronto to address police presence and participation in the annual Toronto Pride parade.

51 Walcott, *Black Like Who?*, 131.

52 See Antonio Benítez-Rojo, *The Repeating Island: The Caribbean and the Postmodern Perspective* (Durham, NC: Duke University Press, 1996).

53 See Walcott, *Black Like Who?*, 131. In this work and others over the past fourteen years, Walcott has argued for a Black diaspora studies that also takes seriously the regional formation of "North American Blackness" and an attendant North American Black studies.

54 See Sylvia Wynter, "The Ceremony Must Be Found: After Humanism," *boundary 2* 12, no. 3; 13, no. 1 (Spring–Autumn 1984): 19–70. See also John Peale Bishop's poem "Speaking of Poetry" in *Now with His Love* (New York: Charles Scribner's Sons, 1933).

55 Sylvia Wynter, "The Ceremony Found: Towards the Autopoetic Turn/Overturn, Its Autonomy of Human Agency and Extraterritoriality of (Self-) Cognition," in *Black Knowledges/Black Struggles: Essays in Critical Epistemology*, ed. Jason R. Ambroise and Sabine Bröck-Sallah (Liverpool: Liverpool University Press, 2015), 198.

56 See Judith Butler, *Gender Trouble: Feminism and the Subversion of Identity* (New York: Routledge, 1990).

57 Sylvia Wynter and Greg Thomas, "*ProudFlesh* Inter/views: Sylvia Wynter," *ProudFlesh* 4 (2006): 31.

58 Wynter and Thomas, "*ProudFlesh* Inter/views," 32.

59 Alexander, *Pedagogies of Crossing*, 208.

60 See Christina Sharpe, *In the Wake: On Blackness and Being* (Durham, NC: Duke University Press, 2016), 41. Sharpe writes about and explains the notion of "residence time," writing, "The amount of time it takes for a substance to enter the ocean and then leave the ocean is called residence time. Human blood is salty, and sodium, Gardulski tells me, has a residence time of 260 million years."

61 Sharpe, *In the Wake*, 40.

62 Leslie Marmon Silko, *The Almanac of the Dead: A Novel* (New York: Simon and Schuster, 1991), 416.

63 Silko, *The Almanac of the Dead*, 421.

64 Silko, *The Almanac of the Dead*, 421.

65 Wynter, "The Ceremony Found," 196.

66 For a discussion of Deleuze and Guattari's "line of flight" and the geo-epistemology of "the Line" as a technologies of binary categorization in Western humanist traditions, see Tiffany Lethabo King, "Humans Involved: Lurking in the Lines of Posthumanist Flight." *Journal of the Critical Ethnic Studies Association* 3, no. 1 (2017): 162–86 .

67 Wynter, "The Ceremony Found," 198.

68 Wynter, "The Ceremony Found," 207.

Epigraph: M. Jacqui Alexander, *Pedagogies of Crossing: Meditations on Feminism, Sexual Politics, Memory and the Sacred* (Durham, NC: Duke University Press, 2005), 322.

1 See Dionne Brand, *A Map to the Door of No Return: Notes to Belonging* (Toronto: Vintage Canada, 2012); Paul Gilroy, *The Black Atlantic: Modernity and Double Consciousness* (Cambridge, MA: Harvard University Press, 1993); Omise'eke Natasha Tinsley, "Black Atlantic, Queer Atlantic: Queer Imaginings of the Middle Passage," GLQ 14, nos. 2–3 (2008): 191.

2 Alexander, *Pedagogies of Crossing*, 322.

3 Black Lives Matter has become a global and international movement that addresses the specific ways that global forms of anti-Blackness emerge within a specific context. The hashtag #BlackLivesMatter, created by Alicia Garza, Patrisse Cullors, and Opal Tometi in the United States, has taken on new and different meanings as it has been appropriated by other groups and forms of political work to address the state-sanctioned killings of Black people around the world.

Agard-Jones, Vanessa. "What the Sands Remember." GLQ 18, nos. 2–3 (2012): 325–46.

Aikau, Hokulani K., Maile Arvin, Mishuana Goeman, and Scott Morgensen. "Indigenous Feminisms Roundtable." *Frontiers* 36, no. 3 (2015): 84–106.

Alexander, M. Jacqui. *Pedagogies of Crossing: Meditations on Feminism, Sexual Politics, Memory, and the Sacred*. Durham, NC: Duke University Press, 2005.

Amparo Alves, Jaime. "From Necropolis to Blackpolis: Necropolitical Governance and Black Spatial Praxis in São Paulo, Brazil." *Antipode* 46, no. 2 (2014): 323–39.

Amadahy, Zainab, and Bonita Lawrence. "Indigenous Peoples and Black People in Canada: Settlers or Allies?" In *Breaching the Colonial Contract*, ed. Arlo Kemp, 105–36. Dordrecht, Netherlands: Springer, 2009.

Arvin, Maile, Eve Tuck, and Angie Morrill. "Decolonizing Feminism: Challenging Connections between Settler Colonialism and Heteropatriarchy." *Feminist Formations* 25, no. 1 (Spring 2013): 8–34.

Ashcroft, Bill. "Archipelago of Dreams: Utopianism in Caribbean Literature." *Textual Practice* 30, no. 1 (2016): 89–112.

Ashcroft, Bill, Gareth Griffiths, and Helen Tiffin. *The Empire Writes Back: Theory and Practice in Post-Colonial Literatures*. New York: Routledge, 2003.

Bailey, M., and R. Shabazz. "Gender and Sexual Geographies of Blackness and Anti-black Heterotopias (Part 1)." *Gender, Place, and Culture* 21, no. 3 (2013): 316–21. Accessed February 14, 2014. doi: 10.1080/0966369X.2013.781305.

Erica Bourquiqnon, "Spirit Possession and Altered States of Consciousness: The Evolution of an Inquiry." In *The Making of Psychological Anthropology*, ed. G. Spindler, 92–93. Berkeley: University of California Press, 1978.

Balfour-Paul, Jenny. *Indigo*. London: British Museum Press, 1998.

Beeson, Kenneth H. "Indigo Production in the Eighteenth Century." *Hispanic American Historical Review* 44, no. 2 (1964): 214–18.

Belcourt, Billy-Ray. "Indigenous Studies beside Itself." *Somatechnics* 7, no. 2 (2017): 182–85.

Benítez-Rojo, Antonio. *The Repeating Island: The Caribbean and the Postmodern Perspective*. Durham, NC: Duke University Press, 1996.

Bersani, Leo. "Is the Rectum a Grave?" *October* 43 (1987): 197–222.

Bishop, John Peale. "Speaking of Poetry." In *Now with His Love*. New York: Charles Scribner's Sons, 1933.

Bradley, Rizvana, and Damien-Adia Marassa. "Awakening to the World: Relation, Totality, and Writing from Below." *Discourse* 36, no. 1 (Winter 2014): 112–31.

Brand, Dionne. *A Map to the Door of No Return: Notes to Belonging*. Toronto: Vintage Canada, 2001.

Brand, Dionne. *Land to Light On*. Toronto: McClelland and Stewart, 1997.

Brathwaite, Kamau. *ConVERSations with Nathaniel Mackey*. Rhinebeck, NY: We, 1999.

Bright, William. "The Sociolinguistics of the 'S-Word': Squaw in American Place Names." *Names* 48, nos. 3–4 (2000): 207–16.

Brooks, Kinitra D. *Searching for Sycorax: Black Women's Hauntings of Contemporary Horror*. New Brunswick, NJ: Rutgers University Press, 2017.

Brooks, Lisa. *The Common Pot*. Minneapolis: University of Minnesota Press, 2008.

Brown, Caroline. "The Representation of the Indigenous Other in *Daughters of the Dust* and *The Piano*." *NWSA Journal* 15, no. 1 (2003): 1–19.

Busia, Abena P. A. "Silencing Sycorax: On African Colonial Discourse and the Unvoiced Female." *Cultural Critique*, no. 14, Construction of Gender and Modes of Social Division II (Winter 1989–90): 81–104.

Butler, Judith. *Gender Trouble: Feminism and the Subversion of Identity*. New York: Routledge, 1990.

Browne, Simone. *Dark Matter: On the Surveillance of Blackness*. Durham, NC: Duke University Press, 2015.

Byrd, Jodi A. *The Transit of Empire: Indigenous Critiques of Colonialism*. Minneapolis: University of Minnesota Press, 2011.

Byrne, Denis. "Nervous Landscapes: Race and Space in Australia." *Journal of Social Archaeology* 3, no. 2 (2003): 169–93.

Cannon, Katie. *Black Womanist Ethics*. Eugene, OR: Wipf and Stock, 2006.

Cavanagh, Edward. "Review Essay: Discussing Settler Colonialism's Spatial Cultures." *Settler Colonial Studies* 1, no. 1 (2011): 154–67.

Cervenak, Sarah Jane. *Wandering: Philosophical Performances of Racial and Sexual Freedom*. Durham, NC: Duke University Press, 2014.

Champagne, Duane. *Notes from the Center of Turtle Island*. Lanham, MD: Alta-Mira, 2010.

Chandler, Nahum Dimitri. *X— The Problem of the Negro as a Problem for Thought*. Oxford: Oxford University Press, 2013.

Chow, Rey. *The Protestant Ethnic and the Spirit of Capitalism*. New York: Columbia University Press, 2002.

Christian, Barbara. "The Race for Theory." *Cultural Critique* 6 (1987): 51–63.

Chrystos. *Dream On*. Vancouver: Press Gang, 1991.

Chrystos. *In Her I Am.* Vancouver: Press Gang, 1993.

Chude-Sokei, Louis, Ariane Cruz, Amber Jamilla Musser, Jennifer Christine Nash, LaMonda H. Stallings, and Kirin Wachter-Grene. "Race, Pornography, and Desire: A TBS Roundtable." *Black Scholar* 46, no. 4 (2016): 49–64.

Churchill, Ward. *A Little Matter of Genocide: Holocaust and Denial in the Americas 1492 to the Present.* San Francisco: City Lights, 2001.

Clarke, John Henrik. *Christopher Columbus and the Afrikan Holocaust: Slavery and the Rise of European Capitalism.* Brooklyn, NY: A&B, 1992.

Clarke, John Henrik. "Christopher Columbus and Genocide." Presentation delivered on January 12, 1992, posted February 17, 2013. Accessed January 7, 2017. https://www.youtube.com/watch?v=vqoTBsgk6gg.

Cooper, Afua. *The Hanging of Angélique: The Untold Story of Canadian Slavery and the Burning of Old Montréal.* Athens: University of Georgia Press, 2007.

Coulthard, Glen Sean. *Red Skin, White Masks: Rejecting the Colonial Politics of Recognition.* Minneapolis: University of Minnesota Press, 2014.

Cvetkovich, Ann. *Depression: A Public Feeling.* Durham, NC: Duke University Press, 2012.

Dash, Julie. *Daughters of the Dust: A Novel.* New York: Penguin, 1999.

Dash, Julie, ed. *Daughters of the Dust: The Making of an African American Woman's Film.* New York: New Press, 1992.

Dash, Julie. "Dialogue between bell hooks and Julie Dash." In *Daughters of the Dust: The Making of an African American Woman's Film,* ed. Julie Dash, 27–68. New York: New Press, 1992.

Dash, Julie, and Houston Baker. "Not without My Daughters: A Conversation with Julie Dash and Houston A. Baker, Jr." *Transition,* no. 57 (1992): 150–66.

da Silva, Denise Ferreira. *Toward a Global Idea of Race.* Minneapolis: University of Minnesota Press, 2007.

Davis, Heather, and Zoe Todd. "On the Importance of a Date, or, Decolonizing the Anthropocene." *ACME* 16, no. 4 (2017): 761–80.

Day, Iyko. "Being or Nothingness: Indigeneity, Antiblackness, and Settler Colonial Critique." *Critical Ethnic Studies* 1, no. 2 (2015): 102–21.

de Azurara, Gomes Eanes, and Charles Raymond Beazley. *The Chronicle of the Discovery and Conquest of Guinea,* no. 95. London: Hakluyt Society, 1899.

Deer, Sarah. "Expanding the Network of Safety: Tribal Protection Orders for Survivors of Sexual Assault." *Tribal Law Journal* 4 (2003): 1–28.

Deer, Sarah. "Federal Indian Law and Violent Crime: Native Women and Children at the Mercy of the State." *Social Justice* 31, no. 4 (2004): 17–30.

Deer, Sarah. "Toward an Indigenous Jurisprudence of Rape." *Kansas Journal of Law and Public Policy* 14 (2004): 121.

Deleuze, Gilles, and Félix Guattari. *A Thousand Plateaus: Capitalism and Schizophrenia.* London: Bloomsbury, 1988.

DeLoughrey, Elizabeth M. *Routes and Roots: Navigating Caribbean and Pacific Island Literatures.* Honolulu: University of Hawai'i Press, 2007.

Denetdale, Jennifer. "Representing Changing Woman: A Review Essay on

Navajo Women." *American Indian Culture and Research Journal* 25, no. 3 (2001): 1–26.

Dennen, Shanya. "Occupying Spaces of Belonging: Indigeneity in Diasporic Guyana." M.A. thesis, University of Texas, Austin, 2013.

Díaz, Junot. *The Brief Wondrous Life of Oscar Wao.* New York: Penguin, 2007.

Díaz, Junot. *This Is How You Lose Her.* New York: Penguin, 2013.

Diaz, Vicente M. "Creolization and Indigeneity." *American Ethnologist* (2006): 576–78.

Diaz, Vincente M. "No Island Is an Island." In *Native Studies Keywords,* ed. Stephanie Teves, Andrea Smith, and Michelle Raheja, 90–108. Tucson: University of Arizona Press, 2015.

Driskill, Qwo-Li. "D4Y DBC (Asegi Ayeti): Cherokee Two-Spirit Peoples Reimagining Nation." In *Queer Indigenous Studies: Critical Interventions in Theory, Politics and Literature,* ed. Qwo-Li Driskill, Chris Finley, Brian Joseph Gilley, and Scott Lauria Morgensen, 97–112. Tucson: University of Arizona Press, 2011.

Driskill, Qwo-Li. "Stolen from Our Bodies: First Nations Two-Spirits/Queers and the Journey to a Sovereign Erotic." *Studies in American Indian Literatures* 16, no. 2 (2004): 50–64.

Driskill, Qwo-Li, Chris Finley, Brian Joseph Gilley, and Scott Lauria Morgensen, eds. *Queer Indigenous Studies: Critical Interventions in Theory, Politics, and Literature.* Tucson: University of Arizona Press, 2011.

Edelman, Lee. *No Future: Queer Theory and the Death Drive.* Durham, NC: Duke University Press, 2004.

Edelson, S. Max. *Plantation Enterprise in Colonial South Carolina.* Cambridge, MA: Harvard University Press, 2006.

Edmonds, Penelope, and Jane Carey. "A New Beginning for Settler Colonial Studies." *Settler Colonial Studies* 3, no. 1 (2013): 2–5.

Edmonds, Penelope, and Jane Carey. "Editors' Introduction." *Settler Colonial Studies* 1, no. 1 (2013): 1–13.

Erhart, Julia. "Picturing What If: Julie Dash's Speculative Fiction." *Camera Obscura* 13, no. 2 (38) (1996): 116–31.

Fanon, Frantz. *Black Skin, White Masks.* New York: Grove, 1952.

Fleetwood, Nicole R. *Troubling Vision: Performance, Visuality, and Blackness.* Chicago: University of Chicago Press, 2011.

Frank, Andrew K. "Taking the State Out: Seminoles and Creeks in Late Eighteenth-Century Florida." *Florida Historical Quarterly* 84, no. 1 (2005): 10–27.

Gilmore, Ruth Wilson. "Fatal Couplings of Power and Difference: Notes on Racism and Geography." *Professional Geographer* 54, no. 1 (2002): 15–24.

Gilroy, Paul. *The Black Atlantic: Modernity and Double Consciousness.* Cambridge, MA: Harvard University Press, 1993.

Glissant, Édouard. *Caribbean Discourse: Selected Essays.* Translated by J. Michael Dash. Charlottesville: University Press of Virginia, 1989.

Glissant, Édouard. *Poetics of Relation.* Translated by Betsy Wing. Ann Arbor: University of Michigan Press, 1997.

Gobin, Anuradha. "Constructing a Picturesque Landscape: Picturing Sugar Plantations in the Eighteenth-Century British West Indies." *Hemispheres: Visual Cultures of the Americas* 4, no. 1 (2011): 42–66.

Goeman, Mishuana R. "In Memorium: Patrick Wolfe (February 18, 2016)." *Amerasia Journal* 42, no. 1 (2016): 140–43.

Goeman, Mishuana R. "Land as Life: Unsettling the Logics of Containment." In *Native Studies Keywords*, ed. Stephanie Teves, Andrea Smith, and Michelle Raheja, 71–89. Tucson: University of Arizona Press, 2015.

Goeman, Mishuana R. *Mark My Words: Native Women Mapping Our Nations.* Minneapolis: University of Minnesota Press, 2013.

Goeman, Mishuana R. "(Re)Mapping Indigenous Presence on the Land in Native Women's Literature." *American Quarterly* 60, no. 2 (2008): 295–302.

Goetschel, Will. "Epilogue: 'Land of Truth—Enchanting Name!' Kant's Journey at Home." In *The Imperialist Imagination: German Colonialism and Its Legacy*, ed. Sara Friedrichsmeyer, Sara Lennox, and Susanne Zantop, 321–36. Ann Arbor: University of Michigan Press, 1999.

Gourdine, Angeletta K. M. "Fashioning the Body [as] Politic in Julie Dash's *Daughters of the Dust.*" *African American Review* 38, no. 3 (Autumn 2001): 499–511.

Grande, Sandy. *Red Pedagogy: Native American Social and Political Thought.* Lanham, MD: Rowman and Littlefield, 2004.

Grosz, Elizabeth. "A Thousand Tiny Sexes: Feminism and Rhizomatics." *Topoi* 12, no. 2 (1993): 167–79.

Gunn Allen, Paula. *The Sacred Hoop: Recovering the Feminine in American Indian Traditions.* Boston: Beacon, 1992.

Hall, Lisa Kahaleole. "Strategies of Erasure: U.S. Colonialism and Native Hawaiian Feminism." *American Quarterly* 60, no. 2 (2008): 273–80.

Haraway, Donna. "Situated Knowledges: The Science Question in Feminism and the Privilege of Partial Perspective." *Feminist Studies* 14, no. 3 (1988): 575–99.

Harney, Stefano, and Fred Moten. *The Undercommons: Fugitive Planning and Black Study.* Wivenhoe, UK: Minor Compositions, 2013.

Harris, LaShawn. *Sex Workers, Psychics, and Numbers Runners: Black Women in New York City's Underground Economy.* Urbana: University of Illinois Press, 2016.

Hartman, Saidiya V. "The Belly of the World: A Note on Black Women's Labors." *Souls* 18, no. 1 (2016): 166–73.

Hartman, Saidiya V. *Lose Your Mother: A Journey along the Atlantic Slave Route.* New York: Farrar, Straus and Giroux, 2007.

Hartman, Saidiya V. *Scenes of Subjection: Terror, Slavery, and Self-Making in Nineteenth-Century America.* New York: Oxford University Press, 1997.

Hartman, Saidiya V. "Venus in Two Acts." *Small Axe* 12, no. 2 (2008): 1–14.

Hartman, Saidiya V., and Frank B. Wilderson III. "The Position of the Unthought." *Qui Parle* 13, no. 2 (2003): 183–201.

Hartsock, Nancy. "Marxist Feminist Dialectics for the Twenty-First Century," *Science and Society* 62, no. 3 (Fall 1998): 400–13.

Harvey, Sandra. "Passing for Free, Passing for Sovereign: Blackness and the Formation of the Nation." Ph.D. diss., University of California, Santa Cruz, 2017.

Haynes, Tonya. "Sylvia Wynter's Theory of the Human and the Crisis School of Caribbean Heteromasculinity Studies." *Small Axe* 20, no. 1 (2016): 92–112.

Holland, Sharon P. *Raising the Dead: Readings of Death and (Black) Subjectivity.* Durham, NC: Duke University Press, 2000.

Horne, Gerald. *The Apocalypse of Settler Colonialism: The Roots of Slavery, White Supremacy, and Capitalism in Seventeenth-Century North America and the Caribbean.* New York: New York University Press, 2018.

Hubbard, Phil, and Rob Kitchin. "Introduction: Why Key Thinkers?" In *Key Thinkers on Space and Place*, ed. Phil Hubbard and Rob Kitchin, 1–17. Thousand Oaks, CA: Sage, 2010.

Hudson, Peter James. "The Geographies of Blackness and Anti-Blackness: An Interview with Katherine McKittrick." *C. L. R. James Journal* 20, nos. 1–2 (2014): 233–40.

Hunziker, Alyssa A. "Toni Morrison, Indigeneity, and Settler Colonialism." *Settler Colonial Studies* 8, no. 4 (2018): 507–17.

Jackson, Shona N. *Creole Indigeneity: Between Myth and Nation in the Caribbean.* Minneapolis: University of Minnesota Press, 2012.

Justice, Daniel Heath. *Our Fire Survives the Storm: A Cherokee Literary History.* Minneapolis: University of Minnesota Press, 2006.

Kaplan, Amy. *The Anarchy of Empire in the Making of U.S. Culture.* Cambridge, MA: Harvard University Press, 2005.

Kelley, Robin D. G. *Freedom Dreams: The Black Radical Imagination.* Boston: Beacon, 2002.

Kelley, Robin D. G. "The Rest of Us: Rethinking Settler and Native." *American Quarterly* 69, no. 2 (2017): 267–76.

King, Tiffany Jeannette. "In the Clearing: Black Female Bodies, Space and Settler Colonial Landscapes." Ph.D. diss., University of Maryland, College Park, 2013.

King, Tiffany Lethabo. "Humans Involved: Lurking in the Lines of Posthumanist Flight." *Critical Ethnic Studies* 3, no. 1 (2017): 162–85.

King, Tiffany Lethabo. "The Labor of (Re)reading Plantation Landscapes Fungible(ly)." *Antipode* 48, no. 4 (2016): 1022–39.

King, Tiffany Lethabo. "Post-Indentitarian and Post-Intersectional Anxiety in the Neoliberal Corporate University." *Feminist Formations* 27, no. 3 (2015): 114–38.

Krauthamer, Barbara. *Black Slaves, Indian Masters: Slavery, Emancipation, and*

Citizenship in the Native American South. Chapel Hill: University of North Carolina Press, 2013.

Lajimodiere, Denise K. "American Indian Females and Stereotypes: Warriors, Leaders, Healers, Feminists; Not Drudges, Princesses, Prostitutes." *Multicultural Perspectives* 15, no. 2 (2013): 104–9.

LaPointe, Charlene. "Boarding Schools Teach Violence." *Plainswoman* 10, no. 4 (1987): 3–4.

Lara, Irene. "Beyond Caliban's Curses: The Decolonial Feminist Literacy of Sycorax." *Journal of International Women's Studies* 9, no. 1 (2007): 80–98.

Lawrence, Bonita, and Enakshi Dua. "Decolonizing Antiracism." *Social Justice* 32, no. 4 (2005): 120–43.

Lefler, Hugh. "Review of *The Letterbook of Eliza Lucas Pinckney, 1739–1762.*" *Florida Historical Quarterly* 51, no. 2 (1974): 185–86.

Leroy, Justin. "Black History in Occupied Territory: On the Entanglements of Slavery and Settler Colonialism." *Theory and Event* 19, no. 4 (2016).

LeVan, Michael. "The Digital Shoals: On Becoming and Sensation in Performance." *Text and Performance Quarterly* 32, no. 3 (2012): 209–19.

Littlehales, G. W. "On the Improbability of Finding Shoals in the Open Sea by Sailing over the Geographical Positions in Which They Are Charted." *Annals of Mathematics* 9, no. 1/6 (1894–95): 163–67.

Lorde, Audre. *I Am Your Sister: Black Women Organizing across Sexualities.* New York: Kitchen Table/Women of Color, 1985.

Lorde, Audre. "The Master's Tools Will Never Dismantle the Master's House." In *This Bridge Called My Back: Writings by Radical Women of Color,* ed. Cherríe Moraga and Gloria Anzaldúa, 94–103. New York: Kitchen Table, 1983.

Lorde, Audre. *Sister Outsider.* Berkeley, CA: Crossing, 1984.

Lorde, Audre. *Uses of the Erotic: The Erotic as Power.* Berkeley, CA: Crossing, 1978.

Maracle, Lee. *I Am Woman: A Native Perspective on Sociology and Feminism.* North Vancouver: Write-On, 1988.

Marshall, Paule. *Praisesong for the Widow.* New York: Plume, 1984.

Mays, Kyle T. "Transnational Progressivism: African Americans, Native Americans, and the Universal Races Congress of 1911." *Studies in American Indian Literatures* 25, no. 2 (2013): 241–61.

McKittrick, Katherine. *Demonic Grounds: Black Women and Cartographies of Struggle.* Minneapolis: University of Minnesota Press, 2006.

McKittrick, Katherine. "Diachronic Loops/Deadweight Tonnage/Bad Made Measure." *Cultural Geographies* 23, no. 1 (2016): 3–18.

McKittrick, Katherine. "Mathematics Black Life." *Black Scholar* 44, no. 2 (2014): 16–28.

McKittrick, Katherine. "On Plantations, Prisons, and a Black Sense of Place." *Social and Cultural Geography* 12, no. 8 (2011): 947–63.

McKittrick, Katherine. "Plantation Futures." *Small Axe* 17, no. 3 (2013): 1–15.

McKittrick, Katherine, and Alexander G. Weheliye. "808s and Heartbreak." *Propter Nos* 2, no. 1 (2017): 13–42.

McKittrick, Katherine, and Clyde Woods. *Black Geographies and the Politics of Place.* Toronto: Between the Lines, 2007.

Menchú, Rigoberta. *I, Rigoberta Menchú: An Indian Woman in Guatemala*, ed. Elisabeth Burgos-Debray, trans. Ann Wright. London: Verso, 2010.

Merskin, Debra. "The S-Word: Discourse, Stereotypes, and the American Indian Woman." *Harvard Journal of Communications* 21 (2010): 345–66.

Mignolo, Walter. "Sylvia Wynter: What Does It Mean to Be Human?" In *Sylvia Wynter: On Being Human as Praxis*, ed. Katherine McKittrick, 106–23. Durham, NC: Duke University Press, 2014.

Miles, Tiya. *The Cherokee Rose: A Novel of Gardens and Ghosts.* Winston-Salem, NC: John Blair, 2015.

Miles, Tiya. *The House on Diamond Hill: A Cherokee Plantation Story.* Chapel Hill: University of North Carolina Press, 2010.

Miles, Tiya, and Sharon Patricia Holland, eds. *Crossing Waters, Crossing Worlds: The African Diaspora in Indian Country.* Durham, NC: Duke University Press, 2006.

Miller, Kei. *The Cartographer Tries to Map a Way to Zion.* Manchester, UK: Carcanet, 2014.

Miranda, Katherine. "Junot Díaz, Diaspora, and Redemption: Creating Progressive Imaginaries." *Sargasso* 2 (2008–2009): 23–40.

Mirzoeff, Nicholas. *The Right to Look: A Counterhistory of Visuality.* Durham, NC: Duke University Press, 2012.

Morgan, Jennifer L. *Laboring Women: Reproduction and Gender in New World Slavery.* Philadelphia: University of Pennsylvania Press, 2004.

Morgensen, Scott Lauria. "The Biopolitics of Settler Colonialism: Right Here, Right Now." *Settler Colonial Studies* 1, no. 1 (2011): 52–76.

Morgensen, Scott Lauria. *Spaces between Us: Queer Settler Colonialism and Indigenous Decolonization.* Minneapolis: University of Minnesota Press, 2011.

Morrison, Toni. *Playing in the Dark: Whiteness and the Literary Imagination.* New York: Random House, 1993.

Morrison, Toni. *Playing in the Dark: Whiteness and the Literary Imagination.* New York: Vintage, 2007.

Moten, Fred. *In the Break: The Aesthetics of the Black Radical Tradition.* Minneapolis: University of Minnesota Press, 2003.

Mowat, Charles, "That Odd Being, 'de Brahm.'" *Florida Historical Quarterly* 20, no. 4 (April 1942): 323–45.

Mustakeem, Sowande. *Slavery at Sea: Terror, Sex, and Sickness in the Middle Passage.* Urbana: University of Illinois Press, 2016.

Musser, Amber Jamilla. *Sensational Flesh: Race, Power, and Masochism.* New York: New York University Press, 2014.

Namjoshi, Seniti. *Sycorax: New Fables and Poems.* New Delhi: Penguin, 2006.

Nelson, Charmaine. "Hiram Powers's America: Shackles, Slaves, and the Racial

Limits of Nineteenth-Century National Identity." *Canadian Review of American Studies* 34, no. 2 (2004): 167–84.

Nelson, Charmaine. *Slavery, Geography and Empire in Nineteenth-Century Marine Landscapes of Montreal and Jamaica.* London: Routledge, 2016.

Nelson, Charmaine. "Slavery, Portraiture and the Colonial Limits of Canadian Art History." *Canadian Woman Studies* 23, no. 2 (2004): 22–29.

Newton, Melanie J. "Returns to a Native Land: Indigeneity and Decolonization in the Anglophone Caribbean." *Small Axe* 17, no. 2 (2013): 108–22.

Pateman, Carole. "The Settler Contract." In *Contract and Domination*, ed. Charles Mills and Carole Pateman, 35–78. Malden, MA: Polity, 2007.

Pateman, Carole, and Charles Wade Mills. *Contract and Domination.* Cambridge, UK: Polity, 2007.

Peters, Jesse. "*The Cherokee Rose: A Novel of Gardens and Ghosts* by Tiya Miles (Review)." *Studies in American Indian Literatures* 27, no. 4 (2015): 135–38.

Philip, M. NourbeSe. *Zong!* Middletown, CT: Wesleyan University Press, 2008.

Pinckney, Elise, and Marvin Zahniser, eds. *The Letterbook of Eliza Lucas Pinckney, 1739–1762.* Columbia: University of South Carolina Press, 1972.

Porteous, J. Douglas. "Bodyscape: The Body-Landscape Metaphor." *Canadian Geographer/Géographe Canadien* 30, no. 1 (1986): 2–12.

Pratt, Stephanie. "From the Margins: The Native American Personage in the Cartouche and Decorative Borders of Maps." *Word and Image* 12, no. 4 (1996): 349–65.

Puar, Jasbir. *Terrorist Assemblages: Homonationalism in Queer Times.* Durham, NC: Duke University Press, 2006.

Raheja, Michelle. "Visual Sovereignty." In *Native Studies Keywords*, ed. Stephanie Teves, Andrea Smith, and Michelle Raheja, 25–34. Tucson: University of Arizona Press, 2015.

Reckin, Anna. "Tidalectic Lectures: Kamau Brathwaite's Prose/Poetry as Sound-Space." *Anthurium: A Caribbean Studies Journal* 1, no. 1 (2003): 1–16.

Reid-Pharr, Robert. *Black Gay Man: Essays.* New York: New York University Press, 2001.

Rifkin, Mark. *Settler Common Sense: Queerness and Everyday Colonialism in the American Renaissance.* Minneapolis: University of Minnesota Press, 2014.

Rifkin, Mark. *When Did Indians Become Straight? Kinship, the History of Sexuality, and Native Sovereignty.* Oxford: Oxford University Press, 2010.

Risser, Paul G. "The Status of the Science Examining Ecotones." *BioScience* 45, no. 5 (1995): 318–25.

Roberts, Elizabeth. "What Gets Inside: Violent Entanglements and Toxic Boundaries in Mexico City." *Cultural Anthropology* 32, no. 4 (2017): 592–619.

Rose, Gilliam. *Feminism and Geography: The Limits of Geographical Knowledge.* Minneapolis: University of Minnesota Press, 1993.

Ross, Luana. *Inventing the Savage: The Social Construction of Native American Criminality.* Austin: University of Texas Press, 1998.

Rowley, Michelle V. "Whose Time Is It? Gender and Humanism in Contemporary Caribbean Feminist Advocacy." *Small Axe* 14, no. 1 (2010): 1–15.

Sale, Maggie Montesinos. *The Slumbering Volcano: American Slave Ship Revolts and the Production of Rebellious Masculinity.* Durham, NC: Duke University Press, 1997.

Scott, David. "The Re-Enchantment of Humanism: An Interview with Sylvia Wynter." *Small Axe* 8, no. 120 (2000): 173–211.

Scott, Darieck. *Extravagant Abjection: Blackness, Sexuality and Power in the African American Literary Imagination.* New York: New York University Press, 2010.

Sedgwick, Eve Kosofsky. "Paranoid Reading and Reparative Reading; or, You're So Paranoid, You Probably Think This Introduction Is about You." In *Novel Gazing: Queer Readings in Fiction,* ed. Eve Kosofsky Sedgwick, 1–40. Durham, NC: Duke University Press, 1997.

Sexton, Jared. "The Vel of Slavery: Tracking the Figure of the Unsovereign." *Critical Sociology* 42, nos. 4–5 (2016): 1–15.

Sharpe, Christina. *In the Wake: On Blackness and Being.* Durham, NC: Duke University Press, 2017.

Silko, Leslie Marmon. *The Almanac of the Dead: A Novel.* New York: Simon and Schuster, 1991.

Simpson, Audra. "Paths toward a Mohawk Nation: Narratives of Citizenship and Nationhood in Kahnawake." In *Political Theory and the Rights of Indigenous Peoples,* ed. Duncan Ivison, Paul Patton, and Will Sanders, 113–36. Cambridge: Cambridge University Press, 2000.

Simpson, Audra. "To the Reserve and Back Again: Kahnawake Mohawk Narratives of Self, Home, and Nation." Ph.D. diss., McGill University, Montreal, 2004.

Simpson, Audra, and Andrea Smith, eds. *Theorizing Native Studies.* Durham, NC: Duke University Press, 2014.

Simpson, Leanne. "The Place Where We All Live and Work Together: A Gendered Analysis of 'Sovereignty.'" In *Native Studies Keywords,* ed. Stephanie Teves, Andrea Smith, and Michelle Raheja, 18–24. Tucson: University of Arizona Press, 2015.

Sirmans, M. Eugene. *Colonial South Carolina: A Political History, 1663–1763.* Chapel Hill: University of North Carolina Press, 2012.

Smith, Andrea. *Conquest: Sexual Violence and American Indian Genocide.* Cambridge, MA: South End, 2005.

Smith, Andrea. "Heteropatriarchy and the Three Pillars of White Supremacy: Rethinking Women of Color Organizing." In *The Color of Violence: The* INCITE! *Anthology,* ed. INCITE! Women of Color against Violence, 66–72. Boston: South End, 2006.

Smith, Linda Tuhiwai. *Decolonizing Methodologies: Research and Indigenous Peoples.* New York: Palgrave, 1999.

Smith, Shanna Louise. "'Tell Me Your Diamonds' Story Bearing in African

American Women's Life History Narratives." Ph.D. diss., University of Maryland, College Park, 2014.

Snorton, C. Riley. *Black on Both Sides: A Racial History of Trans Identity*. Minneapolis: University of Minnesota Press, 2017.

Spencer, Megan [Megan Hamel]. "Cartographies of Haunting: Black Feminist Refusal in Toni Morrison's *A Mercy* and Octavia Butler's *Kindred*." M.A. thesis, Oregon State University, 2016.

Spillers, Hortense. "Mama's Baby, Papa's Maybe: An American Grammar Book." *Diacritics* 17, no. 2 (Summer 1987): 65–81.

Spillers, Hortense J. "Who Cuts the Border? Some Readings on America." In *Black, White, and in Color: Essays on American Literature and Culture*, 319–35. Chicago: University of Chicago Press, 2003.

Spillers, Hortense, Saidiya Hartman, Farah Jasmine Griffin, Shelly Eversley, and Jennifer L. Morgan. "'Whatcha Gonna Do?': Revisiting 'Mama's Baby, Papa's Maybe: An American Grammar Book': A Conversation with Hortense Spillers, Saidiya Hartman, Farah Jasmine Griffin, Shelly Eversley, and Jennifer L. Morgan." *Women's Studies Quarterly* 35, nos. 1–2 (Spring–Summer 2007): 299–309.

Spivak, Gayatri. "Can the Subaltern Speak?" In *Marxism and the Interpretation of Culture*, ed. Cary Nelson, 271–313. Urbana: University of Illinois Press, 1988.

Stallings, LaMonda H. *Funk the Erotic: Transaesthetics and Black Sexual Cultures*. Urbana: University of Illinois Press, 2015.

Stewart, Mart A. "William Gerard de Brahm's 1757 Map of South Carolina and Georgia." *Environmental History* 16, no. 3 (2011): 524–35.

Stockton, Kathryn Bond. *Beautiful Bottom, Beautiful Shame: Where "Black" Meets "Queer."* Durham, NC: Duke University Press, 2006.

TallBear, Kim. *Native American DNA: Tribal Belonging and the False Promise of Genetic Science*. Minneapolis: University of Minnesota Press, 2013.

TallBear, Kim, and Deborah Bolnick. "'Native American DNA' Tests: What Are the Risks to Tribes." *Native Voice* 51 (2004): 3–17.

Tatonetti, Lisa. "Indigenous Fantasies and Sovereign Erotics: Outland Cherokees Write Two-Spirit Nations." In *Queer Indigenous Studies: Critical Interventions in Theory, Politics, and Literature*, ed. Qwo-Li Driskill, Chris Finley, Brian Joseph Gilley, and Scott Lauria Morgensen, 155–71. Tucson: University of Arizona Press, 2011.

Taylor, Diana. *The Archive and the Repertoire: Performing Cultural Memory in the Americas*. Durham, NC: Duke University Press, 2003.

Thomas, Greg. "Sex/Sexuality and Sylvia Wynter's 'Beyond . . .': Anti-Colonial Ideas in 'Black Radical Tradition.'" *Journal of West Indian Literature* 10, nos. 1–2 (2001): 92–118.

Thompson, Krista A. *An Eye for the Tropics: Tourism, Photography, and Framing the Caribbean Picturesque*. Durham, NC: Duke University Press, 2006.

Tinsley, Omise'eke Natasha. "Black Atlantic, Queer Atlantic: Queer Imaginings of the Middle Passage." *GLQ* 14, nos. 2–3 (2008): 191–215.

Trask, Haunani-Kay. "The Color of Violence." In *The Color of Violence: The INCITE! Anthology*, ed. INCITE! Women of Color against Violence, 82–87. Boston: South End, 2006.

Trask, Haunani-Kay. *From a Native Daughter: Colonialism and Sovereignty in Hawai'i*. Honolulu: University of Hawai'i Press, 1999.

Trask, Mililani B. "Hawaiian Sovereignty." *Amerasia Journal* 26, no. 2 (2000): 31–36.

Trotz, D. Alissa. "Rethinking Caribbean Transnational Connections: Conceptual Itineraries." *Global Networks* 6, no. 1 (2006): 41–59.

Tuck, Eve. "Suspending Damage: A Letter to Communities." *Harvard Educational Review* 79, no. 3 (2009): 409–28.

Tuck, Eve, and C. Ree. "A Glossary of Haunting." In *Handbook of Autoethnography*, ed. Stacy Holman Jones, Tony E. Adams, and Carolyn Ellis, 639–68. Walnut Creek, CA: Left Coast, 2013.

Tuck, Eve, and K. Wayne Yang. "Decolonization Is Not a Metaphor." *Decolonization: Indigeneity, Education and Society* 1, no. 1 (2012): 1–40.

Veracini, Lorenzo. "Introducing Settler Colonial Studies." *Settler Colonial Studies* 1, no. 1 (2011): 1–12.

Verstraete, Ginette, and Tim Cresswell. "Introduction." In *Mobilizing Place, Placing Mobility: The Politics of Representation in a Globalized World*, ed. Ginette Verstraete and Tim Cresswell, 11–32. Amsterdam: Rodopi, 2002.

Vimalassery, Manu, Juliana Hu Pegues, and Alyosha Goldstein. "Introduction: On Colonial Unknowing." *Theory and Event* 19, no. 4 (2016). Accessed April 4, 2018. https://muse.jhu.edu.

Wahab, Amar. *Colonial Inventions: Landscape, Power and Representation in Nineteenth-Century Trinidad*. Newcastle upon Tyne, UK: Cambridge Scholars, 2010.

Wallace, David Duncan. *South Carolina: A Short History, 1520–1948*. Chapel Hill: University of North Carolina Press, 1969.

Walcott, Rinaldo. *Black Like Who? Writing Black Canada*. London, ON: Insomniac, 2003.

Walcott, Rinaldo. "The Problem of the Human: Black Ontologies and 'the Coloniality of Our Being.'" In *Postcoloniality — Decoloniality — Black Critique: Joints and Fissures*, ed. Sabine Broeck and Carsten Junker, 93–108. Frankfurt am Main: Campus, 2014.

Walvin, James. *The Zong: A Massacre, the Law, and the End of Slavery*. New Haven, CT: Yale University Press, 2011.

Weheliye, Alexander G. *Habeas Viscus: Racializing Assemblages, Biopolitics, and Black Feminist Theories of the Human*. Durham, NC: Duke University Press, 2014.

Wekker, Gloria. *The Politics of Passion: Women's Sexual Culture in the Afro-Surinamese Diaspora*. New York: Columbia University Press, 2006.

Wilderson, Frank B., III. *Red, White and Black: Cinema and the Structure of U.S. Antagonisms*. Durham, NC: Duke University Press, 2010.

Wolfe, Patrick. "Land, Labor, and Difference: Elementary Structures of Race." *American Historical Review* 106, no. 3 (2001): 894–905.

Wolfe, Patrick. "Settler Colonialism and the Elimination of the Native." *Journal of Genocide Research* 8, no. 4 (2006): 387–409.

Wolfe, Patrick. *Settler Colonialism and the Transformation of Anthropology: The Politics and Poetics of an Ethnographic Event.* London: Cassell, 1998.

Wolfe, Patrick. "'Settler Colonialism': Career of a Concept." *Journal of Imperial and Commonwealth History* 41 (2013): 1–21.

Woods, Clyde. *Development Arrested: Race, Power, and the Blues in the Mississippi Delta.* New York: Verso, 1998.

Wynter, Sylvia. "Beyond Miranda's Meanings: Un/Silencing the 'Demonic Ground' of Caliban's 'Woman.'" In *Out of Kumbla: Caribbean Women and Literature,* ed. Carole Boyce Davies, 355–72. Chicago: Africa World Press, 1990.

Wynter, Sylvia. "Beyond the Categories of the Master Conception: The Counterdoctrine of the Jamesian Poiesis." *C. L. R. James's Caribbean* 69 (1992): 63–91.

Wynter, Sylvia. "Beyond the Word of Man: Glissant and the New Discourse of the Antilles." *World Literature Today* 63, no. 4 (1989): 637–48.

Wynter, Sylvia. "The Ceremony Found: Towards the Autopoetic Turn/Overturn, Its Autonomy of Human Agency and Extraterritoriality of (Self-) Cognition." In *Black Knowledges/Black Struggles: Essays in Critical Epistemology,* ed. Jason R. Ambroise and Sabine Bröck-Sallah, 184–252. Liverpool: Liverpool University Press, 2015.

Wynter, Sylvia. "The Ceremony Must Be Found: After Humanism." *boundary 2* 12, no. 3; 13, no. 1 (Spring–Autumn 1984): 19–70.

Wynter, Sylvia. "1492: A New World View." In *Race, Discourse, and the Origin of the Americas: A New World View,* ed. Vera Lawrence Hyatt and Rex M. Nettleford, 5–57. Washington, DC: Smithsonian Institution Press, 1996.

Wynter, Sylvia. "No Humans Involved: An Open Letter to My Colleagues." *Knowledge on Trial* 1, no. 1 (1994): 42–73.

Wynter, Sylvia. "Novel and History, Plot and Plantation." *Savacou* 5 (1971): 95–102.

Wynter, Sylvia. "On How We Mistook the Map for the Territory, and Re-Imprisoned Ourselves in Our Unbearable Wrongness of Being, of Desêtre: Black Studies toward the Human Project." In *Not Only the Master's Tools: African American Studies in Theory and Practice,* ed. Lewis Gordon, 107–69. Boulder, CO: Paradigm, 2006.

Wynter, Sylvia. "Unsettling the Coloniality of Being/Power/Truth/Freedom: Towards the Human, after Man, Its Overrepresentation—An Argument." CR: *New Centennial Review* 3, no. 3 (Fall 2003): 257–337.

Wynter, Sylvia, and Greg Thomas. "*Proud Flesh* Inter/views: Sylvia Wynter." *ProudFlesh* 4 (2006): 1–36.

Black Lives Matter, 73, 194–95, 208–9, 227n46; Atlanta chapter, 26, 213n12; #BlackLivesMatter hashtag, 66, 68, 206, 262n3; Columbus monument protest (2015), 31–32, 36–45, 73; Toronto chapter, 260n50

Black livingness, 30, 32, 77, 79, 83, 236n23

Black Power movement, 150

Black radical tradition, xii–xiii, 8, 190, 213n12

Black rebellion/revolt, 25, 31, 42–44, 91, 139; slave revolts, 32, 74–75, 83, 90, 108–9, 140, 154, 235nn3–4, 237n24, 238n51, 253–54n47. *See also* fugitivity

Black studies, xiii, 21, 195–96, 220n68, 245n16, 245n19, 257n6; cultural, 134; diaspora and 1, 4, 9, 12–13, 15, 35, 45, 175, 178–79, 191, 193, 202, 261n53; and gender and sexuality, 45, 144, 168, 249n53; history of, 215n12; humanism in, 25, 51, 71, 119, 200, 219n54; interdisciplinarity of, 134–35; Native studies and, 10, 13–15, 28, 31, 35, 44–46, 55, 62, 66, 68, 70, 72, 119, 148, 150, 197, 227n42; ocean in, 5, 165, 207, 216n29; settler colonial studies and, 19, 45; sovereignty in, 13, 62, 147, 150; theft of land in, 58; theorizations of violence, 30

Blokorama, 195, 260n50

blood quantum, 161–62, 165–66

blues epistemology, 130, 138

Boston, Massachusetts: statue of Columbus in, 31–32, 36–38, 179, 197

Bourguignon, Erica, 168

Brady, Jean, 36–38

Brand, Dionne, 35, 175, 256n93

Brathwaite, Kamau, 5–8, 11, 60, 207, 215n21, 217n41

Brooks, Kinitra, 181

Brooks, Lisa, 93–94, 238n42

Brown, Alphonso, 112

Burnett, Charles, 154, 253–54n47

Busia, Abena, 179, 181

Butler, Judith, 134, 199

Byrd, Jodi, 58, 99, 225n22

Byrne, Denis, 107–8, 236n13

Caledonia, 190

Caliban, 14, 176, 179, 181–84, 196, 258n21

Calibana positionality, 182–83

Canada, 24, 34–35, 58, 175–76, 189–97, 260n49; Black Canadian studies, 5, 12–13; murdered native women in, 55, 228n59; Turtle Island and, 211n5, 257n6

Cannon, Katie, 26

Cape Bojador, 1, 19

capitalism, 68, 99, 115, 118, 135, 229n63, 235n10; humanism and, 15; mercantile, 103, 109

Caribana, 194–95, 260n49

Caribbean, 15, 191, 207, 213nn3–4, 215n21, 224n7, 245n16, 245–46n20; Anglophone, 13–14, 102, 182, 195, 257n6; creolization in, 189; diaspora, 11, 47, 194–97, 226n36; feminism in, 183; Indigenous peoples in, 17, 24, 190, 197; poetics, 4–9, 217n41; slave revolts in, 75, 235n3; Sycorax in, 179, 182–83, 193, 195–96

Caribbean studies, 4, 5, 12, 13–14, 119, 178, 179, 195, 217n41

Carnival, 189, 194, 260n49

Cartesianism, 32, 85, 115, 118, 129, 242n82, 247n33; views on land, 52, 79, 88, 124

cartographic I, 85, 87

Casas, Bartolomé de las, 18

Catawba, 90, 93, 97, 238–39n51

Cavanagh, Edward, 59, 64, 69

Césaire, Aimé, 17, 182

Cherokee, xiii, 32–33, 75, 231n93, 252n42, 255n65; British and, 238n51; in *The Cherokee Rose*, 29–30, 34, 142–43, 167–74; in *Daughters of the Dust*, 131, 143–44, 151–66, 173–74; in de Brahm's map, 90–98, 238n51; as one of the Five Civilized Tribes, 212n7; queerness and, 251n5; slavery and, 150, 256n92; tribal nationhood of, 255n71

The Cherokee Rose, 29–30, 34, 142–44, 146, 148, 166–73

Cheyenne, 167

Chickasaw, 93, 141, 212n7, 238n51

Choctaw, 141, 212n7

Chow, Rey, xii

Christian, Barbara, 148

Christianity, 26, 52, 60, 171, 212n7, 234n1; Christian humanism, 16, 18, 39, 79–80; Jesuits, 93–94

Churchill, Ward, 56

Civil Rights Movement, 159, 213n13

Clarke, John Henrik, 36, 213n3

Cliff, Jimmy, 61

coalition, 66, 252n41; Black/Native, xiii, 143, 152, 166, 173, 206; limits of, 26, 58, 148–49, 209, 252n42; women of color, 63

Colebrooke, Henry, 109

colonialism/imperialism, 190, 193–94, 226n36, 234n1; Anglo-American, 106; Anthropocene and, 228n58; British, 19–20, 32–33, 73–102, 106–7, 120, 151; cartography and, 55, 116, 122–24, 128, 170–71, 247n33; in *The Cherokee Rose*, 170–73; in *Daughters of the Dust*, 164; Dutch, 20, 106; French, 20, 90, 93–94, 106, 125; gender norms and, 150; Native studies and, 4, 215n12; neocolonialism, 59, 69; nostalgia for, 99; poetics and, 6–7; Portuguese, 1, 19–20, 135, 213n4, 241n74; sexuality and, 27; slavery

race, 19, 105, 166, 184; gendered, 17, 33, 88, 132–33, 139, 168–70; racialization, xii, 13, 22, 58, 64, 85, 107, 161–62, 194, 196; sexuality and, 132, 148–49, 154, 157–59; violence and, 13, 64, 132

racism, 48, 59, 145; anti-Black, 11, 13, 26, 34–35, 61, 150, 160, 172; opposition to, 133–34, 208; white supremacy, 38, 44, 57–58, 98, 195, 209

Raheja, Michelle, 149, 150

Rastafarianism, 199

Retamar, Roberto, 182

Reckin, Anna, 8

Recovery, 222n97

Red Pedagogy, 64

Red Power movement, 150

Red River Women (BBC), 55

Ree, Christine, x

Renaissance, 15–16, 203–4

"Revisiting Sycorax," 34–35, 175–98, 204–6, 208, 257n7, 258n8, 259n30

rhizome, 99–100

rice production, xiv, 102–3, 234n1, 240n65

Rifkin, Mark, 66, 146, 251n5

Roberts, Elizabeth, 243n3

Rogers, Alva, 141

Rose, Gillian, 129

Rousseau, Jean-Jacques, 247n33

Rowley, Michelle V., 17

The Sacred Hoop, 64

Salole, Abi, xi, 192, 211n4

Santee River, 95

#SayHerName, 66

Schwandt, Marika, xi, xvii, 192, 211n4

Scott, Darieck, 123, 139

Scott, David, 16

secularism, 16, 39, 53, 79–80, 183

Sedgwick, Eve Kosofsky, 134, 217n43, 230n74

self-writing, 76

Seminole, 212n7

Seneca, 10, 232n99

Senegal, 1, 18, 40

Sepúlveda, Juan Ginés de, 18

settler colonialism, x–xv, 18, 32, 54, 102, 118, 150, 153, 208; Blackness and, 13, 19, 26, 39–46, 75–77, 106–7, 109, 179; cartography and, 80, 84, 86–88, 90–98, 106–9; conquistador-settler, xi, xiii, 84, 87, 97, 120, 131, 140; difference from colonialism, 56–59, 69–70; genocide and, 56–57, 62, 65–70, 80, 212n8, 225n22; humanism and, 10, 13, 20–22, 77, 79, 84; labor and, 244n14, 245–46n20; relationship to conquest, 20–21, 65, 68–69, 77, 84; settler colonial turn, 63–67; Settler/Master/Human grammati-

cal structure, 20–21, 67. *See also* colonialism/imperialism

settler colonial studies, xiii, 1, 18–19, 22, 51, 150; Native studies and, 55–56, 65–70, 229n63; settler colonial turn, 63–67; White, 10–11, 20–21, 31–32, 44–45, 66–71, 77, 208. *See also* colonial studies; postcolonial studies

Settler Colonial Studies (journal), 64

"1757 Map of the Coast of South Carolina and Parts of Georgia," 75–79, 86–88, 110, 113–14, 137–39; Atlantic Ocean in, 80, 82–85, 93, 96–98, 100–101, 116; Cherokee in, 90–98, 238n51; fungibility in, 102–3, 124; genocide in, 89–91, 96–98; slavery in, 32–33, 77, 90–91, 96–97, 101–2, 105–9, 125–27

Sexton, Jared, 22, 147–48, 150–51, 228n57

sexual violence, 47–49, 55, 57, 157, 254n53

Shakespeare, William: *The Tempest*, 16, 176, 179, 181–84, 196, 257n7, 259n27

Sharpe, Christina, 5, 116, 146, 163, 202, 243n1, 244n11, 255n64, 261n60

Silko, Leslie Marmon, xii, 56, 198, 200, 232n95; *The Almanac of the Dead*, 21, 50–51, 59–62, 203–4, 227n40

Simpson, Leanne Betasamosake, 114, 149, 191

Sioux Territory: Morton County, xii

Six Nations, 189

slave revolts. *See* Black rebellion/revolt

slavery, ix, 9, 13, 78–79, 134, 138–39, 143, 182, 194, 197; in *The Cherokee Rose*, 167–68, 170, 172; colonialism and, 15, 19–20, 23–24, 45, 51–53, 58–60, 107–8, 118, 122, 140, 166–67, 191, 212n8, 222n110, 245–46n20, 248n48; in *Daughters of the Dust*, 29, 33, 111–13, 117, 128–31, 152–54, 156, 160–61, 163, 248n42, 254n53; in de Brahm's map, 32–33, 77, 82, 84, 90–91, 96–97, 101–2, 105–9, 117, 125–27, 237n28, 242n83; flesh and, 53–54, 120, 132, 137, 222n110, 241n72, 253n44; fugitivity and, 74–75, 107–9, 151; fukú and, 36, 48–49; fungibility and, 22–23, 25–26, 54, 61, 103–4, 118, 122, 128, 135–37, 140, 222n110, 225n24, 228n57; genocide and, x–xv, 10–11, 19–21, 44–45, 48–53, 166–68, 195–96, 200–202; Indigenous enslaving practices, xi, 14, 150, 160, 172–73, 212n7, 256n92; Settler/Savage/Slave trio, 87; slave trade, 1, 5, 39, 48, 54, 62, 105, 109, 135–36, 192, 201–3, 247n32. *See also* abolition; Black rebellion/revolt; wake work

Smith, Andrea, 21, 57–58, 63, 150, 230n87, 231n93

Snorton, C. Riley, 114, 122; on flesh, 104, 120, 240n70; on fungible fugitivity, 25–26, 109–10, 115, 247n31

Somerville, Alice Te Punga, 10, 94